Rapid Application Development with Visual C++

David McMahon

McGraw-Hill
New York   San Francisco   Washington, D.C.
Auckland   Bogotá   Caracas   Lisbon   London   Madrid
Mexico City   Milan   Montreal   New Delhi   San Juan
Singapore   Sydney   Tokyo   Toronto

McGraw-Hill
A Division of The McGraw-Hill Companies

Copyright © 2000 by The McGraw-Hill Companies, Inc. All rights reserved. Printed in the United States of America. Except as permitted under the United States Copyright Act of 1976, no part of this publication may be reproduced or distributed in any form or by any means, or stored in a data base or retrieval system, without the prior written permission of the publisher.

1 2 3 4 5 6 7 8 9 0 AGM/AGM 9 0 4 3 2 1 0 9

P/N 212526-8
part of 0-07-212309-5

The sponsoring editor for this book was Regina Brooks, the editing supervisor was Scott Amerman, and the production supervisor was Clare Stanley. It was set in Century Schoolbook by Don Feldman of McGraw-Hill's desktop composition unit in cooperation with Spring Point Publishing Services.

Printed and bound by Quebecor/Martinsburg.

Throughout this book, trademarked names are used. Rather than put a trademark symbol after every occurrence of a trademarked name, we used the names in an editorial fashion only, and to the benefit of the trademark owner, with no intention of infringement of the trademark. Where such designations appear in this book, they have been printed with initial caps.

> Information contained in this work has been obtained by The McGraw-Hill Companies, Inc. ("McGraw-Hill") from sources believed to be reliable. However, neither McGraw-Hill nor its authors guarantee the accuracy or completeness of any information published herein and neither McGraw-Hill nor its authors shall be responsible for any errors, omissions, or damages arising out of use of this information. This work is published with the understanding that McGraw-Hill and its authors are not attempting to render engineering or other professional services. If such services are required, the assistance of an appropriate professional should be sought.

 This book is printed on recycled, acid-free paper containing a minimum of 50% recycled, de-inked fiber.

CONTENTS

Preface xv

PART 1 SOFTWARE DEVELOPMENT LIFE CYCLE   1

Chapter 1 An Introduction to Rapid Application Development
(RAD) with Visual C++   3

Introduction   4
The Costs vs. Benefits of RAD   4
Avoiding the Pitfalls of RAD   6
Picking the Right Tool for the Job   7
    Visual Basic   7
    Java   8
    Microsoft Access   9
    Visual C++   9
A Brief History of Visual C++   10
Software Life Cycle Models   11
    Waterfall (Linear)   11
    Cyclic Waterfall or Spiral   12
    Brute Force   12
    Hybrids   13
Example Programs   13

Chapter 2 Overview of the Visual C++ Environment and
Advanced Options   15

Introduction   16
The Developer Studio Environment   16
Project vs. Workspace   16
What Is MFC?   17
Project Types   17
File Types in a C++ Project   20
Project Management   21
Project Settings   21
    The General Tab   22
    The Debug Tab   23
    The C/C++ Tab   23
Linker   25
    P-Code   26

	The Tools Menu	26
	The Customize Dialog Box	27
	The Options Dialog Box	28
	The Components and Controls Gallery	29
	Navigating a Project: The Workspace Window	30
	Class Wizard	31
	Custom App Wizard Creation	32
	Version Control	32
	Overview—When and Why You'll Need It	32
	Visual Source Safe	32
	Configuring Source Safe	33
	New Features in Visual C++ Version 6	35
	ActiveX Data Objects (ADO)	35
	ATL Composite Control	35
	Command-Line Builds	36
	Dynamic HTML	36
	New Keywords	36
	OLE-DB Provider Templates	37
	Stored Procedures	37
Chapter 3	Requirements Gathering, Documentation, and Analysis	39
	Introduction	40
	Requirements Gathering	40
	Documentation	40
	End User Documentation	41
	Technical Design Documentation	43
	Analysis	43
	Estimating	44
	Scheduling	44
	Staffing	46
PART 2	**DESIGNING VISUAL C++ SOFTWARE**	**49**
Chapter 4	Systems Architecture vs. Software Architecture	51
	Introduction	52
	Systems Architecture: The Big Picture	52
	Networks	53
	Client/Server Model	53
	Distributed Applications	55

Contents

	General Scalability	55
	Layered Application Development	55
	One-Tiered Model	56
	Two-Tiered Model	56
	Three-Tiered Model	56
Chapter 5	The C/C++ Programming Language	59
	Introduction	60
	Data Types	60
	int	60
	long	61
	short	61
	float	61
	double	61
	char	61
	__int8	62
	__int16	62
	__int32	62
	__int64	62
	bool	62
	wchar_t	62
	Declaring Variables	63
	Rules for Variable Names	63
	Initializing Variables	64
	Declaring Constants	65
	Casting	66
	The Increment and Decrement Operators	66
	Bitwise Operators	68
	AND	68
	OR	69
	Exclusive OR (XOR)	70
	One's Complement	70
	Left and Right Shifts	70
	Defining New Type Names	71
	Pointers	72
	The addressof Operator	73
	A Quick Summary of Pointers	74
	Preprocessor Directives	75
	#error	75
	#if	76
	#pragma	76

#undef	77
The Concatenation Operator ##	77
The Charizing Operator #@	78
Arrays	78
Multidimensional Arrays	79
Initializing Arrays	80
Programming with Strings	80
Comments	81
Control Structures	82
If Statements	82
The ? Operator	84
The Relational Operators	85
For Loops	86
Do Loops	88
While Loops	88
The Switch Statement	89
Modular Programming—Using Functions	90
The Void Return Type	91
Passing Parameters—Pass by Value vs. Pass by Reference	93
Prototyping	94
Variable Scope and Lifetime	96
Variable Lifetime and Static Variables	96
Passing Arrays to Functions	97
Passing Arrays as Pointers	99
Pointers to Functions	100
Function Overloading	101
Dynamic Memory Allocation	102
Defining Data Types with Structures	103
Example: Using Simple Structures	106
Programming Stuctures with Pointers	108
Passing Structures to Functions	109
Example: Passing Structures to Functions	110
Good Programming Practices	115
Avoid the Use of Global Variables	115
Give Your Variables Good Names	115
Comment Your Code	115
Comment Ending Brackets for If Statements, While Loops, and For Loops	116
Indent Your Code	116
Break Code Down into Functions	116

Contents

If a Variable Won't Be Modified in a Function, Use Pass By Value	117
Use Error Trapping	117
Declare All Variables at the Beginning of a Function	117
Plan Your Logic *Before* You Start to Program	117
Some Common Mistakes and How to Avoid Them	118
Failing to Explicitly Convert Data Types	118
Declaring Local Variables with the Same Name as a Global Variable	118
Be Sure to Terminate If Statements, For Loops, and While Loops	118
Memory Allocation Problems	118
Crashing a Program from Memory Problems	119
Going Out of Range	119
Using Keywords as Variable Names	119
Using Functions with a Pointer Return Type	119

Chapter 6 Object-Oriented Design 121

Introduction	122
Software Reuse Speeds Product Development	124
Software Reuse Promotes Reliability	124
Structuring Your Data with Classes	125
The Aspects of Object-Oriented Programming	126
Abstraction	126
Client and Server	126
Encapsulation	127
Information Hiding	127
Inheritance	127
Polymorphism	128
COM	128
COM and the Registry	129
Code Reuse vs. Component Reuse	129
Existing Methodologies	130

Chapter 7 Classes 133

Introduction	134
Creating a Class	134
Data and Function Members	136
Public vs. Private Members	137
Adding Member Functions to a Class	138

Contents

Using Inline Functions	140
Constructors and Destructors	141
Declaring and Using a Class Variable	142
Inheritance-Based and Derived Classes	144
Building a Derived Class	146
Implementing Polymorphism	154
Advanced Class Topics	156
Friend Functions	156
Operators	163
Using Pointers with Classes, *This*	165
Using *This*	165
Virtual Functions	166
Using Multiple Inheritance	167

Chapter 8

Coding Standards	173
Introduction	174
Creating Coding Standards	175
Language Standards	175
Declare All Local Variables at the Beginning of a Function	175
Avoid the Use of "Negative Logic"	177
Don't Use Inline if Statements	177
Explicitly List Parameters in Function Prototypes	177
When Using Shorthand Notation, Be Sure to Comment	178
When Using Overloaded Operators, Be Sure to Comment	178
When Referencing Member Variables and Functions in a Class, Use the *This* Pointer	179
Avoid Ambiguity in Member Names When Using Multiple Inheritance	180
Avoid the Use of Global Variables	180
When Facing a Multiple If-Else-If, Try a Switch-Case Statement Instead	181
Naming Conventions	182
Hungarian Notation	182
Commenting Standards	184
Overview—The Importance of Commenting Code	184
Commenting Function Headers	185
Inline Comments	186
Revision History	187

Contents

Code Construction Standards to Enhance Readability	187
Indenting Block Structures	188
Use of White Space	189
Enforcing Coding Standards	189
Code Reviews	189
Coding up to Standard	190
Enforcing Standards without Constraining Developers	190

Chapter 9 User Interface Design 193

Introduction	194
The Elements of a Good User Interface	195
A Main Window	198
Displaying Data in Grid Format	199
Displaying Individual Records	201
Creating a User Interface with Visual C++	202
Single-Document Interface (SDI) Applications	203
Messages and the Class Wizard	209
Adding New Code and a Menu Item	213
Displaying a Dialog Box to Set the Font	217
Creating a Dialog Box	218
Closing the Dialog	231
Adding a Menu Item for the New Dialog	231
Programming with ActiveX Controls	232
Adding an ActiveX Control to a Project	233
Programming a Control in Code	234
User Interface Prototyping	240
Why Prototype an Application?	241
What to Include in a Prototype	241
Setting Expectations for Prototyping	242

Chapter 10 Database Design 243

Introduction	244
Overview of Database Design	244
Determining the End User's Needs	245
Organizing the Data	246
The Elements of a Database	247
Organizing Data into Tables	248
Data Types in an Access Database	249
Field Properties	251
Ordinal Position	251

Validation Rule	251
Validation Text	252
Allow Zero Length	252
Indexes	252
The Primary Key	253
Foreign Keys and Relating Tables	253
One-to-Many Relationships	254
Queries	255
Views	255
Stored Procedures	255
Normalization	256
First Normal Form	257
Second Normal Form	258
Third Normal Form	260
Denormalizing a Database	261
Using the Visual Data Manager	262
Adding a Table	263
Adding Fields to the Table	264

Chapter 11 Data Access 267

Introduction	268
Flat Files	268
Basic File I/O Using C	269
Using fstream for File I/O	274
Opening a File with fstream	274
Closing a File with fstream	275
Reading from fstream	276
Writing a File with fstream	277
Working with Text Strings	278
Example: Programming with Flat Files	279
Working with Databases	290
A Brief Note on Database Options and File Support	291
Programming with the ADO Data Control	292
Connecting Data Bound Controls	297
Programming the ADO Data Control in Code	298
Important ADO Data Control Events	305
Creating a Database Project	308
Programming a Database with DAO	310
What Type of Data Access Should You Use—ADO, DAO, or ODBC?	316
Structured Query Language (SQL)	316

Contents

Building Select Queries	317
Aliasing	318
Restricting the Records Returned with a Where Clause	318
SQL Example: Searching Text or String Fields, Data Fields, and Numeric Data	319
SQL Example: Fields that Contain Date/Time Data	319
SQL Example: Numeric Fields	320
Using the Like Operator	320
Returning Records that Fall Only within a Certain Range	321
Using the IN operator	321
Sorting the Records Returned by a Query	322
Building More-Complicated Queries with Logical Operators	322
Grouping Records	323
Editing, Adding, and Deleting Records	324
Joining Data from Different Tables	325
Multiuser Considerations	326
Pessimistic Locking	326
Optimistic Locking	326
Read-Only	327
Batch Optimisitc	327
Database Transactions	327

Chapter 12   Putting It All Together   329

Introduction	330
Programming with a Recordset	330
Opening a Recordset with SQL	338

PART 3   **IMPLEMENTATION**   341

Chapter 13   The Microsoft Foundation Class Library   343

Introduction	344
Overview of MFC	344
Window Classes	347
The Application Class	348
Using MFC Wizards	349

Chapter 14   Advanced Topics—Multithreading, DLLs, ActiveX Controls, and Web Programming   351

Threads, Processes, and Asynchronous Program Flow	352
Processes and Threads	352
Advantages of Multithreading Applications	353
Apartment Model Multithreading	355
Multithreading in C++	355
Programming with OLE	355
Creating a Container	356
Creating a Dynamic-Link Library	361
Creating a Win32 DLL	361
Compiling a DLL	366
Importing from a DLL	367
MFC App Wizard DLLs	370
ActiveX Controls	373
Control Basics	374
Overview of Creating an ActiveX Control	375
The Control Class	375
Subclassing a Control	377
Custom Methods, Properties, and Events	377
Ambient, Stock, and Extender Properties	378
Drawing a Control	380
Example: A Simple MFC ActiveX Control	380
Maintaining the Control's Appearance	381
Adding Properties to the Control	383
Adding Custom Methods	385
Adding Events	387
Fixing the OnDraw Member Function	388
Modifying the About Box and Property Page	390
Modifying the Toolbox Icon	392
Compiling the Control	392
Using the ActiveX Control Test Container	393
Testing the Control in a VB App	394
Creating an ActiveX Control with ATL	394
Adding a Property to an ATL Control	396
Adding a Method to an ATL Control	398
Internet Programming	399

Chapter 15

Debugging	401
Introduction	402
Setting Breakpoints and Starting the Debug Process	403
Stepping through Code	405
Step Into	405

Contents

Step Over	406
Step Out	406
Run to Cursor	407
Using Watch Expressions and Examining the Contents of Variables and Memory	407
Adding a Watch	408
Registers	409
Memory	410
The Call Stack	410
Disassembly	411
Error Trapping and Handling Exceptions	412
The try Block	413

PART 4 TESTING AND DISTRIBUTION OF VISUAL C++ SOFTWARE 417

Chapter 16 Testing Applications 419

Introduction	420
The Importance of Documenting the Testing Process	421
Testing for Proof of Concept	422
Unit Testing	422
Integration Testing	423
System Testing	424
Beta Testing	424
Regression Testing	426

Chapter 17 Distribution of Software 429

Identifying the Target Audience	430
Creating a Setup Program for the Application	430
Determining the Dependencies	431
Compiling the Final Version of Your App	432
Getting Started with InstallShield	432
Choose Dialogs	434
Choose Target Platforms	435
Languages	435
Specify Setup Types	436
Specify Components	436
Specify File Groups	437
Specifying the Components	437
File Groups	440

	SetupTypes	440
	Selecting the Media and Building the Install Program	440
	Other Third-Party Utilities	444
	Distribution of the Software—Selecting Media	444
	CD-ROM vs. Floppy Disk	445
	Internet Distribution	445
	Workstation Duplication and Distribution	446
	Patches and Updating Applications	446
Appendix	Appendix	447
	Index 449	

PREFACE

Rapid application development has become the method of choice in the past five years with the introduction of many visual programming tools. Since the early 1990s, Visual C++ has been at the forefront of the technology. However, early versions of Visual C++ were difficult to use from the "visual" perspective; you still had to be a "power programmer" to build applications with Visual C++. However, more-recent versions have made software development for Windows with the C++ language much easier and faster. Much improvement has come about with the development of MFC and improved visual design tools, as well as with the ability to use ActiveX controls and data binding. Despite the increased ease of use, Visual C++ still delivers all the power of the C++ language to those who need it.

The ease and power that a tool like Visual C++ provides to the developer actually creates its own set of problems. It is here that we enter the world of rapid application development. This book attempts to address the issues of developing software with Visual C++, but in a larger context. We will not only see the usual *how-to* explanations about Visual C++, but we will also look at the product in the larger picture.

Visual C++ is a rich and complicated software development tool. Unfortunately, we won't have the space to go into detail on every feature, or explore every type of development. In some cases, our focus will be on getting things done quickly, without worrying about the details.

Part 1 of the book, we examine issues involved in the software development life cycle. This includes an introduction to the issues that programmers may face when they are working with a visual tool like Visual C++. In Chapter 2, we will take a brief look at the Visual Studio IDE and introduce some of the new features found in version 6.0. In Chapter 3, we will take a look at other issues developers will face in the development life cycle, such as requirements gathering, user documentation, and scheduling and team software development.

The next part of the book is "Designing Visual C++ Software." We begin this section in Chapter 4 with an introductory discussion of networks and the three-tiered model of software development. In Chapter 5, we will explore the C++ language. The reader is assumed to have at least some previous exposure to Visual C++, so our review will not go into detail on every feature. However, I hope to provide a ready reference that should cover many useful aspects of the C++ language. We will also tackle some common mistakes and good programming practices to use with Visual C++. In Chapter 6, we will explore the concept of object-oriented programming, before seeing how to use it in practice with classes. After a look at user-interface design, we will take a step back to look at the use of Visual C++ in the larger context. We explore issues such as commenting code and setting up language standards. We are taking the time to discuss such concerns because we recognize that Visual C++ is not used in a vacuum; software development usually involves working with others and sharing your source code. This always brings up issues of readability and standards.

Chapters 10 and 11 will focus on the use of Visual C++ for database development. Visual C++ used to be a difficult tool to use for database applications, but this is no longer the case. For those who haven't had in-depth experience in designing database software, we will explore the basics of database design and plain file handling with Visual C++, using the `fstream` class. Of course, we will also spend some time exploring the new database handling components and features available in version 6.0, such as ADO and OLE DB. We close out this section with a discussion of the coming together of object-oriented software and database programming. This will include a demonstration of using DAO to program with databases in code.

The next phase of the book is implementation. After a brief discussion on the structure of MFC, we begin in Chapter 14 with a discussion of some advanced programming topics, like multithreading, OLE containers, and creating dynamic-link libraries. We will see how to create an ActiveX control with MFC with an example, and then discuss how to do the same thing with the ATL COM Wizard. In Chapter 15, we will discuss debugging your projects and error handling.

Finally, we close the book out by considering the issues involved in testing and distributing software. There are many issues involved in software development that a programmer would rather not deal with, such as testing or user documentation. But all of these considerations are as important as the algorithms and forms that are a part of your project, and that is what this book is attempting to address—looking at software development as a whole.

—DAVID MCMAHON

PART 1

Software Development Life Cycle

CHAPTER 1

An Introduction to Rapid Application Development (RAD) with Visual C++

Introduction

In the old days, and it really wasn't that long ago, a program either had no user interface or the developer put great effort into building one. Applications were often just a command-line prompt, where the user entered input data and waited for a response. Programs were not very intuitive, and certainly they were not user-friendly.

Developing any kind of significant user interface as recently as a few years ago was nothing short of a major headache. Often doing something as simple as placing a button on a screen could involve long lines of code and hard work just to get the button to appear in the right place. Since there was no visual design environment, you had to compile your project and see where the button appeared. If it didn't look right, that meant opening up the text editor, changing your code, recompiling, and testing the program again to see how everything looked. All this work and you're not even talking about solving some type of useful problem yet—which is what software is supposed to do.

With the advent of the Windows operating system, we have seen nothing short of a revolution in the way applications are developed. Programming tools such as Visual Studio have taken away the work required to build a user interface. By designing the interface visually, in much the same way you would with a "what you see is what you get" word processor or graphics program, user interfaces can be designed quickly and easily. Long gone are the headaches of the past. Now you can place the button exactly where you want it to appear and concentrate on the code behind it. The ability to build an interface visually and use event-driven programming to place code behind objects has allowed the development of software to proceed at a faster pace than ever before. The ability to quickly build an application using a tool such as Visual Studio has become known as *Rapid Application Development*, or RAD. When programming with Visual C++, you can combine the advantages of visual programming with the power of the C/C++ language.

The Costs vs. Benefits of RAD

As with anything in life, this ability to build an application quickly can have its downside. Often the first casualty with RAD is careful planning. In the past, when you had to code up everything and your program followed a neat series of steps from start to finish, coding required hours of careful design on paper before you actually sat down to write your program (in theory at least). With a RAD tool such as Visual Basic, a developer can turn on the computer and rush a program out the door, without paying special attention to those kinds of design issues. Fortunately, when it comes to avoiding the pitfalls of RAD, programming in Visual C++ is not as easy as it is with Visual Basic. Programming in Visual Studio with the C++ language requires more attention to detail, which can help put the brakes on sloppy coding. Even so, when developing in Visual Studio, we still need to be aware of the possible weaknesses of RAD:

- Since it's easy to build the user interface, an interface can be designed carelessly and without putting much thought into it. This can result in an unprofessional appearance and can make the program a difficult, frustrating experience for the end user.

- The ease with which forms and controls can be put on screen may make it feel like your program is so intuitive that everyone will know how to use it immediately. This can lead to inadequate effort put into online help and user documentation, again leaving the end user feeling frustrated. Online help and user documentation can also suffer because the RAD tool makes programming seem "fun," so who wants to spend time on boring issues like a help system?

- The wide choice of tools and components can make a programmer go overboard when putting together the user interface, adding too many controls and too many choices for the user.

- The ability to get a program out the door quickly can lead to sloppy coding, which can include avoiding the use of comments and the use of coding standards. RAD tools tempt the programmer with the ability to just turn the computer on and whip out a program, which can lead to problems later on.

- A program can be released without adequate testing. Because the user interface is complete and nice looking, it may give programmers the illusion that they have a solid working piece of code on their hands.

Before we get too down on RAD and dust off the old DOS compiler, let's think back to those old Pascal, COBOL, and FORTRAN days in the computer science lab, when long hours were spent into the early morning slowly stepping through the code. I'm sure no programmer wants to return to the days when building a dialog box was in itself a major project. Let's think about some of the benefits of using a RAD environment:

- RAD promotes good design of a user-friendly interface, as long as careful planning and industry standards are followed.
- RAD allows you to build your user interface quickly and easily, so that the bulk of your time can be spent using the computer for what it's supposed to do—solve problems.
- Since it's easy to build a user interface, you can give the user all the features that he or she needs, keeping the customer happy. This will require effective communication with the customer.
- A RAD tool will help you quickly test and debug your projects, leading to more fail-safe code development.
- RAD tools are easy to learn, allowing you to bring colleagues up to speed quickly on a new development environment and keeping training costs down.

When you compare the good with the bad, especially when thinking back to the days of designing a user interface for a DOS program or with early versions of Windows, the advantages of RAD are clear.

Avoiding the Pitfalls of RAD

With a bit of careful planning and avoiding the temptation to whip out a program, you can use a RAD tool to build successful, robust applications. By sticking to a few good rules, you can ensure that RAD will help you deliver user-friendly, solid Windows applications quickly. Some suggestions are as follows:

- *Stick to effective problem analysis.* MFC wizards and the ease with which you can build a user interface can provide the temptation to simply turn your computer on and draw up a program. You can avoid the problems that this can cause by carefully designing your program before ever loading up Visual Studio. This can include determining what forms the project will contain and what data will be going in and out of the application, and carefully planning your program logic on paper before you code it up. Taking these steps will save you a lot of headaches later on.
- *Avoid implementing applications too quickly.* Again, a RAD tool like Visual Studio can allow the programmer to build an application in a flash, and that usually means that it contains poor logic and a poorly thought out user interface. A programmer can sidestep these problems

by steering clear of the temptation to simply load up Visual Studio and start designing forms. Before beginning a new project, put some time into thinking about it. Ask questions, such as who will use this program? In what way can I make the user interface intuitive? Will my code be readable by another programmer who needs to add a new feature six months from now? Also, spend time thoroughly testing and debugging your code to ensure that it will run smoothly when users get their hands on it.

- *Stick to good coding standards.* Make sure that your code is readable by other programmers. This includes providing careful commenting, avoiding the use of too many global or public variables, and using naming standards for objects and variables. This will save you headaches later on. We'll take up the issue of coding standards in some detail in Chapter 7.

Picking the Right Tool for the Job

These days there are several RAD tools on the market. While virtually all Windows development is easier than it used to be, the different tools available range a great deal in power and ease of use. Your choice of development environment will depend on your level of expertise, what you need out of the application, and who the target audience will be. Let's consider a few of them.

Visual Basic

Now that Visual Basic has a native code compiler along with the ability to develop ActiveX controls and DLLs, it is a good choice for just about any type of Windows application development. Visual Basic is particularly strong when it comes to file processing and the development of a database front end. Some of the strengths of Visual Basic can be summarized as follows:

- Visual Basic is probably the easiest RAD tool to use. The environment makes it very easy to build a user interface, and the Basic language is easy for just about any programmer to pick up.
- Visual Basic is very strong for building database applications, especially those that use Microsoft Access databases.

- Visual Basic now has a native code compiler that allows you to build applications with much better performance. In the past, the lack of the ability to produce a real compiled program was the biggest knock against Visual Basic.
- Visual Basic is more object-oriented than in the past, with the ability to create and use classes and ActiveX controls.
- Visual Basic gives you a wide array of choices in application types. This includes the ability to create dynamic-link libraries (DLLs), ActiveX controls, and Web-based DHTML applications, among others.
- With the ability to create add-ins, the development environment of Visual Basic is extensible.

Weaknesses of Visual Basic include the following:

- Visual Basic is not as strong as other languages for low-level and operating-system type tasks.
- Visual Basic does not allow the direct memory manipulations that are available in C++.
- For numerically intensive applications, Visual Basic will not perform as well.

While Visual Basic is a good choice for many applications, most serious developers will still want to program with C/C++ to take advantage of the powerful language features. This is especially true when you are doing scientific and engineering development or using graphics applications, since C/C++ programs will generally perform number crunching better.

Java

Over the last few years the Java language has taken the programming community by storm. Java is a good language for applet and Internet development. C++ programmers will find it familiar, since it is based on the C language and is strongly object-oriented. Microsoft produces Visual J++, which has the advantage of using Visual Studio, so experienced Visual Studio users will be able to use the same development environment. Java is also platform-independent, relying on a "Java machine" on the user's operating system to interpret the code for that machine. This comes with a trade-off: A Java program won't perform as well. In summary, Java is an option you might consider for doing Internet development.

Microsoft Access

If you are going to be strictly developing database applications that use Microsoft Access databases, especially for in-house use, you might consider using Microsoft Access. While not really a RAD tool, Access has a complete development environment that you can use to build forms and even write Visual Basic code. The advantages and disadvantages of Access can be summarized as follows:

- Good to use if you are only going to develop Microsoft Access database applications.
- May be a good choice if you are developing in-house applications for users that have Access on their machines.
- Cannot build a native compiled application. As a result, applications developed with Access are probably slower than compiled Visual Basic applications and definitely slower than Visual C++.
- Access is not as flexible as Visual Basic. Also, it does not have access to the powerful and advanced features of the C/C++ language.

Visual C++

The power of the C/C++ language still appeals to many developers, and Visual C++ is an ideal choice. It combines visual user interface development in an integrated development environment complete with debugging, compiling, and testing tools. In short, with Visual C++ you get the best of both worlds. Visual C++ is a particularly good choice when you are building scientific and engineering applications, because it still has a large speed advantage over Visual Basic when performing these types of tasks. One drawback is that designing a user interface with Visual C++ is not as easy, and the C/C++ language is not as easy to learn for beginning programmers. Some developers may find that they can use Visual Basic to design their user interface, while using Visual C++ to do any resource-intensive numerical processing in a dynamic-link library. The advantages and disadvantages of Visual C++ can be summarized as follows:

- Even with native code compilation, for many applications Visual C++ will still provide a hefty speed advantage over Visual Basic.
- The power of the C/C++ language is well known to most developers. Visual C++ combines this power with a relatively easy-to-use IDE and visual design capabilities.

- Visual C++ has more multithreading capability than Visual Basic, which still remains rather limited in this area.
- The C++ language functions in some ways like a midlevel language. It provides the control structures and overall format of high-level languages, while allowing the developer to work with individual bits, bytes, registers, and pointers.
- Visual C++ is based on a strongly object-oriented language. By using the C/C++ language, a developer can program with true classes, including the use of inheritance and polymorphism.
- Visual C++ is a good tool for low-level programming tasks, such as building hardware drivers and interacting with the operating system.
- Designing a user interface with Visual C++ can be more difficult and time-consuming.
- If you don't already know the language, learning C/C++ has a longer learning curve than Visual Basic. However, it is worth putting in the extra effort to learn it in order to benefit from the power of the language.

A Brief History of Visual C++

Visual C++ uses the C++ language, which has the C language at its core. The C language was originally created by Dennis Ritchie in the 1970s. As stated above, the C language provided developers with the best of both worlds, by creating a high-level language that incorporated the use of low-level bit, byte, and pointer operations. This is what gives the C language its power.

In the 1980s, Bjarne Stroustrup created the C++ language, which started off as an object-oriented extension of C. C++ quickly developed into a language in its own right. As the Windows environment took hold in the early 1990s, Microsoft introduced Visual C++, which incorporated the powerful C++ language into a visual design environment. Microsoft has greatly extended the language with the Microsoft Foundation Classes, and has made great improvements in Visual Studio, with the addition of class and app wizards. These wizards have made program development much easier, keeping the C++ language on solid ground in the new world of simple development tools like Visual Basic and Delphi.

Chapter 1: An Introduction to RAD with Visual C++

Software Life Cycle Models

A software life cycle model is a method to study, plan, and analyze the development process, from product conception to actual release. A typical software model will have discrete steps, such as design or testing. Of course, these models are idealizations; nobody develops code in a neat fashion like that in the real world. However, using a software life cycle model can be very helpful in keeping the coding process organized. This is especially important in a RAD environment, because the model can help you stick to a carefully planned and organized method of software development, rather than just jumping into the code.

Waterfall (Linear)

In a waterfall or linear software development model, shown in Figure 1-1, the development of a project moves through neatly defined sequential steps. Like a flow chart, each step is listed in an orderly fashion, where it is assumed that the previous step is completed before moving on.

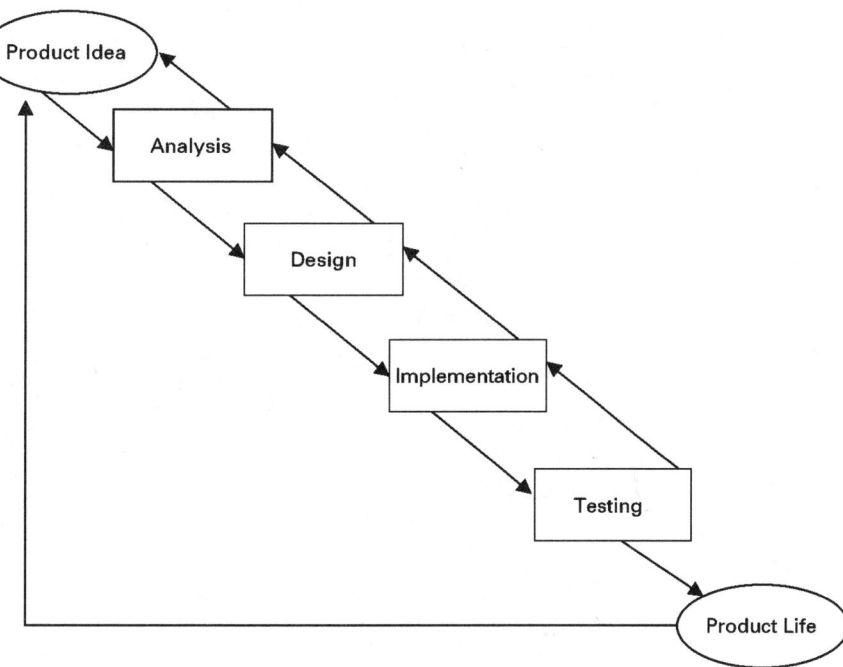

Figure 1-1
Linear software development model.

A drawback to the waterfall model is that this type of progress is unrealistic. The cold, hard truth is that in a real software development environment, the different phases of design overlap, each step will require repeated input from other design steps, and you will probably visit each step more than once.

The waterfall model can be used to divide the software life cycle into phases like the following:

- Product idea
- Software planning stage and analysis
- Coding
- Debugging and testing
- Product life

Despite the shortcomings of the waterfall model, it can be a good starting point to keeping your coding efficient and organized. Just be aware that you will probably never follow such a neat sequence of steps when designing real software.

Cyclic Waterfall or Spiral

The cyclic waterfall or spiral model is a derivation of the linear waterfall model. This model attempts to come to terms with the reality that each phase of the development process will require multiple iterations.

The spiral model was developed at TRW in 1988. Besides allowing for multiple iterations through each phase in the development process, the key idea in this model is that an examination of risk and analysis is performed at each phase. This type of software model is preferred for programmers using object-oriented development. Due to its cyclical nature, it provides designers and managers an opportunity to "loop" through the spiral at each level of abstraction, repeating the same sequence of steps from design to software maintenance. This approach resembles the real world better than the linear waterfall model. As a product is developed, it's more likely that new features will be thought of or designs reconsidered at many phases during the lifetime of the software.

Brute Force

In short, "brute force" is simply turning the computer on and coding up the program. Actually, this really isn't a life cycle model. This is the kind of software development that college professors in freshman computer science classes warn their students about. Unfortunately, with a RAD environment, the temptation to engage in brute-force software development is strong. Since this kind of programming lends itself to errors and poor planning, it should be avoided.

Hybrids

We've only scratched the surface here with software life cycle models. Since none of them is perfect, you're likely to find a hybrid of one or more models useful. Let's consider two possible model hybrids.

Linear Waterfall with Multiple Iterations In real life, there probably aren't many software products that move along so smoothly that someone doesn't think about a design change or a redefinition of the software requirements along the way. While the linear waterfall model offers a neat and organized view of the software development process, this is its biggest weakness. For this reason, a slight twist on the linear model can be thought of that allows each step or phase to be influenced by later phases. This means being able to go back at any point in the development cycle and revisit earlier phases.

Incremental In an incremental model, shown in Figure 1-2, a software product is built up with successive iterations or releases. At each iteration or release, more complexity or functionality is added. Since each step adds a limited amount of functionality, this provides for effective testing and feedback from users. In between releases, a linear waterfall model can be used. As you can note by looking at products released in the software market (i.e., version 1.0, version 1.3, version 2.3), this type of model is popular within computer circles.

Example Programs

Throughout the book we will explore the features of Visual C++ by developing sample code and programs. We will pay special attention to object-oriented development through the uses of classes and illustrate how inheritance and polymorphism might be used. The use of classes will be demonstrated in Chapter 7, while we will tackle user interface design in Chapter 9.

Figure 1-2
Incremental model.

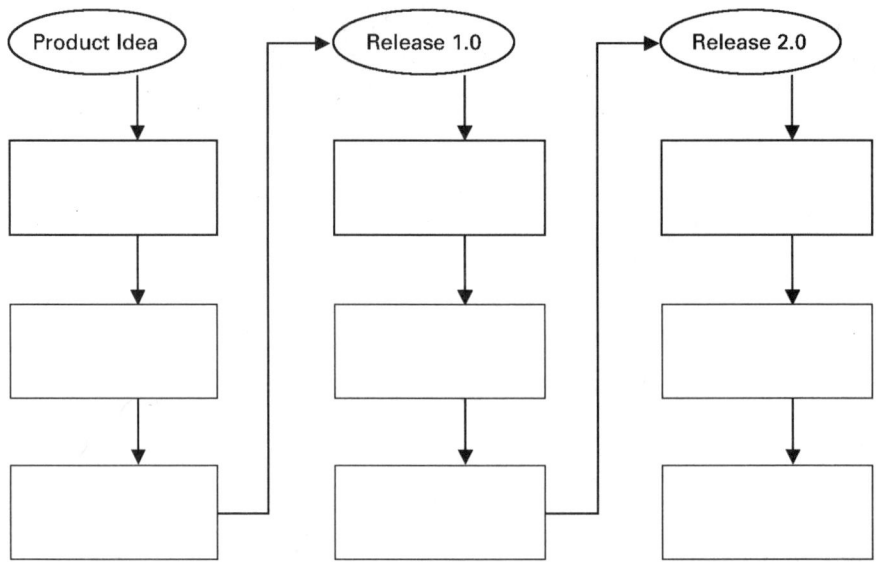

In Chapter 11, we'll explore the file and database handling capabilities of Visual C++. First we will create a simple bank simulator to illustrate the use of the fstream class for easy file handling. We will be paying special attention to the new ADO and OLE DB technologies. We will build sample applications that show how to use the ADO data control and data-bound controls. In Chapter 12, we will see how to use DAO to program with a database in code.

In Chapter 14 we will build three applications. First we'll see how to build a shared statistics library by creating a dynamic-link library, or DLL. We'll also see how to create an ActiveX control. Finally, we will investigate using ATL and MFC when building ActiveX controls.

CHAPTER 2

Overview of the Visual C++ Environment and Advanced Options

Introduction

Visual C++ uses an integrated development environment known as *Visual Studio*. Visual Studio is much more than a C++ compiler; it is a development environment that can be used with a suite of programming languages. For example, it can be used with Java, C++, or even with Digital FORTRAN. Visual Studio provides a seamless environment that you can use to maintain your source code, design a user interface, and compile and link your projects, as well as debug and test them. It is a good idea to familiarize yourself with the development environment before you start working on projects. A development environment such as Visual Studio is known as an *integrated development environment*, or IDE, since all the tools you need are integrated into one application.

The Developer Studio Environment

There are several components or tools of the development environment that you should be familiar with before you start creating projects. First, we need to know the types of projects available and what the elements of a project in Visual C++ are. Next, we need to know how to view and manipulate those elements. We will take a brief look at some useful tools that can enhance the development process.

We'll round out the chapter with a look at version control—specifically how to configure and use — followed by a look at the new features in Visual C++ version 6.

Project vs. Workspace

When working in Developer Studio, you will typically create and use a *workspace*. A workspace contains one or more projects. A project will contain the actual files that you work with, such as C++ source code files or resource files. A project corresponds to an executable file, a dynamic-link library, or an ActiveX control. Many workspaces that you create may only contain a single project, while others may contain several different kinds of projects in the same workspace.

Chapter 2: Overview of the Visual C++ Environment

What Is MFC?

If you are new to programming with Visual C++, you will soon notice that you see the abbreviation MFC all over the place. *MFC* stands for *Microsoft Foundation Classes*. The MFC are C++ classes found in a set of dynamic-link libraries usually placed in your computer's system directory. These classes provide a set of shared classes or objects that can be used in Windows programming. They are used to build Microsoft applications and can be used in your programs as well. By using MFC you can simplify Windows programming by using these prebuilt classes to provide a foundation on which to build your application. In other words, you can avoid reinventing the wheel when doing things such as creating menus, push buttons, and windows. We will be exploring the use of MFC throughout the book.

Project Types

There are several project types available in Visual C++. They range from a simple console program, which is a program with a command-line prompt-type interface, all the way to the creation of ActiveX controls and dynamic-link libraries. To start a new project in Visual C++, select *New* from the File pull-down menu. This will open the New dialog box. To start a new project, select the *Projects* tab (see Figure 2-1).

The main project types that we will be concerned with in this book are as follows:

- *ATL COM App Wizard*   ATL is the *Active Template Library*. You can use the ATL to create COM components, such as ActiveX controls and COM objects. The wizard will guide you through the creation process, providing several options such as whether to make the server an executable (EXE) or dynamic-link library (DLL). ATL provides an alternative to using MFC for ActiveX control development. We will investigate both methods in Chapter 14, "Advanced Topics."

- *Custom App Wizard*   The Custom App Wizard allows you to create your own application wizard for used in the New Project dialog box. The wizard you create can be based on an existing project, the standard MFC wizard steps, or custom steps that you define. This can be

Figure 2-1
Creating a project with the New dialog box.

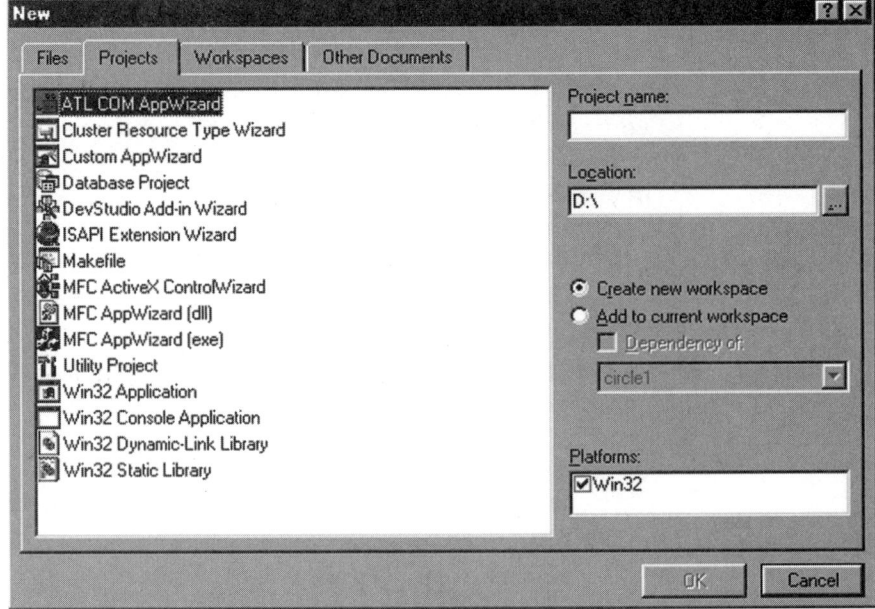

helpful if you are working on the same type of project over and over again.

- *Database Project*   This option can be used to create a database project.
- *Dev Studio Addin Wizard*   This option allows you to create an add-in for the integrated development environment. For example, you can use this to automate a frequently used task.
- *Extended Stored Proc Wizard*   A stored procedure is a procedure in a database that you can execute to provide output to the user. This wizard can be used to create stored procedures. They use the *extended stored procedure* function, which is part of a COM interface.
- *ISAPI Extension Wizard*   This wizard allows you to create Internet Information Server objects.
- *MFC ActiveX Control Wizard*   The MFC ActiveX Control Wizard can be used to build an ActiveX control using the MFC library. ActiveX controls can be used to provide toolbox functionality in other applications and environments, including Visual C++ and Visual Basic.
- *MFC App Wizard (DLL)*   You have probably seen many dynamic-link libraries on your system. These are files with a *.dll* extension. A

Chapter 2: Overview of the Visual C++ Environment

dynamic-link library is a code library that links up with an application at runtime. Dynamic-link libraries facilitate object-oriented development by providing a ready means for efficient code reuse. When you build an MFC DLL, you will be able to use the Microsoft Foundation Classes in your DLL. You have three options: Regular DLL with MFC Statically Linked, Regular DLL Using Shared MFC DLL, and MFC Extension DLL. The wizard will step you through the necessary options when creating your DLL and will create the files necessary to build your library.

- *MFC App Wizard (EXE)* This app wizard will allow you to create a standard windows application using MFC. The MFC App Wizard allows you to create a *single document application, multiple document application,* or *dialog-based application.* A single document type of application will provide the user with one document at a time that can be used to enter and manipulate data. Notepad or Wordpad are examples of Windows applications with single document interfaces. While it only allows the user to work with one document at a time, a single document application can have a functional window with menus and toolbars to enhance the user interface. It can even function as an OLE server or container.

    The next type of MFC application is a multiple documents interface. This is a program with a main window that functions as a container for multiple documents that can be used to enter data. A multiple document interface provides a more flexible environment for the user, because the user can have several documents open at once, and copy and paste information among them. Microsoft Word and Microsoft Excel are examples of multiple document interfaces.

    Finally, the last type of MFC application is the dialog-based application. This type of application uses simple dialog boxes for the user interface. This is similar to an EXE project in Visual Basic, where you design the interface with forms. You can also use the MFC App Wizard to create an HTML-based document application. We will explore each of these application types with examples in future chapters.

- *Win32 Application* You can select this option to create a Windows 32-bit application basically from scratch. This option is not really advisable, since it will involve a lot more work than selecting the MFC App Wizard.

- *Win32 Console Application* This is perhaps the simplest type of application that you can build with Visual C++. A console application is one that uses a command-line user interface. It will run inside a

- *Win32 Dynamic-Link Library* If you select this type of application, you will be able to create a dynamic-link library without using MFC. If you won't need to use MFC for your DLL, this is a good choice. When we discuss advanced topics in C++ in Chapter 14, we will talk about the steps necessary to create a non-MFC DLL.
- *Win32 Static Library* A static library is one that is linked with the source code of another application at compile time. You can create a static library by selecting this option.

File Types in a C++ Project

Each project you create in Visual C++ will contain several files. Files in Visual C++ come in a variety of types. Some of the more frequently used file types are as follows:

- *C++ Source File* This type of file contains C++ source code. A C++ source file has a *.cpp* file extension.
- *C++ Header File* A header file can be used to place C++ code or definitions that will be shared by many different files or even projects. You can define classes in a header file, include compiler constants or directives, or define global variables here. A header file has an *.h* file extension.
- *Icon File* An icon is a type of resource that can be used when designing the user interface for your project. An icon is a graphical file that can be used on command buttons or to represent a program in the Windows environment. Icon files have an *.ico* file extension.
- *Bitmap File* Most Windows users are familiar with a bitmap, or *.bmp* file, which is an image or picture file.
- *HTML Page* This is the basic type of file used in HTML/Internet programming.
- *Text File* You will sometimes need to include text files in your project. For example, when creating a dynamic-link library, you will use a text file with a *.def* file extension to tell the linker which functions to export.

Chapter 2: Overview of the Visual C++ Environment

Project Management

You can manage your open projects from the Project pull-down menu. Each of the menu items is described below.

Set Active Project   If you are doing complex development, you may wish to divide a project into multiple subprojects. Subprojects are related to one another in a treelike hierarchical fashion. You can use the Set Active Project menu to select which project you want to work on.

Add To Project   Selecting the Add To Project menu item allows you to add individual files to a project.

Source Control   You will see the Source Control menu item if you have installed Visual Source Safe. Visual Source Safe is an important tool that can be used to manage projects that are worked on by multiple developers. We will explore Visual Source Safe in more detail at the end of the chapter.

Project Settings

By selecting *Settings* from the Project pull-down menu, you can set several options that will influence the behavior of your project. This includes specifying options for the linker, compiler, debug, and optimizations. Visual C++ allows you to work with two configurations for your project: *debug* and *release*. When a project is in the development stages, you will be working with the debug configuration. This will allow you to include special program arguments or settings that you do not wish to include in the final compiled program. By default, output files for your project when you are working in the debug configuration will be placed in a debug directory, which is part of your projects folder. When you are done testing and debugging your project, you can compile a release version of the project, which may have different settings. The final executable, DLL, or ActiveX files are compiled to a *Release* directory within your project's folder.

When you open the Project Settings dialog box (see Figure 2-2), you will see the General tab and a drop-down list in the upper right corner of the dialog box labeled Settings For. If you click open this drop-down list, you will see three options:

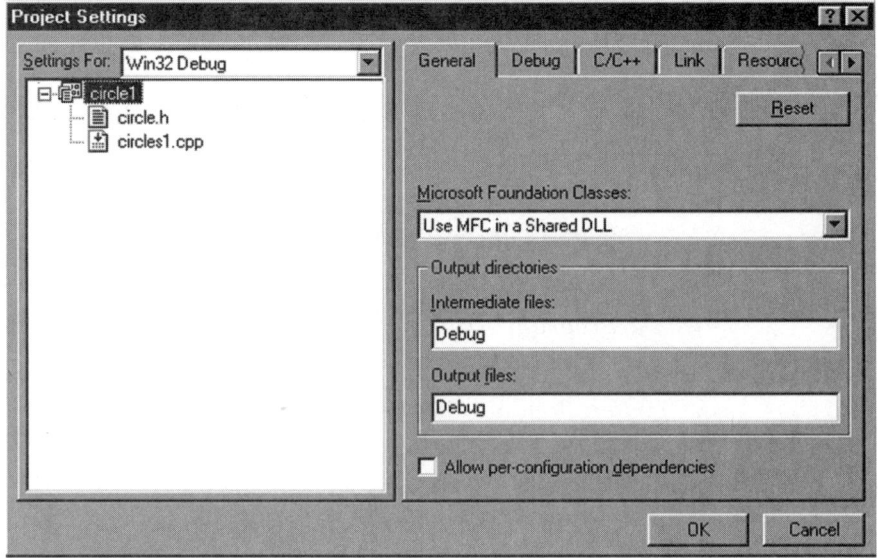

Figure 2-2
Project Settings.

- *Win32 Debug* Select this option to set properties for the debug version of your project.
- *Win32 Release* Select this option to set properties for the release version of your project.
- *All Configurations* Allows you to set options for all configurations.

You can specify the settings for the debug or release versions of your project by clicking on one of the tabs listed below.

The General Tab

The General tab has three important items. First, there is a drop-down list called Microsoft Foundation Classes. You can click open this list and specify the way that your project will use MFC. You will also see two text boxes called Intermediate Files and Output Files. Use these to specify the location where the linker and compiler place the OBJ, DLL, and EXE files for your project. By default, when you are working with the debug configuration for your project, Visual C++ will create a *debug* directory in the folder for your project. Output files will then be placed in this folder. A Release folder will also be created and used when you compile the release version of your project.

Chapter 2: Overview of the Visual C++ Environment

The Debug Tab

To set options for debugging, click on the *Debug* tab (see Figure 2-3). At the top of the window, you will notice a drop-down list called Category. Below this you will find the following options:

- *Executable for Debug Session*   If your project is an ActiveX or DLL, you can specify which executable program to use for testing.
- *Working Directory*   Specify the working directory for your project.
- *Program Arguments*   If your program requires arguments, specify them here.

The C/C++ Tab

This tab can be used to specify several settings for the C++ language, code generation, and compiler optimizations. You can select which options you wish to set by clicking the *Category* drop-down list at the top of the window.

General   Selecting this option allows you to set warning level, debug info, optimizations, preprocessor definitions, and project options.

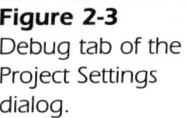

Figure 2-3
Debug tab of the Project Settings dialog.

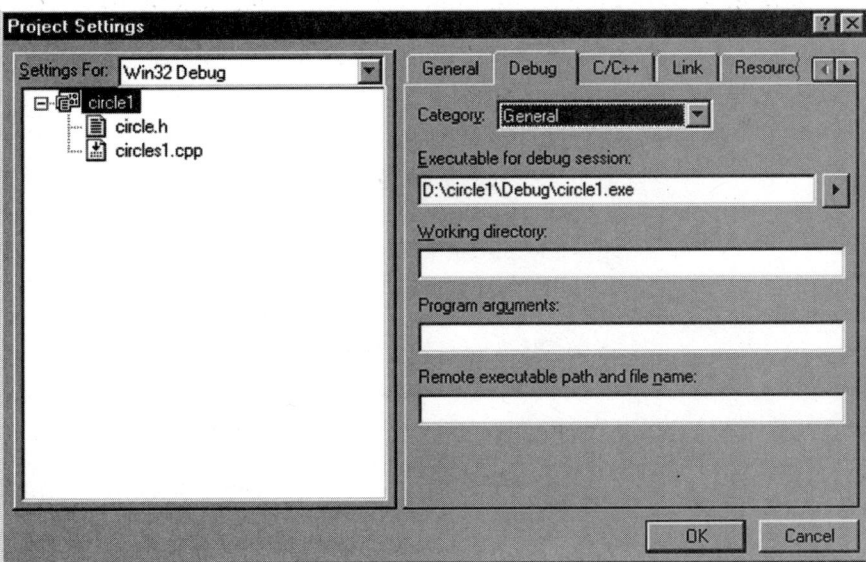

C++ Language Select this option to select the pointer to member representation. Choices include Best Case Always and General-Purpose Always. You can also set exception handling and runtime-type information.

Code Generation Code Generation option allows you to set the processor, runtime library, calling convention, struct member alignment, and project options. Processor allows you to target your application to a specific processor, like 80486 or Pentium Pro. The default selection is Blend, and unless you are writing code for a specific machine, you will probably want to accept this option. Calling Convention can be set to _cdecl, _fastcall, or _stdcall. These modifiers affect the way in which function identifier names are generated and how parameters are passed.

Customize If you select Customize, you can set the following options on or off: language extensions, function level linking, eliminate duplicate strings, enable minimum rebuild, enable incremental compilation, and suppress startup banner and information messages.

Listing Files You can use the Listing Files option to set up a browse file for your project. You can also specify the browse file destination. Optionally, you can exclude local variables from the browse file. The Listing File Type option can be set as Assembly Only, Assembly, Machine Code and Source, Assembly with Machine Code, and Assembly with Source Code.

Optimizations Use Optimizations to set the options for the compiler. In many cases, this is probably the most important setting. For the debug version of your project, the default setting is to disable optimization. For the release version, you may be concerned with attaining the maximum speed or with file size, depending on the nature of your application. The following settings are available:

- *Maximize Speed* This option will produce the fastest application possible. This may increase the file size of your executable.
- *Minimize Size* This option may be important if you are programming for the Internet, where you want fast download times, or if you are programming some specialized hardware, and storage space is at a premium. The compiler will do what is necessary to reduce the file size of your executable, but the trade-off may be reduced performance.

Chapter 2: Overview of the Visual C++ Environment

If you select Customize, you can tweak several individual options to suit your needs. Some of the available options include:

- Assume No Aliasing
- Assume Aliasing Across Function Calls
- Global Optimizations
- Improve Float Consistency
- Favor Small Code
- Favor Fast Code
- Frame Pointer Ommission
- Full Optimization

Also, if desired you can choose to favor inline function expansion.

Precompiled Headers   Precompiled header files, which have a *.pch* extension, allow you to compile and link your projects faster. This category allows you to set the options for using precompiled headers in your project.

Preprocessor   This option allows you to set preprocessor definitions, symbols, and additional *include* directories. *Include* directories are folders which include header files (files with an *.h* extension).

Linker

After your source code is compiled into object code or OBJ files, it must be linked into the final executable file. There are several options that you can set to manage the behavior of the linker. These options include:

- *General*   Here you can set the file name and extension for the final executable, DLL, or OCX file. Object and library files can also be specified. You can also specify incremental linking, profiling, ignoring default libraries, and map file generation.
- *Customization*   You can use the Customization category to specify incremental linking, program database, output file name, process message printing, and startup banner.
- *Debug*   This category can be used to specify the generation of a map file and debug information.

- *Input* The Input category can be used for specification of object/library modules.
- *Output* The Output category is used to set important information about your project. Use the Output category to specify base address, entry point, stack allocation, and version information.

P-Code

The C++ compiler now comes with an option for p-code. You can either compile your project normally (which is recommended, for performance reasons), or by using p-code, which will create object code that is interpreted at runtime. Using p-code can decrease the size of your project significantly. You can use the `#pragma` directive to select some functions for p-code and others for normal compilation when speed is a factor. If you think that reducing the size of your project is a critical factor, you might consider using p-code.

The Tools Menu

The Tools pull-down menu provides several useful tools that you can use when designing and testing your projects. These are as follows:

- *Source Browser* Selecting this option will allow you to create information files for your project that you can browse, for example, for variable names. An SBR, or source browse file, can be created for each OBJ file in your project.
- *Error Lookup* This option will retrieve the error message text corresponding to a value entered. This can be a system error message or a module error message. Values can be in hexadecimal or decimal.
- *ActiveX Control Test Container* Visual C++ provides a test container application that you can use to test your ActiveX controls. All aspects of an ActiveX control can be tested, including setting properties, data binding, and using the control's methods and events. Selecting this menu option will launch the test container application.
- *OLE/COM Object Viewer* Selecting this option will allow you to view the ActiveX controls and OLE objects installed on your system. The

Chapter 2: Overview of the Visual C++ Environment

viewer will show the interfaces supported by each object. This option can also be used to edit the Registry and view-type libraries.

- *Spy++*   This is a Win32 utility that will show you the processes, threads, windows, and messages of your system in a graphical format.
- *MFC Tracer*   This option can be used to debug your projects that use MFC. MFC Tracer will open a debug window and display messages in regard to the operation of the MFC library. If there are problems in your application with regard to MFC, MFC Tracer will display important warnings and errors.
- *Visual Component Manager*   This option can be used to select commonly used commands and to view databases, objects, and folders stored by the Visual Component Manager.
- *Register Control*   Selecting this option will allow you to register an ActiveX control with Windows.
- *Customize*   This option will open the Customize dialog box. It can be used to customize options on the Tools menu, and to set shortcut keys.
- *Options*   Selecting this menu item will open the Options dialog box, which will allow you to customize the Dev Studio environment. We will explore the Options dialog box in more detail below.
- *Macro*   A macro is a series of steps or commands that are executed by issuing one single command. This can be done to automate a series of complex or repetitive tasks in the developer environment.
- *Record Quick Macro*   You can record a series of actions that you perform in Dev Studio to save as a macro.
- *Play Quick Macro*   This option executes a macro.

The Customize Dialog Box

The Customize dialog box is available from the Tools pull-down menu (see Figure 2-4). This dialog can be used to customize the Developer Studio environment. Commands allows you to set up the menus for use in Dev Studio. The Toolbars tab allows you to specify which toolbars are visible in Dev Studio. The Tools option allows you to examine and modify the settings for each element of the Tool's pull-down menu; for example, you can check the command line and arguments for MFC and Tracer, or Spy ++. The Keyboard tab allows you to specify the keyboard shortcuts

Figure 2-4
The Customize dialog.

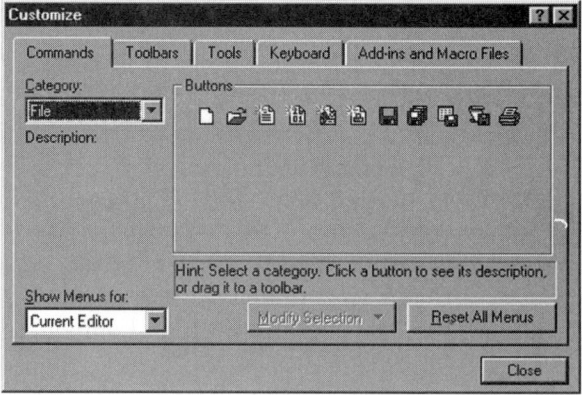

for each menu item in the Dev Studio environment. Add-ins and Macro Files allows you to set up add-ins and macros.

The Options Dialog Box

The Options dialog box can be accessed from the Tools pull-down menu (see Figure 2-5). This dialog can be used to set the options for the Dev Studio environment. For example, you can specify the save behavior for your projects, debug options, workspace options, and more.

Figure 2-5
The Tools Options dialog.

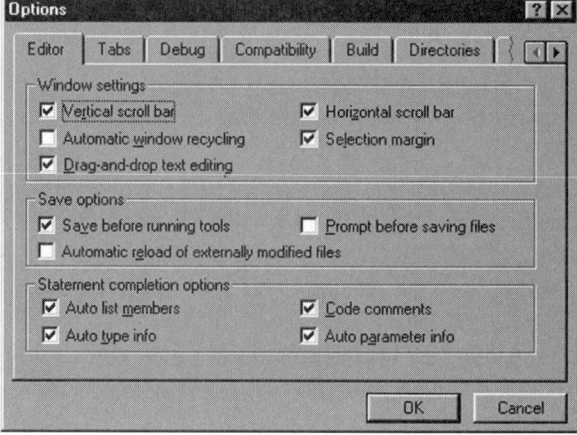

Chapter 2: Overview of the Visual C++ Environment

The Components and Controls Gallery

The components and controls gallery allows you to add components to your project. To open the components and controls gallery, click on the *Project* pull-down menu and select *Add To Project*. Next, select *Components and Controls* from the submenu. The Components and Controls Gallery dialog box will then open on your screen (see Figure 2-6). This window can be used to browse for the components installed on your system. You can look under *Developer Studio Components*, which includes a wide variety of useful prebuilt components. For example, you can use the Clipboard Assistant to add ready-made cut, copy, and paste functions to the Edit menu in your program. There are many useful components, but some other examples include a progress dialog box class, splash screen, status bar, and ToolTip support.

Under Registered ActiveX Controls, you will find all of the ActiveX controls that are installed on your computer. You can then add the desired controls for use in your project. These will vary from system to system.

Figure 2-6
The Components and Controls Gallery.

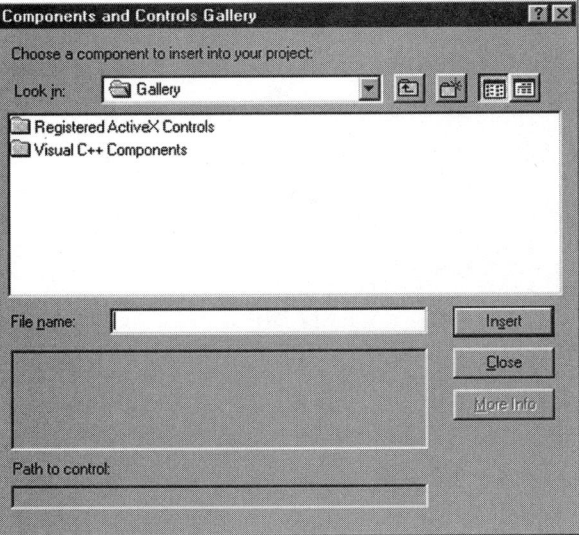

Navigating a Project: The Workspace Window

The Workspace window allows you to view your project in one of several ways. You can use File View, Resource View, or Class View (see Figure 2-7). The Workspace window is typically docked on the left side of the Developer Studio window. If it is not visible, select *Workspace* from the View pull-down menu, or press Alt + O.

When you select File View, all of the files in your project will be listed in an Explorer-type format. You will find a folder for each type of file. A typical file view for a project will show folders for source files, header files, and resource files. You can navigate to a desired file by clicking the folder to open and then double-clicking the file. An Editor window will then open on your screen with the contents of the file displayed.

When you select Class View, if you are using classes in your project, they will be displayed in a treelike hierarchical fashion. This will permit you to view and manipulate your project from a logical point of view. Each class will contain its member variables and functions from one location in the tree.

Resource View allows you to view and manipulate the resources in your project, such as dialogs and icons. For example, if you select a dialog box from Resource View, Developer Studio will display that dialog box

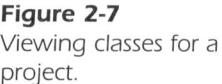

Figure 2-7
Viewing classes for a project.

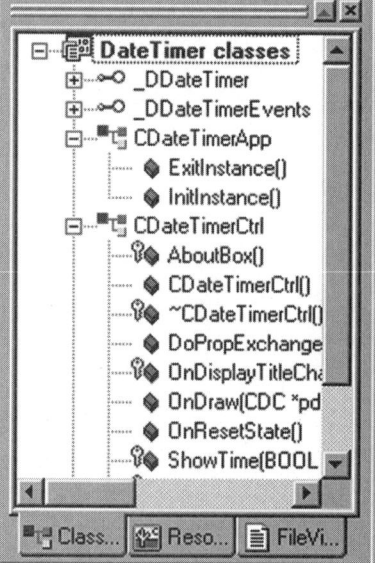

Chapter 2: Overview of the Visual C++ Environment

on your screen so that you can design it visually, in much the same way that you would with Visual Basic.

Info View allows you to access online versions of manuals provided by Microsoft. For example, you will find information on Developer Studio, Visual C++, Platform, and SDK documentation here. These documents can be navigated by clicking on the appropriate links or by selecting a desired topic from the Workspace window.

Class Wizard

You can use the Class Wizard to automate many of the tasks involved in building C++ classes. The Class Wizard can be opened from the View pull-down menu (see Figure 2-8). Class Wizard will only be available if your project is using MFC, and only with classes that are based on MFC. In other words, even if you are using MFC in your project, if you create your own independent classes, you cannot use Class Wizard with them. In summary, you can use the Class Wizard to:

- Add a new class based on MFC
- Manage messages and member variables for your classes

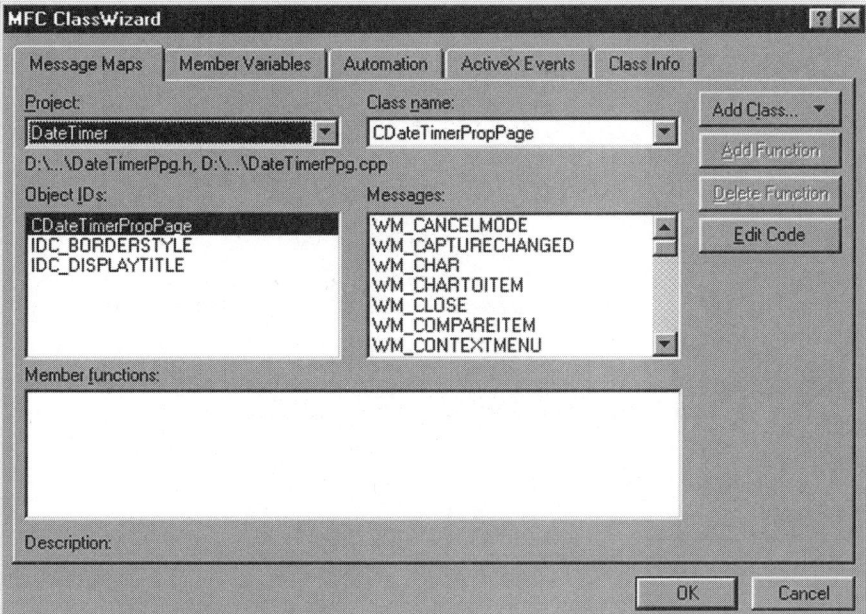

Figure 2-8
The Class Wizard.

- Delete member functions that act as message handlers
- Map messages to functions associated with various user interface elements
- Manage classes that support automation, add methods, properties, and edit code
- Add events to your ActiveX control projects
- View class info, such as header and source files, base class, and resource

Custom App Wizard Creation

If you have application frameworks that you will be using over and over, it might be helpful to automate the process. You can do this by creating a custom app wizard.

Version Control

Overview—When and Why You'll Need It

Version control becomes an important issue if you work in an environment where teams of programmers will be working on the same project. Things can get pretty hairy if each programmer can simply modify the source code whenever they please. Consider a hypothetical company with two programmers, Susan and Bob. Susan might get a copy of the project, make some changes, then copy it back to the central storage location. However, while she was modifying the code, Bob got a copy and put in his own changes. After Susan copied her changes over, Bob copied his changes into the central directory and overwrote the changes Susan made. Of course, good communication can help prevent such mishaps, but in the real world, good communication doesn't always exist, and these types of problems will occur. They can be prevented by using a version control product, such as Microsoft Visual Source Safe.

Visual Source Safe

Visual Source Safe (VSS) is a powerful product in its own right, and discussing all of the features is beyond the scope of this book. However, let's consider some of the main attributes that come with Source Safe to find out how it can protect code in a team developer or enterprise environment.

You can load Source Safe while running Visual C++ by selecting *Source Control* from the Tools menu. Once a project is loaded into Source Safe, to modify the source code of that project you have to "check out" the project or file. When a file is checked out, others can look at the latest version of the file and find out who checked it out, but they can't modify the source code themselves. In our little hypothetical example, if Susan would have checked out the source code of her project, Bob would not have been able to modify the code until Susan "checked in" the project. This prevents the mishap that we described from occurring. Not only does Source Safe prevent such conflicts from arising, but when Bob goes to Source Safe in an attempt to open the source code, he will be able to see that Susan has the code checked out. In this way, Source Save protects the source code from being changed by multiple developers at the same time, and it improves communication by allowing other developers to see who has the code.

Visual Source Safe also allows you to maintain a historical record as the code is checked back in. That way, every programmer can make a note of what he or she did to the code, and the date will be noted. This historical record is a valuable tool in any multideveloper environment.

Configuring Source Safe

To configure the way that Source Safe works with Visual C++, you need to open the Source Code Control Options dialog box. From the Tools menu in Dev Studio, select *Source Control*, and then choose the *Options* submenu. There are four basic options available:

- Get latest checked-in versions of files when opening a project?
- Check in files when closing the project?
- Add files to source control when adding them to a project?
- Remove files from source control when deleting them from the project?

You can select Yes, No, or Ask for each of these options. The best choice is to select Ask, so that you can determine how the project will work with VSS on a case-by-case basis.

Source Safe comes with an Admin utility, which allows the setup of user accounts and maintenance of databases. An administrator should be chosen to run the Admin utility. That person should set up an Admin account with a password to maintain security. Once this is done, the administrator can create a Visual Source Safe database. This is done by selecting *Create Database* from the Tools menu.

The administrator must set up an account for each of the developers that will be working on the projects stored in Source Safe. This is done by selecting *Add User* from the Users menu, where you can set up the user name and a password. Once a user has been created, it can be changed by selecting *Edit User*. The user names and passwords of all users can be changed, with the exception of the Admin account.

Once Source Safe is configured with a database and user accounts, users can use the Visual Source Safe Explorer to check out, modify, and check in Visual C++ projects. To open Explorer, click on the *Tools* menu in Visual C++ and select *Source Safe*. Next, choose *Run Source Safe*. Once you log in, the Source Safe Explorer will open on your screen. Just like the Windows Explorer, Source Safe has two window panes, which work in much the same manner. The window pane on the left displays a list of projects as a series of file folders. By clicking open a folder, you can see its contents in the right window pane. One or more files can be selected in the right window pane. You can click on *Select All* from the Edit pull-down menu to select every file. Source Safe also has a third pane at the bottom of the screen that will show the results of actions performed, such as checking out a set of files.

To check out one or more selected files, right-click on the selected files and choose *Check Out*. Visual Source Safe will then prompt you for the location on your computer where you want the files to be copied. Once a location is chosen, Source Safe will mark the files as checked out and copy them to your hard disk. You can then work on the project and make modifications without having to worry about another developer losing your changes.

When you are done working on the project, you can reverse the process by selecting *Check In* from the right-click pop-up menu. Source Safe will then prompt you to enter a note about what was done to the source files. This is where the historical record is built, so it's important to make detailed notes about what you did to the code. Once you click *OK*, Source Safe will copy the files from your computer into the Source Safe database and make the files available to other users. Note that once you check in a file, the files remain on your computer, but they will be marked as read-only.

Source Safe also provides an option called Get Latest Version. If you need to examine changes that other users have made to the code or simply wish to include the latest version of some code in your own version of the project, you can choose this option. This will copy the files onto your computer, but it will not allow you to put any changes you make into the Source Safe database.

Finally, when you have Source Safe installed and configured, note that you can interact with it from inside Visual C++. You can right-click on the file or files in the File View window, and there will be menu options for checking in, checking out, or getting the latest versions of the files.

In summary, if you are developing in an enterprise or team environment, a tool such as Source Safe should be used. This will guard against the types of conflicts that can arise in an environment with multiple programmers, as well as provide an accurate historical record of product development.

New Features in Visual C++ Version 6

With each release of Visual Studio, Microsoft continues to enhance each language with the addition of new features. Visual C++ is no exception, and it comes with several new features to enhance Windows development. Some of the new features are listed below.

ActiveX Data Objects (ADO)

ADO is the latest incarnation of Microsoft's database access technologies. ADO allows you to build database programs by using the ADODC data control and data-bound controls. Visual C++ comes with several data controls previously only found in Visual Basic, such as grids and combo boxes. With this enhancement, it is almost as easy to build database apps with Visual C++ as it is when using Visual Basic.

ATL Composite Control

Visual C++ allows you to create an ActiveX control using the Active Template Library, or ATL. An ATL composite control allows you to create an ATL-based control using other controls.

Command-Line Builds

The MSDEV utility can be used to command-line compile projects without creating a *Make* file. MSDEV uses the following syntax:

```
MSDEV <FileName> [/MAKE "<Project Name> -<Configuration Name> ALL"]
[/REBUILD /CLEAN /NORECURSE /OUT <Log File> /USEENV]
```

- `FileName` is a project (*.dsp*) or workspace (*.dsw*) file name.
- `MAKE` is used to specify which project and configuration (i.e., debug or release).
- `REBUILD` removes all intermediate files before compiling, and then rebuilds them.
- `CLEAN` also removes intermediate files but does not rebuild them.
- `NORECURSE` compiles the current project but not any dependent projects.
- `OUT <Log File>` can be used to send the output to a log file, rather than to the screen.
- `USEENV` will cause the directory settings found in tools options as specified in the project or workspace file to be ignored; the current environment options will be used instead.

Dynamic HTML

As the Internet works its way deeper into people's lives, development for the World Wide Web becomes more important. Recognizing this fact, Microsoft has included the CHTML MFC class as an aid in developing Web programs.

New Keywords

Visual C++ has added a set of new keywords to improve and extend the language. These include `bool`, `explicit`, `false`, `mutable`, `true`, and `typename`.

- `bool`   You can declare variables of type `bool`, which are simply Boolean variables that take on true/false values.

- `explicit` You can use the `explicit` keyword with constructors to specify that the constructor will only be used when the initialization explicitly matches that of the constructor.
- `mutable` The `mutable` keyword can only be used in C++ files. This keyword allows you to create a member of a `const` object that can be manipulated.
- `true` This is just a Boolean constant. The `false` keyword is also a Boolean constant.
- `typename` The `typename` keyword is supported in C++. This can be used to specify an undefined type.

OLE-DB Provider Templates

This allows you to build a remote connection to a database with an OLE-DB interface. OLE-DB is part of Microsoft's latest incarnation of its database technology.

Stored Procedures

The Extended Stored Procedure Wizard can be used to help you create stored procedures for use with SQL Server. Stored procedures created with the wizard use a COM interface.

CHAPTER 3

Requirements Gathering, Documentation, and Analysis

Introduction

In this chapter we tackle some issues many programmers would rather not think about. This includes requirements gathering, documentation, and technical support for the end user, and management issues such as estimating, scheduling, and staffing. While as a programmer you would rather just hack away, the ability to provide good, efficient, and user-friendly code requires that we think about the larger picture.

Requirements Gathering

Requirements analysis involves identifying the needs that the software program is supposed to fulfill. Requirements analysis is a crucial step in the software development process. If not done properly, the entire development cycle is compromised. During the requirements gathering phase, the following data needs to be determined:

- The type of system that will be developed.
- The skill level of the end user.
- How data will be stored.
- What tools will be used to develop the system.

Thinking about these issues needs to be done from the beginning of a software project. This means that communication with the end user is important throughout the entire life cycle of the project. Effective communication ensures that the concept of the system is the same for the software team as well as for the end user. It also keeps the skill level of the customer in mind throughout the process. Failure to do so can lead to added costs later on, such as having to redesign the user interface.

Documentation

Documentation can take two forms. The first is documentation for the end user. Without adequate documentation, the best software product in the world will fall flat on its face. Documentation for the end user includes users manuals and online help. These days it may also include a Web page. While we won't specifically address using Web-based documentation, the same principles described here will apply.

Chapter 3: Requirements Gathering, Documentation, Analysis

Documentation doesn't just include the end user. Don't forget that you'll need to document the code itself. This might be for other programmers or members of the design team. In the technical world, communication often gets lost, despite the fact that it's as important as ever.

End User Documentation

Documentation for the end user is probably one of the most unpleasant aspects of the software design process, but it is also one of the most important. Without good software documentation, the user may feel frustrated and unhappy with the product. Good software documentation for the end user includes:

- A printed users manual.
- Online help.
- Context-sensitive help

When a software project is finished and debugged, the tendency is to feel that it's all over. A software team probably would not rather think about it, but think about it we must.

Manuals   These days, some software companies are trying to keep costs down by skimping on the manual. However, this can actually damage your relationship with the customer. When a person buys a software product, they want to feel like they're "getting something." We know that what they're buying is the bits and bytes on the CD-ROM or disk, but the customer needs to feel they are getting something "solid." A thick users manual contributes to this feeling.

Besides aesthetics, a users manual can reduce cost in the long run. By having a ready reference, users will feel less tempted to reach for the phone and call tech support. In practice, things don't always work this way. We all know that many users won't open the manual; they'll just call tech support anyway. Even so, by having a clear, concise manual, you will give the majority of your users a ready source of information about your program and provide a professional appearance. Here are some suggestions for what you should incorporate into a users manual:

- Include clear, concise step-by-step directions. Set off step-by-step tasks with bulleted or numbered text.
- Identify menus, buttons, or commands clearly by using bold or italic text, or another typeface.

- Use plenty of screen captures and good illustrations.
- Include arrows and pointers in your illustrations so the user can see important features quickly.
- Avoid a condescending tone.
- Don't think completing any task is obvious; remember, the users of your program may not spend their lives on the computer.
- Don't be too technical. The inner workings of a software product should be invisible to the user.
- Include a "frequently asked questions" section, where users can turn to address technical problems. Since several users will typically run into the same problems, addressing those situations in a central location can reduce tech support calls.
- Make sure that contact information such as phone number, Web address, and e-mail are easy for the user to find in the manual, for those times when they do need direct help.

Online Help   Online help is just as important in documentation as the users manual. Online help should mirror the manual if possible, but may not necessarily be an exact copy. Don't skimp with online help. Again, this leads to frustrated customers who won't buy future products. There are several good online help tools available that make developing online help as simple as using a word processor. You should consider using HTML Web-type help to keep up with current technology. When developing online help, use the same guidelines as you would when developing a users manual. Be sure to use detailed explanations, a lot of screen captures, and illustrations, and don't leave anything out that you assume the end user should know. You can specify the help file for your application to use by setting the HelpFile property of the application object, or from the General tab of the Project Properties dialog box.

Context-Sensitive Help   The goal of user interface design is to be friendly. When designing help systems, the need to maintain a user-friendly approach is still there. This includes designing context-sensitive help. You can set context-sensitive help by setting the HelpContextID property of most controls. This property can be used to link a specific control or form to a specific topic in a help file. HelpContextID is type `long`, and must correspond to the context ID that you place in your help file. When the user has that form open, and he or she presses F1, the help file will open on that topic.

Chapter 3: Requirements Gathering, Documentation, Analysis

Technical Design Documentation

Technical design documentation is a process that follows the software project throughout its lifetime. This includes commenting code, defining algorithms with flow charts, communicating the structure of a project through diagrams, and maintaining scheduling and staffing requirements.

In Code Documentation   In Chapter 6, we'll spend some time talking about commenting code. Commenting code is really documentation. This provides a record of the software development process, provides an accessible place to explain your code, and keeps communication among the software team at a high level.

Documentation as a Living Process   Documentation is a living process because its lifetime follows the lifetime of the software project very closely. This starts at the very beginning. In Chapter 1, we discussed the various software life cycle models. No matter what life cycle model you choose, the first step involves defining the problem and planning the allocation of resources among other things. This is where the documentation process begins. Documentation can include:

- Clear definitions of the problem at hand. In other words, what task will the software perform, or what problem will it solve?
- Staffing and scheduling estimation.
- Algorithm definitions.
- Progress notes.
- A record of customer requests for new features.
- A record of changes made to the software.

Analysis

In this section we'll think about analysis issues that will come into play not only in the planning process but throughout the entire development cycle. The important first step is estimating the resources required to complete a project. This will impact and involve our second topic, scheduling. Finally, we'll talk about staffing requirements.

Estimating

When it comes to software design, estimating is a tricky business. When determining how long a project will take or how many people will be required to complete it, you're always talking about a large amount of uncertainty. The risk of uncertainty varies from project to project, but there are three main areas where this risk lies. The first of these is the complexity of the project. This is not a hard-and-fast rule; an experienced manager will have a good grasp of how the complexity of a project will impact development time. For example, software to run a spaceship is going to be more complicated than a desktop database program, but a manager with 20 years of experience at NASA will have a reasonable grasp on how long it should take, despite the increased complexity. In today's world, however, the uncertainty risk is higher with any task because of the rapid pace of technological change.

Another important factor that has been identified as a risk factor in estimation is the size of a project. A large software project has a larger number of interwoven parts. This makes the estimating process more difficult, and therefore gives rise to more error. Even if a large project can be made highly modular, each module may in itself be complex, injecting its own risk of error into the overall estimation process.

The third factor that can be identified as a risk to getting a good estimate is project structure. This means the ability to break down a project into a hierarchical and modular structure that is well suited to the use of different development teams. If a project fits this model well and your business has the resources necessary to build the required software teams, then it will be easier to provide a more accurate estimate.

Estimating is a complex process. Like software design, estimating can be made more effective and accurate by breaking the process down into smaller pieces. Once this is done, each task can be compared to tasks done in the past. Previously done tasks can then be used to provide a baseline estimate.

A detailed discussion of estimating is beyond the scope of this book. Readers who want to learn more should consult *A Manager's Guide to Software Engineering* by Roger S. Pressman, available from McGraw-Hill, for more information.

Scheduling

If you asked a randomly selected computer programmer what was the most common feature that all software products have, he or she might

Chapter 3: Requirements Gathering, Documentation, Analysis

say that the typical software project never gets completed on time. As I'm sure you're aware, the development of software never seems to go according to schedule. The causes of this problem are many, but we can probably identify a few that are common to most projects:

- *An unrealistic goal was set by management.* It's more likely that the time required to write software will be underestimated, especially by those not directly involved in writing code.
- *Unforeseen technical problems can arise.* This might include difficulties with a new language or technology.
- *Customer demands or rethinking of the software design.* This often requires continually retooling the code.
- *Bad communication among staff members or from management.* If it's not clear what management wants done, software may have to be redesigned after developers have already put in considerable effort.
- *New ideas don't pan out.* Sometimes a new technology or idea might look good until it's actually placed in the code. When it's decided to backtrack, this results in lost time.

Many scheduling problems can be resolved with careful planning. While we can never totally eliminate these problems, we can minimize them by taking the appropriate steps. Let's think about some of the ways we can do so.

Identifying Critical Tasks In any given software project some tasks will have a greater role in determining whether or not the project can be completed on time. Some tasks may be peripheral or simply easy to complete, so you know that they won't cause any bottlenecks. In contrast, a critical task will be one such that the time required to complete this task will determine the length of the entire software development cycle. This means that it is important to lay out which tasks are critical and then follow those tasks more closely.

Make a Careful Match between Staff and Technologies Time can be wasted by including a long learning curve in the development of a software product. For example, let's say your team has a product out that is running a bit slow according to the customers. Everyone on the team is a Visual Basic programmer, but the management decides to increase the speed of the project by moving some of the code to a dynamic-link library written in C++. After three months, no progress has been made. The reason? The programmers assigned to complete the task, who assured management it would be no problem, have been busy learning

C++ instead of attending to the task at hand. This kind of conflict can be avoided by making sure that everyone is comfortable with the technologies used before code development begins. This applies whether it's a new language, an ActiveX control, or an Internet app. Management has to be thorough when considering this problem; a programmer probably doesn't want to admit he or she doesn't know how to do something.

Communication among the Software Team Bad communication among members of the software team can result in missing scheduled deadlines. While this seems obvious, this is an area that is often overlooked in the software world. This is because programming can be a loosely defined, independent activity. Programmers don't want someone peering over their shoulder as they work, and often management wants programmers to be independent and take the initiative. If this mode of operation is taken too far, communication can break down. A programmer might leave a kickoff meeting feeling clear about what the software requirements are, and then two months later, it turns out he or she is totally off course. The result: lost development time and a late project. It's important to keep in touch with the members of the software team to make sure that everything is doing what it's supposed to, and that scheduled deadlines are being met.

Meeting Customer Demands or Inside Suggestions If a customer demands a new feature but requires that the product still meet scheduling deadlines, obviously you can't just dismiss them out of hand. Keeping the customer happy is the number-one goal, so if customer demands exceed your capacity to meet schedules, you may consider adding staff to solve a problem. The increased cost can be offset by increasing the unit price or by spreading the cost out over many product sales. Compare this to the damage done by missing scheduled deadlines: unhappy customers, reduced market impact, and a bad reputation. Balance, however, rears its ugly head again. If you are selling to multiple clients, you simply can't add a new feature every time a customer requests one or someone in the company has a bright idea. Weigh each new feature against how many customers have requested it and how it will impact the existing software, and ask yourself how innovative that bright new idea really is.

Staffing

When working on a computer, it's easy to forget the human element in the design process. However, staffing for a new software project is one of the most important tasks that will be done in the development life cycle. Staffing will involve not only determining how many people will be required to complete a project, but also evaluating each individual.

Evaluating the individual will involve a consideration of the following:

- *Knowledge* This is a straightforward analysis of what tools each member of the team needs to know. This might include computer languages, familiarity with ActiveX controls, DHTML, database access, or the ability to write a DLL, to name a few examples. Knowledge can be outweighed by experience. If a software engineer has a great deal of experience, he or she will pick up new tools quickly, while a software engineer who knows a lot of tools but has little experience can be a liability without proper guidance.

- *Experience level* Knowledge is one thing, but putting it into practice to solve a difficult problem may not be so easy without experience. The key is to build a software team with an experienced leader, especially if it is a critical task. Once an experienced leader is in place for guidance, the rest of the team may be easier to assemble.

- *Performance level* Not all employees will perform at the same level or with the same intensity. Knowing how fast or effectively a member of the software team can work is an important factor in any requirements analysis. It is generally thought that the most productive employees will be three times more productive than average. As a result, knowing who the top performers are can be of great importance when delegating speed or mission-critical tasks.

- *Personality characteristics* The personality characteristics of each staff member can have a big impact on the success of the team. It's important to consider personality characteristics when putting a team together and allocating tasks. There are several skills and characteristics to evaluate. Some questions to ask include: Does the employee have good communication skills? Is the employee a team player, or a loner? Can the person adapt well to change? Is he or she optimistic?

Putting together the right software team can be a complicated process. Once that has been done, the next issue to face is keeping the software team motivated. Some important issues in keeping the team motivated include:

- *Foster communication* We discussed this earlier. This is an important issue, so I'm listing it again as a factor to keep in mind when thinking about keeping the software team motivated. If a programmer isn't clear about responsibilities, this will create tension. It doesn't hurt to regularly meet with each team member to see how things are progressing.

- *Address burnout* Everyone gets burned out from time to time, and if schedules are too tight or the pressure is too high, the risk of burnout increases. Paradoxically, if the environment is too laid-back, programmers can burn out as well. This is because programmers tend to be driven people who like a challenge. In a soft or laid-back environment they will get bored. But if everyone is putting in 12 hours per day for weeks on end, they'll start to question if it's worth it. The trick is, of course, to develop an environment with a middle-of-the-road course. Keep it challenging, but realize that employees have lives outside of work.

- *Avoid jargon and too many diagrams* We've spent some time talking about software models and analysis. In the real world, this approach is important, but it must be kept in perspective. Programmers tend to be practical people, and if overwhelmed by too many flowcharts and diagrams, they won't take the project seriously.

- *Establish clearly defined roles* Make sure each member of the team knows his or her role. Roles should also be flexible to allow interaction and to effectively cover if an important team member cannot complete the project.

- *Keep meetings focused* If there's one thing that wastes time in a business, it's endless meetings. It's important to keep the intended purpose of the meeting in focus. Meetings can often deteriorate so much that by the end of two hours of discussion, the original problem was completely neglected. So you've wasted time, and you still have an unsolved problem on your hands. In short, stay on track in software meetings.

- *Provide a helpful atmosphere* The development environment should be one in which members of the team are encouraged to ask for help if necessary. Developers should be encouraged to ask questions or to ask for help without being made to feel incompetent.

In summary, putting together a software team with just the right mix is not an easy task. However, you can build effective software teams by keeping balance in mind. This means balance of experience and performance level, as well as balancing personality characteristics to keep things running smoothly.

PART 2

Designing Visual C++ Software

CHAPTER 4

Systems Architecture vs. Software Architecture

Introduction

Chances are you will have to face the issues entailed in developing client/server software sometime during your programming career. This means that you will have to take the structure of the network into account when designing your software. Software should be designed in a flexible way so it can be used on a system of any size, from a single laptop to a large enterprise network. This means that you will have to break your software down into components. With this flexible design, an application can be scaled to work in a larger environment simply by distributing the components among different server computers.

Systems Architecture: The Big Picture

Since Windows applications are built with components, you should be able to design your application and have it run on a single desktop or in a client/server environment without much, if any, modification. This is done by building your application in three distinct layers:

- *The user interface (UI) layer*   This layer is used to present and accept data to and from the end user. This layer of the application will not do any data processing or perform any business logic. The underlying structure of the data is hidden from this layer.
- *Business logic layer*   This middle layer will perform the application logic and act as an interface to the data layer. The business logic layer can be implemented as a component that resides on an intermediate server. You can implement the business logic by designing your software with classes, which we will cover in Chapter 7.
- *Database layer*   In an enterprise environment, this layer will typically be placed on a server. The database layer does not interact directly with the UI layer. Instead, it interacts with the classes you create to model the data.

By splitting an application into three separate layers that more or less correspond to the hardware configuration of the network, the application is flexible enough to be scaled and modified with minimal pain on the part of the developer. Each layer interacts with another layer through an interface. For example, if the business logic changes, the classes designed to create the middle-layer component can be swapped out and replaced. Since the UI layer and database layer only interact with the business logic layer though an interface, things will go on running as before. In other words, as far as the other layers are concerned, nothing has changed.

The three-layered approach allows us to scale the application to different-sized organizations. If it's a single user, all three components can fit nicely on a single machine. In a moderately sized two-tiered network, we can run two tiers on the client machine and have the server perform data services. In a large network, each tier will be put on a different component of the network.

Developing software to run on the network means that you will have to have a general understanding of how a network functions. You will also need to know about communicating with server computers, which may have specialized services. An in-depth treatment of client/server architecture is beyond the scope of this book. However, in this chapter a brief overview of the client/server structure will be given, hopefully to justify the need to build three-tiered applications. For a detailed treatment of the client/server architecture, see *Second Generation Client/Server Computing* by D. Travis Dewire (McGraw-Hill, 1997).

Networks

Computer networks began with large mainframes that did all the processing, while users sat at what was known as a "dumb" terminal. The terminal did not store any data; it simply provided the user with access to the mainframe. As the cost of computing power has fallen, the trend has been toward more-distributed designs. Early versions of distributed computing involved connecting together a relatively small group, say, a single department. Files and devices such as printers were shared among the group. Thus, the concept of a local area network, or LAN, was born.

Client/Server Model

The idea of a client/server architecture is based on specialization. Certain computers, known as servers, are specialized to perform certain tasks. With application software, this usually involves fulfilling data requests. When a request is made for data, the server returns the result of the request rather than the entire database file. Processing the data and presenting it to the user is done on the client machine. With the server machine handling data services, in a first-generation client/server environment the client takes care of the following:

- Presentation of data to the user
- Application and business logic
- Data logic

Second-generation client/server takes further advantage of the concept of distributed access by adding additional servers to the mix. By including multiple servers on the network, different servers can be specialized to provide solutions to different tasks. The client machine will still be involved in presentation services as before. However, in second-generation client/server, application logic and business rules can be moved to a server computer. Still another server handles data requests. This type of architecture is known as a *multitiered client/server architecture*. A server is no longer a machine that is set up to perform a wide variety of tasks. Instead, you have several servers, each of which is specialized and optimized for a single task. The network is now divided into three tiers:

- *User interface tier*   Implemented on the client machine
- *Application logic and business rules*   Implemented on a specialized server, sometimes known as the "intermediate server"
- *Database access*   Implemented on yet another server

The client machine is typically a single-processor computer running Windows NT workstation. This is connected through a LAN to a departmental or application server. An application server can be a single processor or multiprocessor machine and may handle up to 100 users. This machine is connected through a wide area network, or WAN, to an enterprise or data server.

A multitier architecture allows an organization to maintain specialized or dedicated servers. Servers can be optimized for one particular task. For example, a high-performance computer can be used for computation-intensive operations. The architecture can be expanded as other needs are identified. New servers can be added that provide functions in the form of objects or components that are accessible to every application on the network. The network can include a data warehouse server that functions as a dedicated data processing server.

Chapter 4: Systems Architecture vs. Software Architecture

Distributed Applications

Today's software applications are broken down into components. Many of these components are shared by several different applications. This is as true on your desktop as it is in a client/server environment. However, in a distributed or client/server environment, common components can be maintained on a server. Typically, components that are common to several applications can be executed on the server, with the results sent back to clients as needed. A distributed application may need to know how to interact with the specialized services of a server computer.

A distributed application can be one that has either distributed data or distributed processing. In a multitier environment, an application can have both data and processing distributed. During the design phase, the application must be broken down into separate units that can run independently. The first step involves defining the three tiers: user interface, business logic, and data processing. Each tier may be broken down and refined even further. The goal is to allow the organization to replace individual components without affecting the operation of the application as a whole.

General Scalability

Scalability depends on a modular architecture. This means the ability to upsize or downsize an individual component without changing the system as a whole. The system can adapt to the resource demands it encounters. For example, we can increase disk capacity or replace a server by another with more power. Scalability also means that servers are specialized for a specific function such as data warehousing.

Layered Application Development

An application should be designed in a modular fashion. By dividing an application into several modular components, the robustness and flexibility of the software is ensured. This is because we can modify any one component without having any impact on the rest of the application. Each module interacts with other components only through the interface it presents.

When building a modular application, you assign each component a specific task to perform. All computing tasks can be classified into three general areas: user interface tasks, logic tasks, and data processing tasks. This type of breakdown leads to the multitiered development model promoted by Microsoft. Each tier of the application is responsible for performing one aspect of the overall software model. At this point, we can consider three types of n-tier applications.

One-Tiered Model

The first type of model is known as a one-tiered model. This is just an application running on a single PC. The data, business rules or logic, and user interface are all implemented on the same machine. If data sharing is not a requirement, this is a desirable model, since speed is optimized. No time is wasted going out to retrieve data. However, in today's world there aren't many useful applications that don't need to share data in some way. As a result, there aren't very many one-tiered applications in existence.

Two-Tiered Model

The two-tiered model is based on the client/server concept. In this model, the user interface and business logic are in an application stored on each client machine. The data is stored on a server computer. The user sends requests to the server in the form of queries, which the server fulfills and returns to the client. The client application formats the data and presents it to the user either by using forms or in reports. The user can then manipulate the data, print reports, and so on. The business logic layer can also be placed on the server in this manner. No matter where the business logic layer is placed, a compromise has to be made. This is because if we place it on the client machine and modifications are made as business logic changes, we have to redistribute the software to each client machine. If the business logic is placed on the server, downtime can result as the server is updated and database programming is changed.

Three-Tiered Model

The most recent incarnation of n-tiered development is the three-tiered model. The model has been developed primarily because of the rising popularity of the Internet. With a Web server, data is processed and formatted before being presented to the client, which in this case is a Web browser. This led to the idea of using a middle layer to implement data formatting before sending it to the client. The middle layer also functions to validate data before returning it to the server. This middle tier is known as the *business services tier*. The benefit of having the middle tier is that it can be changed as the business logic changes. This simplifies updates because the client does not have to receive new front-end software, while the server side database can remain unchanged.

Don't think this type of model is restricted to use on the Internet. The three-tiered model is a flexible model that can be used in all software development, even on a single machine. The way each tier is distributed will depend on how large the business is in which the application is used. In any case, the three-tiered model can be used in application development with three phases. Each phase should be completed before moving on to the next.

- *Define the object model*   In this phase, we define the objects that will be used in the program. Objects can be represented by constructing classes (see Chapter 7).
- *Build the database*   The design of a database is just as important as the other phases of software development. Pay special attention to the construction of file formats, table design, relationships between tables, and indexes.
- *Build the user interface layer*   The UI layer should be built in the last phase of development. This runs counter to the temptations offered in a visual programming environment. By developing the business logic and database layers first, we can ensure that an application will be more robust.

The three tiers in this model are the UI layer, the business logic layer, and the data layer.

UI Layer   The first tier is the client application that the end user sees on his or her computer. The client application is usually a standard EXE program. This layer will include windows, dialog boxes, and ActiveX controls that provide the user with a means to manipulate the data. The UI layer will manipulate the data through the objects provided by the middle tier. With three-tiered development, the underlying structure of the database is invisible to the UI layer.

Business Logic Layer   The business logic layer is based on an object model, which in C++ means creating classes. The main purpose of the business logic layer is to encapsulate the data interface. This will permit us to hide the data layer from the rest of the program. It will then be easier to manipulate each layer of the software without affecting the other layers.

The business logic layer is built on business objects. These objects are abstract representations of something in the real world. This can be a model of a person, an object, or a process. For example, we can model employees, customers, a manufacturing process, or a machine.

Once each object that we need to model is identified, we need to define an interface for the object. The interface of each object is the way that other objects or layers of the system can communicate with it. The interface should be as independent of the underlying architecture as possible. This means that the "internals" of the object can be changed while maintaining the same interface, which keeps communication between objects and layers unchanged.

One way to build the middle tier is to create a dynamic-link library, or DLL. A dynamic-link library can include the classes used to define the objects in an application. These objects can be "wrapped" by functions which are exposed to other layers or applications. The UI layer, or the application presented to the end user, can access the objects of the DLL through the wrapper functions. When a business object is changed, the DLL is modified by changing the underlying classes, but the client application can continue to operate as before, since the communications interface remains unchanged.

Data Layer The final piece of the three-tiered model is the database layer. This layer is placed on a server computer. This is where the actual data processing takes place. Information from the data layer is passed to the objects in the business layer, or middle tier. There is no direct link between the client application or UI layer and the data layer.

In conclusion, keep in mind that the three-tiered model of application development is not restricted to business or Internet applications. If you are developing a scientific or engineering type of program, the same breakdown of the software can be used.

CHAPTER 5

The C/C++ Programming Language

Introduction

In this chapter a quick review of the C/C++ programming language will be provided. We will cover the following topics:

- C/C++ data types
- Variable declaration
- Constants
- Pointers and arrays
- Control structures
- Programming with functions
- Structs and enumerated types
- The basic structure of a C program
- Using #include and other preprocessor directives
- Using Visual Source Safe with your projects

It is assumed that you already have some exposure to C++ programming, so we will not go into detail here. For a more detailed look at the C/C++ programming language, see *Visual C++ 6: The Complete Reference* by Chris H. Pappas and William H. Murray III (McGraw-Hill, 1998).

Data Types

The C++ programming language provides a wide range of data types that can be used for any programming task. These include several numeric types, types for handling characters, and more. We briefly review each type here.

int

The `int` data type can be used to track whole numbers. The size and range of an `int` varies depending on the system; for Windows 95, an `int` requires 2 bytes of storage and has a range between −32,768 to 32,767. Under Windows 98 or Windows NT, an `int` is 4 bytes or 32 bits, with a range from −2,147,483,648 to 2,147,483,647. An `int` can also be declared with the `unsigned` keyword, for zero or positive values only. This doubles the range of an int; for Windows 98 and NT, the range becomes 0 to 4,294,967,295.

long

The long data type is also used to track whole numbers, but over a wider range. A long requires 4 bytes of storage and has a range from −2,147,483,648 to 2,147,483,647. On a Windows 98 or Windows NT system, this is the same as an int. Like an int, you can declare a long with the unsigned keyword, which has a range of 0 to 4,294,967,295.

short

The short data type is another type that can be used for whole numbers. A short requires 2 bytes of storage and has a range between −32,768 to 32,767. If you declare a short with the unsigned keyword, the range becomes 0 to 65,535.

float

A float is used for fractional or floating-point numbers, such as *pi* (3.14159). A float requires 4 bytes, and the range is ±3.4 E ±38. This provides 7 digits of precision.

double

Like a float, a double tracks fractional or floating-point values. A double is allocated 8 bytes of memory space, however, giving it a larger range, from 1.7 ± 308, or 15 bits of precision. You can also declare a long double, which is allocated 10 bytes of storage and has a range of 1.2E ± 4932 (19 digits).

char

A char can be used to hold individual characters or can be used to track whole numbers over the range −128 to 127. A char is allocated a single byte. You can also declare an `unsigned char`, which has a range from 0 to 255. To handle strings, you can declare an array of `char`s, with each element of the array holding a single character in the string.

__int8

This data type is the same as `char`. The range is −128 to 127, and `__int8` requires 1 byte of storage space.

__int16

This data type is the same as `short`. The range is −32,768 to 32,767, and `__int16` requires 2 bytes of storage space.

__int32

This data type is the same as `int` (on Windows 98 or Windows NT systems) or as `long`. The range is −2,147,483,648 to 2,147,483,648. `__int32` requires 4 bytes of storage.

__int64

This type requires 8 bytes of storage and has a range from −9,223,372,036,854,775,808 to 9,223,372,036,854,775,807. There is no correspondence between the `__int64` type and any of the other basic types.

bool

This data type can be used to track Boolean, or true/false, values.

wchar_t

This data type can be used for wide characters, which are 16 bits long, as opposed to a `char`, which is 8 bits long.

Chapter 5: The C/C++ Programming Language

Declaring Variables

In C++, variables are declared by specifying the data type followed by a listing of variable names. Variables are declared at the beginning of a function. In Visual Basic, you can declare a variable wherever you need it. In C++, if your variables are not declared at the beginning of a function, this will cause an error. The syntax for a variable declaration is as follows:

```
Data_Type variable_name;
```

Each variable declaration is terminated with a semicolon. For example, to declare an integer, we write:

```
int max;
```

This declares a variable named max of type integer, which can be used to track whole numbers. We can declare multiple variables of the same type on one line by separating each variable name with a comma. In the next example, we declare three integers, max, min, and sum:

```
int max, min, sum;
```

To declare more than one data type, we place the variables of each type on a separate line. In the next example, we declare three variables of type int like we did in the previous example, but this time we add the variable average, which will track real or floating-point values:

```
int max, min, sum;
float average;
```

Rules for Variable Names

In C++, variable names, function names, and names used for user-defined types are known as *identifiers*. There are certain rules the identifiers you use in your programs must adhere to, but C++ is pretty flexible about the names you use. In general, when naming your variables, keep the following rules in mind:

- Identifiers can contain letters, numbers, and underscore characters.
- An identifier can be as short as a single character.

- In C, only the first 31 characters are guaranteed to provide a unique name.
- Identifiers can begin with a single underscore, but C++ reserves the use of names that begin with two underscore characters.
- Identifiers are case-sensitive. `Max`, `MAX`, and `max` are all recognized by C++ as representing three different variables.

It is often customary to use a single underscore for clarity with variable names. For example, we could declare a `short` to function as a loop counter:

```
short _counter;
```

Also, remember to always terminate variable declarations with a semicolon.

Initializing Variables

In Visual Basic, numeric variables are initialized to zero and strings are set to blank text. This is not the case in C++. When a variable is declared and used the first time, it will contain whatever happens to be in the memory location that was allocated by the compiler. For this reason it is a good idea to always initialize your variables before you use them. We can initialize variables after they are declared, as shown in this example:

```
int sum, deviation;
sum = 0;
deviation = 0;
```

C++ also permits you to initialize a variable at the same time you declare it. This is a handy feature that can save typing. In the next example, we declare a variable of type `double` named `average` and initialize it in the declaration statement:

```
double average=0;
```

As you can see from this example, you simply follow the variable name with an equal sign and the initial value you want to set.

Declaring Constants

There are many times in software development when you will use the same value over and over. This can be a text string, or more often it will be a numeric value. You could type out the value explicitly throughout your code, but that would be a nightmare in even a moderately sized program if the value needed to be changed. Doing so would require a careful search through every line of code to see where it was used. Another option would be to declare a variable and initialize it to the constant value. This provides the advantage of referring to the value by a symbol rather than typing the value explicitly, but then you might inadvertently change it later on in your code.

Fortunately, most programming languages provide a better means to declare constants, and C++ is no exception. There are really two ways to define a constant. The first is to use the #define directive at the beginning of a file. The #define directive is a macro that tells the compiler to substitute one text string for another in your source code. For example, we can use the #define directives to define TRUE and FALSE:

```
#define TRUE -1
#define FALSE 0
```

When you use a #define statement, leave off the terminating semicolon. Later in our code, we can set a variable using the symbol used in the #define statement:

```
IsLate = TRUE;
```

In C++, we can also declare constants using the const keyword. This keyword is used in conjunction with a data type. This essentially allocates the correct memory space for a quantity and gives it a symbolic name, much like a variable. The difference is that the compiler will not let you modify any identifier you declared using the const keyword. In the next example, we declare a constant to track the number pi:

```
const double pi=3.14159;
```

You can include your constant definitions with the variable declarations in your functions, or if you require more global scope, you can include them in a header file.

Casting

A *cast* can be used to convert the data type of a variable or expression to another type. You can cast by enclosing the data type you want to convert to in parentheses before the expression or variable name. The syntax of a cast is as follows:

```
(new data type) expression
```

In the next example, we convert the `intensity` variable to a `double` before completing the operation:

```
int intensity=0;
double x,y;

//code here to read in values

x = (double)intensity + y;
```

In this example, `intensity` is converted to type `double` before the operation is performed. When you are mixing data types in arithmetic statements, it is a good idea to use casts to explicitly convert each variable or expression to the appropriate type.

The Increment and Decrement Operators

When you write a program, chances are you will perform the operation:

```
x = x + 1;
```

or perhaps:

```
x = x - 1;
```

over and over again. C++ provides the increment and decrement operators to provide a shorthand notation and speedier way to perform these kinds of operations. The increment operator is used by including two "+" signs before or after the variable name. For example, we can replace the following expression:

Chapter 5: The C/C++ Programming Language

```
x = x + 1;
```

with the increment operator:

```
x++;
```

Or we can replace the line:

```
x = x - 1;
```

with the decrement operator:

```
x--;
```

The increment and decrement operators can also be used within any assignment statement. Where the operator is placed is of primary importance; this tells the compiler when to do the operation. For example, if we write:

```
sum = max + y++;
```

the variable named y will be incremented by one *after* the assignment statement is executed. However, if we write:

```
sum = max + (++y);
```

the value of y will be incremented by one *before* the assignment statement is executed. The parentheses around the increment operator were included for clarity.

C++ also provides a shorthand you can use to compute basic arithmetic operations. We can start by looking at addition. For example, we can write:

```
sum = sum + j;
```

Or, using the more concise shorthand, we can write:

```
sum += j;
```

This also works with other operations such as subtraction or multiplication. For example, we can convert:

```
max = max * k;
```

into the concise statement:

```
max *= k;
```

Bitwise Operators

You can use the bitwise operators to act on the value contained in a single variable. The bitwise operators may be familiar to readers who have used logic tables or to those who have done computer hardware design. Each of the bitwise operations is described below.

AND

The & symbol is used to "AND" two values together. Logical AND is defined by the following table:

X	Y	X AND Y
0	0	0
0	1	0
1	0	0
1	1	1

For example, we can apply the & operator to two `char` variables in code:

```
char result, x, y;

...

result = x & y;
```

Suppose that the contents of each variable were defined by:

```
x = 0101 0111
y = 1001 1110
```

We obtain the result by applying the AND operation to each bit at a time. Starting from left and working our way to the right, the result is as follows:

```
result = 0001 0110
```

OR

Logical OR returns "true," or 1, if one or both values are 1. The truth table for OR is as follows:

```
X    Y    X OR Y
0    0    0
0    1    1
1    0    1
1    1    1
```

We can apply the OR operator in code by writing:

```
result = x | y;
```

Recall that the contents of each variable were defined by:

```
x = 0101 0111
y = 1001 1110
```

We obtain the result by applying the OR operation to each bit at a time. Starting from left and working our way to the right, the result is as follows:

```
result = 1101 1111
```

Exclusive OR (XOR)

Exclusive OR or XOR is almost like OR, except that XOR returns zero if both values are 1. The truth table for XOR is as follows:

```
X    Y    X XOR Y
0    0    0
0    1    1
1    0    1
1    1    0
```

We can apply the XOR operator in code by writing:

```
result = x ^ y;
```

Recall that the contents of each variable were defined by:

```
x = 0101 0111
y = 1001 1110
```

Again, we obtain the result by applying XOR to each pair of bits:

```
result = 1100 1001
```

One's Complement

One's complement allows us to toggle each bit, changing a 1 to a 0 and a 0 to a 1. To take the one's complement of a variable in code, we write:

```
x = ~x;
```

If the variable x contained the following bit sequence before the operation:

```
0110 0101
```

the one's complement operation will toggle the value of each bit, so that afterwards x contains:

```
1001 1010
```

Left and Right Shifts

C++ also allows you to shift the bits in a variable by a specified amount. Bits will be shifted off one end, while 0's are brought in the opposite side. Each shift to the right is the same as dividing a number by 2, while each shift to the left is the same as multiplying a number by 2. To shift a value in code, you use the << operator for a left shift and the >> operator for a right shift, followed by a whole number that tells the compiler how many times to do the shift. For example, to left-shift a variable three times, we can write:

```
int y;
y = 30;
y = y << 3;
```

To right-shift the variable one time, we write:

```
y = y >> 1;
```

When looking at the bits contained in a variable, remember that a right shift will bring in 0's from the left side, shift bits over to the right, with the rightmost bits "falling off." For example, if we have the following bit pattern:

```
1100 0101
```

and we right-shift two times, the pattern becomes:

```
0011 0001
```

When shifting to the left, 0's are shifted in the right side, while the leftmost bits are dropped off. A left shift by three positions of the bit pattern:

```
1001 1101
```

results in:

```
1110 1000
```

where you can see that three zeros were shifted in on the right side.

Defining New Type Names

C++ allows you to define your own type names by using the `typedef` keyword. This keyword will create a new name for an existing type. This can be used to make your code more readable and clear; in other words you can specify the meaning of your variables by creating a new type definition. The syntax for using `typedef` is as follows:

```
typedef type newname;
```

In the next example, we create our own type name called `meterspersecond`, which we will use in place of `double`:

```
typedef double meterspersecond;
meterspersecond speed;
```

The second statement is a regular variable declaration. Our source code makes it clear that the variable `speed` tracks meters per second, but the compiler knows this is just a name used in place of `double`, and so creates the speed variable to be type `double`.

Pointers

C/C++ has a special way to declare variables, known as a *pointer*. When a variable is declared as a pointer, the variable actually stores the *memory address* of the data, rather than the data itself. As you will see, this ability leads to a more flexible way to build software. You can declare a pointer by prefixing an asterisk character (*), which is known as the *indirection operator*, to the beginning of the variable name. In the next example, we declare a pointer to an integer named `sumtotal`:

```
int *sumtotal;
```

Suppose that we decided to print `sumtotal` to the screen:

```
//code here to calculate the sum total
...

//print it out
cout << "The Total Value is : " << sumtotal;
```

If we ran this code, we would see something like this on the screen:

```
The Total Value is : 0x00000001
```

This is because when you refer to a pointer value without the asterisk, you are referring to the memory address of the variable. To access the actual data the memory address has, you must append the asterisk to the beginning of the pointer variable name, just like we did when declaring it. If we change the code to:

```
//code here to calculate the sum total
...

//print it out
cout << "The Total Value is " << *sumtotal;
```

when we ran the program, we might see something like this:

```
The Total Value is : 42
```

Chapter 5: The C/C++ Programming Language

Pointers are very useful when programming with characters and when passing variables to functions. We will cover each of these topics below.

The addressof Operator

There will be times when you will be required to set a pointer to point at the memory location of a regular variable. Or perhaps a function will expect a memory address (i.e., a pointer) as an argument, but the variables you are passing are plain variables. How do you resolve this problem? The answer is you use the *addressof* operator, which is just the ampersand character (&) appended to the beginning of the variable name.

In this example, we declare two variables of type double. The first variable, NumItems, is a pointer. The second variable, _Count, is not. We can set NumItems to the memory location of _Count by using the address of operator:

```
double *NumItems, _Count;

_Count = 8;

*NumItems = 42;

cout << "COUNT IS : " << _Count;
cout << "\nLocation of NumItems " << NumItems;
cout << "\nNumItems is : " << *NumItems;

NumItems = &_Count;
cout << "\nNumItems is : " << *NumItems;
```

After we declare the variables, we assign initial values to each variable. Then we print them out. The output on the screen looks like this:

```
COUNT IS : 8
Location of NumItems 0x0000121
NumItems is : 42
```

Remember that when you refer to a pointer variable without the asterisk, you are referencing the memory address it contains. That is what prints when the first output statement for NumItems is executed. In the second statement, we use the asterisk before the variable name, so the value that memory address contains prints out, which in this case is 42.

After these statements are executed, we use the addressof operator to set `NumItems` to point to the *memory location* identified by the variable `_Count`:

```
NumItems = &_Count;
```

You will recall that `_Count` was assigned the number 8 after we declared the variables. Now `NumItems` points to the same memory location, so when we print it out the second time, the screen displays:

```
NumItems is : 8
```

A Quick Summary of Pointers

In summary, the addressof operator (`&`) returns the address of the object or variable that it precedes. Suppose that a variable `max` is set to memory location 1000. Consider the following statements:

```
max = 42;
mypointer = &max;
```

This places the address of the variable `max` into the pointer variable `mypointer`. The indirection operator (`*`) is used to declare and reference a pointer variable. When you refer to a pointer variable without the indirection operator, you are referring to the memory address it contains. In the example we just listed, the following is true:

- `max` refers to the value assigned to the variable, in this case 42
- `&max` refers to the address of the variable `max`, which is 1000
- `mypointer` refers to the memory address of the pointer. After we assign it to the address of `max` using the `&` operator, `mypointer` contains the value 1000
- `*mypointer` refers to the data contained in the memory location referenced by the pointer variable `mypointer`. So `*mypointer` returns 42.
- After we make the assignment `mypointer = &max`, `mypointer`, and `&max` refer to the same value (1000), while `*mypointer` and `max` refer to the same value (42)

Preprocessor Directives

A *preprocessor* statement or directive is an instruction to the compiler. Preprocessor statements are placed at the beginning of a file. Typical uses include defining constants with the `#define` statement which was described earlier, or including code stored in another file. Files that are included in this manner are known as *header files*, and they end with an *.h* file extension. For example, to do simple input/output operations to the screen, you can use a file named *iostream.h*. To include this file in a program, we write:

```
#include "iostream.h"
```

Notice that a preprocessor statement begins with the pound character (#). An `include` statement tells the compiler to insert the code from the listed file into the line where you have placed it. Header files typically include declarations of global or file-wide variables, definitions of constants, or function prototypes. The file name that you want to include must be enclosed between double quotation marks or brackets. If the file name is enclosed in brackets, like:

```
#include <iostream.h>
```

this tells the compiler to look for the file in a special `include` directory defined by the compiler. If the file is placed somewhere else, you can enclose the file name inside double quotes, which will tell the compiler to start the search for the file in the current directory.

The `#include` and `#define` preprocessor statements are the directives used most often. However, there are many others, which we briefly describe below.

#error

The `#error` directive tells the compiler to stop the compilation process. This directive can be used while debugging a project. You specify a message that is displayed when the `#error` statement is encountered. The syntax for using a `#error` statement is as follows:

```
#error message
```

#if

C++ includes several preprocessor directives that can be used like `if` statements to selectively compile different blocks of code. If the expression used with a #if, #ifdef, or #ifndef statement is true, the code between this and the next #endif statement will be compiled. Otherwise, the code is ignored. When you use an `if` statement, you can specify an alternative course of action by using an accompanying `else`. The same rule applies here; we can include a #else statement to include an alternative block of code to execute if the expression evaluates to false. Typical uses of #if statements include compiling code for different target platforms or including code that is only compiled for debug purposes. For example, we might print out the value of a variable if we are in debug mode:

```
#define DEBUG

int n=0;

//code to process the variable here

...

#if defined DEBUG
    cout << "\n TESTING THE VALUE OF n : " << n;
#endif
```

To construct more complicated branching, you can use the #elif directive, which means "else if." Other shorthand notations include #ifdef which means "if defined," and #ifndef which means "if not defined."

#pragma

Many C++ programs will contain #pragma directives. A #pragma directive is a statement that can be used to provide the compiler with a set of instructions. This directive is used to give compiler implementation-specific instructions. Visual C++ supports the set of #pragma instructions listed below:

```
alloc_text
auto_inline
check_pointer
check_stack
```

Chapter 5: The C/C++ Programming Language

```
code_seg
comment
data_seg
function
hdrstop
init_seg
inline_depth
inline_recursion
intrinsic
linesize
loop_opt
message
native_caller
optimize
pack
pagesize
skip
subtitle
title
warning
```

#undef

The #undef directive can be used to change a previous definition of an identifier. For example, we can undefine an identifier and then give it a new definition if we are in debug mode:

```
#ifdef DEBUG
#undef MAXSIZE 1000
#define MAXSIZE 50
#endif
```

The Concatenation Operator

Two pound signs in a row are used in preprocessor statements as a *concatenation* operator. This can be used to build macro names dynamically. In the next example, we define a macro that depends on a parameter defined later:

```
#define SETVALUE(max)    myvalue ## max

...
int SETVALUE(a);
```

The compiler will view this as:

```
int myvaluea;
```

The Charizing Operator #@

The *charizing* operator can be used to instruct the compiler to view an argument to a macro as a character enclosed by single quotes. For example, if we wanted the compiler to see:

```
mychar = `a';
```

we can use the charizing operator like this:

```
#define USECHARIZE(c) #@c
mychar = USECHARIZE(a);
```

Note that the #@ character sequence is the charizing operator; the `USECHARIZE` macro is a definition we created. You could do the same operation and substitute your own macro name.

Arrays

Arrays in C++ are declared by listing the data type and the name of the array, followed by brackets that contain the number of array elements. All the elements in an array are of the same data type. Arrays may be declared for any data type, and array names follow the same rules used for variable names. The general syntax for an array declaration is as follows:

```
Data_Type array_name[num];
```

where `num` is the number of elements in the array. Arrays always start at element 0 and go up to one fewer than the number of elements specified in the declaration statement. For example, if we declare the integer array as:

```
int x[120];
```

the index of the elements of x ranges from 0 to 119. Often, we will use a `#define` statement to specify the number of elements used in array declarations. For example:

```
#define MAX 100
...
```

Chapter 5: The C/C++ Programming Language

```
int x[MAX];
```

To assign values to an element of the array, you can reference a specific element with an index. To assign a value to the first element of the array we declared above, we write:

```
x[0] = 99;
```

You can also refer to the elements in an array with a variable. This is what is usually done. For example, we can initialize the elements of an array in some kind of loop structure. If the loop counter was an integer variable name j, we can refer to each element of x in succession with the line:

```
X[j] = 0;
```

Multidimensional Arrays

Multidimensional arrays are declared by including an additional set of brackets for each array dimension. To declare a two-dimensional array of type double, we write:

```
double voltages[10][100];
```

In this example, the array voltages contains 10 rows and 100 columns. To declare arrays with more dimensions, simply add a new set of brackets with the number of elements in that dimension. You refer to the elements in a multidimensional array by specifying an index for each dimension of the array. In this example, we refer to the third row and second column of the voltages array:

```
x = voltages[2][1];
```

Remember that array indexes always start at 0. We can also specify the index of a multidimensional array with variables:

```
double voltages[10][100];
int x,y;

x = 5;
y = 12;

voltages[x][y] = 54.3;
```

Initializing Arrays

C++ provides a nice way to initialize an array at the same time that you declare it. In this example, we declare an array named `testscores` and initialize each element of the array. The array has 5 elements:

```
double testscores[5] = {3, 4, 5, 5, 1 };
```

You set off the initial values with curly braces and separate each initial value with a comma. Note as always we terminate the declaration statement with a semicolon.

Programming with Strings

The most common method of programming strings in C++ is to use a null-terminated character array. The first step is to declare an array of `chars` in the same way that you do other types of arrays:

```
#include "string.h"
#define maxsize 12

char mystring[maxsize];
```

You can then assign text strings to the array by using the `strcpy` (string copy) function:

```
strcpy(mystring,  "Hello World");
```

Notice that we included the *string.h* header file. This file is required if you are using any of the string processing functions. A string can be initialized in a declaration statement, just like other data types:

```
char mymessage[] = "Hello World!";
cout << mymessage;
```

Simply include a set of brackets after the variable name, then follow with an equal sign and the string you want to use in your initialization. We can concatenate two strings together by using the `strcat` function, which is illustrated in the next example:

```
char firstname[] = "John ";
char lastname [] = "Smith";
```

Chapter 5: The C/C++ Programming Language

```
char fullname[12];

strcpy(fullname, firstname);
strcat(fullname, lastname); //concatenate the last name

cout << fullname;
```

To compare two strings, use the `strcmp` function. This function takes two arguments that are of type `string` and returns an `int`. If the result is less than 0, this means that the first string is less than the second string. If the result is greater than 0, this means the first string is greater than the second string. If the result is 0, we have two strings that match. We'll illustrate the use of the `strcmp` function as follows:

```
char name1[12] = "John Jones";
char name2[12] = "John Jones";
int result;

= strcmp(name1, name2);

if(result == 0)
   cout << "\n We have the same name.";
```

We will explore the use of strings in more detail later throughout the book.

Comments

A *comment* is a line of text that is ignored by the compiler. The purpose of a comment is to explain the program code, either to yourself (later on when you no longer remember why you wrote the code) or to other programmers. Comments are ignored by the compiler and have no effect on the size or performance of your program. The simplest way to comment code in C++ is to use two backslashes, as illustrated in this example:

```
//initialize counter
j = 0;
```

A comment can be included on the same line as program code:

```
sum = sum + 1000; //adjust value to threshold
```

For long comments that may take several lines, you can use a forward slash combined with an asterisk to start the comment. The compiler will ignore all the text until it finds the corresponding asterisk and slash that terminates the comment:

```
/*
   This is an example
   Of a comment on
   Multiple lines, all text ignored by the compiler
*/
```

We will have more to say about commenting code in Chapter 8, "Coding Standards."

Control Structures

If a program is going to do something useful, it must provide a means to control the flow of execution. This is done with control structures, such as `if` statements or `while` loops. There are several control structures available in the C++ language. We review each of them here.

If Statements

An `if` statement is used to execute a block of code if a condition evaluates to true. The most basic form of an `if` statement is as follows:

```
If (condition)
Statement;
```

This says that if the condition is true, execute the line of code following the `if` statement. For example, we can print out the value of a variable if it is greater than 10:

```
if( x > 10)
   cout << "VALUE OF X : " << x;
```

If x is less than 10, the `cout` statement will not execute. To include more than one statement in the `if` block, we enclose the statements in brackets. We can modify the previous example to also set the variable y equal to x and print the value of x to the screen if x is greater than 10:

```
if( x > 10)
{
  y = x;
  cout << "VALUE OF X : " << x;
}
```

Chapter 5: The C/C++ Programming Language

The condition in an `if` statement can be any value or expression that will evaluate to true or false. If you want the program to take action if the expression evaluates to false, you can include an `else` statement following the end of the `if` program block. Building on the previous example, we will print out the value of the variable y if x is less than 10:

```
if( x > 10)
{
  y = x;
  cout << "VALUE OF X : " << x;
}
else
{
   cout << "X LESS THAN 10. Y IS : " << y;
}
```

The brackets around the `else` block are not strictly necessary, since only one statement is executed, but we have included them for clarity. If there are several conditions to be evaluated, you can use an `if-else if-else` block. You can include multiple `if-else` statements, but the entire block must end with an `else` statement. In the next example, the code takes different actions depending on the value of a variable named average:

```
if (average < 60)
{
   failure = true;
   rank = 0;
   next = 10;
}
else if(average > 60 && average <= 80)
{
   failure = false;
   rank = 1;
   next = 20;
}
else if(average > 80 && average < 90)
{
   failure = false;
   rank = 2;
   next = 25;
}
else
{
   failure = false;
   rank = 3;
   next = 30;
}
```

The `else` condition takes care of the case where average is greater than or equal to 90.

The ? Operator

C++ provides the *ternary* operator (?) which is a way to use a shorthand notation for `if-else` statements and provide faster code. The ternary operator takes three operands and uses the following syntax:

```
Expression1 ? expression2 : expression3;
```

The first expression is a logical condition that can be evaluated to true or false, just like in an `if` statement. If the expression is true, then the code in `expression2` is executed. If it is false, the expression following the colon, `expression3`, is executed in its place. To see how this works, we can convert the following `if-else` statement into one using the ternary operator:

```
if(x > 100)
   max = x/10;
else
   max = 0;
```

Using the ternary operator, this becomes:

```
max = (x > 100) ? x/10 : 0;
```

For simple `if-else` statements, the ternary operator saves typing and allows the compiler to build faster code. Be sure to include a comment explaining what the statement means.

The Relational Operators

When you are building `if` statements or any statement that uses logical conditions, you may need to use the relational operators to build compound statements. We already did this in the previous example; we tested for values that fit within a specified range.

The basic operators are listed here:

Operator	Definition
>	Greater than
<	Less than
>=	Greater than or equal

Chapter 5: The C/C++ Programming Language

Operator	Definition
<=	Less than or equal
==	Equal
!=	Not equal

Logical operators are used to build compound statements like "apples less than 5 and oranges equal to 10." The logical operators used in C++ are as follows:

Operator	Definition
&&	AND
||	OR
!	NOT

The logical operators work the same way as the AND/OR truth tables we described in the section on bitwise operators. Take the following example:

```
If(a < 100 && b > 20)
{
   max = a;
}
```

In this example, there are two logical conditions to be evaluated. If you recall the truth table for AND, you will recall that true (represented by 1) only results if both arguments are true. This means that the code inside the `if` statement block will only execute when a is less than 100 and b is greater than 20. If either of those conditions are false, the statement will not execute.

If we change the logical operator to OR, then only one of the two conditions needs to be true. The code would look like this:

```
If(a < 100 || b > 20)
{
   max = a;
}
```

In this case, the statement in the `if` block will execute if one condition or the other (or both) evaluates to true. For example, if a is 50 and b is 5, the statement in the `if` block will execute because one of the conditions evaluated to true. The statement would also execute if a was 50 and b was 21, or if a was 200 and b was 50. The only time the statement will not execute is when both conditions evaluate to false.

The NOT operator can be used for "reverse" logic. In other words, when you want something to execute when the logical condition evaluates to false, use the NOT operator. In the following example, the code in the `if` block will execute when the Boolean variable *done* is false:

```
If( !done)
{
   cout << "Processing Not Complete";
}
```

For Loops

The `for` loop can be used to iterate through a set of program statements a fixed number of times. The syntax of a `for` loop is as follows:

```
for(initialize counter; stop condition; increment)
{
    //code block
}
```

The code block can be one or more valid C++ statements. If only one statement is used, the enclosing brackets are not required. In the following example, we compute the sum of the numbers 1 to 1000:

```
int sum=0;
int counter;

for(counter=1; counter <= 1000; counter++)
   sum = sum + counter;

cout << "\nThe sum total is : " << sum;
```

`For` loops are typically used to manipulate or initialize arrays, since you know ahead of time how many times you'll need to iterate the loop. In the next example, we initialize an array so that each element is set to `-1`:

```
#define MAX 1000
#define STARTVAL -1

double rdata[MAX];
int counter;

for(counter = 0; counter < MAX; counter++)
   rdata = STARTVAL
```

Chapter 5: The C/C++ Programming Language

The counter used in a `for` loop can start at any value, and you can also loop backward. In the next example, we loop through the array in reverse order, decrementing the counter each time through the loop:

```
#define MAX 1000
#define STARTVAL -1

double rdata[MAX];
int counter;

for(counter = MAX; counter >= 0; counter-)
   rdata = STARTVAL
```

For loops can also be nested. You typically do this when working with multidimensional arrays. In the next example, we copy the values in one two-dimensional array into another one:

```
#define MAX_SIZE 200
#define MROWS 10
#define AVAL 100

double VX[MROWS][MAX_SIZE];
double TESTVALUES[MROWS][MAX_SIZE];
int i,j;
for(i=0; i < MROWS; i++)
{
    for(j=0; j < MAX_SIZE; j++)
    {
        TESTVALUES[i][j] = VX[i][j] - AVAL;
    }
}
```

You can also declare and initialize the counter variable in the loop, as follows:

```
for(int j = 0; j < 100; j++)
   sum = sum + j;
```

Do Loops

When the number of times you will need to iterate through a block of code statements cannot be determined until runtime, a `Do` loop is the appropriate choice. The structure of a `Do` loop is as follows:

```
Do
{

    //statement block
}while(condition)
```

A Do loop will execute at least once. At the bottom of the loop, the condition for termination is evaluated. If it evaluates to true, the loop is executed again. In this simple example, we loop until the counter variable is greater than 10:

```
int mycounter=0;
int dval=0;

Do
{
   mycounter = mycounter + 1;
   dval = dval + mycounter * 5;
}while(mycounter <= 10)
```

Any logical condition that evaluates to true or false can be used in the while statement.

While Loops

The while loop is similar to a Do loop; however, the logical test condition is at the top of the loop instead of at the bottom. This means that the loop may not execute, unless the condition evaluates to true the first time control enters the loop. The next example reads numbers into an array until either the user enters a "q" to terminate the loop or until the maximum number of allowed elements is reached:

```
#define MAX 100

int MyVals[MAX];
int counter=0;
char c;

cout << "\nPlease Enter a Number(q to quit) : ";
cin > c;

while( c != 'q' && counter < MAX)
{
   MyVals[counter] = c;
   counter = counter + 1;
   cout << "\nPlease Enter a Number(q to quit) : ";
   cin > c;
}
```

The Switch Statement

The switch statement can be used in a multiway branching situation. While you can use an if-else if-else statement for testing multiple

Chapter 5: The C/C++ Programming Language

branching, sometimes a `switch` statement is more appropriate. The syntax for a `switch` statement is as follows:

```
switch(expression)
{
  case constant1 : statement block;
                   break;
  case constant2 : statement block;
                   break;
  ...
  case constantn : statement block;
                   break;
  default : statement block;
}
```

The `break` statement is used to exit the `switch` statement and bypass the remaining code. Once a break is encountered, program control is transferred to the statement following the closing bracket of the `switch` statement. The expression at the top of the `switch` statement is evaluated and compared to each case until a match is obtained. Then the statements in that block are executed. The default at the bottom of the `switch` statement is optional, but it can be included to account for the case when a match is not obtained. In this example, the user selects a menu item by entering a single character. The character is tested to see which menu item was selected, and the appropriate function call is then made:

```
Switch(c)
{
   case `o' : openfile();
              break;
   case `n' : newfile();
              break;
   case `p' : printfile();
              break;
   case `x' : exitprogram();
              break;
   default : << "\nPlease Select a valid menu item.";
}
```

Modular Programming— Using Functions

Almost all modern programming languages are built upon the concept of using subroutines or procedures. In the C/C++ languages, this is done by programming with functions. The function is the key element in a C or

C++ program; you can't have one without at least one function. A *function* is a self-contained programming module that can accept and modify parameters, and return a value. Like a variable, a function is identified by a name that you assign to it. The general syntax of a function is as follows:

```
return_type function_name(parameter list)
{
    body of function;
}
```

Each C/C++ program has at least one function, called `main`, which has a return type of `int`. The following "hello world" program illustrates the use of the `main` function:

```
#include "iostream.h"

int main()
{
    cout << "\nHello World!";

    return(0);

}
```

The function `main` is the starting point for any C++ program. Without `main`, there is no C++ program. While you could write a complex program by simply writing a long series of statements in the `main` function, this is not advisable. It is better to break down a problem into simpler subproblems, which will form the basis of your own functions.

The body of the function is one or more program statements, including local variable declarations. The `return` type of the function is one of the basic C++ types or a type that you define. A function includes a parameter list, which is zero or more arguments that are passed to the function. The variables passed to a function can be modified, or the values of the variables can be used in calculations and returned by the function. The concept of a function is at the heart of all C++ programs.

In the following example, the function `Area` returns the area of a circle:

```
double Area(double Radius)
{
    const double pi = 3.14159;
    double result=0;
    double radius_squared=0;

    radius_squared = Radius * Radius;
    result = pi * radius_squared;
```

Chapter 5: The C/C++ Programming Language

```
        return(result);
}
```

The last statement of the function is the `return` statement. This statement is used to return a value to the calling program. This function also takes one parameter, `Radius`. Each parameter that you pass to a function must have a declared data type. To call a function, you use it in an assignment statement just like a variable name. The following example calls the `Area` function and stores the result in the variable named `TotalArea`:

```
double TotalArea;
double MyRadius=0;

cout << "\nPlease Enter the Radius : ";
cin > MyRadius;

//call the Area function
TotalArea = Area(MyRadius);

out << "\nThe Area of the circle is : " << TotalArea;
```

The `Void` Return Type

Many programming languages allow the programmer to create subroutine-type procedures. C++ does not have a subroutine-type procedure. You can, however, create functions that behave like subroutines. This can be done by creating a function with a return type known as `void`. Any function that is declared with the `void` return type can be thought of as a subroutine, which is a procedure that does not return a value. In the following example, we declare a function of type `void` that calculates the average of two variables:

```
void Average(int a,b; double ave)
{
    const int count=2;

    ave = (double)((a + b)/count);

}
```

To call a function with a `void` return type, simply list the function name as a program statement. For example, to call the `Average` function, we can use the following code:

```
int one, two;
double myaverage;
one = 14;
two = 20;

Average(one,two,myaverage);
```

If a function takes no parameters, simply list the function name with an empty set of parentheses. In this example, we call a function that closes down a program:

```
//user selected exit, shut down the program
shutdown();
```

This also works when a function has a return type other than void. Consider a `print` function that sends output to the printer, takes no arguments, and returns an `int`, which indicates success or failure:

```
#define SUCCESS 1
#define FAILURE 0

int result;

//code here to process data to print
...
//print out the data
result = print();

if(result == SUCCESS)
{
    cout << "\n FILE PRINTED SUCCESSFULLY.";
}
else
{
    cout << "\n ERROR: UNABLE TO PRINT FILE>";
}
```

Passing Parameters—Pass by Value vs. Pass by Reference

There are two ways to pass a parameter to a function. The first method, *pass by value*, is the default method. This is what we used in the `Area` function. When you use pass by value, a copy of the parameter is made and passed to the function. In this case, the variable passed to the function cannot be modified. The value that the variable contains is copied and passed to the function that can use that value in calculations. That is exactly what was done in the `Area` function, when it is called by passing the `MyRadius` variable, a copy is made and the `Area` function uses that copy inside the function as the parameter `Radius`.

Sometimes it is necessary to change the value of a variable in a function. To do this, you must pass the memory address of the variable to the function. In the previous example, we calculated the average of two variables. We stored the result in the `ave` parameter, but since this parameter was passed by value, we are actually working with a copy of whichever value is passed to the `Average` function. As a result, the calculated average cannot be passed back from the function. Let's modify the code that called the `Average` function to print out the value of the variable we passed into it:

```
int one, two;
double myaverage;

one = 14;
two = 20;

myaverage = 8;

Average(one,two,myaverage);

cout << "\nAverage is : " << myaverage;
```

In this case, the value of `myaverage` has been changed. When the variable is printed out, we will see the following:

```
Average is : 8
```

The reason is that with pass by value, the contents of the parameter that is passed are unchanged. A copy of the `myaverage` variable was made inside the function. It was the copy that was modified, not the variable we passed to the function.

To remedy this situation, we can use pass by reference for the `ave` parameter. This is done by declaring the parameter with the indirection operator, making it a pointer. In this case, the function becomes:

```
void Average(int a,b; double *ave)
{
    const int count=2;

    *ave = (double)((a + b)/count);

}
```

Now the memory location is passed to the function, and the value calculated in the function will be returned to the caller.

Let's see how we would call the function when the variable used to hold the average is not a pointer. We will need to use the addressof operator (&) to pass the memory location used for the variable. The code would then look like this:

```
int one, two;
double myaverage;

one = 14;
two = 20;

myaverage = 8;

Average(one,two,&myaverage);

cout << "\nAverage is : " << myaverage;
```

In this case, the value of `myaverage` has been changed. When the variable is printed out, we will see the following:

```
Average is : 17
```

Prototyping

Before you use a function call in a program, you must provide a *prototype* for that function. A prototype is simply a listing at the beginning of a source code file that includes the header of the function, without the code in the function body. Prototypes can be included in the text of the source code file or in a header file that is included in the project. The body of the function is located somewhere else; it can be later in the same file or even in another source code file. The purpose of the prototype is to allow the compiler to resolve the name, return type, and parameters of the function before it is encountered in code.

To list a function prototype, simply make a copy of the function header and place a semicolon on the end. In the next example, we demonstrate the use of a function prototype for the `Average` function:

```
#include "iostream.h"

void Average(int a,b; double *ave); //prototype for Average
                                    //function
int main()
{
```

Chapter 5: The C/C++ Programming Language

```
    int one, two;
    double myaverage;

    one = 14;
    two = 20;

    myaverage = 8;
    Average(one,two,&myaverage);

    cout << "\nAverage is : " << myaverage;

    return(0);

}
void Average(int a,b; double *ave)
{
    const int count=2;

    *ave = (double)((a + b)/count);

}
```

The function prototype is listed at the top of the file, before the main program. The actual function body is included in the same file after the end of the main function. The function body can be placed anywhere, but I put mine at the end of the file for clarity. We can also move the Average function and its prototype to a separate file. Suppose this code is moved to the file *average.h*. Now we access the prototype by including the *average.h* file:

```
#include "iostream.h"
#include "average.h"   //average.h file includes function
                       //body and prototype

int main()
{
    int one, two;
    double myaverage;

    one = 14;
    two = 20;

    myaverage = 8;

    Average(one,two,&myaverage);

    cout << "\nAverage is : " << myaverage;

    return(0);

}
```

Variable Scope and Lifetime

Variables can be defined in many places in a C++ project. They can be defined inside a function, inside the main function, or in a header file, for example. The range over which a variable name is valid is known as its *scope*. Variables should be given as limited scope as possible, which generally means that you should declare variables inside functions and exchange information by passing parameters to each function. Variables with wider scope are subject to corruption and can lead to unstable code.

Variables defined inside a function have *local scope* and are not known outside that function. They can only be modified inside the function, and if a variable with the same name is declared outside the function, that variable is treated as a separate memory location. Modifying that variable will have no impact on the local variable.

In C++, you can define a file-wide variable by either declaring it before the function `main` or by including it in a header file. You can also create variables with global scope, which means that it is accessible throughout an entire program. Global variables should be avoided if possible, since they can lead to confusion and corrupted data. This is because the variable can be modified anywhere in the program.

Variable Lifetime and Static Variables

A variable inside a function has a lifetime that is limited to the lifetime of the function in which it is declared. When a function is finished executing, all the memory allocated for the variables is released. When the function is called again, the variables are reinitialized. For example, the variable named `counter` in the following function is reset to 1 each time the function is called:

```
void CountIt()
{
   int count=1;

   count = count + 1;

}
```

If we wanted to count how many times the function was called, this would not be very useful behavior. We can solve this dilemma by declaring `count` as a `static` variable. When a variable is declared as static, it is stored in a standard memory location rather than on the stack, and the memory is not released with each function call. We declare a variable as static by including the `static` keyword in the variable declaration, as illustrated here:

```
void CountIt()
{
   static int count=1;

    count = count + 1;

}
```

Using the `static` keyword ensures that the variable will retain its value in between function calls. This way we would be able to count the number of times that the function is called.

Passing Arrays to Functions

We can pass an array as an argument to a function. We can pass an array to a function by passing the address of the first element of the array. Keep in mind that the function won't know how many elements are in the array; it can only view the array as an ordered sequence of memory locations. If we want to step through all of the elements of the array, we will need to pass the number of elements to the function. In this example, the average value of an array is calculated:

```
#include "iostream.h"
#define MAX 500

double getaverage(double inarray[], int array_size);

int main()
{
   double MyData[MAX];
   int Count;
   double average=0;
   Count = MAX;

   //code to load array here
   ...

   //get the average and print
   average = getaverage(MyData,Count);

   cout << average;

   return(0);

}
```

```
double getaverage(double inarray[], int array_size)
{
    double sum=0;
    double result=0;

    int j;

    for(j=0; j < array_size; j++)
        sum += inarray[j];
    result = sum / array_size;

    return(result);
}
```

The first statement to notice in this program is the function prototype:

```
double getaverage(double inarray[], int array_size);
```

Notice that the array is declared in the function header as an empty pair of brackets. When we call the function, we simply use the name of the array as the parameter:

```
average = getaverage(MyData,Count);
```

Now examine the function body. Remember we said that the number of elements in the array must be passed to the function; otherwise, it has no way of knowing this information. This information is passed to the sample function through the `array_size` parameter. Once inside the function, the elements of the array can be accessed in the normal way.

Passing Arrays as Pointers

An alternative method is to declare the array as a pointer. This would change the function header of the `getaverage` function to the following:

```
double getaverage(double *inarray, int array_size);
```

We still need to tell the function how many elements are contained in the array. Inside the function body, the array can be accessed in one of two ways. The first way is to simply use the standard array notation:

```
double getaverage(double *inarray, int array_size)
{
```

Chapter 5: The C/C++ Programming Language

```
    double sum=0;
    double result=0;

    int j;

    for(j=0; j < array_size; j++)
       sum += inarray[j];

    result = sum / array_size;

    return(result);
}
```

This can be done because the pointer serves to pass the address of the first element of the array, which is also done when you simply pass the name of the array.

A more sophisticated way, however, is to treat the array name as a pointer inside the function. We can loop through the array using pointer arithmetic, because the address of each element of the array is obtained by simply adding one to the previous address each time through the loop. This can be seen more clearly in code:

```
double getaverage(double *inarray, int array_size)
{
    double sum=0;
    double result=0;

    int j;

    for(j=0; j < array_size; j++)
       sum += *(inarray + j);

    result = sum / array_size;
    return(result);
}
```

This adds the appropriate amount to the base address of the array, which is represented by the array name `inarray`. We use the indirection operator (*) to get the contents at that memory location; otherwise, we would be accessing the memory address itself. When you are passing an array to a function that expects a pointer, all you have to do is pass the array name as we did before.

An alternative method you can use is to pass the address of the first element of the array, like we have in this example:

```
double getaverage(double *inarray, int array_size);

int main()
{
```

```
    double MyData[MAX];
    int Count;
    double average=0;

    Count = MAX;

    //code to load array here
    ...
    //get the average and print
    average = getaverage(&MyData[0],Count);

    cout << average;

    return(0);
}
```

You can also pass arrays with higher dimensions to functions using the same techniques. Just be sure to pass the number of elements in each dimension to the function.

Pointers to Functions

You can use a function that returns a memory address instead of a value by declaring the return type of the function to be a pointer. For example, we can declare a function that returns a pointer to an `int`:

```
int *Sum(int myarray[]);
```

A value can be returned by returning an address:

```
return &localresult;
```

While this can be done, it is not a good programming practice. Remember that the memory address allocated inside the function is on the stack and might be used for another variable when a new function call is made. If you require the result of a function to be a pointer, pass it as an argument instead.

Function Overloading

Overloading is a situation in which more than one function prototype is given the same function name. The appropriate function to use is recognized by the compiler by the return type and argument list of each func-

Chapter 5: The C/C++ Programming Language

tion. Function overloading is a means you can use when the same function will be used with different data types. For example, we can calculate the average of the elements of an array using a function. To overload the function, we will write two function prototypes: one will calculate the average for an array of `int`, while the other will calculate the average for an array of type `double`. The code is listed here:

```
#include "iostream.h"

int average(int mydata[]);
double average(double mydata[]);

int main()
{
   int wholenums[5] = {1,2,3,4,5};
   double reals[5] = {1.2, 2.3, 3.4, 4.5, 5.6};

   int aveints=0;
   double avedbls=0;

   aveints = average(wholenums);
   avedbls = average(reals);

   cout << "\nAverage of Ints " << aveints;
   cout << "\nAverage of Doubles " << avedbls;

   return(0);

}
int average(int inarray[])
{
   int sum = 0;

   for(int i = 0; i < 5; i++)
      sum += inarray[i];

   return(sum/5);
}
double average(double inarray[])
{
   int sum = 0;

   for(int i = 0; i < 5; i++)
      sum += inarray[i];

   return(sum/5);

}
```

Here we see that we can write the same code for both data types, even though they are calling two different functions. This makes for neater code, since your function names should reflect the purpose of the function. The only restrictions for function overloading are you cannot overload two functions that take the same types of arguments but have different return types.

Dynamic Memory Allocation

There will be many times in a C++ program when it will be necessary to allocate the memory used for a variable or complicated structure. This can be done with the `malloc` function. Memory that is available for dynamic allocation is known as *free memory*, which is obtained from an area known as the *heap*. The `malloc` function takes one parameter, which is an integer specifying how many bytes to return. By default, `malloc` has a return type of (void *). However, you will usually cast this return type to the type of variable or structure for which you are allocating the memory.

To determine how many bytes you need, you don't have to go look up the byte requirements of each type. Instead, you can use the `sizeof` function, which will return the number of bytes required for a complicated structure or any basic data type. In the following example, we allocate memory for a block of 1024 doubles:

```
#define SZ 1024

double *mymemblock;  //pointer to a block of memory
                    //containing doubles

mymemblock = (double *)malloc(SZ * sizeof(double));
```

First, you will notice that we declared a pointer variable. The function of the pointer is to point to the starting location of the memory that `malloc` will return. Next, notice that we have used a cast so that `malloc` will return a pointer to a double. For the argument to `malloc`, we have used the `sizeof` function to determine how many bytes are required for a double, and since we want 1024 of them, we multiply by the constant we defined earlier.

When memory is no longer in use, it is a good idea to return it to the heap so that it can be used elsewhere. This is done by calling the `free` function. The `free` function takes one argument, the pointer to the memory location used. We can free up the memory allocated above for `mymemblock` by passing the pointer to the `free` function:

```
free((void *)mymemblock);
```

The `free` function expects the argument to be a pointer of type `void`, so we have used a cast to make the conversion. Be careful when using the `free` function; make sure the memory was actually allocated before this function is called. Otherwise, you might run into serious problems.

Defining Data Types with Structures

When you think about many of the objects used in everyday life, you soon realize that most of them are characterized by more than one variable. For example, suppose a program needs to be written to track the employees for a small company. The company will want to track several items for each employee. These might include:

- Name
- Social Security number
- Age
- Phone number
- Address
- Job title
- Wage

There might be others, but this is sufficient for the purposes of this example. We could define a set of arrays to track each item, like this:

```
#define NUM 100

double wage[NUM];
int age[NUM];
char Name[NUM];
char SSN[NUM], phone[NUM], Address[NUM], JobTitle[Num];
```

Then we could refer to each employee by the index; say we have an integer variable named `icount`. To access each piece of data, we would have to use the appropriate array. For example, we could print some information about an employee to the screen:

```
cout << "Employee Number " << icount << " is " << Name[icount];
cout << "Job Title : " << JobTitle[icount];
cout << "Pay Rate : " << wage[icount];
```

Obviously, this method is not a very effective way to track a set of related data. The code would be messy, unreliable, and hard to keep track of. A better way is to define an employee with a *struct*. A struct is a special C/C++ data type that can be used to group a set of variables together as a single data type. The syntax for a struct is the following:

```
struct struct-name {

   //data declarations

}object-list;
```

Each variable that you want to include in the structure is declared in between the braces. The name you assign to the structure is sometimes known as the *tag field*. For example, we can build a struct to represent an employee:

```
struct Employee{
   char name[30];
   char address[30];
   char phone[13];
   char SSN[11];
   int age;
   double wage;
   char job[20];
};
```

This type of arrangement allows us to track the information about each employee as a single, unified entity. Here the tag field is `Employee`, which we will use to declare variables. We can declare a variable of the new type with a statement like this one:

```
struct Employee NewEmployee;
```

This declaration has declared a variable named `NewEmployee` of the type `Employee`. To access the individual members of an `Employee`, we use the *dot syntax*, which is also known as the *member operator*. This is simply done by writing the structure name followed by a period, which is then followed by the name of the member variable we want to access. For example, to set the age of the `NewEmployee` variable:

```
NewEmployee.age = 44;
```

Here we print the name of the employee on the screen:

```
cout << "Hired Employee is : " << NewEmployee.name;
```

Chapter 5: The C/C++ Programming Language

We can define the structure and declare a variable at the same time. Here we will declare the `NewEmployee` variable at the same time as we define the structure:

```
struct Employee{
  char name[30];
  char address[30];
  char phone[13];
  char SSN[11];
  int age;
  double wage;
  char job[20];
}NewEmployee;
```

You can also declare more than one structure variable simply by separating each variable name with a comma:

```
struct Employee{
  char name[30];
  char address[30];
  char phone[13];
  char SSN[11];
  int age;
  double wage;
  char job[20];
} NewEmployee, Manager, Supervisor;
```

This example has declared three variables of type `Employee`. These are `NewEmployee`, `Manager`, and `Supervisor`. You refer to each variable in the usual way. Here we set the wage field of each variable:

```
NewEmployee.wage = 6.50;
Manager.wage = 10.50;
Supervisor.wage = 8.25;
```

C++ also allows you to create structures without a tag field. This is known as an *anonymous structure type*. If you use this method, you must declare at least one variable of the structure type when you define it. For example, we can define the structure used to represent an employee without using a tag field like this:

```
struct{
  char name[30];
  char address[30];
  char phone[13];
  char SSN[11];
  int age;
  double wage;
  char job[20];
} Manager;
```

In this case, we have one variable named `Manager`, which includes the fields listed in the structure. If you define a structure without a tag field, you cannot declare any other variables of this type anywhere else in the program. If you will need to create other struct variables or pass them to functions, you will need to include a tag name.

Example: Using Simple Structures

In this section we will create a simple program to illustrate the use of structures. This simple example will show how to declare and use an array of structures. First, we start a new Win32 console project. When programming with structures, I prefer to place the definitions of structures in a header file. Our header file looks like this:

```
struct Employee{
  char name[30];
  char address[30];
  char phone[13];
  char SSN[11];
  int age;
  double wage;
  char job[20];
};
```

The header file simply holds the definition of our structure. The code for our program is placed in a CPP file. The code looks like this:

```
//demonstrate the use of structures

//header files
#include <iostream.h>
#include "employee.h"

//define the maximum number of employees hired
#define MAX 5

int main()
{
    //array to store new employees
    Employee NewEmployees[MAX];

    //loop counter
    int counter;

    //loop through and enter the data
    for(counter=0; counter < MAX; counter++)
    {
```

Chapter 5: The C/C++ Programming Language

```
            cout << "\nEnter the Employees Name : ";
            cin > NewEmployees[counter].name;
            cout <<"\nEnter the Employees Job Title : ";
            cin > NewEmployees[counter].job;
            cout << "\nEnter the Employees Rate of Pay : ";
             cin > NewEmployees[counter].wage;
        }

        //print out data to the screen
        cout << "/nHere is the data you entered\n";

        for(counter=0; counter < MAX; counter++)
        {
         cout << "\n Information for : " << NewEmployees[counter].name;
         cout << "\n Job Title : " << NewEmployees[counter].job;
         cout << "\n Hourly Rate of Pay : " <<
NewEmployees[counter].wage;
        }

        return(0);

}
```

The first two lines of the file are `include` directives that tell the compiler we will be using the iostream and employee header files. The employee header file includes the `Employee` structure definition. Next, we define a constant named `MAX`, which will be used to set an upper limit on the number of employees entered:

```
//header files
#include <iostream.h>
#include "employee.h"

//define the maximum number of employees hired
#define MAX 5
```

Inside the `Main` function, the first item of business is to declare our variables. First, we declare an array of `Employee` structures named `NewEmployees`. To declare an array of structures, you simply use a declaration statement the same way you would when declaring an array of basic types. In this case, you substitute the name of your structure:

```
//array to store new employees
Employee NewEmployees[MAX];

//loop counter
int counter;
```

The next part of the program is a `for` loop, which allows the user to enter the data for each new employee. Each time through the loop, the iostream operator `cout` is used to prompt the user for the appropriate data. Next, the `cin` operator is used to read the data that was entered with the keyboard. If you examine this line, you can understand how to access the elements in an array of structures:

```
cin > NewEmployees[counter].name;
```

To reference each element, you simply list the variable name. In this case, we have an array of type `Employee` named `NewEmployees`. After the variable name, you enclose the array index in brackets. You can then use the dot syntax or member operator to access the actual members of this element of the array. The rest of the program simply reports to the user the data that was entered.

Programming Stuctures with Pointers

In the previous chapter we discussed the use of pointers with the basic data types. Pointers provide many advantages to the programmer, and when programming with structures, you will find this to be the case as well. Using pointers with structure variables involves minor changes in syntax. Instead of using the dot operator to access the members of the structure, we use the *arrow* operator. To see how this works, let's return to the `Employee` structure we used earlier. You may recall the definition we developed for an `Employee` structure:

```
struct Employee{
  char name[30];
  char address[30];
  char phone[13];
  char SSN[11];
  int age;
  double wage;
  char job[20];
};
```

In the following code example, there are two variables of type `Employee` declared. The first variable, `Manager`, is a regular variable, while the second variable, `Worker`, is declared as a pointer:

```
Employee Manager, *Worker;
```

We refer to the members of the `Manager` variable in the usual way:

Chapter 5: The C/C++ Programming Language

```
Manager.age = 48;
Manager.job = "Night Manager;
```

When referring to the members of the `Worker` variable, which is a pointer, we use the arrow operator:

```
Worker->age = 23;
Worker->job = "Desk Clerk";
Worker->wage = 7.5;
```

As you can see, the only difference when programming a pointer to a structure variable is using the arrow operator in place of the dot syntax. We can also assign the address of one structure to another. In this example, we set the `Worker` variable pointing to the address of the `Manager` structure:

```
Worker = &Manager;

cout << Worker.job;
```

Now the `Worker` pointer points to the memory location of the `Manager` structure. When the code executes, the string `Night Manager` will be printed on the screen, since that is the value that was set for the `Manager` variable.

Passing Structures to Functions

As is the case with any variable in a program, there will be many cases when a structure needs to be passed as an argument to a function. When passing a variable to a function in a C/C++ program, the default behavior is to use pass by value, which means that a copy of the structure is passed to the function. Making copies of structures can be time-consuming and take up a lot of memory, so it is a good idea to pass a pointer to the structure instead. With structures, we also have the option of passing only individual variables of the structure to functions. Both examples will be illustrated below.

Example: Passing Structures to Functions

In our next example, we will create a simple program that stores data in an array of structures. This program will include two functions to do

Part 2: Designing Visual C++ Software

some calculations with the data; they will illustrate two different methods we can use when passing data contained in a structure to a function.

The program keeps track of a set of characteristics for a group of dogs. The program lets the user enter the information about each dog and then prints out the average weight of the dogs. The program will also convert the height of the first dog from inches to centimeters.

```
#include "iostream.h"

struct dog{
      char Name[25];
      char Breed[10];
      int height;      //height in inches
      int weight;      //weight in pounds
      int age;         //age in years
      char sex;
};

//function declarations
int AveWeight(dog *dogs, int NumDogs);
float ConvertHeight(int Height);

int main()
{
      const int DogCount = 5; //Max number of dogs
      int counter; //loop counter
      dog Canines[DogCount];   //array of type struct dog
      float centimeters, AvWeight;

      //read in the data for the dogs
      for(counter=0; counter < DogCount; counter++)
      {
         cout << "\nEnter The Dogs Name : ";
         cin > Canines[counter].Name;
         cout << "\nEnter the Breed : ";
         cin > Canines[counter].Breed;
         cout << "\nEnter the Dogs Height : ";
         cin > Canines[counter].height;
         cout << "\nEnter the Dogs Weight : ";
         cin > Canines[counter].weight;
         cout << "\nEnter the Dogs Sex(M or F) : ";
         cin > Canines[counter].sex;
         cout << "\nEnter the dogs age in years : ";
           cin > Canines[counter].age;

      }

      //convert the first dogs height to centimeters
    centimeters = ConvertHeight(Canines[0].height);

      cout << "\nHeight in Inches : " << Canines[0].height;
      cout << "\nHeight in Centimeters : " << centimeters;

      //find the average weight of the dogs
      AvWeight = AveWeight(&Canines[0], DogCount);
      cout << "\nAverage Weight : " << AvWeight;
```

Chapter 5: The C/C++ Programming Language

```
        return(0);
}

int AveWeight(dog *dogs, int NumDogs)
{
    //Function AveWeight
    //Description : Computes the average weight in the array
    //pointed to by the dogs structure. NumDogs contains
    //the number of elements in the array.

    int Average=0;
      int TotalWeight=0;

    for(int i=0; i < NumDogs; i++)
            TotalWeight = TotalWeight + dogs[i].weight;

      Average = TotalWeight/NumDogs;

      return(Average);

}//End Function Average

float ConvertHeight(int Height)
{
    //Function : InchesToCentimeters
    //Description : Converts the dogs height from inches to
    //centimeters
    //works on a single dog

      const float Cents = 2.54;

    float result=0;

    result = (float)Height*Cents;

      return(result);

}//End Function ConvertHeight
```

The first part of the listing defines the structure we will use to track the data. The structure has variables to track important information about each dog, such as the age and breed:

```
struct dog{
    char Name[25];
    char Breed[10];
    int height;      //height in inches
    int weight;      //weight in pounds
    int age;         //age in years
    char sex;
};
```

Next, we see two function declarations we will need to convert a dog's height into centimeters and to compute the average weight of the dogs:

```
//function declarations
int AveWeight(dog *dogs, int NumDogs);
float ConvertHeight(int Height);
```

In the `AveWeight` function, a pointer to a variable of type `dog` is passed. In this case, we are using pass by reference; that is, we are passing the actual memory address of the structure. The function will actually be set up to work with an array of structures of type `dog`. Recall from the last chapter that you can pass an array as a pointer, and then simply access each element in the normal way inside the function. That is what we will do in this case. The second function expects one parameter, `Height`, as an integer. When we call this function, we will pass an individual component of the structure.

Now let's take a look at the beginning of the main program.

```
int main()
{
        const int DogCount = 5; //Max number of dogs
        int counter; //loop counter
        dog Canines[DogCount]; //array of type struct dog
        float centimeters, AvWeight;

        //read in the data for the dogs
        for(counter=0; counter < DogCount; counter++)
        {
            cout << "\nEnter The Dogs Name : ";
            cin > Canines[counter].Name;
            cout << "\nEnter the Breed : ";
            cin > Canines[counter].Breed;
            cout << "\nEnter the Dogs Height : ";
            cin > Canines[counter].height;
            cout << "\nEnter the Dogs Weight : ";
            cin > Canines[counter].weight;
            cout << "\nEnter the Dogs Sex(M or F) : ";
            cin > Canines[counter].sex;
            cout << "\nEnter the dogs age in years : ";
              cin > Canines[counter].age;

        }
```

At the top are the variable declarations. First, a limit is set on the number of dogs that can be entered. This is done by defining the constant integer `DogCount`. Next, we declare an array named `Canines`. The data type of this array is the struct named `dog` that we defined earlier. Finally, we declare two variables to report the results of the function calls we are going to make. The variable declarations are followed by a `for` loop, which lets the user enter the data.

Chapter 5: The C/C++ Programming Language

The `for` loop gives us an opportunity to review the way in which arrays of structures are handled. For example, to enter the height for a given dog, we use the line:

```
cin > Canines[counter].height;
```

Notice that we list the name of the structure, followed by the index enclosed in brackets. Then we use the dot syntax to reference the variable we want to set, which in this case is the `height` parameter.

After the `for` loop is completed, the height of the first dog can be converted into centimeters. This is done by calling the `ConvertHeight` function. For convenience, the function header is listed again here:

```
float ConvertHeight(int Height);
```

This function has a return type of `float` and expects one parameter of type `int`. To call this function using a stucture, we will need to pass just one variable of the structure. First, to access the first element of the array, we write:

```
Canines[0]
```

Next, we use the dot syntax to specify which variable we want, which in this case is height:

```
Canines[0].height
```

The complete code looks like this:

```
//convert the first dogs height to centimeters
centimeters = ConvertHeight(Canines[0].height);

cout << "\nHeight in Inches : " << Canines[0].height;
cout << "\nHeight in Centimeters : " << centimeters;
```

The next part of the code computes the average weight for all the dogs. To do this, we will need to pass the entire array of dog structures to the function. We can do this by passing the first element of the array. The function header for `AveWeight` tells us it is expecting a pointer of type dog:

```
int AvWeight(dog *dogs, int NumDogs);
```

When we call the function, we use the address of operator &, which will pass the address of the first element of the array. The function will be able to access the remaining elements of the array by simply using an index, like we described in the last chapter. The function call looks like this:

```
//find the average weight of the dogs
AvWeight = AveWeight(&Canines[0], DogCount);
```

where the notation:

```
&Canines[0]
```

tells the compiler to pass the address of the first element of the array. We can see how this is used inside the `AveWeight` function:

```
int AveWeight(dog *dogs, int NumDogs)
{
        //Function AveWeight
        //Description : Computes the average weight in the array
        //pointed to by the dogs structure. NumDogs contains
        //the number of elements in the array.

    int Average=0;
    int TotalWeight=0;

   for(int i=0; i < NumDogs; i++)
      TotalWeight = TotalWeight + dogs[i].weight;

    Average = TotalWeight/NumDogs;

       return(Average);

}//End Function Average
```

Inside the function, the parameter is simply treated as an array. The address that is passed to the function as a pointer gives the function the location of the first element in the array. The remaining elements are accessed by using an array index, which is equivalent to incrementing the address by one each time through the loop.

In C++, you can add additional complexity to a structure by including member functions as well as public and private declarations. Once you get to that point, however, you are so close to the concept of a class that you may as well use a class in place of a structure. We take up the concept of a class in Chapter 7.

Chapter 5: The C/C++ Programming Language

Good Programming Practices

In this section we'll review some good programming practices that you should stick to when developing your Visual C++ projects. We've mentioned some of these issues already in our discussions of the C++ programming language, and we will be talking about more of them throughout the book.

Avoid the Use of Global Variables

When you define the variables you will be using in your programs, try for the most local or limited scope possible. This means you should attempt to define your variables inside functions rather than file-wide or global variables. Pass values between functions to exchange information. This makes for more robust and stable code.

Give Your Variables Good Names

All identifiers used in C++ programs should have good, descriptive names. This includes the names used for variables, constants, arrays, and functions. Give each identifier a meaningful name that represents the function of that variable in the program. We will be examining standard naming conventions used for variables and objects in Chapter 8.

Comment Your Code

This is one of the most important tips any programmer can keep in mind. All code should be commented, unless it is immediately obvious what the code does. Comments do not add to the file size or decrease the performance of your program; the compiler simply ignores them. They are used simply for your benefit. So comment liberally. We will discuss comments in more detail in Chapter 8.

Comment Ending Brackets for `If` Statements, `While` Loops, and `For` Loops

It is a good idea to place a little comment on the ending bracket of an `if` statement or loop in a C++ program. When your programs start to get more complicated and therefore are much larger, it can get confusing matching each ending bracket to the beginning bracket. For example:

```
if ( x > 10)
{
    //large code block here
    ...
    if( y < 0 )
  {
     //more code here
     ...
   }//end if y <0
}//end if x > 10
```

In this example we have identified each ending bracket by the `if` statement that it belongs to. When debugging the code or tracing the logic, this can be very helpful.

Indent Your Code

When you are including a statement block inside an `if` statement, `while` loop, `for` loop, or as part of the body of a function, indent the code by at least three spaces. This will help clarify what the block is a part of and make your code more readable.

Break Code Down into Functions

If you are using a block of code over and over again in a program, this is a good indicator that code needs to be put in a function. Breaking a program down into functions makes it more efficient and easier to debug and maintain, and makes the code in the program reusable, since you can cut and paste the functions into other projects.

If a Variable Won't Be Modified in a Function, Use Pass By Value

Pass by value is the default method used to pass variables in C++. This protects the contents of memory, since a variable passed in this way cannot be altered by a function. You should stick to this method of parameter passing unless you really need to modify a variable.

Use Error Trapping

Throughout the book we will see how to test for error conditions. It is important to check for error conditions and take corrective action when necessary so that your program will not crash or exhibit unpredictable behavior.

Declare All Variables at the Beginning of a Function

While you can declare a variable in C++ anywhere you feel like it, this is a sloppy programming practice. You should declare all of your variables in a special section at the beginning of each function. Include comments that describe what each variable does. Also initialize your variables in the declaration statement or immediately afterwards.

Plan Your Logic *Before* You Start to Program

Programmers have always been susceptible to the temptation to sit down and start typing out a program without planning it out on paper first. In today's world of easy visual programming, this temptation is as strong as ever. Avoid this temptation and plan out the logic and flow of your programs before you open up Visual C++.

Some Common Mistakes and How to Avoid Them

In this section, we will go over a few common mistakes many new C++ programmers make and provide suggestions on avoiding them.

Failing to Explicitly Convert Data Types

Be sure to use casting to convert data types when you are mixing them in the same assignment statement. Failure to do so can result in a compiler error.

Declaring Local Variables with the Same Name as a Global Variable

If your program uses global or file-wide variables, make sure there are no naming conflicts with local variables. This can result in problems if you think that the code using the local variable is modifying the variable with wider scope. To keep yourself out of this situation, try to avoid using global variables in the first place, and if you do need to use them, try to give them unique names. You may wish to use your own special naming convention with global variables; for example, instead of naming a variable `Temperature`, name it `gTemperature` so that you will know it has global scope.

Be Sure to Terminate `If` Statements, `For` Loops, and `While` Loops

Many beginning programmers may start a long code block and forget to include the closing bracket. To avoid this simple error, add both the starting and ending brackets for code blocks like `if` statements before you write your code, then place your code inside the brackets.

Memory Allocation Problems

If you are programming with complicated structures or predefined C++ data types and you get strange behavior, such as you assign a value to it and nothing is there, you may need to allocate the memory for that structure. In fact, you should use the `malloc` function after you declare a variable of a complicated type to make sure the system allocates the memory for it.

Crashing a Program from Memory Problems

Be careful in your use of memory. Be sure to free up any memory you take from the heap with the `malloc` function. Also make sure that you never use `free` on a pointer that has not been allocated memory.

Going Out of Range

Be careful when working with arrays; you can easily exceed the bounds of the array. You might just get garbage out of unused memory, or you might end up crashing the program. When passing arrays to a function, be sure to pass the number of elements in each dimension.

Using Keywords as Variable Names

It's a syntax error to use a keyword as a variable name. The compiler will catch this error.

Using Functions with a Pointer Return Type

If you return the address of a local variable when a function has a pointer return type, this can result in data corruption or loss. Future function calls that will use up the stack may end up using that memory address. Instead of using a pointer return type for a function, pass a variable by reference to accept the result of the function.

CHAPTER 6

Object-Oriented Design

Introduction

In recent years the traditional method of software development has been supplanted by *object-oriented programming*. In the context of software development, an *object* is a software component that combines data and the procedures that act on that data together into a single entity. Objects provide a ready means to model the real world in software; after all, the real world is made up of a series of objects. With each object we can think of the characteristics or attributes it has, which will make up the data of the object. We can also consider what happens to the object or what kind of actions the object can initiate. These will be the procedures for the object.

Let's consider a specific example and think about the data and procedures that can be used to define the object. A familiar object from everyday life is the family automobile. We can start thinking about modeling a car in software by breaking a car down into data and procedures. First, we consider the data of the car object, which are the characteristics or *properties* of the car. Here is a list of some of the properties the average car might have:

- Make
- Model
- Year
- Fuel capacity, in gallons
- Miles per gallon, city
- Miles per gallon, highway
- Current fuel, in gallons
- Oil type required
- Number of cylinders
- Money spent on fuel

Each of these data elements or properties of the car can be modeled by a simple data type. For example, we can define the model and fuel capacity in the following manner:

```
Dim Model As String
Dim FuelCapacity As Byte
```

For the procedures that the car object will have, we can think about what happens to the car during its existence. Some of the things that happen to a car might include:

Chapter 6: Object-Oriented Design

- General driving
- Going in for repairs
- Refueling
- Getting in an accident

Each of the items we've identified here can be modeled as software procedures. For example, we could develop a function that modeled general driving. If we were interested in fuel consumption, we might track how many miles of city travel or highway travel the car went on, and have the driving function return the number of gallons used. Our function definition might look something like this:

```
Function Drive (HighwayMiles As Integer, CityMiles As Integer) Return GallonsUsed
```

By analyzing each of the data elements and procedures in this way, we can build up a car object to model the behavior of a car under different driving conditions, or to study its fuel use. While this is a good start, you might notice that many properties of the car object will have to be set over and over again in code. Say, for instance, we were continually modeling Ford trucks. Since all of these trucks will have similar values for several of their properties or similar behavior for many of the procedures, it might make sense to have an object named "Truck." You might also notice that a truck has characteristics that a car does not have. Rather than having to redefine a new object that used all of the characteristics of a car with a few additions, it would be nice if we could use the car object as the basis of the truck object, and *extend* it.

This brings us to the idea of *inheritance*. With inheritance, we can define a generic car object with the properties and procedures that we defined above. We can then define new types that inherit the car object, but add their own additional data and procedures. Let's call the original object the *base* object. When the new object type inherits from the base object, it will have all of the data and procedures as part of its characteristics. In other words, the truck object will already have *Model* and *FuelCapacity* without having to redefine them. However, the truck object might extend the car object by extending it, say, with the following properties and methods:

- *Diesel*   A Boolean variable that can be set to true if the truck uses diesel fuel
- *Tow capacity*   An integer that tells us how many pounds the variable can tow

- *Load capacity*   An integer that tells us how many tons the truck can hold

I'm sure that you can think of some more. In the same way that we can use the car object as the base object for developing a truck object, we can use it to define several other objects as well, such as a sedan, minivan, or any other type of automobile.

From the preceding discussion, you are probably beginning to see some of the power that an object-oriented approach to programming provides. By putting software code in objects, we have a reusable component. By reusing components, we can build software in much shorter time periods, with less cost, and with more reliability.

Software Reuse Speeds Product Development

Once a piece of software is packaged in a reusable object, it can be plugged into a new program without having to reinvent the wheel. This will save an enormous amount of time when developing new software. An object-orientated approach can also provide a standardized way for interoperability, which means that components can be simply dropped into a program and used immediately without having to deal with the nuances of using code libraries. When you use objects—for example, a calendar object—you save a great deal of time by being able to simply drop the calendar into your project without having to code up a calendar yourself. Being able to choose from a wide collection of objects allows the speedy development of software at a lower cost.

Software Reuse Promotes Reliability

Once an object is designed, debugged, and thoroughly tested, it can be used over and over again without having to worry about the code that represents the object causing problems. Entire software projects can be built entirely from objects that are already known to be reliable. This means that the reliability of the project as a whole is increased. The time spent debugging and testing can also be reduced, because this has already been done for each object in the program.

Chapter 6: Object-Oriented Design

Structuring Your Data with Classes

When we thought about the car object, we *classified* the objects, such as car or truck. This is the origin of the term *classes*. By using a class to define an object in software, we can classify objects by behavior (procedures or methods) and data (properties). We can also think about what might happen to an object; we can call this an *event*. An object is an *instance* of the class.

In the C++ language, a class is modeled on a type declaration or struct. Without getting into the details of how a class is used in C++ right now, let's think about how we can represent a class in an abstract fashion. Let's return to the car example. Using the properties and methods that we defined in the introduction, we could build the class like this:

```
Class Car

Properties

    Make As String
    Model As String
    Year As String
    FuelCapacity As Integer
    CityMPG As Integer
    HwyMPG As Integer
    Fuel As Integer
    FuelCost As Currency
    MoneySpentOnRepairs As Currency

Methods

Function Drive (HighwayMiles As Integer, CityMiles As Integer) Return GallonsUsed
Function GetRepairs (RepairType As Integer) Return Cost
Function Refuel (Gallons As Integer) Return Cost

Events
Crash()

End Class
```

We can then declare variables of type `car`, as defined by the `car` class above. Each of these variables will be an object, and we say that each object is an instance of the `car` class. For example:

```
Car Van, Sedan;
```

The function of the class is to *define* the object. Once the object is defined, we can declare the individual instances of the object in our program. Because all of the objects of a particular class share the same properties, methods, and events, they will behave in the same way.

We can also use a class that functions only as a template. In this case, the class is known as an *abstract* class. Objects of the abstract class are never declared; the class is only used to define other classes, through inheritance. The methods and events of the abstract class may not even do anything. We can place blank function definitions and only add the code to the inherited classes.

The Aspects of Object-Oriented Programming

The world of object-oriented programming is one that's filled with terminology. This terminology can make object-oriented programming seem a lot more complicated than it really is.

Abstraction

By viewing a problem in a black box or hierarchical fashion, we can simplify software development by concentrating only on certain details of a problem. We can build an object as a series of black boxes without worrying about what's happening inside each box. This process is known as *abstraction*. Abstraction involves temporarily ignoring the details of how the black boxes work while we concentrate on structuring the object. Once the object is built at a higher level, we can fill in the details of each black box. The roots of abstraction go back to the idea of building modular software. In that case, we could define a software program as a series of steps represented only by function headers. Once the overall flow of the program was developed, then we could move on to filling in the details—that is, writing the code behind each of the functions.

Client and Server

This term is not really a part of the object-oriented language, but I've put it here because it's important you know what we mean by the terms *client* and *server* in the context of objects. In the Windows environment, an application will make its objects available to other applications—this is called *exposing* the objects. The application that exposes its objects is known as the *server*. The applications that use these objects are known as *client* applications. When you develop a Windows application that uses the Word Basic object library, Microsoft Word functions as the server, while your application is the client. We'll see later that Visual C++ allows you to develop server applications by building your own objects and making them available to other apps.

Encapsulation

Encapsulation means that the user of an object does not worry about how that object goes about performing its functions. Encapsulated data is not accessible outside of the object. The data in the object can only be manipulated by the methods of that object. The methods of the object can either be invoked by a message from another object, or by another method that is part of the object itself. The goal of encapsulation is to hide the details of how the object works.

Information Hiding

In object-oriented software development, the user interacts with an object by performing certain operations on that object. The user cannot see the data or the implementation behind that object. The goal of information hiding is to promote software reuse. By hiding the details, we can modify the object without having any impact on any applications that use the object. The goal of object orientation is to reduce the interaction between the object and the user to an interface. The details of the object may change, but the interface stays the same. If the object is updated or changed, the user application does not care; to the user, the object seems the same. This saves time and money, and keeps software headaches to a minimum.

Inheritance

In our introduction we showed how we could use the car object to define other objects that were similar but had their own characteristics, such as a truck. The central characteristic of *inheritance* is the ability to use a set of characteristics and behaviors that are common to a wide variety of objects. We call a class that inherits the characteristics of the base class a *subclass*. The subclass is defined in terms of the base class that already exists. The subclass inherits all of the characteristics and behaviors of the base class as its own and can extend the functionality of the class by adding new characteristics and behaviors. Inheritance is a characteristic of object-oriented programming that contributes to faster and cheaper software development.

Polymorphism

Polymorphism means that a software operation can be applied to many different situations. For example, we might have a class called *shape* that represents three-dimensional objects. A useful method for 3D shapes would be *volume*, which returns the volume of the object. Different classes of shape objects, such as cubes and spheres, will use different methods for calculation of volume. As another example, think about using the + symbol to concatenate strings or to add two numbers together. We can think of this as using the same object to perform two very different operations. When an operation can be used in several different ways, we call this *overloading*. Polymorphism allows a subclass to *override* a method of the base class to suit its own purposes. For example, we can have a base class called Circle. The Area method for the circle class will return Pi* (Radius squared) for the area. We can develop a Sphere class and override the Area method to return the area of a sphere, 4*Pi* (Radius squared).

The idea of polymorphism contributes to the abstract approach of object-oriented development by letting the developer focus on using the method without worrying about how the method is implemented. Once it's figured out how the method will be used, the details inside can be built.

COM

If you've been anywhere around the software development world in the last couple of years, no doubt you've heard about *COM* and *DCOM*. If you've been programming in Windows, you're already somewhat familiar with COM through OLE and ActiveX. COM stands for *component object model*, and it represents a standardized method of communication

Chapter 6: Object-Oriented Design

between objects. Under COM, objects can only communicate by means of an interface that they provide. The internal workings of the object are invisible to clients—they can only see and manipulate the interface. COM provides this standard through a set of base classes upon which all objects are built. Developers use a set of abstract classes that define the component interface. Recalling the definition of abstraction in an object-oriented environment, this means that COM builds these classes as if they were a set of black boxes—or function headers. COM specifies how information gets in and out of the box, but the internal workings of the box are defined by the developer. Since the implementation details are hidden from the client, and the client knows the interface of the object through COM, the client can communicate with the object through the use of the COM standard.

One of the benefits of COM is that it allows objects to evolve while maintaining the same interface for backward compatibility. Client applications can continue to use new versions of an object without worrying about how the internal implementation has changed. This permits developers of objects to increase the functionality of the object while at the same time promoting software reuse.

Another term floating around software circles these days is *DCOM*. DCOM is the *distributed* component object model. This is an extension of COM that allows objects to work across a network. This is done by using what is known as a *remote procedures call*, or *RPC*. This allows a client application to access objects that are on a remote machine without having to worry about the fact that it is on a network.

COM and the Registry

In Windows, each COM object uses a unique 128-bit number that is known as the *ClassID*. This value is stored in the Registry, where it can be used by client applications to look up the component. As long as the component maintains the same ClassID and interface, the client application can continue to use newer versions of the component. This is an important means by which COM promotes software reuse.

Code Reuse vs. Component Reuse

Throughout this discussion of objects, you may be thinking back to the concept of a code library. A *code library* is a set of related software functions that other programmers can use in their development. This provides some of the benefits of object-oriented programming, especially by providing reusable code. However, the concept of code reuse does not provide a standardized means of communication that is imposed by component reuse. A standard like COM imposes an interface that is used by all objects. This means that any object in Windows automatically knows how to communicate with any other object.

Another problem with code reuse is that it does not provide true abstraction and encapsulation. In many cases, you might even have the source code of the library available for modification. This prevents the library from keeping its internal implementation hidden from the user. Code reuse also does not depend on the notion of classes, which means that the code cannot be extended through the use of inheritance and polymorphism. Component reuse, on the other hand, depends on these concepts in a fundamental way. This makes software reuse easier and less costly.

Existing Methodologies

There are several object-oriented design methods known throughout the industry, and here a brief overview of some of the well-known techniques will be given. One of the most famous of these is the *Grady Booch* object-oriented design method. This method uses Booch diagrams, which show the interactions between different objects. Object-oriented design allows the developer to show how objects are derived from base classes and how these objects interact. The Booch method provides object diagrams and object partitioning, along with the relationships of the behavior of each object. This method is the most matured method of object-oriented design.

The *Coad/Yourdon* method illustrates the behavior of objects by naming methods on classes. These methods are defined by what is known as a *service chart*. A service chart has flowcharts and state transition charts. Interactions among objects are tracked by message connections. This method allows the entire system to be described in a single diagram, with a system built-in layers.

The *Object Modeling Technique* or *Rumbaugh* method, consists of three models. These are the object model, the dynamic model, and the functional model. The object model displays classes and their properties that include operations and relationships between classes, such as inher-

Chapter 6: Object-Oriented Design

itance and association. The dynamic model provides state transition diagrams for each class. The functional model is a data flow diagram. This method is considered easy to follow, but it is a relatively new model that is still in development.

The *unified modeling language* is a methodology that combines Booch, Rumbaugh, and the Jacobsen use-case driven object-oriented model. Use-case diagrams are used to show the software as seen by the end user. Class diagrams show the structure of the classes within the system, while object diagrams are used to show the objects in the system (remember, an object is a specific *instance* of a class). This model also includes state diagrams to show the states an object can have, along with any state transitions.

CHAPTER 7

Classes

Introduction

In Chapter 5 we saw how you can create your own data types with a struct. In Chapter 6 we found out how object-oriented programming is used to model the real world and to provide developers with robust and reusable objects through the concepts of inheritance, encapsulation, and polymorphism. To do object-oriented programming in C++, you will use a construct known as a *class*. A class is a lot like a struct, in that you can use it to define your own data types and objects. However, a class can do much more than a struct. Most importantly, a class can be used to implement object-oriented programming to the fullest, using each of the characteristics described in the previous chapter, such as inheritance.

Creating a Class

In Chapter 5, we described the C++ struct, which can be used to create your own data types. Each struct is known by a name assigned by the programmer called the tag field, and the struct contains one or more member variables declared between braces. To review, an example struct we created in Chapter 5 is shown here:

```
struct Employee{
  char name[30];
  char address[30];
  char phone[13];
  char SSN[11];
  int age;
  double wage;
  char job[20];
};
```

A struct is a very useful device, and it goes a long way when we need to create our own data types to represent real-world objects like employees. However, a struct does not implement all of the features of object-oriented programming. Among other things, you cannot develop a struct and then define new structs based on it using inheritance. Also, you will not find that a struct implements polymorphism. To build real object-oriented software, we need to turn to the C++ class. The class has the following characteristics, which make it a true object-oriented development tool:

Chapter 7: Classes

- *A class provides encapsulation.* That is, a class provides both a state (member variables) and an operation that can be performed on that state (member functions).
- *A class provides information hiding.* With a class, we can declare member variables and functions as *Private*, which means that they are hidden from the outside world. Private members can only be accessed by code that is part of the class.
- *A class provides inheritance.* A class can be defined as a base class or a subclass that inherits characteristics of the base class.
- *A class provides polymorphism.* C++ classes can be defined for several related objects, like shapes. Each of the classes, which are derived from the same base class, will have the same methods, such as Area. However, the function that implements the area for each shape is different.
- *A class provides an efficient means of software reuse.* Each class defines an object that can be reused across software projects.

These properties of the class make it the ideal tool for object-oriented programming. Defining a class is a lot like defining a struct. The syntax for a class is as follows:

```
class class-name : Inheritance-list
}
    //private members
protected:
    //private members which can be inherited
public:
    //public members accessible outside the class
} object-list;
```

The class keyword is used in place of the struct keyword. The class-name field is the name that you assign to the class, like the tag field for a struct. This is the name that you will use to define variables and objects of the class in code. The inheritance list is optional. If a class is inherited from other base classes, you list the names of those classes here. The colon is only included if you have an inheritance list.

The members of the class are defined between the enclosing braces, just like they are when we are defining a struct. However, in a class there are three categories for the members of a class. Each category is specified by a special keyword known as an *access specifier*:

- private A private member is one that cannot be accessed by code outside the class. By default, if you list variables or functions in a class without using an access specifier, they are considered private. For clarity, it is a good idea to always explicitly show that the members are private by using the `private` keyword.

- `protected` A protected member is also private, but it can be inherited by other classes.
- `public` A public member is accessible outside the class.

When you use an access specifier, follow the keyword by a colon and start your member definitions on the next line.

Data and Function Members

The first step in developing object-oriented software is to define your objects. Basically this means defining two sets of items. First we need to define what the characteristics of the object are. As we discussed in the last chapter, this involves defining the properties of the object. The second task we face is defining what operations can take place on those properties; these are the member functions of the object. We now proceed to illustrate how this is done by defining a simple class to represent a circle. This will be an extremely simple class, but it will illustrate many of the things you need to know to be on your way to developing object-oriented software. Our goal is to define a `circle` class that can be used to declare objects of type `circle` in C++ programs.

First of all, let's think about what data can be associated with a circle. This data includes:

- pi—The constant used in circle calculations.
- Radius
- Diameter

There are two calculations that can be performed on the data of the circle. These include:

- Area
- Circumference

We can build the `circle` class by implementing `area` and `circumference` as member functions. Since the diameter is defined in terms of the radius, we can also implement `diameter` as a member function. This way, we can protect the `circle` object from corruption, since we only

Chapter 7: Classes

want the user to be able to set one parameter of the circle, which we choose to be the radius.

The first step is to create the `circle` class and add the member variables. We will declare our member variables as type `float` because chances are the user will need to perform calculations on floating-point values. The class definition could start out as:

```
class circle{
    float pi;
    float radius;
};
```

As we said earlier, a class looks a lot like a struct, but the `struct` keyword has been replaced by a new keyword, `class`. We have defined `pi` as a constant, which we will use to help implement the `area` and `circumference` functions. It is a good idea to have each class you define in its own header file, which is named for the class. To create the circle class, we will use a file named *circle.h*.

Public vs. Private Members

You will recall that the default access that C++ defines for class members is `private`. This means that both class members we have added to the `circle` class have private access and are only available within the class. That means that the following code will not compile:

```
circle mycircle;

mycircle.radius = 6.5;
```

Radius is the defining property of a circle, so we want the user to be able to modify it. To remedy this situation, we need to change the `circle` class so that the radius can be set outside the class. This means we need to give it public access. We will also add the `private` keyword to our class. As we stated earlier, private access is the default. But it's always a good idea to write clear code, so it won't hurt to include the `private` keyword in our definition. The `circle` class now looks like this:

```
class circle{
private:
    float pi;
```

```
public:
   float radius;
};
```

We could, of course, define pi as a constant, but we will declare it as a variable here for the purposes of instruction. It has been declared as a private member because it will be used in the calculations on the circle, but it isn't necessary to make it available outside the class. Now we have made the radius member public, so it can be set and read at will by code outside the class.

Adding Member Functions to a Class

Now that we have defined the data members of the class, we are ready to include the member functions that will act on that data. There will be three member functions that we will add:

- Area
- Circumference
- Diameter

We will start by only including the function members inside the class. Since we defined the `radius` variable as type `float`, and each function will act on the `radius` variable, we will give each function a return type of `float`. The functions will only act on the radius of the circle and will therefore not need to accept any parameters. The final point to keep in mind is the type of access that we want for each function. These functions will need to be available outside the class, so we will give them public access. We can therefore modify the class to look like this:

```
class circle{

private:
   float pi;

public:
   float radius;
   float area();
   float circumference();
   float diameter();

};
```

Chapter 7: Classes

The empty parentheses included with each function name indicate to the compiler that these are function names, not member variables. Where is the function body? Well, a common practice is to put the function body for each function immediately *after* the class definition. This will make the class definition nice and compact. We will need a way to tell the compiler that functions defined outside of the class actually belong to that class. This is done by using the *scope resolution operator*. The scope resolution operator is simply made by typing two colons. The syntax is as follows:

```
return-type class-name::member-name
```

When we include the scope resolution operator with the functions that we write to implement the circle, the compiler will know that the code is part of the class. For clarity the member functions should be included immediately following the class definition. When we add functions to implement the `area` and `circumference` of the circle, the class looks like this:

```
class circle{

private:
    float pi;

public:
    float radius;
    float area();
    float circumference();
    float diameter();

};

float circle::area()
{
    float result=0;

    result = pi*(radius*radius); //return pi*r^2
    return(result);

}

float circle::circumference()
{
    float result=0;

    result = 2 * pi * radius;

    return(result);

}
```

Using Inline Functions

Up to this point the `diameter` function has been left out on purpose. This is because C++ provides another way to define a function, called an *inline function*. An inline function is created by including the code for the function on a single line with the function header. We could have defined all of the functions for the `circle` class in this way, but we used both methods to illustrate how a class can be built. The `diameter` function will be implemented as an inline function. All we need to do is enclose the function code in braces on the same line where the function header was defined in the class. The class with the code for the `diameter` function looks like this:

```
class circle{

private:
   float pi;

public:
   float radius;
   float area();
   float circumference();
   float diameter() { return(2*radius); };

};

float circle::area()
{

    float result=0;

    result = pi*(radius*radius); //return pi*r^2

    return(result);

}

float circle::circumference()
{

    float result=0;

    result = 2 * pi * radius;

    return(result);

}
```

The `diameter` function is defined as an inline function:

```
float diameter() { return(2*radius)};
```

Chapter 7: Classes

When a function is defined as an inline function, this tells the compiler to attempt to expand the function inline rather than calling the function. Functions that are part of a class are automatically inline functions, if possible. A function can only work as an inline function generally if it is extremely simple. Functions that contain complex statements like loops cannot be expanded inline.

Constructors and Destructors

There is one more task we need to do before the `circle` class can be used: We must set the value for the private variable `pi`. This can be done by using a *constructor function*. The constructor function is called automatically whenever an object of your class type is created. You give the constructor the same name as your class, and you can include code in the constructor to initialize member variables. You can write the constructor function to accept variables, which are passed to the constructor for the purposes of initializing member variables. However, in this case, we will simply use the constructor to set the value of pi. We will list the constructor as the first function in the class. The class definition now looks like this:

```
class circle{

private:
   float pi;

public:
   circle() { pi=3.14159; } //class constructor
   float radius;
   float area();
   float circumference();
   float diameter() { return(2*radius);};
};
```

Notice that no semicolon follows the constructor function.

We can also add a *destructor function* to the class as well. The destructor is called when the object of the class is destroyed or goes out of scope. To add a destructor to the class, you also add a member function with the same name as the class, but you add a ~ character to the beginning of the name. The purpose of the destructor is to free up any resources that were in use by the class. Note that the constructor and destructor functions do not have a return type. With the destructor, the final version of the class definition looks like the following:

```
class circle{

private:
   float pi;

public:
   circle() { pi=3.14159; }
   ~7Ecircle() { cout << "\nClass Destroyed.";}
   float radius;
   float area();
   float circumference();
   float diameter() { return(2*radius);};

};
```

The destructor does not have to do anything, and it is common to see a destructor with an empty set of braces. Again, note that the constructor and destructor functions are not terminated with a semicolon, unlike the other elements of the class.

Declaring and Using a Class Variable

Now that the `circle` class is complete, we are ready to use it in a program. The following program illustrates the use of the `circle` class.

```
#include <iostream.h>
#include "circle.h"

//Circle1.cpp : Program to illustrate
//the use of a circle object

int main()
{
    //declare two circle objects

    circle small_circle, big_circle;
    float myarea, mycircumference, mydiameter;
    float totalarea;
    //set the respective radii
    small_circle.radius = 2.5;
    big_circle.radius = 40;

    //retrieve the area, circumference and diameter
    //of the small circle
    myarea = small_circle.area();
    mycircumference = small_circle.circumference();
    mydiameter = small_circle.diameter();

    //display results on screen
    cout << "\nSmall Circle Area : " << myarea;
```

Chapter 7: Classes

```
            cout << "\nSmall Circle Circumference : " << mycircumference;
            cout << "\nSmall Circle Diameter : " << mydiameter;

            //retrieve the area, circumference and diameter
            //of the big circle
            myarea = big_circle.area();
            mycircumference = big_circle.circumference();
            mydiameter = big_circle.diameter();

            //display results on screen
            cout << "\nBig Circle Area : " << myarea;
            cout << "\nBig Circle Circumference : " << mycircumference;
            cout << "\nBig Circle Diameter : " << mydiameter;

            //get the total area and print it
            totalarea = small_circle.area() + big_circle.area();

            cout << "\nTotal Area is : " << totalarea;

            return(0);

        }
```

You will recall that we placed our class in a header file which has the same name as the class. For this reason the first line of the program is an #include statement, which tells the compiler to include that file. We use double quote marks because the file is found in the working directory of the program:

```
#include "circle.h"
```

The next line to look at is the line of code where we declare two variables of type `circle`:

```
//declare two circle objects
circle small_circle, big_circle;
```

Class objects are declared in the same way as normal variables. The line begins with the name of the class and is followed by the variable list. Here we declared two variables of type `circle`, `small_circle`, and `big_circle`. When an object of the class is declared, the constructor function is automatically called. This means that this line will call the `circle` constructor function and initialize pi for each variable.

After declaring some variables, we set the radius for each circle. To refer to the value of a member variable in a class, you use the same dot syntax that we used with types defined with a struct:

```
//set the respective radii
small_circle.radius = 2.5;
big_circle.radius = 40;
```

Next, we call the member functions of the `small_circle` object. This is also done by using the dot syntax. The member functions we defined for the `circle` class do not accept any parameters, so we will list each function name with a set of empty parentheses. If you don't include the parentheses, you will get a compiler error. The code looks like this:

```
//retrieve the area, circumference and diameter
//of the small circle
myarea = small_circle.area();
mycircumference = small_circle.circumference();
mydiameter = small_circle.diameter();
```

The results are then printed on the screen, and we perform the same operations for the `big_circle` object. The final line of code that is of note is this one:

```
//get the total area and print it
totalarea = small_circle.area() + big_circle.area();
```

Here we obtain the total area of both circles by adding together the areas of each one, which is done by invoking the `area` member function for each object. The important thing to note is that you can use the `public` member functions of a class in assignment statements just like you can with regular functions.

At this point, you have a good understanding of classes. While the `circle` class was very simple, we were able to illustrate the methods used to create a class, defining `public` versus `private` member variables and functions, using the scope resolution operator, using inline functions, using constructors and destructors, and declaring and using class objects in code. In the next section we will expand on the basic ideas of the class by exploring more-advanced capabilities like inheritance.

Inheritance-Based and Derived Classes

One of the most powerful features of classes, and one that clearly separates a class from a struct, is the ability to use inheritance. As we discussed in the last chapter, inheritance allows you to define a base class that has properties that are common to a wide variety of different but related objects. For example, we can have a general object called `shape` to represent three-dimensional shapes, like spheres and cones. No matter what the shape is, it is going to have many common properties, like area, volume, and perhaps radius. You can derive new objects like the ones we mentioned—spheres, cones, and cylinders, for example, which are based on the `shape` object. If we implement the `shape` object as a class, it will function as the base class. We can then define a new class to represent each specific type of shape. The new classes would inherit methods and properties from the base class and provide their own specific implementations for calculations like area or volume. Classes based on inheritance can use members of the base class, as well as add members of their own. The ability to extend and reuse your classes in this way is part of the power that the C++ language provides.

Let's illustrate how various shapes might be implemented by using inheritance. The shapes that we implement will include a sphere, a cylinder, and a cone. We begin by imagining the member data and functions that each of these objects will have in common. These will include:

- Radius
- All will use the constant pi
- Area
- Volume

We can also imagine that our software will be able to draw the shapes on the screen, so we can include a draw method as well. We will start by defining a new class named `shape`, which will be the base class for the specific shape classes we want to implement. Our base class will contain only empty function definitions, as well as a definition of pi. One thing we need to think about is how do we want to define the access for each member function and variable? Since we will allow the user to set the radius and read the area and volume of each object, we will make these members public. Therefore, we can write the `shape` class like this:

```
class shape
{

public:

    double radius;
    shape() {} //constructor
    ~7Eshape() {} //destructor
    double area() { return(0); };
    double volume() { return(0); };
    void draw() {};

}; //end class shape
```

We also need to add a variable that will hold the value of pi. This variable will be private to the class; it will be used by the member functions of the class, but it will not be accessible outside the class. In a class that is not going to be used as a base class or if the variable was only going to be used by shape, we could make this variable `private`. However, we want all of the classes that inherit shape to have the ability to access and use the variable. For this reason, we will use the `protected` access specifier to declare the variable `pi`. This will ensure that the classes that inherit shape have access to it, but code that is outside the class does not. The `shape` class can be rewritten like this:

```
class shape
{

protected:
    double pi;
public:

    double radius;
    shape() { pi = 3.14159; } //constructor
    ˇ7Eshape() {} //destructor
    double area() { return(0); };
    double volume() { return(0); };
    void draw() {};
}; //end class shape
```

Now we have everything we need to implement specific objects like cylinders. Notice that the shape constructor initializes the `pi` variable. You can add code to your base class that is common to all inherited classes. When we build our derived classes, they will be able to use the code in the constructor without building that code as an explicit part of the derived class definition. This is part of the beauty of inheritance; we get some code for free. Since our base class is representing the abstract idea of a shape, the member functions like `area` and `volume` will have no code here. When we create each inherited class, we can add the code there that is specific to each object we model. We won't be implementing the `draw` function in this example, but we have included it here to show that you can add abstract function definitions that can be implemented later on.

Building a Derived Class

The next step is to build each derived class. The first thing we will do is create the class definition with the member function headers without

Chapter 7: Classes

actually adding any code just yet. We will also add any new members we need that are specific to each derived class.

First, let's tackle a sphere. A sphere can be defined simply in terms of its radius, so there isn't really much to add here. However, for the purposes of instruction, let's recall that the volume of a sphere is as follows:

```
Volume = 4/3*π*r3
```

We will define a new constant specific to the `sphere` class to represent the value 4/3. Since this constant is specific to spheres and is only used in calculations by member functions, we will make this constant a private member. With this in mind, we write the definition of the `sphere` class like this:

```
class sphere : public shape
{
public:
    sphere() { vol = 4.0/3.0; }
    ~7Esphere() {}
    double area();
    double volume();
    void draw() {};
private:
    double vol;
};
```

The first item to notice is the following:

```
class sphere : public shape
```

The class definition starts out like any other, but we have added an inheritance list. We are telling the compiler that the `sphere` class will be inherited from the `shape` class. We include the `public` keyword to tell the compiler that we want our derived class to inherit the public members of `shape`. Otherwise, it would just inherit the protected members.

At the bottom of the class, notice that we have added a new variable named `vol`, which is not a part of the `shape` base class:

```
private:
    double vol;
```

As we stated earlier, this constant will be used to represent the constant 4/3, which is used in the volume calculation for a sphere. The constant will only be used by member functions of the class, so we have declared it with the `private` access specifier. We can use the constructor for the `sphere` class to initialize the constant:

```
sphere() { vol = 4.0/3.0; }
```

Even though we have defined a constructor for the `sphere` class, keep in mind that the `sphere` class inherits from the `shape` class, so we get the code in the `shape` class constructor for free. The `pi` variable defined as protected in the `shape` class will be initialized automatically, and we will have access to it throughout the `sphere` class.

Once the derived class is defined, it is time to put the specifics for each member function into code. The member functions for the class are placed immediately following the end of the class definition. We will tell the compiler which class each function belongs to by using the scope resolution operator, like we did with the `circle` class. The `area` and `circumference` classes for the `sphere` class look like this:

```
double sphere::area()
{
    double result=0;
    double rsquared=0;

    rsquared = pow(radius,2);

    result = 4*pi*rsquared;

    return(result);

}
double sphere::volume()
{
    double result=0;

    double rcubed=0;

    rcubed = pow(radius,3);

    result = vol * pi * rcubed;

    return(result);

}

//*******************End Class Sphere***************************//
```

These functions are fairly simple; they simply do the appropriate calculation based on mathematical formulas and return the result as type

Chapter 7: Classes

double. Both functions are listed under the `public` access specifier for the class, so they will be accessible to code outside of the class. Also notice that we include a comment at the bottom of the class that clearly indicates the end of the class; we will add the code for the next derived class immediately following the comment. There is one new function we have used, the `pow` function:

```
double rcubed=0;

rcubed = pow(radius,3);
```

The `pow` function is found in the C++ header file *math.h* that ships with Visual C++. You can include it in your projects by adding the line:

```
#include <math.h>
```

at the beginning of the file. The `pow` function takes two arguments. The first argument is called the *base*, and the second argument is called the *exponent*. The function has a return type of `double` and returns base^{exponent}.

The next class we will derive from the `shape` class is the `cylinder` class. The `cylinder` class will also use the public members of the `shape` class, and we indicate this by adding the line `: public shape` immediately after the `class` keyword and tag specifier. The class definition looks like this:

```
class cylinder : public shape
{

public:
    cylinder() { height = 0; }
    ~7Ecylinder() { }
    double height;
    double area();
    double volume();
    void draw() {};

};
```

We have also added one new variable to the `cylinder` class, `height`. The variable should have public access, since we want the programmer who is using our class to be able to set the height of the cylinder he or she creates. We use the `cylinder` constructor to initialize the `height` variable. Recall that the `shape` base class has a `public` variable named `radius`; the `cylinder` class is inheriting all of the public and protected members of the `shape` class, so it gets `radius` and `pi` for free. The code to implement the `area` and `volume` functions for the `cylinder` class is added immediately after the class definition. The code is listed here:

```
double cylinder::area()
{
    double result=0;

    result = 2* pi * radius * height;

    return(result);

}
double cylinder::volume()

{
    double result=0;
    double rsquared=0;

    rsquared = pow(radius,2);

    result = pi * rsquared * height;

    return(result);
}
```

Like the `sphere` class, the `cylinder` class simply implements the mathematical formulas used to calculate the area and volume of the sphere.

The final class that we will derive from the `shape` class is the `cone` class. The `cone` class, like the `cylinder` class, will have a variable to represent height. We will also need to add a variable to track the surface length along the side of the cone. These two variables can be set by the user, so we will give them `public` access. The class definition looks like this:

```
class cone : public shape
{
public:
    cone() { height = 0; surfacelen = 0;}
    ˜7Econe() { }
    double height;
    double surfacelen;
    double area();
    double volume();
    void draw() {};

};
```

Notice that we use the `cone` constructor to initialize both variables. The `cone` class also inherits the public and protected members from the `shape` class, so it gets the `radius` and `pi` variables for free. Remember

Chapter 7: Classes

that since they are inherited, we do not have to explicitly list them in the class definition. However, they will be available to member functions, and the public shape member `pi` will be available when we declare objects of type `cone`. The code to implement the area and volume functions is shown here:

```
double cone::area()
{
    double result=0;

    result = pi * radius * surfacelen;

    return(result);

}
double cone::volume()
{
    double result=0;
    double rsquared=0;

    rsquared = pow(radius,2);

    result = (pi/3) * rsquared * height;

    return(result);

}

//*********************End Class Cone***************************//
```

Notice again that we list the return type, class name, and member function name in the header of each function:

```
double cone::volume()
```

Now we have the complete definition of our base class and three derived classes that we can use to declare objects. We can use each of these classes in the main program, like the one below:

```
#include <iostream.h>
#include "shapes.h"

int main()
{
    //declare objects
    sphere ball;
    cylinder cokecan;
    cone icecreamcone;

    //variables to hold results of calculations
    double area, volume;
```

```
//prompt the user for the radius
cout << "\nEnter the radius of the sphere: ";
cin > ball.radius;

//find the area and volume for the given radius
area = ball.area();
volume = ball.volume();

//report the results
cout << "\nThe Surface Area of the Sphere : " << area;
cout << "\nThe Volume of the Sphere : " << volume;
cout << "\n";

//now do the cylinder
cout << "\nEnter the radius of the cylinder: ";
cin > cokecan.radius;
cout << "\nEnter the height of the cylinder: ";
cin > cokecan.height;
area = cokecan.area();
volume = cokecan.volume();

cout << "\nThe Surface Area of the cylinder: " << area;
cout << "\nThe Volume of the cylinder : " << volume;
cout << "\n";
//now do the cone
cout << "\nEnter the radius of the cone: ";
cin > icecreamcone.radius;
cout << "\nEnter the height of the cone: ";
cin > icecreamcone.height;
cout << "\nEnter the surface length of the cone: ";
cin > icecreamcone.surfacelen;

area = icecreamcone.area();
volume = icecreamcone.volume();

cout << "\nThe Surface Area of the cone: " << area;
cout << "\nThe Volume of the cone : " << volume;
cout << "\n";

return(0);

}
```

The first step is to include the header file where we defined the classes. This is done by including *shapes.h*:

```
#include <iostream.h>
#include "shapes.h"
```

Recall that by using the `#include` directive, we are telling the compiler to insert the contents of that file at this location. We will also be doing some input/output, so we have included the *iostream* header file as well.

Once we have the *include* file, we are free to declare variables and work with the objects of our class. In the main program you will see that

Chapter 7: Classes

we declare three objects, one to represent each type of derived class that we created earlier:

```
//declare objects
sphere ball;
cylinder cokecan;
cone icecreamcone;
```

Recall that sphere, cylinder, and cone are the names that we assigned to each of the derived classes. So ball is an object of type sphere. You will also remember that each class has two member functions that we can use: area and volume. The next line declares two variables of type double, which will be used to accept the results of the area and volume functions:

```
//variables to hold results of calculations
double area, volume;
```

The names of these variables do not have to be the same as the names of the class member functions, but we have given them the same name for clarity. Next, we prompt the user to enter the radius of the sphere. We then use the dot syntax to reference the radius member variable of the ball object:

```
//prompt the user for the radius
cout << "\nEnter the radius of the sphere: ";
cin > ball.radius;
```

If you go back and look at the definition of the sphere class, you will notice that the radius member variable was not listed. We can use it here because the sphere class inherits all of the public and protected members of the shape class, where radius is defined.

In the next two lines, we use the area and volume member functions of the sphere class to return the appropriate results:

```
//find the area and volume for the given radius
area = ball.area();
volume = ball.volume();
```

Once we have the results, we print them to the screen so the user can see them:

```
//report the results
cout << "\nThe Surface Area of the Sphere : " << area;
cout << "\nThe Volume of the Sphere : " << volume;
cout << "\n";
```

The rest of the program performs the same operations for the `cylinder` and `cone` objects. The only thing to notice is that we used the member variables that were defined specifically for those classes. For example, we set the height and surface length for the cone:

```
cout << "\nEnter the height of the cone: ";
cin > icecreamcone.height;
cout << "\nEnter the surface length of the cone: ";
cin > icecreamcone.surfacelen;
```

Implementing Polymorphism

In this simple example, we have illustrated not only the use of inheritance, but another important concept of object-oriented programming: polymorphism. We discussed polymorphism briefly in Chapter 6, but let's restate the concept here. Strictly speaking *polymorphism* means "many forms." When applied to object-oriented software development, polymorphism means that a derived class can modify or add to the member data and functions that it inherits from the base class. Function names are overloaded, which means that we will have several object types with the same function name, but the actual implementation of that function depends on the type of object in use. However, by keeping the same function names for the same operation performed on different types of objects, we keep our code more readable. For example, we have illustrated that here with the `area` function. We can find the area of a sphere or a cone using the same line of code:

```
area = ball.area();
area = icecreamcone.area();
```

Yet each object implements the `area` function differently, calling its own `area` function, which overrides the `area` function of the base class, shape. This is polymorphism in practice. To see how we might override a member function more explicitly, let's create a new class. This time we will create a class called `square`:

```
class square
{
public:
    double side;
    square() { side = 0;}
    double area() {};
}
```

Chapter 7: Classes

```
double square::area()
{
    double result=0;

    result = side*side;

    return(result);
}
```

Now suppose that we want to create a class named `rectangle` that inherits the public members of the `square` function. The class definition looks like this:

```
class rectangle : public square
{

public:
    double length;
    double width;
    rectangle() { length = 0; width = 0; }
    ~7Erectangle() {}

};
```

Remember that when we inherit from a base class, we get everything from that base class for free. So we *could* actually program `rectangle` objects without writing any more code, because each `rectangle` object inherits the `area` member function from the `square` class:

```
rectangle x;
x.side = 7;
cout << "\nAREA OF RECTANGLE IS : " << x.area();
```

Of course, this gives us the incorrect answer. What we need to do is implement the `area` function for the rectangle, which will override the code in the `area` function for the `square` class. The function looks like this:

```
class rectangle : public square
{

public:
    double length;
    double width;
    rectangle() { length = 0; width = 0; }
    ~7Erectangle() {}
    double area();

};
```

```
double rectangle::area()
{
    double result = 0;
    result = length * width;
    return(result);
}
```

Notice that the class definition of rectangle has changed; we must include the function header for any member function from the base class that we will override. After the `rectangle` class is defined, we can implement the function to override the base class `area` function. Now we can write the code that will return the proper value for the area of a rectangle:

```
rectangle x;
x.length = 7;
x.width = 4;
cout << "\nAREA OF RECTANGLE IS : " << x.area();
```

Advanced Class Topics

In the previous sections, we have laid down the foundation needed to program with classes. Already you can see the many advantages and extra power that a class provides over a struct. There is much more that a class can do, however. In this section we will consider some of the more-advanced capabilities that can be used with classes. We begin our discussion by introducing *friend functions*.

Friend Functions

The purpose of a `friend` function is to override private member access. In other words, by declaring a function to be a `friend` function, you are giving nonmember functions access to the private members of the class. A `friend` function is not defined as part of the class. However, they have access to all of the private resources of a class that a class member function does. A `friend` function is declared by using the keyword `friend` preceding the function prototype. The function prototype is included in the class definition, but the body of the function is not a part of the class. To see how this works, let's look at an example.

Chapter 7: Classes

Our next program will illustrate how to use a `friend` function with a class. We have developed a class that can be used in an astronomy program to track the characteristics of the planets, as shown here:

```
//structure to track the period of rotation of a planet
struct period
{
     short hours;
     short minutes;
     short seconds;

};

//structure to track the inclination of a planet
struct inclination_angle
{
     short degrees;
     short minutes;

};

class planet
{

private:

     long int radius; //radius in km
     double mass;     //mass in kg
     friend double density(planet); //friend function to
                                    //return planet density
public:

     float distance; //distance in AU's
     float surface_gravity;
     float escape_speed;
     short temperature;  //temp in kelvins
     inclination_angle inclination;
     period rotation_period;
     char name[25];

     //functions to allow user to set private variables
     void setradius(long int newradius) { radius = newradius; };
     void setmass(double newmass)   {   mass = newmass; };
     //functions to allow user to read private variables
     long int read_radius() { return(radius); };
     double read_mass() { return(mass); };

     double distance_in_kilometers();
     double distance_in_miles();

}; //end class planet

//class planet member functions
double planet::distance_in_kilometers()
{
```

```
        double result=0;
        const double AU_TO_KM = 1.496E8;

        result = distance * AU_TO_KM;

        return(result);

}

double planet::distance_in_miles()
{
        double result=0;
        double kms=0;
        const double kms_to_miles = 1.61; //1 mile = 1.61 kilometers
        kms = distance_in_kilometers(); //call member function to get kms

        result = kms/kms_to_miles; //convert from kms to miles

        return(result);

}
```

The important thing to notice is in this class definition, we have included a `friend` function named `density`. This `friend` function has its prototype listed in the `private` section of the class:

```
private:

        long int radius; //radius in km
        double mass;     //mass in kg
        friend double density(planet); //friend function to
                                       //return planet density
```

Notice that we have preceded the function prototype with the `friend` keyword. The function body of the `friend` function is not included as a part of the class. A `friend` function is written in the same way that a traditional C++ function is written. You will see below that the main program will also include a prototype of the `density` function, and we will write the function body after the main function. The `density` function takes one parameter, of type `planet`, as we have indicated in the prototype.

In the `public` section of the class, notice that we have defined the following two functions:

```
double distance_in_kilometers();
double distance_in_miles();
```

In the `distance_in_miles` function, we have called the distance_in_kilometers function for the sake of illustration. This shows

Chapter 7: Classes

how you can call other member functions of a class within any member function, in the same way that you would call a function in any C++ program:

```
double planet::distance_in_miles()
{
    double result=0;
    double kms=0;
    const double kms_to_miles = 1.61; //1 mile = 1.61 kilometers
    kms = distance_in_kilometers(); //call member function to get kms

    result = kms/kms_to_miles; //convert from kms to miles

    return(result);

}
```

The code in the main program is as follows:

```
#include <iostream.h>
#include <math.h>
#include "planets.h"

double density(planet); //function prototype for class friend

int main()
{
    planet jupiter;
    double mydensity;
    double miles, kilometers;

    //set some properties of the planet jupiter
    //set mass and radius. These are private member
    //variables, must use wrapper functions to set them
    jupiter.setmass(1.89E27);
    jupiter.setradius(71492);

    //set public member variables
    jupiter.distance = 5.2; //distance in AU's
    jupiter.escape_speed = 60; //escape speed in km/s
    jupiter.surface_gravity = 2.54;
    jupiter.temperature = 130;

    //set values for member variables which
    //are structs
    jupiter.inclination.degrees = 3;
    jupiter.inclination.minutes = 7;

    jupiter.rotation_period.hours = 9;
    jupiter.rotation_period.minutes = 50;
    jupiter.rotation_period.seconds = 30;

    //call the friend function to get the density
    mydensity = density(jupiter);
```

```cpp
        //call member functions to convert distance
        //to miles and kilometers
        miles = jupiter.distance_in_miles();
        kilometers = jupiter.distance_in_kilometers();

        //print the results to the screen
        cout << "\nDensity of the Planet Jupiter " << mydensity;
        cout << "\nSemi-major Axis in Miles " << miles;
        cout << "\nSemi-major Axis in Kilometers " << kilometers;

        return(0);

};

double density(planet myplanet)
{
        double volume=0;
        double const pi = 3.14159;
        double rcubed =0;
        double planet_density=0;
        double myradius=0;

        //get the volume of the planet
        //note that this is a friend function,
        //so has access to private member variable
        //radius

        //convert planet radius to meters
        myradius = myplanet.radius * 1000;

        rcubed = pow(myradius,3);

        volume = (4/3)*pi*rcubed;

        //calculate the density, using private
        //member function mass
        planet_density = myplanet.mass/volume;

        return(planet_density);

}//end function density
```

Take a look at the code immediately following the `#include` statements. Here we have included a prototype for the `friend` function density:

```cpp
double density(planet); //function prototype for class friend
```

The prototype for the `friend` function must also be declared here because the function is really a traditional C++ function. Now turning our attention to the code inside the function `main`, notice that we declare an object of type `planet` near the beginning of the function:

```cpp
planet jupiter;
```

Chapter 7: Classes

Now take a second look at the class definition. Notice that the member variables `mass` and `radius` have been declared with `private` access. You will recall that this means that these variables cannot be accessed by code that is outside of the class definition. We have provided two `public` member functions that can be used to set these values, and that is what is done in the next two lines of code:

```
//set some properties of the planet jupiter
//set mass and radius. These are private member
//variables, must use wrapper functions to set them
jupiter.setmass(1.89E27);
jupiter.setradius(71492);
```

Note that if we wrote a line like the following in the main program:

```
jupiter.radius = 71492;
```

the compiler would generate an error, since `radius` is a `private` member variable. Keep this in mind when we look at the code for the `friend` function. The `public` member variables of the class, however, can be set from anywhere in our code:

```
//set public member variables
jupiter.distance = 5.2; //distance in AU's
jupiter.escape_speed = 60; //escape speed in km/s
jupiter.surface_gravity = 2.54;
jupiter.temperature = 130;
```

If you recall, we also defined two structs at the beginning of the program. The `planet` class has two member variables that are structs. These member variables are accessed in the normal way by using the dot syntax. First, we need to tell the compiler which member variable we are accessing, and then since these member variables are structs, we also need to use the dot syntax to specify which member of the struct is being accessed:

```
//set values for member variables which
//are structs
jupiter.inclination.degrees = 3;
jupiter.inclination.minutes = 7;
```

Now let's turn our attention to the `density` function. The code is listed here:

```
double density(planet myplanet)
{
```

```
double volume=0;
double const pi = 3.14159;
double rcubed =0;
double planet_density=0;
double myradius=0;

//get the volume of the planet
//note that this is a friend function,
//so has access to private member variable
//radius

//convert planet radius to meters
myradius = myplanet.radius * 1000;

rcubed = pow(myradius,3);

volume = (4/3)*pi*rcubed;

//calculate the density, using private
//member function mass

planet_density = myplanet.mass/volume;

return(planet_density);

}//end function density
```

This function takes one parameter of type `planet`, which we have called `myplanet`. Since this is a `friend` function, we have access to the private member variables of the `myplanet` object. We use this to access the `radius` member variable:

```
//convert planet radius to meters
myradius = myplanet.radius * 1000;
```

If we attempted to use this line of code anywhere else in the program that was outside of the class, this would generate a compiler error.

In summary, a `friend` function allows you to circumvent the usual data hiding provided for `private` member variables in a class. A `friend` function has the following requirements:

- A function prototype must be included in the class definition. The `friend` keyword precedes the function prototype.
- A standard function prototype must be included in the file where the function is actually called. This is the same requirement that is applied to traditional C++ functions.
- The function body is written in the same way as a traditional C++ function. However, inside the `friend` function, access to `private` member variables of the class is allowed.

Operators

Earlier we discussed the possibility of overloading the name of a function. For example, we had two classes named sphere and cone, which overloaded the common function named area:

```
area = ball.area();
area = icecreamcone.area();
```

The C++ language also allows the developer to overload operators. This means that you can give symbols such as < , > , + , - , or * new meanings inside a class. You cannot overload all operators, but C++ does allow you to overload a large subset of them. These are listed here:

C++ Operators That Can Be Overloaded

+	−	<	>	<=	=>	+=	-=	==	!=	<<	>	<<=	=>	~	|	||	!=	/=	/
&	&&	&=	%	%=	new	delete	^=	^^	++	—	!	*0	*0=	=	[]	()			

C++ does not permit you to create a new operator. In addition, the following operators cannot be overloaded:

- The preprocessor directive operators # and ##
- The operators . : .* and ?

Other restrictions apply to overloading as well. C++ maintains the same precedence for operators, and you cannot change the number of arguments for an operator. To create an overloaded operator, you write a function with the operator keyword. The overloaded operator function is a part of a class:

```
return type class-name::operator#(parameter list)
{
//function body here
...

}
```

where # is the operator that you want to overload. The parameter list for an operator function contains no parameters when you are overloading a unitary operator and one parameter when overloading a binary operator. We will add a binary operator to the planet class we created in the last section. The operator we will overload is the % operator. For the planet class, the % operator will sum the mass of two planets. First, we add the following function prototype to the `public` section of the `planet` class definition:

```
//operator returns name of planet
//with larger mass
double operator%(planet a);
```

Notice that we have used the `operator` keyword and told the compiler that we want to overload the % operator. The operator will act on a planet, so the function accepts one parameter of type `planet`. The body of the function looks like this:

```
double planet::operator%(planet a)
{
    return(mass + a.mass);
}
```

When you overload a binary operator, the code in the function has access to the members of the left-hand object. This is how we are able to refer to the `mass` member variable. The second operand is passed as an argument to the function. To see how this works, let's add some more code to the main program. First, we declare some new variables:

```
planet earth, venus;

double totalmass=0;
```

Next, we set the mass for the planets `earth` and `venus`. You will recall that `mass` is a `private` member variable, so we need to make a call to the `setmass` wrapper function:

```
earth.setmass(5.974E24);
venus.setmass(4.87E24);
```

Next, we apply the overloaded operator % to `earth` and `venus` to return the sum of their masses:

```
totalmass = venus%earth;
```

Now take another look at the code in the overloaded operator function. In this case, any references to member variables without an object qualifier refer to the `venus` object. This means that `mass` refers to `venus.mass`. The second operand, `earth`, is passed as the parameter `a` in the overloaded operator function.

Chapter 7: Classes

You can use overloaded operators to provide shorthand for use in operations on your classes.

Using Pointers with Classes, `This`

In Chapter 5 we showed how to use a pointer to a struct. For example, if we had the following code:

```
struct dog
{
   char type[20];
   int weight;
   int age;
};

dog *lab;
```

we would use the `->` operator to reference the members of the `dog` struct rather than using the dot syntax. To set the `age` and `weight`, we write:

```
lab->weight = 70;
lab->age = 4;
```

The same rule applies to classes. This is true whether we are referencing a member variable or a member function. For example, let's return to the `planet` class and declare a pointer:

```
planet *saturn;
planet Neptune;

saturn->setmass(5.68E26); //call member function
saturn->distance = 9.52;  //set public member variables
saturn->escape_speed = 36;
saturn->inclination.degrees = 26; //set struct member var

//now do same for Neptune, which is not a pointer
Neptune.setmass(1.03E26);
Neptune.distance = 30;
Neptune.escape_speed = 24;
Neptune.inclination.degrees = 29;
```

Using `This`

There is one special pointer you need to be aware of when programming with classes, the `this` pointer. The `this` pointer references the object that generated a call to a member function. Every member function of a class gets the `this` pointer for free; you do not have to explicitly pass it to any functions. When we referred to the `mass` member variable in the overloaded operator function, we were implicitly referring to the `this` pointer. We can explicitly show the `this` pointer by changing the code to the following:

```
double planet::operator%(planet a)
{
    return(this->mass + a.mass);
}
```

The syntax here is a little clearer than simply listing the member variable. This explicitly shows that we are referring to a member of the object for which the member function is invoked. The `this` pointer can be used in any member function, not just overloaded operators. For example, in the `distance_in_kilometers` function, we referenced the member variable `distance`. We can use the `this` pointer to explicitly show that `distance` is a member variable of the object that invoked the call to the `distance_in_kilometers` function:

```
//class planet member functions
double planet::distance_in_kilometers()
{
    double result=0;
    const double AU_TO_KM = 1.496E8;

    result = this->distance * AU_TO_KM;
    return(result);
}
```

Virtual Functions

Virtual functions are useful in implementing polymorphism. A function is declared as `virtual` by preceding the function prototype with the `virtual` keyword. Virtual functions are used in classes that will function as a base class. The `virtual` function can be overridden by any derived classes. The derived class does not have to override the function; in that case, the definition of the function in the base class is used. You can also declare a pure `virtual` function by using the `=0/` operator. The syntax is as follows:

Chapter 7: Classes

```
virtual return type function_name(parameter list) =0;
```

This syntax tells the compiler that this function has no definition in the base class.

Using Multiple Inheritance

Inheritance is a powerful way to extend the code behind your objects. As we saw earlier, you can define a base class that acts as a template for multiple derived classes of similar objects, or you can derive a new class from a base class and override functions specific to the new class. C++ also provides a way that you can use to increase code reuse known as *multiple inheritance*. When you develop a class using multiple inheritance, the derived class inherits from more than one base class. You specify the base classes you want to use in the inheritance list part of the class. Each base class is separated by a comma and includes the appropriate access specifier (`public`, `private`, `protected`).

By using multiple inheritance, you can build derived classes more quickly. There are many objects that may have the characteristics and functions of more than one base object. For example, we could write a program to model the sun. We could have two base classes:

- `Sphere`
- `Star`

The `sun` class could inherit characteristics from each class. This will save effort and promote code reuse by allowing us to take advantage of member functions like `volume` and `area` already defined in the `sphere` class, as well as the member functions and variables in the `star` class that apply to the sun.

In our next example, we create a program that tracks students for the local high school. The program includes the file *schools.h*, which defines three classes:

```
#define GRADUATION 40

enum classes {freshman, sophmore, junior, senior };

class person
{
public:
    char name[30];
```

```
        char SSN[11];
        char address[30];
};

class grade_level
{
public:
    classes class_level;
    int year_of_graduation;
};

class student: public person, public grade_level
{
public:
    int credits;
    int grade_points;
    student(int hours, int gp) { credits = hours; grade_points = gp;}
    ~7Estudent() {}
    float GPA();
    bool CanGraduate();
};

float student::GPA()
{
    float result=0;

    result = (float)this->grade_points/(float)this->credits;

    return(result);

}
bool student::CanGraduate()
{

    if(this->credits < GRADUATION)
        return(false);
    else
        return(true);
}
```

The `student` class, found at the bottom of the file, inherits both the `person` class and the `grade_level` class. This is indicated in the first statement of the `student` class definition:

```
class student: public person, public grade_level
```

Following the name of the class, we include a colon and then begin the inheritance list. Each base class is listed with an access specifier. The list is comma-delimited. You will recall that when a derived class inherits members from its base class, it gets those members for free. With multiple inheritance, this benefit applies to all base classes. This means that when we declare objects of type `student`, we will be able to automati-

Chapter 7: Classes

cally use the members defined in both the `person` and `grade_level` classes.

Take a look at the constructor of the `student` class:

```
student(int hours, int gp) { credits = hours; grade_points = gp;}
```

This time, we have built the constructor so that it can accept parameters. This will allow us to initialize a `class` object when we declare it. We will see how this works in the main function of the program.

In the member functions of the `student` class, notice that we are using the `this` pointer to reference members of the class as they are needed:

```
float student::GPA()
{
    float result=0;

    result = (float)this->grade_points/(float)this->credits;

    return(result);

}
```

You may recall that this is not strictly necessary, but it makes the code clear. In other words, it is clear that we are accessing member variables.

The main program is as follows:

```
#include <iostream.h>
#include <string.h>
#include "schools.h"

int main()
{
    student mystudent(20,65);
    student *bill;
    float gpa=0;

    bill = &mystudent;

    //set members inherited from
    //person class
    strcpy(bill->name,"Bill Jones");
    strcpy(bill->SSN,"999-99-9999");
    strcpy(bill->address,"99 Main ST");

    //set members inherited from
    //grade_level class
    bill->class_level = junior;
    bill->year_of_graduation = 99;
```

```
    //set members defined in
    //student class
    bill->credits += 3;
    bill->grade_points += 9;
    gpa = bill->GPA();

    //print
    cout << "\nBills GPA : " << gpa;

    if(bill->CanGraduate())
        cout << "\nBill Can Graduate ";
    else
        cout << "\nBill Cannot Graduate yet.";

    return(0);

}
```

The first line of code to notice is the declaration statement:

```
student mystudent(20,65);
```

Here we use the fact that the constructor allows us to initialize the member variables of the `student` class. We do so by passing the values `20` for credits and `65` for grade points. On the next line, we declare a `pointer` variable of type `student`:

```
student *bill;
```

We then set the pointer to point to the `student` variable we declared in the first line. This is done by using the address of operator `&` (see Chapter 5) to return the address of the `my student` variable:

```
bill = &mystudent;
```

Note that if you wrote the code like this:

```
student *bill(20,65);
```

the compiler would generate an error. That is why we have decided to declare the variables the way we did, so that we could take advantage of the initialization and work with a `pointer` variable. Recall that when we work with pointers to a class or a struct, we use the -> operator rather than the dot syntax to access member variables and functions.

The next section of the code shows how we can take advantage of the inheritance we received from both classes. First we set the member variables of our student pointer that are inherited from the `person` class.

Chapter 7: Classes

Remember these variables do not need to be explicitly listed in the student class; we get them from the person class by listing person in the inheritance list. For our student pointer variable, we can reference these members as if they were declared right in the student class definition:

```
//set members inherited from
//person class
strcpy(bill->name,"Bill Jones");
strcpy(bill->SSN,"999-99-9999");
strcpy(bill->address,"99 Main ST");
```

Next, we set the members that are inherited from the grade_level class:

```
//set members inherited from
//grade_level class
bill->class_level = junior;
bill->year_of_graduation = 99;
```

Now say that Bill took another class and got a B. We can adjust his credits and grade points by setting the member variables that are defined in the student class. These are the members that are not inherited:

```
//set members defined in
//student class
bill->credits += 3;
bill->grade_points += 9;
```

On the next line, we call the GPA member function to see how bill is doing:

```
gpa = bill->GPA();
```

Finally, we call the member function CanGraduate to see if bill is eligible for graduation:

```
if(bill->CanGraduate())
    cout << "\nBill Can Graduate ";
else
    cout << "\nBill Cannot Graduate yet.";
```

While this is a simple example, it illustrates how you can define more than one class which can be used as base classes for one derived class. The derived class has access to all of the public and protected members of the base classes. This type of programming promotes code reuse and other goals of object-oriented programming. At this point we have covered class basics. We will be using classes throughout the remainder of the book, and we will use and build on the ideas presented in this chapter. In the next chapter, we will take some time to explore good programming practices in more detail before jumping into Windows programming with C++.

CHAPTER 8

Coding Standards

Introduction

Writing software is in many ways a subjective process. Every programmer is an individual, and that means they think in their own unique way. This fact will manifest itself in many different aspects of a software project. For one thing, some programmers will write neat and tidy code, with consistent indentation of blocks within `if` statements and `do` loops, while others will just sit down and type, so absorbed in the problem at hand that they aren't giving a thought to how their code looks. Some programmers will give long, descriptive names to variables, while others will use short, cryptic names, and still others will use names with no meaning at all.

When designing a user interface, everyone will have different ideas of what looks good. One programmer may think the user interface is a trivial, unimportant aspect of the project and may not give any thought to how the end user feels about it. Another programmer may feel a bit too creative and produce a user interface with bright colors that are difficult to look at or arrange the controls in a completely nonstandard way that leaves the user confused.

When it comes to logic, everyone thinks differently, so unless you're doing something really simple like adding 2 + 2, chances are, multiple programmers will produce multiple solutions to a given problem. This can lead to many misunderstandings. Show your logic to another programmer, and that programmer may not have a clue why you take the steps that you take.

All of these difficulties make it clear that in any organization with more than one programmer, or even with a single programmer who is not likely to be available for the next 50 years to explain what he or she did, coding standards are essential. When developing a large-scale project, you need to consider the likely possibility that another programmer will need to understand what you're doing, maybe sometime in the future when you're not there to explain it. With a visual design environment like Visual C++, coding standards can impact two areas. First, they will promote the design of professional, user-friendly interfaces. Second, good coding standards will promote better communication among the design team, and it will speed development. The other programmers in your team should be able to look at your code and be able to easily figure out for themselves what it's doing.

Chapter 8: Coding Standards

Creating Coding Standards

When you are creating coding standards, it's important that you don't tie a programmer's hands too much. You want to make sure that code is understandable by all and follows some type of industry standard, but you don't want to stifle the creativity of the individual programmer. Coding standards will impact four general areas:

- Designing the user interface
- Applying language standards and naming variables
- Commenting code
- Making code more readable

We'll spend some time discussing the design of a user interface in the next chapter. In this chapter, we'll be focusing on the other three issues.

Language Standards

In this section we will consider some standards you may wish to adopt for use with the programming language itself. Next to user interface design, this is probably the most tricky aspect of creating coding standards, because a programmer may think that you're stepping on his or her creativity. Let's consider a few examples of the types of language standards you might want to adopt. The following are merely suggestions so that you can think about the types of requirements you can include in your own coding standards. Some of these were mentioned in Chapter 5.

Declare All Local Variables at the Beginning of a Function

While C++ lets you declare a variable wherever and whenever you feel like it, this is not really a good idea. This unfortunate benefit gives a programmer the opportunity to write sloppy code and encourages one to code "on the fly," without carefully planning out an algorithm beforehand. While the language doesn't require it, it's a good idea for your organization to require that programmers declare and initialize all variables at the beginning of a function, before starting the actual coding. Consider the following example:

```
void Stats (double InputData[], double *Average, double *Min , double *Max, double *Sum, int max)
{
   //variable initialization
     *Min = 0;
     *Max = 0;

   int j;

   Sum = 0;

    for ( j =0; j < max; j++)
    {
      *Sum = *Sum + InputData[j];
      if ( InputData[j] < *Min )
        *Min = InputData[j];

      If ( InputData[j] > *Max )
        *Max = InputData[j];
    }

*Average = Sum/max;

}
```

This function will look better and be easier to read if we place all variable declarations at the beginning of the routine and follow this by any required initialization. The routine would then look like this:

```
void Stats (double InputData[], double *Average, double *Min , double *Max, double *Sum, int max)
{
   //local variable declarations
   int j; //loop counter

   //variable initialization
     *Min = 0;
     *Max = 0;
     *Sum = 0;
     for ( j =0; j < max; j++)
     {
      *Sum = *Sum + InputData[j];
      if ( InputData[j] < *Min )
        *Min = InputData[j];

      if ( InputData[j] > *Max )
        *Max = InputData[j];
     }

*Average = Sum/max;

}
```

This example is a small and simple function. However, in the real world, chances are the code you're going to write will be long and complicated. It makes more sense to have all variable declaration and initialization in one central location, rather than having to jump around to find every variable in the procedure.

Avoid the Use of "Negative Logic"

By "negative logic," I mean saying "If NOT Condition Then" rather than "If Condition Then." In many cases, using If NOT is simply not as clear. There are times when you may want to use If NOT, such as testing for an end-of-file condition. In that case you probably would say "If NOT End of File." But in many other situations, using negative logic is not as clear. Consider the following `if-else` statement:

```
if (!(A > B))
  A = A + 1;
else
 B = B + 1;
```

It's much better to write this as:

```
if ( A <= B )
  A = A + 1;
else
 B = B + 1;
```

This makes for code that's easier to understand.

Don't Use Inline `if` Statements

By clearly delimiting `if` statements in an `if-end-if` block, you make your code clear and easy to follow.

Explicitly List Parameters in Function Prototypes

C++ does allow you to write function prototypes that only specify the data types of the arguments, without listing the parameter names. For readability, it is a good idea to explicitly include the parameter names.

For example:

```
bool userstats(double *, double *, int, double *, double *);
```

could be written more clearly as:

```
bool userstats(double users[], double *ave, int count, double *max,
double *min);
```

Although both methods are legal, the second method is clear and readable, while the first method is ambiguous. The second method gives us an idea of what variables are being passed. Always choose the clear and readable way to write software.

When Using Shorthand Notation, Be Sure to Comment

C++ provides many shorthand ways of doing things that not only save typing but also allow the compiler to develop faster code. For example, we can use the ternary operator (?) in place of an if statement. A C++ programmer *should* recognize this, but keep in mind that maybe not everyone will be familiar with it, or maybe they will just be debugging your code late at night and won't recognize it right away. Avoid ambiguity by commenting shorthand code. For example:

```
//if y is less than 10,

//set x to 5, -1 otherwise
x = (y < 10) ? 5 : -1;

...
//set sum = sum + max
sum += max;
```

By adding simple comments that clarify each operation, we can ensure that the intent of the code is clear to everyone.

When Using Overloaded Operators, Be Sure to Comment

Another situation that requires the use of brief explanatory comments is the use of overloaded operators. You will recall in the last chapter we

Chapter 8: Coding Standards

overloaded the % operator to add the masses of two planet objects. The code:

```
Total = earth%venus;
```

is not immediately clear. A comment should be inserted to explain that an overloaded operator is being used and what that operator does. For example, we can modify the above line of code to read:

```
//Find the total mass with
//overloaded % operator. Same as
//Total = earth.mass + venus.mass
Total = earth%venus;
```

When Referencing Member Variables and Functions in a Class, Use the This Pointer

Code that you write in a class member function automatically gets access to all member variables and functions. However, it is a good idea to use the this pointer when referencing class members. Using this ensures that there is no ambiguity in the code. For example, consider the following code in the header file *person.h*:

```
class person
{
public:
    int salary;
    int age;
    char name[25];
    char ssn[11];
    person() {}
    ~7Eperson() {}
    void addsalary(int);
    //more member functions
    ...
};

//later on in the code
...
void person::addsalary(int amount)
{
    salary += amount;
}
```

Now consider that the program uses the following header file, *globals.h*:

```
int salary;
int NumEmployees;
```

The main program looks like this:

```
#include "globals.h"
#include "person.h"

int main()
{
    person theboss;

    ...
}
```

The code will work perfectly fine, but in a large program that could have large classes with hundreds or thousands of lines of code, confusion might result. This can be avoided by using the `this` pointer, which makes it immediately obvious that the variable or function is a member of the class. We can rewrite the `addsalary` function using the `this` pointer:

```
void person::addsalary(int amount)
{
    this->salary += amount;
}
```

Now anyone knows immediately which salary you are referring to, without having to check the class definition.

Avoid Ambiguity in Member Names When Using Multiple Inheritance

If you will create derived classes from more than one base class, make sure that the member variables and functions that are public or protected in each base class have unique names. Avoid the ambiguity and problems that may arise if a member has the same name in both parent classes.

Avoid the Use of Global Variables

Each variable that is declared in your programs should get the most local scope possible. Try to track and exchange information by passing param-

Chapter 8: Coding Standards

eters to functions. Only declare file-wide or program-wide variables when absolutely necessary. This can cut down on confusion and errors.

When Facing a Multiple `If-Else-If`, Try a `Switch Case` Statement Instead

A `switch case` statement is often preferable to using multiple `if-else-if` branches. Not only can a `switch case` statement be more efficient, it simply looks better. For example:

```
//State is an int that holds code representing a state, i.e., Texas,
California, etc.
if ( State = = 0)
  //code for Texas
else if ( State == 1)
  //code for Arizona
else if ( State == 2)
  //code for New York
else if (State == 3)
  //code for New Jersey
else if (State == 4)
  //code for Florida
else
  //code for everyone else
```

This could be handled better with a `switch case` statement:

```
switch (State)
{
  case 0 :
     //code for Texas
     break;
  case 1:
     //code for Arizona
     break;
  case 2:
     //code for New York
     break;
  case 3:
     //code for New Jersey
     break;
  case 4:
     //code for Florida
     break;
  default:
     //code for everyone else
}
```

By following a common set of language standards, you can help ensure that all the code in your organization is uniform and easy to follow.

Naming Conventions

Variable naming is one thing that many programmers tend to overlook. To save typing, they may use cryptic or even meaningless names. When others look at your code, they'll have to ask themselves such questions as "What does H do? What kind of data is x storing?" In today's world of cheap memory and large hard drives, this is not necessary. Names should be clear and descriptive. In addition, every name should convey the following two characteristics of a variable:

- The type of data the variable holds
- The function of that variable

Also, some naming standards will include some means to specify whether the variable is a public or private variable, a local variable, or even what file the variable belongs to. While this information might be useful, it will lead to naming conventions that are too hard for programmers to follow. In the end, the programmer will become frustrated and you'll be back to cryptic, hard-to-understand names.

Hungarian Notation

Hungarian notation is a favorite naming convention among programmers created by Charles Simonyi. Hungarian notation attaches a prefix to variable names to identify the type of variable or object being used. You can use Hungarian notation by following two simple rules:

- A prefix, usually the first three letters of a variable name, is lowercase and is used to indicate the variable's data or object type.
- The rest of the variable name is a descriptive name that tells you what the variable does or stores.

By specifying the data type of the variable, you can help ensure that a programmer won't make avoidable errors such as assigning a value to a variable that's outside its range. Hungarian notation also makes code easier to read. If the name of the variable specifies its data type, you won't have to search for the variable declaration to see what it is.

Let's consider an example of variable names that can be improved by the use of Hungarian notation:

```
char deps;
double avg, wg;
```

Chapter 8: Coding Standards

Using Hungarian notation, we would declare the variables like this:

```
char chDependents;
double dblAverage, dblWage;
```

The second declaration is much clearer. The data type of each variable is specified. There is no question as to what data each variable will track.

In Visual C++, you should use Hungarian notation for the naming of variables and class objects. This will allow you to identify the type of each object, as well as what it does. For example, when declaring objects of the `Planet` class, which we defined in the last chapter, we could use the notation:

```
Planet plJupiter;
```

Table 8-1 provides some suggested abbreviations that can be used with Hungarian notation.

There are many naming conventions. Which one you use and if you use one at all is completely up to you. But no matter what you do, always use clear variable and object names so that the purpose of the variable is clear.

TABLE 8-1

Abbreviations for Hungarian Notation

Data/Object Type	Abbreviation	Example
Char	ch	chNumChildren
int	int	intSalary
long	lng	lngPopulation
Float	f	fVoltage
Double	dbl	dblAverage
Short	s	sNum
String	sz	szName
Pointer	P	pEmployee
Long double	ld	ldSum
Unsigned Short	us	usItems
bool	bln	blnEndofFile

Commenting Standards

Overview—The Importance of Commenting Code

The importance of clear and meaningful comments can't be emphasized enough. One thing we've talked about is the likelihood that another programmer will have to modify or debug code that you write. Even if this isn't the case, it's quite possible you'll have to modify your own code several months after you've written it. If the code you write is even of moderate complexity, without comments, chances are, later on either you or someone else will look at it and not understand what it's doing. Time will have to be wasted in an attempt to find out what the code means. By commenting the code effectively, you can save development and debugging time by making the intent of the code as clear as possible. Commenting extensively has no effect on the size or performance of your executables, so if you think a detailed comment is necessary, don't hesitate to put it in. Comments in Visual C++ are denoted either with double slashes like:

```
//this is a comment
```

or by using a slash and asterisk character. In the latter case, the comment can be continued on multiple lines until another corresponding asterisk and slash is found. For example:

```
/*
   The lines in here
   Are all comments
   And ignored by the compiler

*/
```

Consider the following code:

```
for (int j=0; j < Num; j++)
{
 Mtot = Mtot + M[j];
 Mk = Mk + M[j] * X[j];
}

K = Mk/Mtot;
```

This code could be made a little clearer by inserting a few comments. Before we enter the loop, we add a comment to explain what the loop does and introduce the function of each variable. Inline comments in the loop explain what specific calculation is being performed. With comments, the code looks like the following:

```
// The following loop calculates the center of mass, which is
// given by the formula (Sum of each mass * position)/(total mass of
all objects)
// M is an array of type double which contains the mass of each
object.
// X is an array of type double which contains the position of each
object.
// There are a total of Num Objects. Num can be at most 100.
// K will hold the center of mass for the objects.

for(int j = 0; j < Num; j++)
{
 Mtot = Mtot + M[j]; //Mtot is the total mass
 Mk = Mk + M[j]*X[j]; //Mk is the sum of each mass multiplied by its
position
}

K = Mk/Mtot; //calculate the center of mass
```

You can see from this simple example how adding comments will make the code more readable. The following are tips for effective commenting:

- Insert comments at the beginning of each file used in your project. Include the files' purpose, type, location, the date of creation, and who created it.
- Insert function headers that tell you what the function does, as well as describe the parameter list.
- Use inline comments when an operation is not immediately clear or elementary.
- Use comments when declaring variables, explaining the variables' purpose, data type, and lifetime.
- Use a detailed comment to explain any complicated algorithm. Don't assume that others will understand what you're doing.
- Maintain a revision history for your project. By tracking who did what and when, it will be easy to keep things moving smoothly.

In the following sections, we'll explore some uses of comments in more detail.

Commenting Function Headers

Every function header should have a comment that provides a general description of what that function does. This includes all functions, including standard C++ functions, class member functions, and event functions, which we will take up in the next chapter. The function header comment should include the following information:

- The purpose of the function.

- The author's name and date when the function was first written.

- The names and data types of all variables passed as parameters, along with what each variable will do.

- The revision history for the function. When a modification is made, include your initials, the date, and a brief description of what was changed.

The following example shows how a function header should be commented:

```
void Average (double *MyData, double *Average, short NumItems)
{

/*******************************************************************

    Procedure : Average
    Author : John Jones
    Date Created : 5/5/98
    Description: Computes the average of the elements in an array of
type double.

    Parameter List:
    MyData : Array of Type double, the function finds the average of the
elements in this array. The array is assumed to start at element 1.
    Average : Type double. The average will be returned in this
variable.
    NumItems : The number of elements in the array.
    Revision History:
    6/2/98 : JJ Changed NumItems from type byte to type Integer.
    8/1/98 : KL Changed loop variable to type long.

*******************************************************************/
```

Notice that we've inserted blank lines to separate each section and make the comments more readable. We have also added several asterisk characters. Although they aren't required, they make it very clear where the comment begins and ends. Comments in Visual C++ are usually set off with the color green by the editor.

Inline Comments

Inline comments can be used to explain operations that aren't immediately clear, to explain the purpose of a variable, or to explain any limitations that the code may encounter. You can place inline comments at the end of a line of code by simply adding an apostrophe character. The following example illustrates the use of an inline comment:

```
Vol = 4/3*pi*pow(R,3); //calculate the volume of the sphere
```

Revision History

When you are commenting code, one useful bit of information that should be tracked is the revision history for the project. In the previous section, we discussed keeping a revision history for each procedure. Some programmers may prefer to maintain a single revision history for the entire project. This can be done by including a text file in your project whose only function is to store the revision history of the project. You can require that each programmer enter his or her name or initials, the date, and what the programmer did every time the project is modified. With the revision history centrally located, it's easy to see who did what and when it was done, which can be especially important if bugs start creeping into a large project, or if an unauthorized change was made. You may wish to include a central revision history along with a revision history for each procedure.

Code Construction Standards to Enhance Readability

When you've got multiple programmers working on a project, an important issue that will have to be dealt with is the readability of the code. By *readability*, we're simply talking about neatness, good spacing, and indentation that basically makes the code pleasant to look at. This sounds like a frivolous issue, but it's actually pretty important. You just have to consider the likelihood that either someone else will need to modify code you write or you'll have to fix up your code months later. Efficiency can be maintained at a higher level, not just by including comments and by following a set of adopted language standards, but by making the code easy to read and follow. In the following sections, we'll discuss two areas that impact the readability of code. These are indenting block structures and using white space.

Indenting Block Structures

If you took any freshman computer science courses in college, you were probably annoyed by a professor who deducted 5 points for not indenting code. But the fact is, indented code is easier to read and clearly delimits what code is part of a block and what isn't. You should be able to look at a piece of code and almost see the logic flow. In the following piece of code, it's not immediately clear where one block begins and another ends:

```
if (x > y ){
Max = x;
Temp[j] = Temp[j] + 1;}
else
Max = y;

do{
MyData[j] = MyData[j] + Total;
Total = Total - 1;
}
loop while ( Total > Min)
```

We can make this code more readable by indenting the blocks of code in each control structure by three or four spaces. I also prefer to insert my opening brackets on the line after an `if` statement or `while` statement. I will also add brackets around the `else` clause just to make the code look more symmetrical:

```
if (x > y)
{
  Max = x;
  Temp[j] = Temp[j] + 1;
}
else
{
  Max = y;
}

do
{
  MyData[j] = MyData[j] + Total;
  Total = Total - 1;
}
loop while ( Total > Min)
```

Use of White Space

Spacing can also be helpful in making code more readable. This can include placing spaces between operators and equal signs, as well as including blank lines to separate logical blocks. C++ does allow you to write code like the following:

```
int sum=0;
int total;

total+=1;

sum=total + j;
```

Although many C++ programmers do refuse to add white space, it doesn't take much work, and it makes code easier to read. Don't forget that someday someone else might read your code. The code above would look a little better if it was written like this:

```
int sum = 0;
int total;

total += 1;

sum = total + j;
```

Enforcing Coding Standards

Once you've decided on a set of coding standards for your organization, you've got to enforce them. This can be a difficult road to follow. I've seen plenty of resentment by programmers when coding standards are imposed. The trick is to enforce the standards without putting programmers on the spot or infringing on their creativity. Many organizations use code reviews to enforce standards. We'll discuss how a code review works, and then address the issue of balance in coding standards.

Code Reviews

A code review is a process where a team leader, or perhaps the entire software team, reviews new code to make sure that it fits the standard. One way to run a code review is to have a supervisor check the code when it is close to completion to see how close it is to meeting the standard. Shortcomings can be pointed out to the programmer to give him or her a chance to fix up the code. This may include noting bad variable names, the failure to indent block structures, or the use of global variables. Once the programmer has had a chance to fix the errors, copies of the code can be distributed to the entire team for review. Then in a group meeting, members of the team can bring up issues that they see in the code.

If a code review involves the entire team, it can be hard on the programmer, as well as a waste of time and resources. A better approach is to have a supervisor do the code review one-on-one. This way, the programmer won't be embarrassed in a roomful of people or feel undue pressure over every `if` statement, variable name, or comment. I've seen programmers dreading code reviews; it lowers morale, disrupts productivity, and often leads to an environment in which resources are wasted counting spaces or complaining about variable names. If you stick to one-on-one code reviews with a supervisor or manager who is skilled at constructive criticism, these problems can be avoided.

Coding up to Standard

The best defense is a good offense, so it's a good idea to have your standards clearly laid out beforehand. Standards should not be too "tight"; they should be easy to follow and not place too large a burden on the programmers. Language standards should be kept to a minimum. Variable naming and comments are important standards to enforce, and it's a good idea to make sure programmers indent blocks of code and avoid long lines of code.

Enforcing Standards without Constraining Developers

Earlier in the chapter I stated that you don't want to step on a programmer's creativity. This means that, in general, coding standards should not involve forcing programmers to use a particular method of logic, unless it causes some undue problem such as slowing performance or giving an unexpected answer. Programmers should be free to use their own thought processes to solve problems, as long as they comment thoroughly so that someone else can clearly see how the code works.

When it comes to issues such as indenting blocks of code, don't take that too far. I've actually worked in places where they sit down and count the spaces. This is a complete waste of time and energy, and it leaves everyone on edge, making them focus on minutia rather than on writing

Chapter 8: Coding Standards

good code. When enforcing neatness, just make sure that the code looks neat and is indented—without becoming neurotic about it. In summary, a good rule of thumb is to make the standards simple and easy to follow. The developer should be able to look up all the coding standards on one or two sheets of paper.

# CHAPTER 9

User Interface Design

Introduction

Up to this point, we have been designing Win32 console applications that use a command-line-type interface in an MS-DOS window. As anyone reading this book knows, in today's world of graphical programs, that type of user interface is not of much use. With that in mind, we now turn our attention to the problem of designing a graphical user interface with Visual C++.

Programming in Windows with C++ is a lot more complicated than it is when writing console applications. However, with Visual C++ most of the hard work can be done by the wizards you can use to create new projects. This saves the developer a great deal of time when creating a Windows app. While designing the user interface (UI) in Visual C++ is not as easy or straightforward as it is when using Visual Basic, it is easy enough, once you get used to it, that it won't take up too much of your efforts.

We begin this chapter with a general discussion of the elements that a good user interface should have. While Visual development tools give the programmer a great deal of flexibility in designing the interface, this can sometimes backfire when programmers get too carried away or when they aren't keeping the end user in mind. For this reason, it is always crucial to be thinking of the least-experienced user who will be working with your program when designing the UI.

Next, we will talk about the three general types of executable programs that we can build with Visual C++. These include:

- *Single-document interface (SDI) program*   This is a program that may include a menu system, a toolbar, and a status bar, with a single document work area in the middle of the screen. Notepad is a good example of an SDI application.

- *Multiple-document interface (MDI) program*   The MDI application is one of the most common types of programs in Windows. This type of app has the same overall structure of the SDI app, but it allows the user to open multiple documents at the same time. Each document is contained in a *child window*, while the main window is known as the *parent*. MS Word and Excel are examples of MDI-type applications.

- *Dialog-based interface program*   Designing a dialog-based application in Visual C++ is similar to using forms in Visual Basic.

In this chapter we will mainly focus on how you can use the App Wizard to build an SDI application. Once you understand that, you will

Chapter 9: User Interface Design

be able to easily create the other types. We will close the chapter with a discussion of application prototyping.

The Elements of a Good User Interface

One of the fortunate facts of life when programming with a visual tool like Visual Basic or Visual C++ is that Microsoft has made many of the tools that they use in building GUIs available as controls. Another free benefit we get from programming in Windows is that Windows *defines* many of the user interface elements, such as forms, command buttons, and common dialogs. But this brings us to a mild conflict: Within the constraints set by Windows, a visual programming tool often gives the developer complete freedom to design the user interface. This is both good and bad. It promotes creativity, which helps propel the art of designing user interfaces to new heights. On the other hand, too much freedom can lead to programmers developing UIs that are downright ugly. This might mean a screen that has bright colors or one that is cluttered with too many controls. The choices made may hinge on a variety of factors, including the preferences of the developer as well as constraints set by the data the program is working with. This means that it's important to add a user interface design protocol to your set of coding standards.

When thinking about the elements of a good user interface, we can start by considering what is already popular in the software world. Many large companies have spent a lot of money trying to figure out how to build a user-friendly interface, so it's a good idea to follow their lead. By sticking to a *general* method of user interface design, we can ensure that any computer user with a reasonable level of experience will be able to use your application without being confused by the layout of the forms. If we're talking about building a program for use in the business world or by scientists and engineers, we also want to build a professional-looking application. Let's identify some of the elements of popular software products that we can incorporate into a Visual C++ application:

- *Splash screen* Almost every off-the-shelf or professional application displays a "splash screen" when it launches. The origin of this practice came about as a means to keep the user happy while the program went about time-consuming initialization business. The splash screen displays the program name, the company that developed it, and copyright and version information, as well as some type of graphics. Splash screens are so ubiquitous in Windows that every program is expected to have one. If a program doesn't have one, it feels unprofessional. You don't want your users to think that you're some backyard hacker, so it is a good idea to include a splash screen even if your program doesn't need it.

- *Main window* If your program has more than one form, it should have a centralized main screen where the user can access just about every function that the program has. There are a few options available for the main window, but they will all have several elements in common. As mentioned, we can have an MDI, or multiple-document interface, where the main window functions as a container for document forms that contain the actual data with which the user interacts. We can also have an SDI, or single-document interface. This is similar to the MDI in that the main form is a container for a document window; however, in this case there can only be one document open at a time.

- *Pull-down menu system* Even though Windows has been moving to a more and more graphical approach with push buttons and icons, you should include a pull-down menu system that at least duplicates some of the functions available on toolbars or with buttons. A user of a Windows application expects it.

- *Toolbar* Toolbars have become a popular user interface element, particularly since the release of Windows 95. A toolbar provides a user-friendly one-step access to frequently used functions. These days just about every Windows application has a toolbar on the main window. You shouldn't build a form that has a menu system without a toolbar to accompany it.

- *ToolTips* A ToolTip is a text string that will display on screen when the user rests the mouse pointer over a control. The ToolTip provides a description of what the control does, for example, *Save* if the user clicks the button with a floppy disk on it.

- *Status bar* A status bar gives a main window a complete feel and can be used to display helpful or important information to the user. For example, if you're using a word processor to type a document, the status bar might tell you what page you are on or what line of the page you're currently typing.

In addition to these elements, you should do the following to ensure a professional-looking and user-friendly user interface:

Chapter 9: User Interface Design

- *Maintain good tab order.* Users expect to be able to move around the controls of a form by using the TAB key. Make sure that you keep the tab order moving in a logical fashion, especially if you go back later and add new controls in the middle of the screen.

- *Add a control box and min/max buttons.* It's a good idea to follow Windows convention and put these buttons on every form, providing the user with the ability to minimize, maximize, and close the form. Since these buttons are standard in Windows, users will know what to do with them if they have any computer experience, and placing them on your forms helps give your application a professional appearance.

- *Follow conventions used for command buttons.* Most Windows programs follow the same convention for the arrangement given to common command buttons. These include OK-Cancel, Yes-No-Cancel, Save-Cancel, and Abort-Retry-Ignore. The buttons should be shown on the screen in the same left-to-right order that they are listed here. Users get accustomed to using a specific order and might move around the screen clicking buttons quickly. For example, if the buttons are out of the expected order, the user may end up clicking the *No* button when they meant to click the *Yes* button. In addition, the way that command buttons are arranged on your forms will give the user an impression about the level of professionalism the application has. The arrangement of standard command buttons is no place to be creative, so follow the conventions that Microsoft uses.

- *Follow clear screen layout.* If a screen gets too crowded, that means it's a bad user interface design. This is a pressing problem that is seen in customized database apps for the business world. It's important to learn what a good data input screen should look like. To find out, look at the top sellers in areas such as personal finance or accounting software.

- *When displaying data, display at most two tables on a single form.* It may be tempting to display a series of related data tables on the same screen. However, this can result in too much clutter. If you are working with two tables in a master-dependent relationship, this is acceptable. However, if there are more than two tables, use command buttons to allow the user to view the other tables, either on a separate screen or on an area of the screen that is normally hidden. The goal is to keep forms as clutter-free as possible. People digest information better when it is given to them in smaller bits rather than in large chunks.

A Main Window

To illustrate these principles, let's consider an application written to help run a carpet-cleaning business. The application tracks customers, gives job estimates, and tracks equipment. The main window of the application is a form that provides a menu system and buttons that can be used to access the rest of the application (see Figure 9-1). There are a few things to notice about the layout of the screen:

- *There is a standard menu system.* This window has a standard Windows pull-down menu system that is found in almost any application.

- *There is a toolbar.* A toolbar with user-friendly buttons is found just below the menu system. The buttons on the toolbar are large so that they are easy to spot (obviously, the size that can be given to each button will depend on how much functionality you need to put on the toolbar. Try to keep it at a minimum so the program is clear and straightforward. My experience has been that users prefer the larger buttons by a substantial margin.) The function of each button is made clear by a one-word description of what part of the program the button will

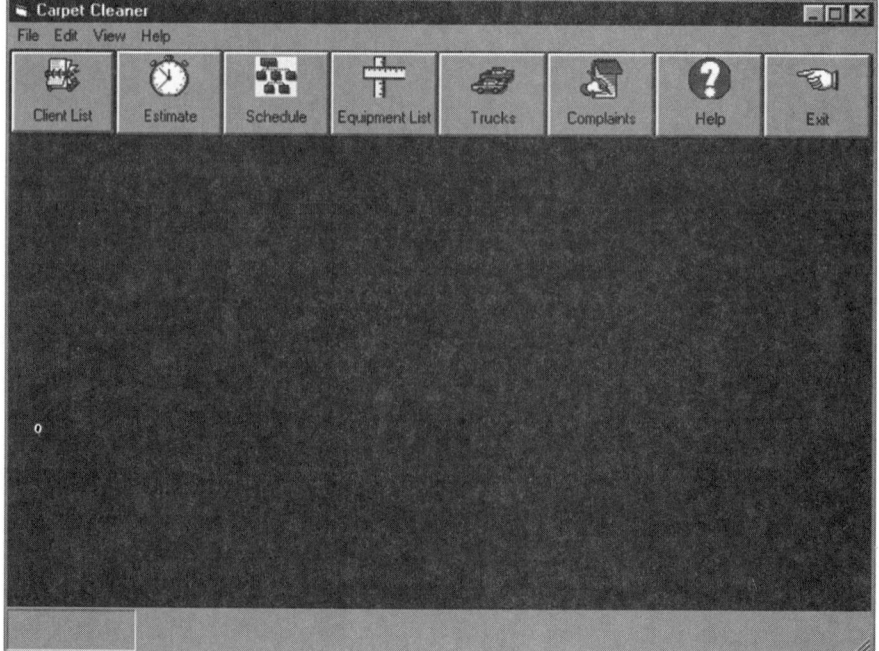

Figure 9-1
A sample main window.

Chapter 9: User Interface Design

open. The buttons are given a pleasant appearance with colorful, but not overwhelming, icons.
- *The middle of the window is blank.* For a database application like this one, the middle of the main window will function as a work area of sorts, where the other forms that contain the data will be displayed. In many applications (SDI or MDI) the work area of the main window will contain documents.
- *There is a status bar.* A status bar is found at the bottom of the screen. We can use the status bar to display a message to the user.
- *Help is easily accessed.* The user can clearly spot a Help button on the main toolbar, as well as the Help pull-down menu.

As mentioned earlier, the main window acts as a gateway to the rest of the application. This can be true in a wide variety of contexts, including both scientific/engineering or database applications. We will use the example of a database application here to see how that type of structure might be used.

In a database application, the user will typically be tracking several tables of related data. For example, in our carpet cleaning application this might include:

- Employees
- Customers
- Scheduled jobs
- Inventory

We can break down the application by having a different toolbar item or menu to represent each of these separate data areas. Other menu items might let users build queries or perform other operations that can relate data from different tables. But the main concern here is to see how we might organize the toolbar to build a user-friendly application. If they want to add a new customer to the database, for example, they should be able to simply click a button on the toolbar to open the Customers window. Now let's examine how the data might be displayed once they do click that Customers toolbar button.

Displaying Data in Grid Format

When we are talking about database applications, the way in which the data is displayed is of central concern. There are many ways to arrange data, and I will suggest just one way. This method, however, is a good user-friendly method. The goal of our user interface design is to keep users from being overwhelmed by the data, while at the same time trying to show them as much data as possible and giving them a means to move quickly through it. One way you meet these goals is to break the data down into two windows. The first window, which is accessible directly from a button on the main screen, displays the data in a grid-style format. The grid will display either the results of a query or the contents of an entire table; this choice will depend on the particular program at hand. Figure 9-2 is an example of what a well-designed grid window should look like. This window has several key elements:

- The caption of the window displays either the name of the table that is open or a descriptive name reflecting the results of a query.
- A grid displaying the data is centered in the middle of the window. The grid is for viewing purposes only, and the user can select a row or record by clicking on the grid with the mouse.
- A series of command buttons is placed in the lower portion of the window, providing the user with commands they can execute to manipulate the data. For our example, we have a New button, which the user can click to add a new record. The Edit button lets the user edit the currently selected record. Other buttons that may be included are Delete, Query, and Print. The specific nature of most of the buttons will be determined by each specific application. The form should have a Close button that the user can click to return to the main screen.

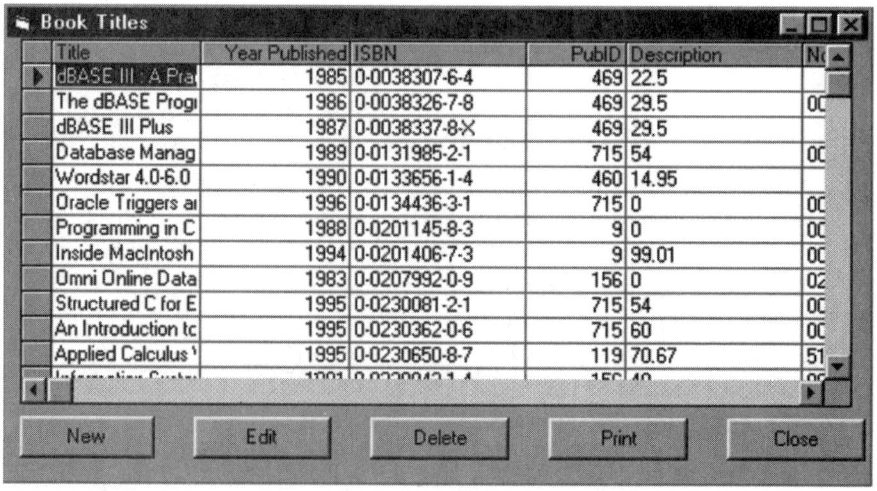

Figure 9-2
Displaying data in a grid format.

Chapter 9: User Interface Design

- The New and Edit buttons will open another window, which displays a single record. This secondary window can be used to add new records or edit the contents of an existing record.

A window that displays data in a grid format should also have a means for the user to search the database. There are many extended data controls available on the market that have built-in searching capabilities. It is a good idea to use these in your projects. Otherwise, you should add your own Find or Search button that will let the user search the data grid based on the values of one or more fields. The Find button can be implemented by using the Find methods of a recordset object.

Displaying Individual Records

The grid window is a type of gateway. It lets the user browse through the data and perform actions on that data as required. However, many of the actions are not actually performed by this window but are instead done with a second window which acts on individual records. One of those actions is to add new records to the table or to edit an existing record. An example of a window used to display a single record is shown in Figure 9-3. A window of this type has the following elements or characteristics:

- The caption contains the table name. You can also include an identifying characteristic of the individual record here, such as an ID number or name.
- The fields of the record are displayed neatly in textboxes, which the user can edit.
- Each textbox is clearly labeled.
- An OK button lets the user save any changes.

Figure 9-3
Displaying an individual record.

- A Cancel button lets the user back out or abandon the changes.
- A Help button lets the user access help from this dialog box.
- The form uses good tab order. When the form loads, the cursor is present in the Author ID text box. When the user presses the TAB key, the cursor will move in this order: Author Name, Year Born, OK, Cancel, and Help.

Notice what the window does not show or allow:

- A data control, which acts as the data source and allows the user to move through the records, is not visible.
- This form can only be used to display one record: the grid form that we discussed in the previous section to navigate the records of the database. Users select the records that they are interested in viewing on the grid form and click the edit form. This form then opens, displaying that particular record. If users click *New* from the grid form, the data control on this form will add a new record, which will blank out all of the data-bound controls so the user can enter new data.

We will delay the specifics of designing a database application until Chapter 11. The point here was to provide you with a set of general principles that you can use when displaying data of any kind to the user. We will now turn to the specifics of designing applications with Visual C++.

Creating a User Interface with Visual C++

Earlier I mentioned that when creating a Windows application with Visual C++, there are three general categories of applications. These were as follows:

- Single-document, or SDI, applications
- Multiple-document, or MDI, applications
- Dialog-based applications

In the next section, we will explore the creation of an SDI application in detail. Once you understand the SDI application, creating the other types will follow easily. We will be developing dialog-based applications in future chapters.

Chapter 9: User Interface Design

Single-Document Interface (SDI) Applications

A single-document interface application lets the user work with only one document at a time. The document is displayed in the middle area of a window that may have a menu system, toolbar, and status bar. A good example of a single-document application is WordPad, shown in Figure 9-4. Unlike Microsoft Word, WordPad does not allow the user to open multiple word-processing documents. However, WordPad does have a fully developed user interface, including pull-down menus and a toolbar.

The easiest way to get started with a Windows application in Visual C++ is to open the MFC App Wizard. This is done from the Projects tab of the New dialog box (see Figure 9-5). The first thing we need to do when using the wizard is to tell Visual C++ the name of our new project. Use the following steps:

- Select the MFC App Wizard (EXE) from the Projects list on the left-hand side of the screen.

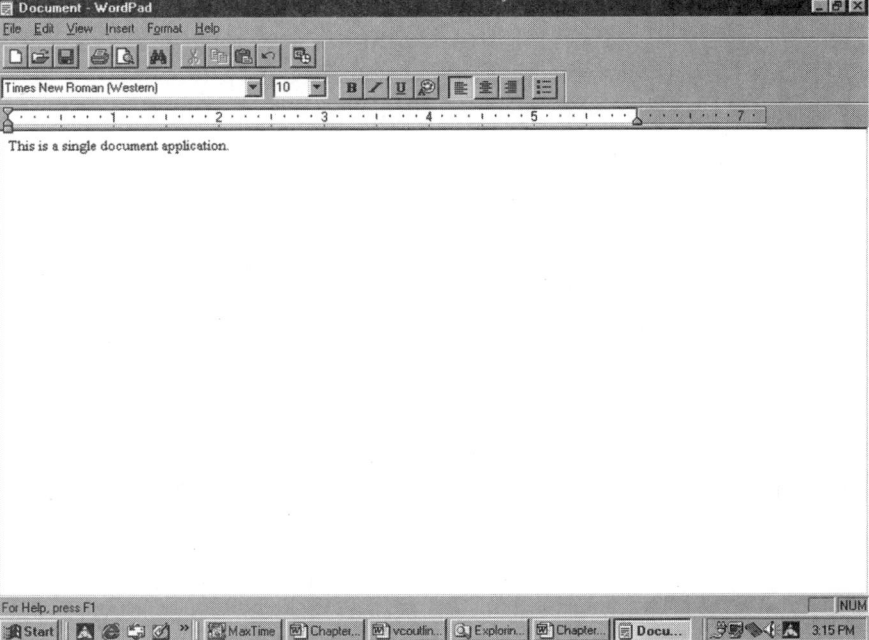

Figure 9-4
A single-document application.

Figure 9-5
Starting the MFC App Wizard.

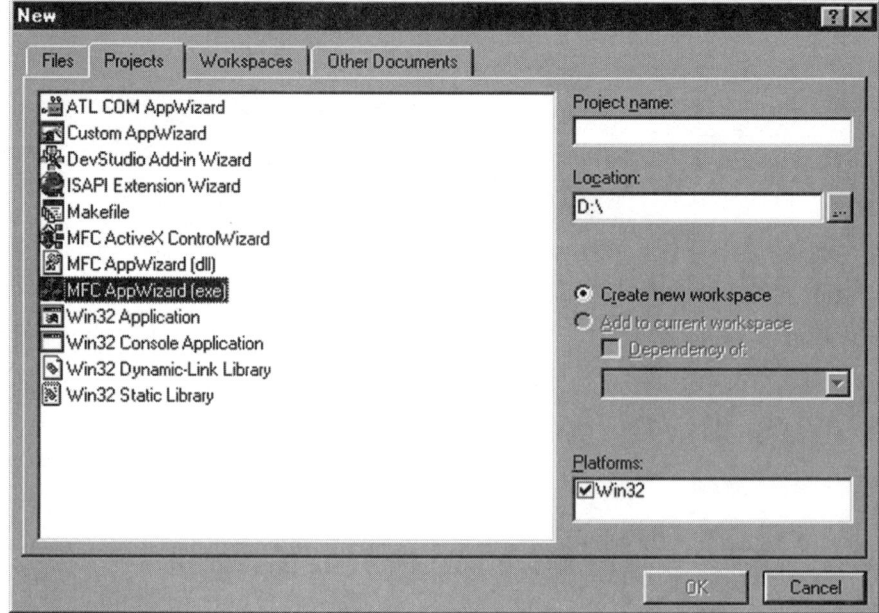

- Type the name you want for the application in the Project Name input box. We will call our first application SingleDoc.
- In the Location input box, specify the folder where you want the source code for the project to be stored.
- Click the *OK* button.

The next step in the process is to select the type of application you want to create. This is where you select between SDI, MDI, or dialog-based (see Figure 9-6). For this example, select *Single Document*. You can also specify which language you want your resources in by clicking on the drop-down list near the middle of the dialog. Click *Next* to continue.

The next screen of the wizard allows you to select a database, if any, to use with your application. We will not be using databases just yet, so select *None* and click *Next* to continue.

On the next screen, you can select the type of OLE or ActiveX support you will use with your application. If you decide to use OLE, there are four basic choices:

- *Container* Selecting Container allows your application to provide the most basic level of OLE support. A container can act as a client for OLE objects, and it can also store linked and embedded objects.

Chapter 9: User Interface Design

Figure 9-6
Selecting the type of application with the App Wizard.

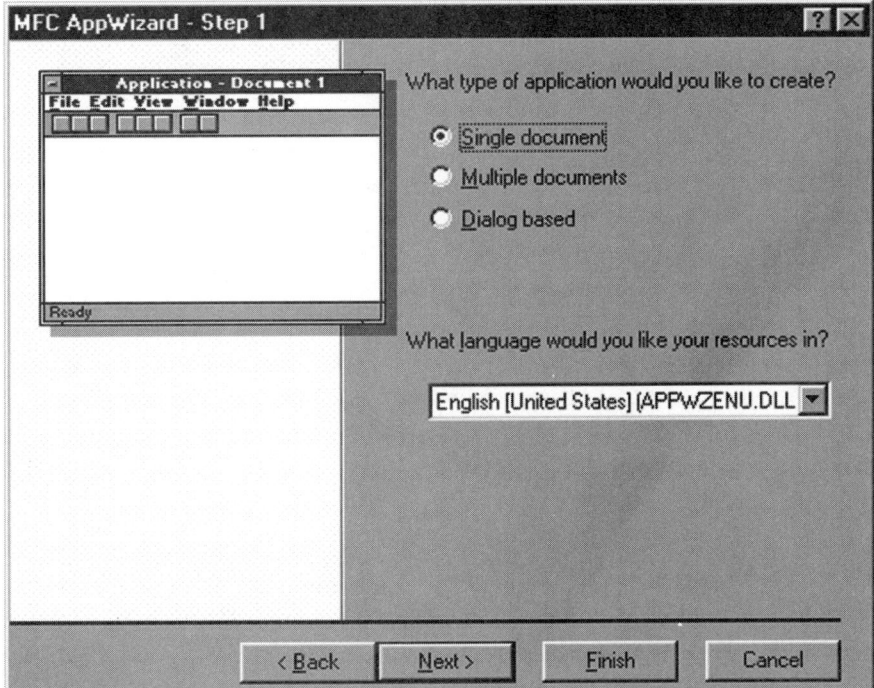

- *Mini-server* A mini-server can create and work with embedded documents.
- *Full Server* If you select Full Server, your application can act as a full OLE server, but it cannot act as a container. In other words, your application can create objects that other applications can use, but your application will not be able to use OLE objects created by other programs.
- *Both Container and Server* Selecting this option will give your application complete OLE support. It will be able to act as a container, holding objects from other applications, and it will also be able to act as a server. If you select this option, you can also make your application an ActiveX document server or an ActiveX document container. If you select the ActiveX Document Container box, your application will be able to host documents from programs like Microsoft Word or Excel. If you select ActiveX Document Server, your application will be able to create and support its own ActiveX documents.

Keep in mind that the type of OLE support you choose can influence the size and performance of your program. Only use the minimal OLE support necessary to keep your applications as efficient as possible. We won't be discussing the use of OLE until Chapter 14, so for now select *None*.

At the bottom of the window you will notice that there are two checkboxes under the heading What Other Support Would You Like to Include? These are as follows:

- *Automation* If you select this option, your application will be able to work with objects that were created by other applications.

- *ActiveX Controls* An ActiveX control is an encapsulated component or object that you can plug into your program to add some type of user interface capability. An ActiveX control is stored in a file with an *.ocx* file extension. Typical examples of ActiveX controls include calendar controls, database controls, list boxes, and combo boxes. There are a wide variety of ActiveX controls available, many from third-party companies.

You will find ActiveX controls valuable in just about any type of application. So we will allow our applications to have ActiveX controls by checking this box. We will ignore automation for the time being.

The next step in the wizard is selecting which types of user interface elements to include in the application (see Figure 9-7). Here you can use the checkboxes to select what user interface elements to include in your application. This includes a docking toolbar, printing and print preview, context-sensitive help, and 3D controls. You can also decide if you want Internet Explorer-style toolbars or normal toolbars. If you decide to use an Internet Explorer-type toolbar, you will be able to add Windows controls to the toolbar, rather than just having it correspond to items in the pull-down menu.

If you click the *Advanced* button, you will see a dialog box open like the one shown in Figure 9-8. This window allows you to specify several parameters about the documents used in your application, such as the file extension, the file filter name, and the caption displayed in the main window (called the *main frame*). We will use *.dat* for our file extension. If you click on the *Window Styles* tab, you can set options for the main window, such as whether to include a minimize or maximize box. If this were an MDI application, you would be able to set these options for the child windows as well.

The next screen will ask you if you want the wizard to generate source code comments. It is a good idea to accept the default setting Yes, Please.

Chapter 9: User Interface Design

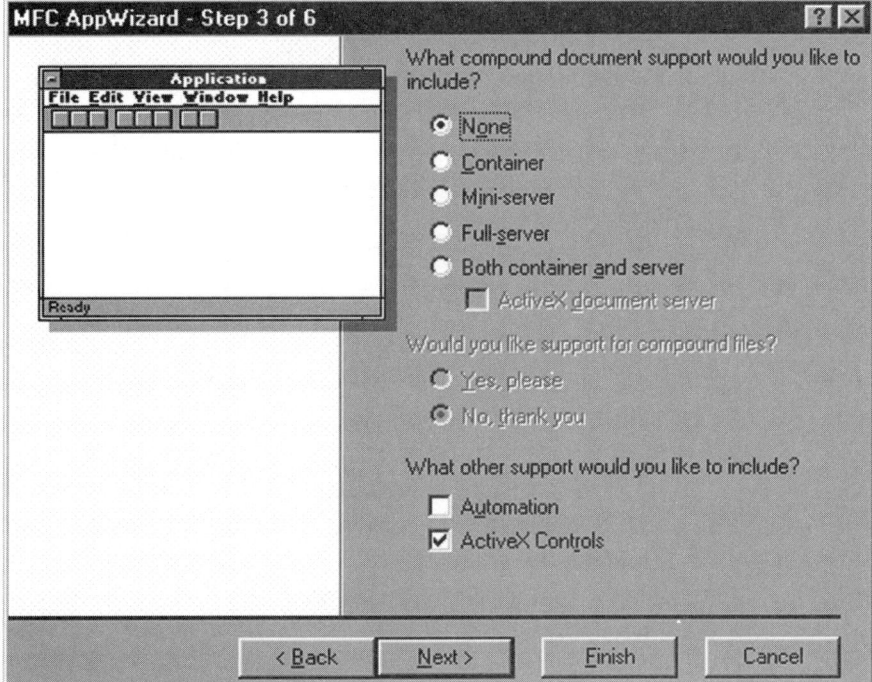

Figure 9-7
Selecting the type of ActiveX support for your application.

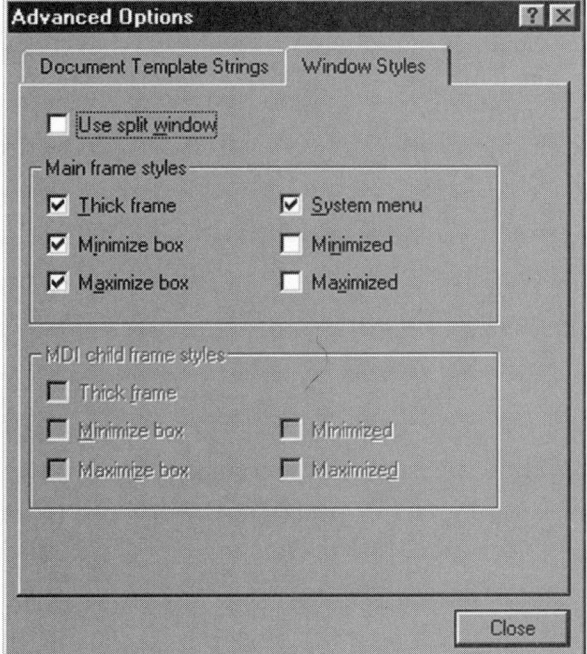

Figure 9-8
Advanced Options.

Part 2: Designing Visual C++ Software

If you do, the wizard will add some comments to the code it will generate that will be behind all of the toolbars and menus you have selected. It will also ask you if you want to use the MFC as a shared DLL or as a statically linked library. It is a good idea to use it as a shared DLL, since this will cut down on your executable size. However, you will need to ship the DLL file with your applications. This DLL is found in the file *MFCXX.DLL* where *XX* is the file version.

The final screen, shown in Figure 9-9, will show you a list of classes that it will create for your application. If you click on each class in the list, you will see the header file (*.h*) and implementation file (*.cpp*) for each class. You will also see the base class used. We can ignore the base class for most of the classes generated; however, we want to pay special attention to the base class used for the document view class. In our case, we named our project *SingleDoc*, so the class is named `CSingleDocView`. The default base class is `CView`, which isn't much help if you want your program to have much functionality, unless you want to create an entirely new type of document (which could mean some hefty coding). If you click open the *Base Class* drop-down list, you will see the following choices:

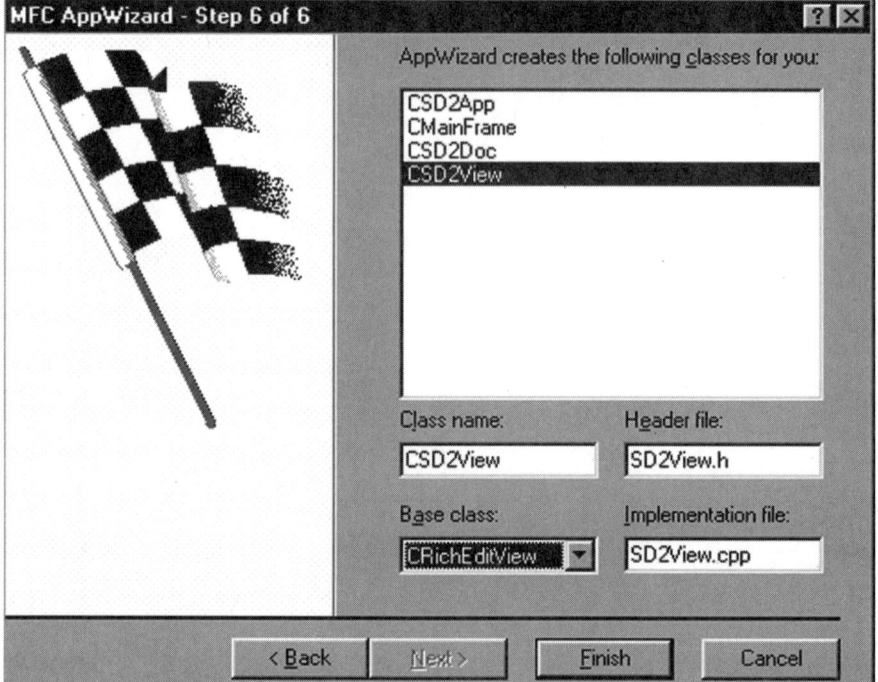

Figure 9-9
Selecting the Base class.

Chapter 9: User Interface Design

- `CFormView` Creates a scrollable dialog-type view and dialog box controls. With an SDI project, this basically creates a single form that you can enhance with ActiveX controls.
- `CHtmlView` Creates a view that will function as an HTML document.
- `CEditView` Creates a plaintext editor, like Notepad.
- `CListView` Creates a List View-type view.
- `CRichEditView` Creates a more sophisticated text editor.
- `CScrollView` This is a derivative of the plain `CView` class, which has scrolling capabilities.
- `CTreeView` Creates an application that is based on a `TreeView` control. This is like the Windows Explorer interface.

For this example, we will select `CRichEditView`, in which case the wizard will basically create a simple word-processing application for us. Here you see the power of inheritance and reuse in action; Visual C++ provides the framework of your application with classes you can use in your own applications.

When you click the `Finish` button, the wizard will open a summary screen for your new project. When you click *OK*, the project will be created. When it is finished, you can run the program right away, and you'll find that it already has many built-in functions. The program will already open and save files or open a Print Preview window without your adding a single line of code. Since you used the `CRichEdit` class as the base class, the program already has many word-processing capabilities, such as the ability to open a rich text file (*.rtf*) and to accept images (see Figure 9-10). This is the beauty of RAD, the basic structure of the software is prebuilt for you, allowing you to concentrate on *your own* software tasks without having to worry about Windows or the user interface.

Messages and the Class Wizard

Now that we have the basic framework in place for a Windows application, we will turn our attention to putting our own code behind it. In this section, we will add a menu item to allow the user to manipulate the font used in a document. Before we do that, however, let's take a look at the code that is already in this program. How does this program know how to display an About box or save a file? To find the answer, we need to open the *Class Wizard* (see Figure 9-11). The Class Wizard can be used to

Figure 9-10
Running our rich text document application.

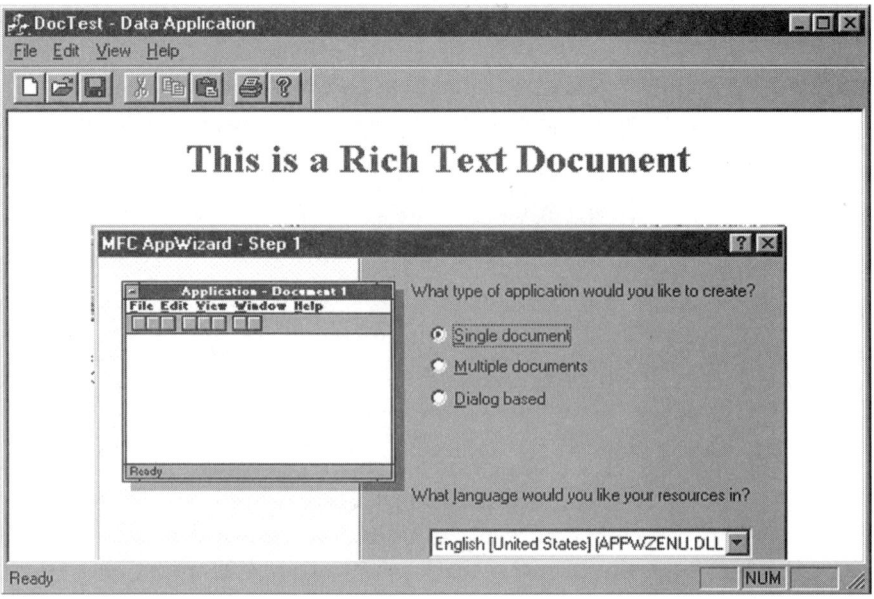

Figure 9-11
MFC Class Wizard.

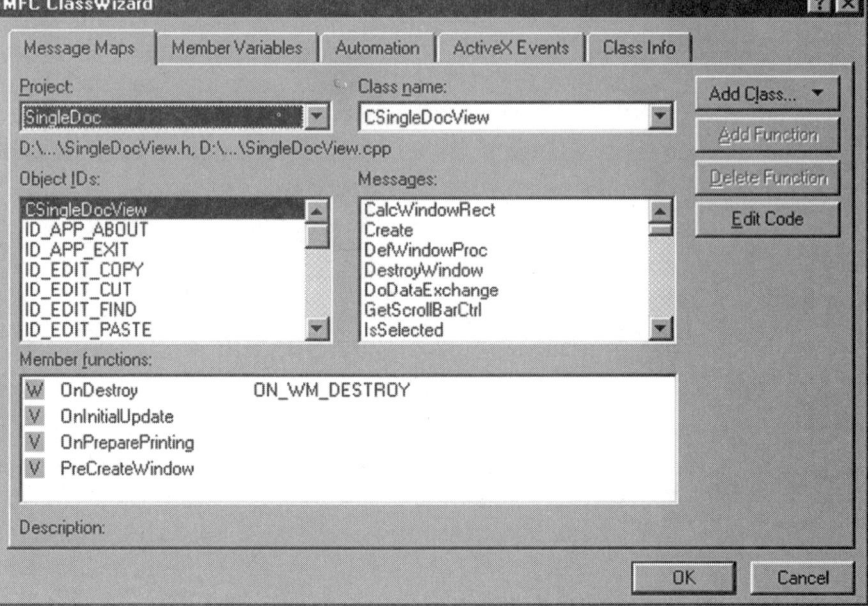

Chapter 9: User Interface Design

view, edit, or add new code to the project. Keep in mind that the Class Wizard can be used with any type of project, not just SDI applications.

On the first tab, Message Maps, you will see a drop-down list in the upper right-hand corner of the screen that you can use to select the class to view. When you select a class, such as CMainFrame, you will see the object IDs for that class displayed in the list box on the middle left portion of the screen. An object ID is exactly what it sounds like; it identifies the objects in your program, such as a menu command. You can select an object ID and view the messages for that object in the Messages list box. This is similar to the events that a Visual Basic program puts behind each object.

A *message* is a notification from Windows that an event important to that object has occurred. This might be a mouse click, or the object might have to redraw itself when it is redisplayed on the screen, which it can do through the Paint event. Messages that already have code behind them are listed in boldface text. Like an event in Visual Basic, a message might be generated by user action, or it might be generated by the operating system.

The interesting thing is that when you create a Visual C++ project with the MFC App Wizard, it does a lot of work for you and generates a great deal of code. If you are new to Windows programming with C++, this might seem a bit intimidating. However, my advice to newcomers is to ignore all of that mess. We won't be worrying about the details involved in the code the wizard generates or how Windows works here. What we are concerned with in this book is *rapid* application development, so the focus will be on getting the software to do what we want, rather than dealing with the intricacies of Windows.

When you run the SDI application created with the App Wizard, you will find that it automatically displays an About box when you click *Help* then *Help...About* pull-down menu. To see how this works, we can look at the message for this menu item. To open the code, follow these steps. This example assumes that you have named your project *SingleDoc*:

1. Click open the *Class Name* drop-down list and select *CSingleDocApp*.
2. Select *ID_APP_ABOUT* from the Object IDs list.
3. Select *Command* from the Messages list. You will notice that the member functions for this message are displayed in the list at the bottom of the window.
4. Select the *OnAppAbout* member function if it is not selected already.

5. Click the *Edit Code* button on the right.

A code window will open on your screen that looks like the following:

```
// App command to run the dialog
void CSingleDocApp::OnAppAbout()
{
    CAboutDlg aboutDlg;
    aboutDlg.DoModal();
}
```

This code displays the About dialog box for our program. Visual C++ works a little differently than Visual Basic in this regard. In Visual Basic, you can design forms and then run a program and just show the form with a line such as:

```
frmAbout.show
```

However, Visual C++ doesn't quite work that way. You cannot automatically work with the dialog boxes you designed in Visual C++ in the same way you can in Visual Basic. To work with a dialog box in Visual C++, you must declare an instance of that dialog box. The dialog box is represented by a class, which in this case is `CAboutDlg`. The first line of code in this event declares an object, `aboutdlg`, of type `CAboutDlg`. The second line of code uses a method of the class, `DoModal`, to display the dialog box.

You will also notice the following code just before the `OnAbout` member function:

```
BEGIN_MESSAGE_MAP(CAboutDlg, CDialog)
    //{{AFX_MSG_MAP(CAboutDlg)
        // No message handlers
    //}}AFX_MSG_MAP
END_MESSAGE_MAP()
```

This is a *message map*. The message map is used to link the message of an object ID, such as `ID_APP_ABOUT` to a member function, which in this case is the `OnAppAbout` function. In the following message map you can see how the message map connects several IDs to member functions:

```
BEGIN_MESSAGE_MAP(CSingleDocView, CRichEditView)
    //{{AFX_MSG_MAP(CSingleDocView)
        // NOTE - the ClassWizard will add and remove mapping macros here.
        //    DO NOT EDIT what you see in these blocks of generated code!
```

Chapter 9: User Interface Design

```
    ON_WM_DESTROY()
    //}}AFX_MSG_MAP
    // Standard printing commands
    ON_COMMAND(ID_FILE_PRINT, CRichEditView::OnFilePrint)
    ON_COMMAND(ID_FILE_PRINT_DIRECT,
CRichEditView::OnFilePrint)
    ON_COMMAND(ID_FILE_PRINT_PREVIEW,
CRichEditView::OnFilePrintPreview)
END_MESSAGE_MAP()
```

Message maps are generated automatically by C++, so we won't worry about them here.

This is how the user interface side of Visual C++ works. First, we find the class that we are interested in working with. Then we select the object we need and select the appropriate message. Next, we choose the member function where we will edit or place code.

Adding New Code and a Menu Item

Now that we have seen how to open a member function, along with the code the wizard generated to show a dialog box, let's add some code of our own. Our first stab at Windows programming will be very simple. We will add a menu item that displays a "Hello World" message to the user.

To add a new menu item, we need to go to Resource View. Resource View lets you design and manipulate the visual aspects of your program, such as dialog boxes, icons, and menu items. In Resource View you will see a folder corresponding to each of these types. You can view the individual items of each type, such as a dialog box, by opening the appropriate folder and selecting the item you want. In Figure 9-12, we have opened the Menu folder and selected the IDR_Mainframe menu item, which shows us the menus that are displayed on the main form. Now let's see how to add a new menu item.

In Resource View you can click and view the menu items for the program almost like you could when running the program. For example, if you click open the File menu, the menu opens and displays the menu items that belong under that header. We will add our "Hello World" item to the Help menu. You can add a new menu item with the following steps:

1. Click the *Help* pull-down menu. You will notice a blank slot at the bottom of the menu. We will place the new menu here.
2. Click once on the blank slot to select it.

Figure 9-12
Editing menus.

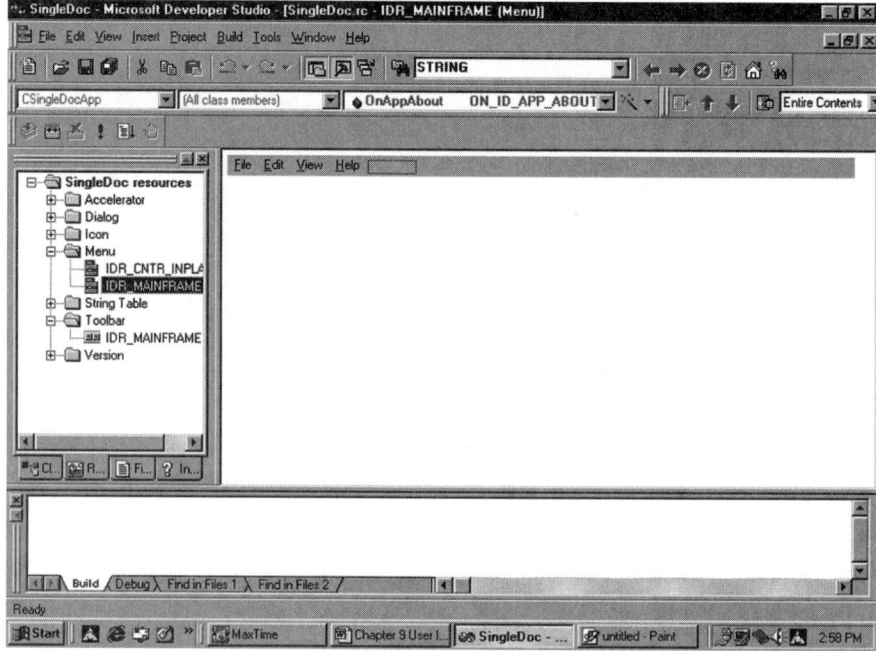

3. Right-click and select *Properties* (see Figure 9-13). The Properties dialog for this menu item will open (see Figure 9-14).

Here we can set the properties of the menu. There are only two properties that we are interested in right now, the ID and Caption properties. Fill in the following:

- Set the caption property to *Hello World*.
- The ID property will be set automatically by Visual C++. Just close the Properties window. If you reopen it, you will see the text ID_HELP_HELLOWORLD has been inserted. We can accept this, or you can add your own ID. For now, we will accept the default.

To put code behind the menu item, we need to reopen the Class Wizard. Use these steps:

1. Select the `CSingleDocApp` class.
2. Choose *ID_HELP_HELLOWORLD* from the Object IDs list.
3. Select the *COMMAND* message.
4. Click the *Add Function* command button on the right side of the screen. When programming with Visual C++, we need to explicitly add each member function we are going to work with.

Chapter 9: User Interface Design

Figure 9-13
Setting the properties for a menu.

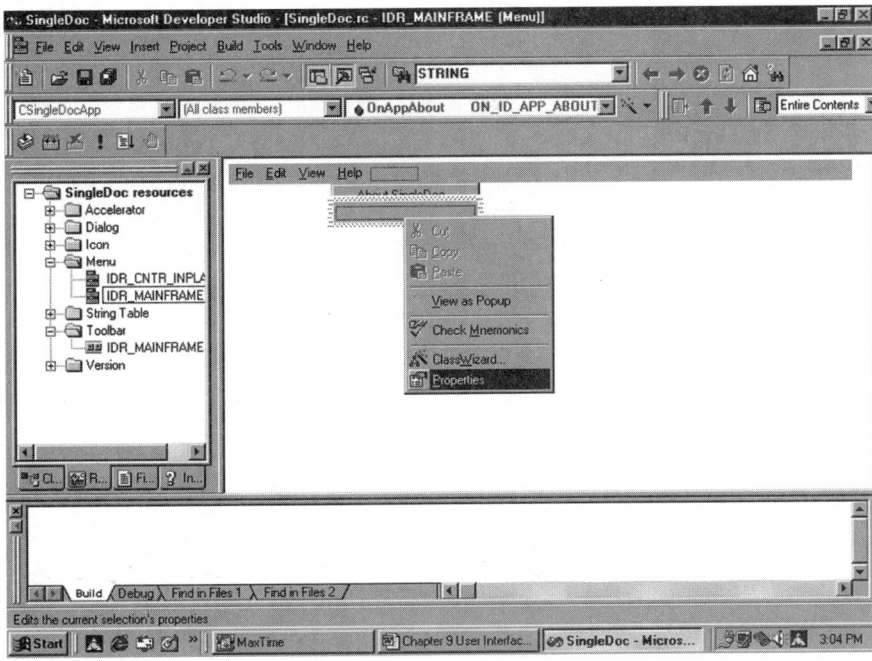

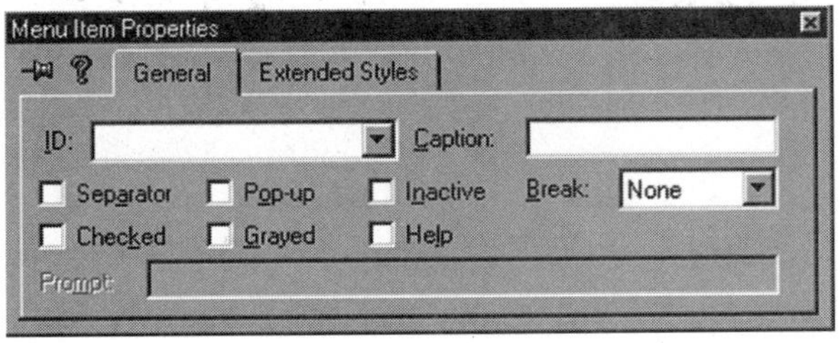

Figure 9-14
The Menu Properties dialog.

5. Visual C++ will prompt you for a name for the member function. In this case, it will say *OnHelpHelloWorld*. You can accept this by clicking OK, or you can add your own name in first and then click *OK*.

You will then see the member function just created in the member function list at the bottom of the screen. Now we can edit the code in that function in the same way that we did for the `OnAppAbout` function. Select that function from the list, and click *Edit Code*. The Class Wizard will close and a code window will open, showing a blank function where we can enter code:

```
void CSingleDocApp::OnHelpHelloworld()
{
    // TODO: Add your command handler code here

}
```

We will use a *message box* to display the "Hello World" message to the user. A message box is a common object in Windows; they are used by many programs to display important messages. For example, a message box might be used to inform the user that an error has occurred or that a file was saved. A message box may have OK and Cancel buttons, or perhaps the ubiquitous Yes/No/Cancel arrangement. We can display a message box by calling the `MessageBox()` function. The syntax of the `MessageBox` function is as follows:

```
MessageBox(HWND hWnd, LPCSTR message, LPCSTR Caption, Unsigned
Int style);
```

where `hWnd` is the handle of the window that owns the message box, `message` is the text string that you want to display to the user, `Caption` is the caption of the message box window, and `style` is an integer representing the type of message box displayed.

You can ignore the `hWnd` argument by passing the constant NULL. There are several options for style, which include simply displaying an OK button, OK and Cancel buttons, or images like an exclamation point or stop sign icon. Each type is represented by a different constant. You can add the constants together to display combinations. For example, the constant for Yes/No/Cancel is `MB_YESNOCANCEL`, and the constant for showing a stop sign is `MB_ICONSTOP`. To display a message box with both elements, we use:

```
MB_YESNOCANCEL + MB_ICONSTOP
```

For our program, we will display an OK button with an exclamation icon. The code looks like this:

```
void CSingleDocApp::OnHelpHelloworld()
{
    // Say Hello to the User
    MessageBox(NULL,"Hello World", "Hello", MB_OK +
MB_ICONEXCLAMATION);

}
```

When users run the program and click the *Hello World* menu item, they will see a message box like the one displayed in Figure 9-15. Now

Chapter 9: User Interface Design

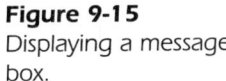
Figure 9-15
Displaying a message box.

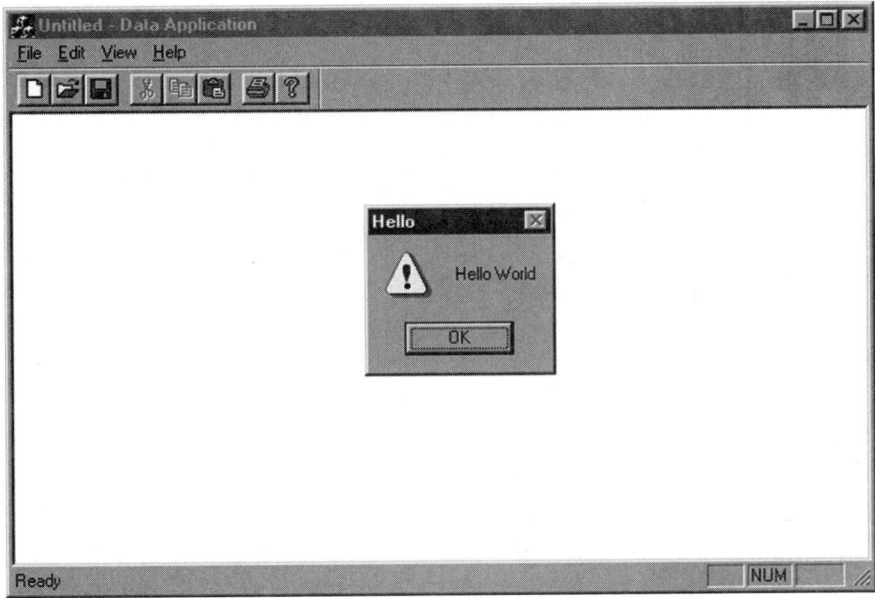

that we know how to do some simple program actions like displaying a message, let's go about designing our own dialog box that will allow the user to select some text and set the font.

Displaying a Dialog Box to Set the Font

One of the benefits of developing an application with the MFC App Wizard is that we get a few things for free. This includes standard dialogs and behavior like printing and print preview. While the wizard already included these two items for us, we will see how we can add other common dialogs to our project by simply adding a menu item. We will include a Font dialog box to allow the user to set the font of the text displayed in the document window.

To provide a Font dialog box for the user, we will add a menu item to the main window. To do this, return to the IDR_MAINFRAME menu item in the Resources list. When the Menu editor comes up, select the rightmost menu item, which is blank. Now set the Caption property to *Format*. For the first menu item, set the Caption property to *Font*. You can tell Visual C++ to use this menu item to display a font dialog by choosing one of the existing items from the ID drop-down list. For a font dialog, select *ID_FORMAT_FONT*. You can specify many types of standard behavior for menu items this way. To see how the wizard has used this to construct the other menu items, open them and check the properties of each one. You will see standard menu items with IDs such as ID_FILE_PRINT and ID_FILE_SAVE. This is another example of the ability to reuse objects in a visual design environment.

A Format menu is usually to the left of the Help menu, so we need to reposition it. To do this, drag the Format menu to the left by clicking on it and holding down the left mouse button. Now insert it just before the Help menu. The menu should look like that shown in Figure 9-16. No code is required; the menu item will automatically display the Font dialog box.

Creating a Dialog Box

Chances are the applications you build with Visual C++ will have one or more dialog boxes. If you've used Windows, you are already familiar with

Figure 9-16
Adding a menu.

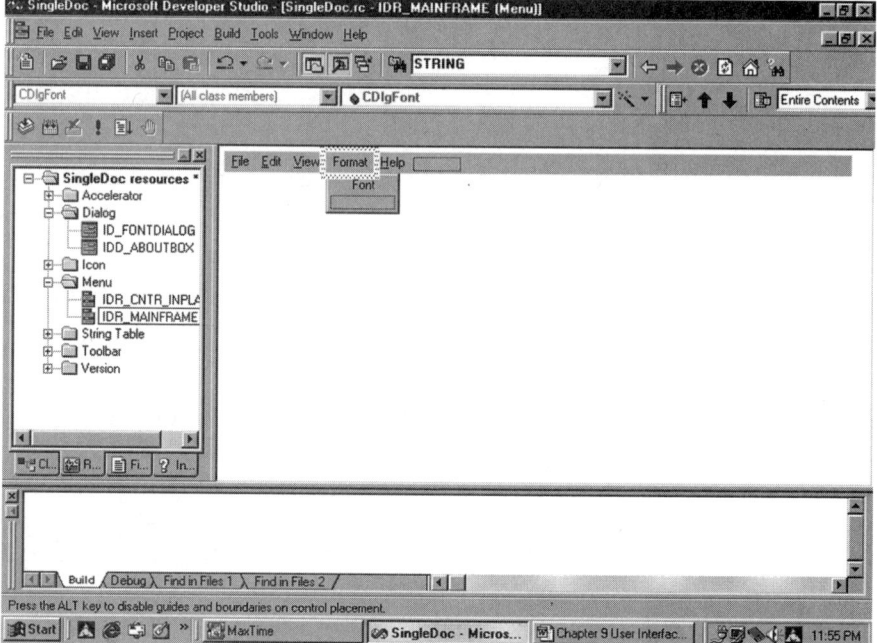

Chapter 9: User Interface Design

dialog boxes. You will see dialog boxes when you print a document, set the font, or set the options for a program like Microsoft Word. There are many dialog boxes in Developer Studio. If you click the Project | Settings menu or the Tools | Options menu, you are opening dialog boxes. Basically, a dialog box is a small window that is used to get input from the user.

Let's see how to add a new dialog box to the application. Our dialog box won't do anything particularly useful, but we will use this example to illustrate how we can get information from the user and display information on the screen. You will recall that earlier I said that a dialog box is one of the resources in the project. So to add a new dialog box, we need to add a new resource. You can do this with the following steps:

1. Click the *Insert* pull-down menu.
2. Select *Resource*. The Insert Resource dialog box will open (see Figure 9-17).
3. Choose *Dialog*.
4. Select *New*.

Figure 9-17
Editing a dialog box.

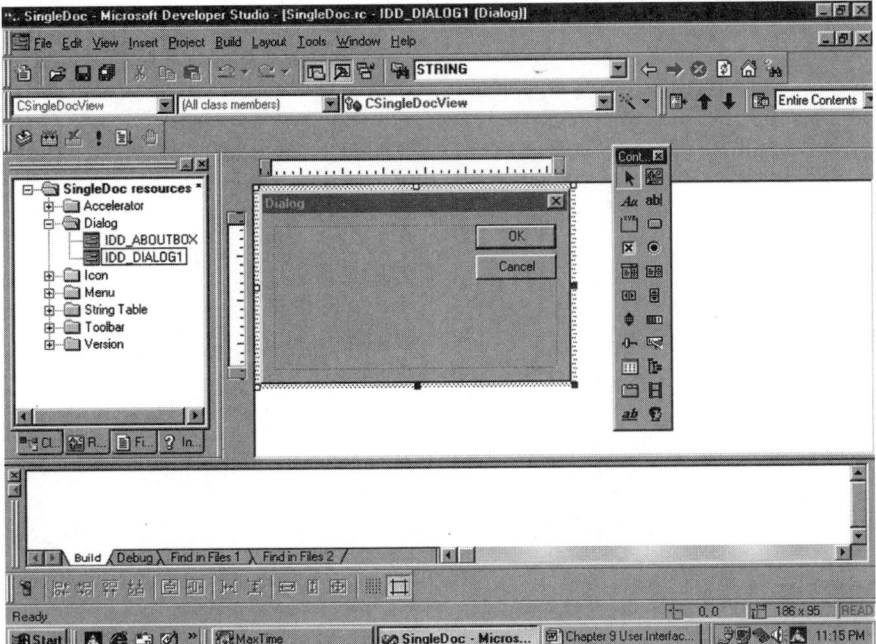

Visual C++ will open the new dialog and display it, as shown in Figure 9-17. You can start designing the dialog, adding controls and setting properties just like you would in Visual Basic. This is why Visual C++ has the Resource Editor, to save you the time of having to edit the actual script. Here you can use graphical methods instead.

The first thing we might want to do is resize the dialog. The dialog box is too small for most applications as it is arranged now, so we will resize it by dragging on the border with the mouse. Now we need to reset some properties of the dialog.

Our dialog will report the sum of two numbers that the user enters. First, we want to give the dialog a meaningful name and have it display a useful caption. We will set the following properties:

- Set the ID property to *IDD_SUMDIALOG*.
- Set the Caption property to *SUM*.

A user enters information into a dialog box through the use of controls, like edit boxes or list boxes. You can find controls in the Toolbox, which is a floating toolbar found in the Resource Editor (see Figure 9-18). The toolbox has several important controls that can be used to create a user interface. Here is what each of these controls can be used for:

- *Pointer* The pointer is the small arrow icon in the upper left corner of the toolbox. This is not actually a control; instead, it is used to size

Figure 9-18
The Toolbox.

Chapter 9: User Interface Design

and move controls that have already been placed on the surface of a dialog box.

- *Picture* The Picture control will create a rectangular delimited area on the dialog box that can be used to display an image.
- *StaticText* Statictext can be used as a label for another control or to display information to the user.
- *Edit Box* An edit box can be used to accept alphanumeric input from the user.
- *GroupBox* A groupbox creates a frame that can be used to group a set of controls together on a dialog box. Typically this is used to display a set of related checkboxes or option buttons.
- *Button* This is the familiar command button found in Windows with such labels as OK, Cancel, Yes, and No. A command button can be placed on a dialog box and given any label you desire. You can then use the Class Wizard to place code behind it.
- *CheckBox* A checkbox is used to give the user a Yes/No selection. Checkboxes are not exclusive.
- *Radio Button* A radio or option button is also used to give the user a Yes/No selection; however, in a group of option buttons only one can be selected.
- *Combo Box* A combo box is a drop-down list.
- *ListBox* A listbox provides the user with a list of choices.
- *Horizontal Scroll Bar* A scroll bar can be used in conjunction with other controls to allow the user to set some value or to control graphics information.
- *Vertical Scroll Bar* A vertical scroll bar displays vertically on the dialog box.
- *Spin* A Spin control allows the user to click up and down.
- *Progress* This control allows you to display a progress bar to the user.
- *List Control* This control displays a list of items, which can be icons or text.
- *Tree Control* This control displays data in a treelike structure. This is similar to a Windows Explorer-type interface.
- *Tab Control* You can use a Tab control to build forms that contain a lot of data. The Tab control is used to create index tabs.
- *Rich Edit* This control adds a rich edit textbox to the dialog box. A rich edit box is like an edit box; however, it has the advantage of being

able to use the fonts and formatting of a rich text file. This means you can set the font of the text it contains to bold, italic, and underline, and use different fonts and colors.

- *Custom Control* This selection allows the use of custom controls. This is a leftover from older versions of C++. Chances are you will be using ActiveX controls.

To add a control to a dialog box, use these steps:

1. Select the control that you want to add in the toolbox.
2. Position the mouse pointer over the area where you want to place the control.
3. Hold down the left mouse button and "draw" the control on the surface of the dialog box.
4. Release the mouse button.

We will add the following controls to the dialog box:

- A static text object to label the first edit box.
- An edit box to accept the first number.
- A static text object to label the second edit box.
- An edit box to accept the second number.
- A list box that records the results.

We can use meaningful names for the ID property of each object. For example, the edit box that accepts the first number has its ID property set to *IDC_edtFirstNum*. We have used a variant of Hungarian notation here; the character sequence *edt* tells us this is an edit box, while the rest of the string tells us what it does. We can use this naming style for the ID property of each control. For example, we set the ID for the list box to *IDC_lstResults*.

We will also rename the OK and Cancel command buttons. We change the ID property of the OK button to *IDADDBUTTON* and the Caption to *ADD*. The ID and Caption properties of the Cancel button are set to *IDCLOSE* and *Close*, respectively. The dialog box is shown in Figure 9-19.

Once you have added the controls to a dialog box, you will need to bring up the Class Wizard. The wizard will tell you that you have added a new resource to the project and ask you if you want to create a new class for it or select an existing class. In this case we will create a new class and click *OK*. The New Class dialog box will open, where you can enter the name of the class (see Figure 9-20). We will call the class `CDlgAddNumbers`. The

Chapter 9: User Interface Design

Figure 9-19
Customized dialog box.

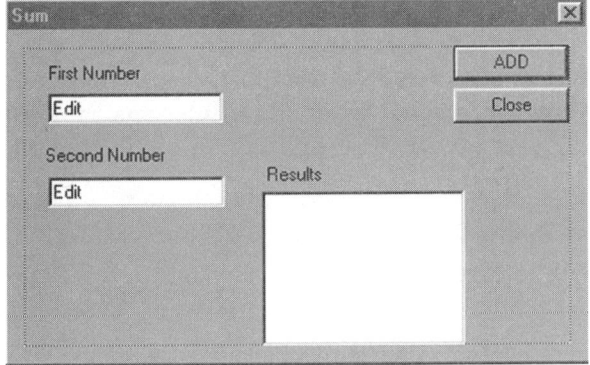

Figure 9-20
The New Class dialog.

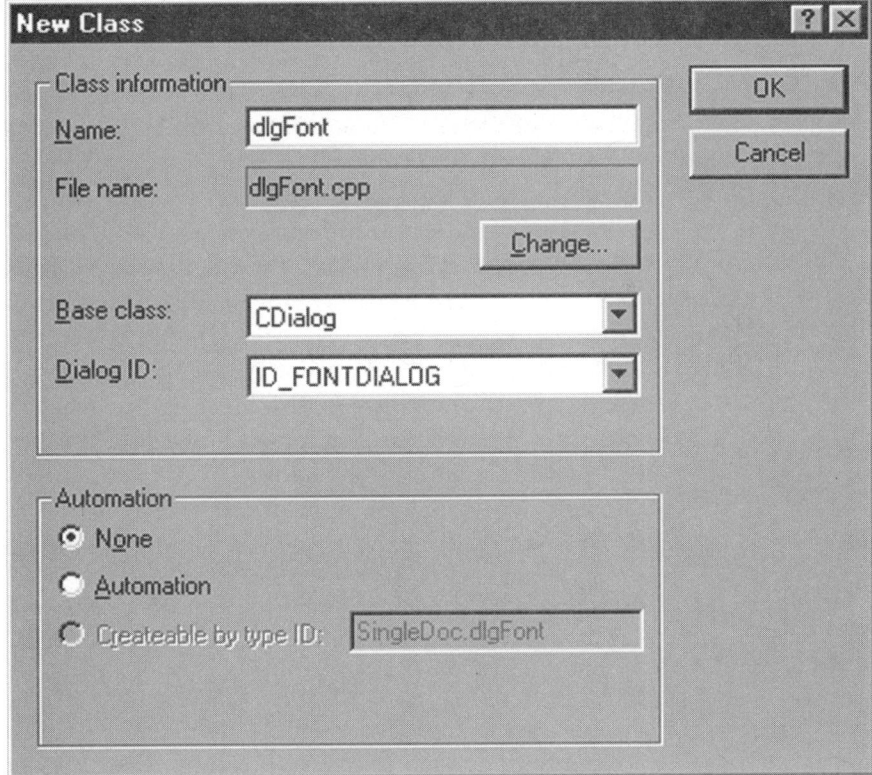

Class Wizard will create two files that will contain the class for this dialog, *DlgAddNumbers.cpp* and *DlgAddNumbers.h*.

The first step is to put code behind the command buttons on the dialog. We will need to add member functions that will be called when the user clicks a button. You can add a member function for the Add button by following these steps:

1. Make sure that the `CDlgAddNumbers` class is shown in the Class Name drop-down list.
2. Click *IDADDBUTTON* in the Object IDs list.
3. Select *BN_CLICKED* from the Messages list.
4. Click the *Add Function* button on the right side of the Window.
5. Accept the OnAddButton name by clicking the *OK* button.

The `OnAddButton` member function will be shown in the Member Functions list at the bottom of the screen. Before we edit the code for this function, we need to add member variables to represent the controls we have placed on the form.

Unlike Visual Basic, where a form "knows" which controls you have placed on it, a Visual C++ dialog box does not automatically get this information. Perhaps we could say that Visual C++ is not as "smart" as Visual Basic in this regard, but this is a result of the strong object-oriented nature of the C++ language.

To add member variables, click on the *Member Variables* tab of the Class Wizard. You will see the project name and class name displayed at the top of the wizard (see Figure 9-21). The class name should be listed as `CDlgAddNumbers`. The ControlIDs list box in the middle of the screen displays the controls that you added to the dialog (note that static text objects are not included in this list). We will need to add member variables to represent the edit boxes and the list box. This will allow us to work with the controls in code.

First, we will add a member variable to represent the IDC_edtFirstNum edit box. This can be done by using the following steps:

1. Select the *IDC_edtFirstNum* item from the *Control IDs* list box.
2. Click the *Add Variable* button.
3. The Add Member Variable dialog box will open (see Figure 9-22).
4. Specify the member variable name. The convention is to begin a member variable name with the m_ character combination, which Visual C++ has already inserted for you. Name this variable `m_edtFirstNum`.

Chapter 9: User Interface Design

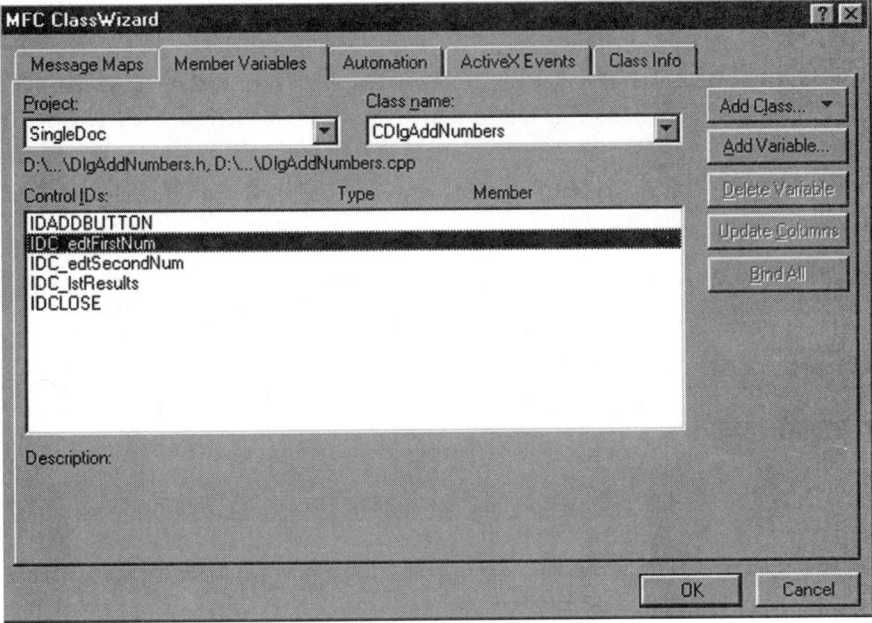

Figure 9-21
Adding member variables with the Class Wizard.

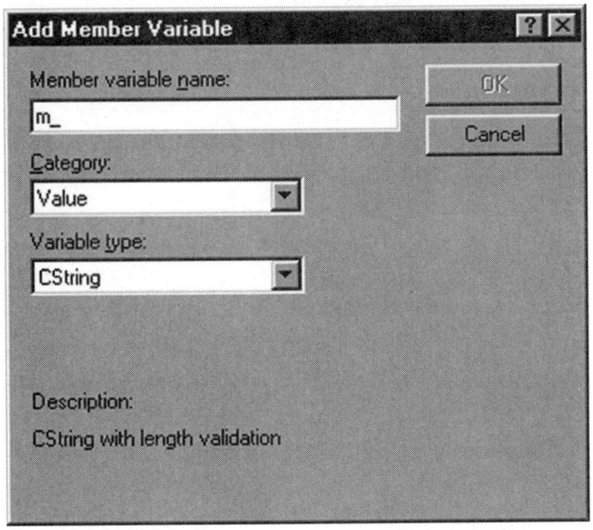

Figure 9-22
The Add Member Variable dialog.

5. Next we need to set the Category. Click open the list and select *Control*. When you do, the Variable Type option should automatically be set to the proper type of control.

6. Click the *OK* button. You will see the new member variable listed, properly associated with the IDC_edtFirstNum control ID.

The member variables for the other controls can be added by using the same procedure. Note that we will not need to add member variables for the Add and Close buttons. When done, click the *Message Maps* tab of the Class Wizard. Now we can add code to the Add command button's `BN_CLICKED` member function. Open the code for this member function.

When the user clicks this button, we will need to complete the following steps:

1. Retrieve the text the user entered into each edit box.
2. Convert the text to numerical values.
3. Add the numbers.
4. Convert the result to text.
5. Report the result by adding it to the list box.

To see how this is going to work, take a look at the header file that the Class Wizard has created for the dialog box. The class that defines the dialog box includes the member variables that we just created, and it looks like this:

```
// CDlgAddNumbers dialog

class CDlgAddNumbers : public CDialog
{
// Construction
public:
    CDlgAddNumbers(CWnd* pParent = NULL);   // standard constructor

// Dialog Data
    //{{AFX_DATA(CDlgAddNumbers)
    enum { IDD = IDD_SUMDIALOG };
    CListBox   m_lstResults;
    CEdit      m_edtSecondNum;
    CEdit      m_edtFirstNum;
    //}}AFX_DATA

// Overrides
    // ClassWizard generated virtual function overrides
    //{{AFX_VIRTUAL(CDlgAddNumbers)
    protected:
    virtual void DoDataExchange(CDataExchange* pDX);    // DDX/DDV support
    //}}AFX_VIRTUAL

// Implementation
protected:

    // Generated message map functions
    //{{AFX_MSG(CDlgAddNumbers)
    afx_msg void OnAddbutton();
    //}}AFX_MSG
    DECLARE_MESSAGE_MAP()
```

Chapter 9: User Interface Design

```
};
//{{AFX_INSERT_LOCATION}}
// Microsoft Developer Studio will insert additional declarations
immediately before the previous line.
#endif //
!defined(AFX_DLGADDNUMBERS_H__CEF42959_5C60_11D3_856B_8361827A9B65__IN
CLUDED_)
```

Notice the two member variables `m_edtFirstNumber` and `m_edtSecondNumber`. Each variable is an object of a class named `CEdit`. The `CEdit` class is used to implement an edit box, and we can use the members of this class to figure out how to set and retrieve text from one of these controls. We find that the edit box gets these functions from the Window base class that it is derived from. There are two functions that we need to use:

- `GetWindowText`
- `SetWindowText`

The headers for these two functions are as follows:

```
int GetWindowText(CString& StringVar) const;

void SetWindowText( LPCTSTR lpszString);
```

These member functions can be accessed by using the dot syntax for the member variables that we created to represent the controls placed on the dialog. This is because these member variables are class variables of the `CEdit` class. Before we see how to do that, however, notice the `LPCTSTR` and `CString` data types. These are string data types that we can use in a C++ program in a similar manner to a plain `String` in Visual Basic. `CString` is a way to represent `const char *`-type strings in C++ and use overloaded operators for easy string manipulation. For example, we can do the following:

```
CString First, Last, Name;

First = "John"; //use the = overloaded operator to copy a string
Last = "Jones";

Name = First + Last; //use the overloaded + operator for string con-
catenation
```

This is easier and more natural than using arrays of type `char`. The `CString` data type will make it very easy to extract and use data from the edit boxes. Let's review the tasks we need to complete when the user clicks the Add button and go over each of them in turn:

- Retrieve the text the user entered into each edit box.
- Convert the text to numerical values.
- Add the numbers.
- Convert the result to text.
- Report the result by adding it to the list box.

We can accomplish these tasks with the following code:

```cpp
void CDlgAddNumbers::OnAddbutton()
{
    //Function : OnAddbutton
    //Description : Called when user clicks
    //the add button. Adds two numbers
    //user entered in edit boxes and displays result.

    //strings to retrieve values
    //from edit boxes
    CString strNumberOne, strNumberTwo;

    //string to return result
    CString strResult;

    long one, two, result; //variables to complete
                           //arithmetic operation

    char temp[10]; //temporary variable to hold result
                   //will be used in ltoa function

    //read text the user typed in
    m_edtFirstNum.GetWindowText(strNumberOne);
    m_edtSecondNum.GetWindowText(strNumberTwo);

    //convert to numbers
    one = atol(strNumberOne);
    two = atol(strNumberTwo);

    //add the numbers
    result = one + two;

    //convert result to string
    _ltoa(result, temp, 10);

    //build result string with complete equation
    strResult = strNumberOne + " + " + strNumberTwo + " = " + temp;

    //Add result to list box
    m_lstResults.AddString(strResult);

    //clear the textboxes
    m_edtFirstNum.SetWindowText("");
    m_edtSecondNum.SetWindowText("");
}
```

Chapter 9: User Interface Design

Our first task is listed as:

- Retrieve the text the user entered into each edit box.

We can do this by using the `GetWindowText` member function of the `CEdit` class that we described earlier. To call this function, we use the dot syntax with the member variables we declared to represent each edit box. We pass a variable of type `CString` to the member function to retrieve the value:

```
//read text the user typed in
m_edtFirstNum.GetWindowText(strNumberOne);
m_edtSecondNum.GetWindowText(strNumberTwo);
```

The next task on our list is as follows:

- Convert the text to numerical values.

Since we are using variables of type `long` to hold the numbers, we can do this by calling the `atol` function. This function is found in the header file *stdlib.h* and accepts one parameter of type `string`. The function definition is as follows:

```
#include <stdlib.h>
long atol(const char * str);
```

First, we make sure that the *stdlib.h* file has been included in our source file for the dialog, and it has. We use the following two lines of code to convert the values read into the strings to type `long`:

```
//convert to numbers
one = atol(strNumberOne);
two = atol(strNumberTwo);
```

Our next tasks on the list are as follows:

- Add the numbers.
- Convert the result to text.

Adding the numbers together is easy. Once we've done that, we need to convert them back into a string so that we can display the result in a list box. One way we can do that is by calling the `_ltoa` function, which converts a `long` into an array of type `char`. The `_ltoa` function takes three parameters:

```
char * _ltoa(long inval, char *str, int base);
```

where `inval` is the number you want to convert to a string, `str` is the pointer to a `char` that will hold the result, and `base` is the base or radix of `inval`. In this case, it is base `10`.

A `CString` is type `const char *`, so we cannot pass a variable of type `CString` to this function. We will call the function with a temporary variable that is a character array, and then we can use this array of `char`s in a concatenation statement to build the result string:

```
//add the numbers
result = one + two;

//convert result to string
_ltoa(result, temp, 10);
```

Our next task is to build the output string. We want to display the entire equation to the user. For example, if the user enters 2 and 2, we want to display:

```
2 + 2 = 4
```

We can do this easily by using the overloaded concatenation operator `+`, which works with variables of type `CString`. Since we can mix an array of `char`s in the concatenation operation, we can include the `temp` variable we used to convert the result into a string. We store the concatenated string in a variable called `strResult`, using the overloaded `CString` operator `=` for string copy or assignment:

```
//build result string with complete equation
    strResult = strNumberOne + " + " + strNumberTwo + " = " + temp;
```

Our final task is to display the result to the user in the list box. We can look at the `CListBox` class to find the method we need and use the member variable we created to represent the list box when we built the class for our dialog box. This is done easily by calling the AddString method of the `CListBox` class, which takes one parameter, the string we want displayed in the list box:

```
//Add result to list box
m_lstResults.AddString(strResult);
```

The final line of code clears the edit boxes so that the user can add two more numbers. This is done by passing a blank string to the SetWindowText method of the `CEditBox` class members:

Chapter 9: User Interface Design

```
//clear the textboxes
m_edtFirstNum.SetWindowText("");
m_edtSecondNum.SetWindowText("");
```

Closing the Dialog

There will come a time when the user grows tired of adding numbers together, so we have provided a Close button that the user can click with the mouse. Now we have to add some code to make this button do exactly that. First, we need to add an `OnCloseButton` member function to the dialog box class with the Class Wizard. An easy way to close the dialog box is to use the OnCancel method of the `CDialog` class, which our dialog box has inherited as its base class. We use the `this` pointer to explicitly show that the code in this member function is referring to the object that owns the class:

```
void CDlgAddNumbers::OnClosebutton()
{
    // Close the dialog box
    this->OnCancel();

}
```

Adding a Menu Item for the New Dialog

Now we have the dialog box completed. All we need to do is provide the user with a way to open it. To do this, we will add a new menu item under the View menu. First, we go to the IDR_Mainframe menu resource and add a new menu item under the View menu with caption set to *Add Nums* and ID set to *ID_ SHOWADD*. Next, we open the Class Wizard, select the *CSingleDocApp* class, and choose the ID_SHOWADD object ID. We then choose the COMMAND message and create an `OnShowadd` member function. This member function will be called when the user clicks the menu.

When we click the *Edit Code* button for the `OnShowadd` member function, the code window will open, where we can add code to display the new dialog. You will recall that when the wizard automatically added code to display the About box, it declared a variable of type `CAboutDlg`. We will use the same method to show our dialog box. In the last section you will recall that we defined a new class to represent the dialog box,

`CDlgAddNumbers`. To work with the dialog, we will declare a new object of this class. When the wizard creates a new class for our dialog box, we get the methods of a generic dialog box "for free" from inheritance. We will use the DoModal method to display the dialog box to the user. The code looks like this:

```
void CSingleDocApp::OnShowadd()
{
    // Show the addnumbers dialog
    CDlgAddNumbers dlgAddNums;
    dlgAddNums.DoModal();
}
```

Before this code will work, however, we need to tell the compiler to include the files that define the `CDlgAddNumbers` class in the *CSingleDoc.cpp* file. Otherwise, the compiler will not recognize the variable declaration. The Class Wizard created two files to implement the new class for the dialog box. These are as follows:

DlgAddNumbers.h

DlgAddNumbers.cpp

Therefore, we will add the following `#include` statement to the *CSingleDoc.cpp* file:

```
#include "DlgAddNumbers.h"
```

This tells the compiler to add the contents of this file into the *CSingleDoc.cpp* file when it compiles it. That way, it will understand our declarations and code that use the `CDlgAddNumbers` class. With these changes, we can compile the program and display the dialog by clicking on the View menu.

Programming with ActiveX Controls

In this section we will briefly explore programming with ActiveX controls. Almost every Windows program that you can imagine developing will probably use one or more ActiveX controls. In the last section we explored the built-in controls that come with Visual C++, such as edit boxes, list boxes, and radio buttons. Many developers have created their

Chapter 9: User Interface Design

own controls, which are stored in a file format with an *.ocx* extension. These controls are known as *ActiveX controls* and can be inserted and used in much the same way as a basic C++ control.

To illustrate the use of an ActiveX control, we have created a dialog-based project with the MFC App Wizard called *mydialogs*. We will use this project to show you how to:

- Add an ActiveX control to a project
- Place the control on a form
- Program the control in code

Adding an ActiveX Control to a Project

To add an ActiveX control to a project, use the following steps:

1. Click open the *Project* pull-down menu.
2. Select *Add to Project*.
3. Select *Components and Controls*.

This will open the *Components and Controls Gallery* (see Figure 9-23). To add an ActiveX control, click open the *Registered ActiveX Controls* folder. This folder will display all of the registered controls on your system To

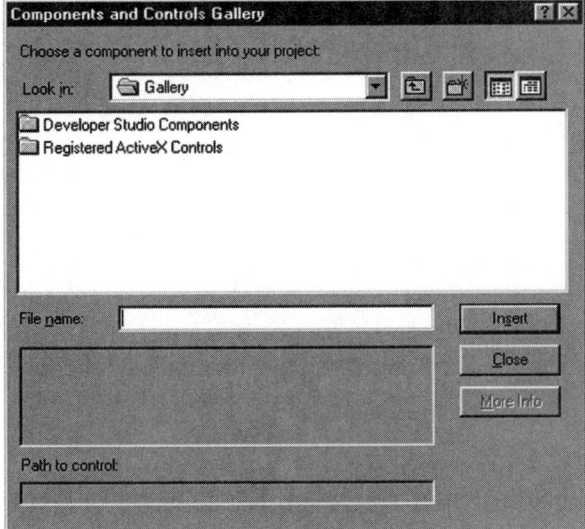

Figure 9-23
Inserting a component.

add a control, select the control you want and click the *Insert* button. The Confirm Classes dialog will open (see Figure 9-24). Visual C++ will create a wrapper class for you to use the control in code. The Confirm Classes dialog will tell you the class name, header file, and implementation file for the control. Once Visual C++ is done creating a wrapper class for the control, you will find the control available in the toolbox. It can then be added to a dialog just like any other built-in control. You can resize, move, and set the properties of the control as well.

When you are done adding controls, click *Close*. For our example, we will insert an ActiveX control that comes with Visual Basic, the *MsFlexGrid.OCX*, or flex grid, control.

Programming a Control in Code

Once you have the ActiveX control inserted into your project and placed on a dialog, you can program it just like any other control. First, you must use the Class Wizard to create a member variable to represent the control, just like we did when we used the edit and list boxes in our SDI project. We will use our FlexGrid to display a set of numbers, so we will create a member variable that is of the control category named

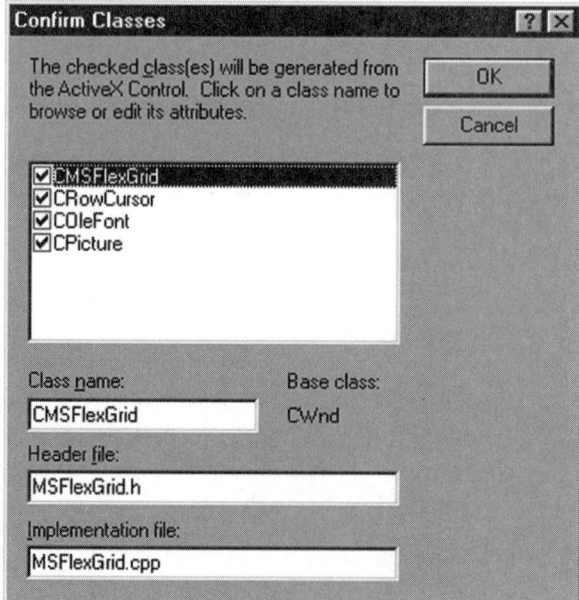

Figure 9-24
The Confirm Classes dialog.

Chapter 9: User Interface Design

m_NumberGrid to represent the FlexGrid. To see how we will work with this member variable in code, we can look at the header file created for the control, which is the *MSFlexGrid.h* file:

```
#if !defined(AFX_MSFLEXGRID_H__168F4357_5D54_11D3_856B_97DBF5135E65__INCLUDED_)
#define AFX_MSFLEXGRID_H__168F4357_5D54_11D3_856B_97DBF5135E65__INCLUDED_

#if _MSC_VER >= 1000
#pragma once
#endif // _MSC_VER >= 1000
// Machine generated IDispatch wrapper class(es) created by Microsoft Visual C++

// NOTE: Do not modify the contents of this file.  If this class is regenerated by
//  Microsoft Visual C++, your modifications will be overwritten.

// Dispatch interfaces referenced by this interface
class COleFont;
class CPicture;
class CRowCursor;

/////////////////////////////////////////////////////////////////////////////
// CMSFlexGrid wrapper class
class CMSFlexGrid : public CWnd
{
protected:
    DECLARE_DYNCREATE(CMSFlexGrid)
public:
    CLSID const& GetClsid()
    {
        static CLSID const clsid
            = { 0x6262d3a0, 0x531b, 0x11cf, { 0x91, 0xf6, 0xc2, 0x86, 0x3c, 0x38, 0x5e, 0x30 } };
        return clsid;
    }
    virtual BOOL Create(LPCTSTR lpszClassName,
        LPCTSTR lpszWindowName, DWORD dwStyle,
        const RECT& rect,
        CWnd* pParentWnd, UINT nID,
        CCreateContext* pContext = NULL)
    { return CreateControl(GetClsid(), lpszWindowName, dwStyle, rect, pParentWnd, nID); }

    BOOL Create(LPCTSTR lpszWindowName, DWORD dwStyle,
        const RECT& rect, CWnd* pParentWnd, UINT nID,
        CFile* pPersist = NULL, BOOL bStorage = FALSE,
        BSTR bstrLicKey = NULL)
    { return CreateControl(GetClsid(), lpszWindowName, dwStyle, rect, pParentWnd, nID,
        pPersist, bStorage, bstrLicKey); }

// Attributes
```

```cpp
public:

// Operations
public:
    long GetRows();
    void SetRows(long nNewValue);
    long GetCols();
    void SetCols(long nNewValue);
    long GetFixedRows();
    void SetFixedRows(long nNewValue);
    long GetFixedCols();
    void SetFixedCols(long nNewValue);
    short GetVersion();
    CString GetFormatString();
    void SetFormatString(LPCTSTR lpszNewValue);
    long GetTopRow();
    void SetTopRow(long nNewValue);
    long GetLeftCol();
    void SetLeftCol(long nNewValue);
    long GetRow();
    void SetRow(long nNewValue);
    long GetCol();
    void SetCol(long nNewValue);
    long GetRowSel();
    void SetRowSel(long nNewValue);
    long GetColSel();
    void SetColSel(long nNewValue);
    CString GetText();
    void SetText(LPCTSTR lpszNewValue);
    unsigned long GetBackColor();
    void SetBackColor(unsigned long newValue);
    unsigned long GetForeColor();
    void SetForeColor(unsigned long newValue);
    unsigned long GetBackColorFixed();
    void SetBackColorFixed(unsigned long newValue);
    unsigned long GetForeColorFixed();
    void SetForeColorFixed(unsigned long newValue);
    unsigned long GetBackColorSel();
    void SetBackColorSel(unsigned long newValue);
    unsigned long GetForeColorSel();
    void SetForeColorSel(unsigned long newValue);
    unsigned long GetBackColorBkg();
    void SetBackColorBkg(unsigned long newValue);
    BOOL GetWordWrap();
    void SetWordWrap(BOOL bNewValue);
    COleFont GetFont();
    void SetRefFont(LPDISPATCH newValue);
    float GetFontWidth();
    void SetFontWidth(float newValue);
    CString GetCellFontName();
    void SetCellFontName(LPCTSTR lpszNewValue);
    float GetCellFontSize();
    void SetCellFontSize(float newValue);
    BOOL GetCellFontBold();
    void SetCellFontBold(BOOL bNewValue);
    BOOL GetCellFontItalic();
    void SetCellFontItalic(BOOL bNewValue);
    BOOL GetCellFontUnderline();
```

Chapter 9: User Interface Design

```
void SetCellFontUnderline(BOOL bNewValue);
BOOL GetCellFontStrikeThrough();
void SetCellFontStrikeThrough(BOOL bNewValue);
float GetCellFontWidth();
void SetCellFontWidth(float newValue);
long GetTextStyle();
void SetTextStyle(long nNewValue);
long GetTextStyleFixed();
void SetTextStyleFixed(long nNewValue);
BOOL GetScrollTrack();
void SetScrollTrack(BOOL bNewValue);
long GetFocusRect();
void SetFocusRect(long nNewValue);
long GetHighLight();
void SetHighLight(long nNewValue);
BOOL GetRedraw();
void SetRedraw(BOOL bNewValue);
long GetScrollBars();
void SetScrollBars(long nNewValue);
long GetMouseRow();
long GetMouseCol();
long GetCellLeft();
long GetCellTop();
long GetCellWidth();
long GetCellHeight();
long GetRowHeightMin();
void SetRowHeightMin(long nNewValue);
long GetFillStyle();
void SetFillStyle(long nNewValue);
long GetGridLines();
void SetGridLines(long nNewValue);
long GetGridLinesFixed();
void SetGridLinesFixed(long nNewValue);
unsigned long GetGridColor();
void SetGridColor(unsigned long newValue);
unsigned long GetGridColorFixed();
void SetGridColorFixed(unsigned long newValue);
unsigned long GetCellBackColor();
void SetCellBackColor(unsigned long newValue);
unsigned long GetCellForeColor();
void SetCellForeColor(unsigned long newValue);
short GetCellAlignment();
void SetCellAlignment(short nNewValue);
long GetCellTextStyle();
void SetCellTextStyle(long nNewValue);
short GetCellPictureAlignment();
void SetCellPictureAlignment(short nNewValue);
CString GetClip();
void SetClip(LPCTSTR lpszNewValue);
void SetSort(short nNewValue);
long GetSelectionMode();
void SetSelectionMode(long nNewValue);
long GetMergeCells();
void SetMergeCells(long nNewValue);
BOOL GetAllowBigSelection();
void SetAllowBigSelection(BOOL bNewValue);
long GetAllowUserResizing();
void SetAllowUserResizing(long nNewValue);
long GetBorderStyle();
```

```cpp
    void SetBorderStyle(long nNewValue);
    long GetHWnd();
    BOOL GetEnabled();
    void SetEnabled(BOOL bNewValue);
    long GetAppearance();
    void SetAppearance(long nNewValue);
    long GetMousePointer();
    void SetMousePointer(long nNewValue);
    CPicture GetMouseIcon();
    void SetRefMouseIcon(LPDISPATCH newValue);
    long GetPictureType();
    void SetPictureType(long nNewValue);
    CPicture GetPicture();
    CPicture GetCellPicture();
    void SetRefCellPicture(LPDISPATCH newValue);
    CString GetTextArray(long index);
    void SetTextArray(long index, LPCTSTR lpszNewValue);
    short GetColAlignment(long index);
    void SetColAlignment(long index, short nNewValue);
    long GetColWidth(long index);
    void SetColWidth(long index, long nNewValue);
    long GetRowHeight(long index);
    void SetRowHeight(long index, long nNewValue);
    BOOL GetMergeRow(long index);
    void SetMergeRow(long index, BOOL bNewValue);
    BOOL GetMergeCol(long index);
    void SetMergeCol(long index, BOOL bNewValue);
    void SetRowPosition(long index, long nNewValue);
    void SetColPosition(long index, long nNewValue);
    long GetRowData(long index);
    void SetRowData(long index, long nNewValue);
    long GetColData(long index);
    void SetColData(long index, long nNewValue);
    CString GetTextMatrix(long Row, long Col);
    void SetTextMatrix(long Row, long Col, LPCTSTR lpszNewValue);
    void AddItem(LPCTSTR Item, const VARIANT& index);
    void RemoveItem(long index);
    void Clear();
    void Refresh();
    CRowCursor GetDataSource();
    void SetDataSource(LPDISPATCH newValue);
    BOOL GetRowIsVisible(long index);
    BOOL GetColIsVisible(long index);
    long GetRowPos(long index);
    long GetColPos(long index);
    short GetGridLineWidth();
    void SetGridLineWidth(short nNewValue);
    short GetFixedAlignment(long index);
    void SetFixedAlignment(long index, short nNewValue);
    BOOL GetRightToLeft();
    void SetRightToLeft(BOOL bNewValue);
    long GetOLEDropMode();
    void SetOLEDropMode(long nNewValue);
    void OLEDrag();
};

//{{AFX_INSERT_LOCATION}}
// Microsoft Developer Studio will insert additional declarations
immediately before the previous line.
```

Chapter 9: User Interface Design

```
#endif //
!defined(AFX_MSFLEXGRID_H__168F4357_5D54_11D3_856B_97DBF5135E65__INCLU
DED_)
```

The members of the `CMSFlexGrid` class are the variables and functions we can use. To load the grid with integers, we'll set the number of rows and columns in the grid, and then use the `SetText` member function to load the data into the grid. The code is placed in the `OnOK` member function for our dialog:

```
void CMydialogsDlg::OnOK()
{
    int i, j;
    CString strValue;
    char temp[10];

    //set the number of rows and columns
    //for the grid. The grid will have
    //100 rows and three data columns.
    //add one for column headers
    //and row index
    m_NumberGrid.SetRows(101);
    m_NumberGrid.SetCols(4);

    //load the column headers
    m_NumberGrid.SetCol(0);
    m_NumberGrid.SetRow(0);
    m_NumberGrid.SetText("Row");
    m_NumberGrid.SetCol(1);
    m_NumberGrid.SetText("One");
    m_NumberGrid.SetCol(2);
    m_NumberGrid.SetText("Two");
    m_NumberGrid.SetCol(3);
    m_NumberGrid.SetText("Three");

    //load the data
    for(i=0; i < 100; i++)
    {
        for(j=0; j< 4; j++)
        {
            //set the row number
            m_NumberGrid.SetRow(i+1);

            //set the column
            m_NumberGrid.SetCol(j);

            //if this is the first
            //column, insert the row
            //number, otherwise insert
            //data
            if(j == 0)
                _itoa(i,temp,10);
            else
```

```
                _itoa((i + j)*10, temp,10);
                m_NumberGrid.SetText(temp);

        }//next j

    }//next i

}
```

The completed application with the MSFlexGrid control is shown in Figure 9-25. Most third-party vendors will provide documentation that will show you how to use their particular control. However, the general procedure used here is the method you will use; the only difference will be in the member functions and variables that belong to the class that represents the control. At this point, we have the basics we need to use Visual C++ for rapid application development.

User Interface Prototyping

In the era of rapid application development, prototyping is taking on an ever-larger role in dealing with the customer. Since it's easy to patch together a user interface, it makes sense to prototype an application. In this section we explore the importance of prototyping.

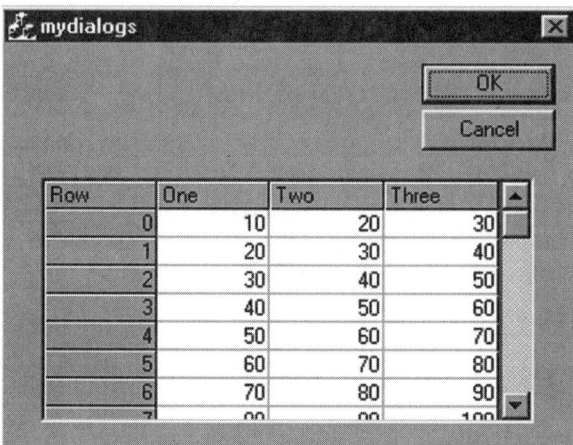

Figure 9-25
Program with MSFlexGrid running.

Why Prototype an Application?

The main function of a prototype is to define system requirements. Prototyping helps build communication with the customer. When an application is prototyped, it will go through several successive iterations of increasing complexity. By providing the customer with a mock-up of the application early on, we can gauge and react to the customers' desires before the software is too developed. This process is continued throughout the development of the application, keeping the customer involved in the design process. This is better than surprising them with a piece of fully developed software after six months of programming. If they aren't happy, that's six months wasted. Prototyping helps maintain communication with the customer and helps ensure that progress is being made in a timely fashion, keeping the customer happy.

What to Include in a Prototype

The idea of prototyping is to show the customer what appears to be a complete version of the software. Behind the scenes, all we have is a shell—in other words, a mock-up or model. This is easy to accomplish with a visual programming language. For example, we can design several dialogs and load them with bogus data. The dialogs can be compiled into a "program" that we can show to the user, giving the customer a chance to see how the application would work before any real effort has been applied to the project.

It's important to approach prototyping as you would any aspect of software development. That means one thing: don't rush. RAD environments tempt a developer to rush out a real program as it is. If we are talking about throwing together a few screens, the temptation to rush is even larger. The downside is that a poor design choice may be included in the prototype that ends up being part of the final product.

The key to avoiding these problems is to approach prototyping with a requirements-gathering approach. Meet with the customer and have the customer define what they want. They can lay out what data will be tracked, how they expect to access it, and how they want the screens to look. The format of printed reports may be discussed. You then take this information to patch together a hollow shell of a Visual C++ program that will display the forms and some artificial (or maybe even real) data. A sample report can be included.

When this is completed, you meet with the customer again and determine if the requirements have been met. If not, more work is put into the prototype. Once the customer is satisfied, work on the real project can begin. The prototyping process may involve several hit-and-miss attempts. How well things go will depend on the level of communication with the customer. In many cases the prototype will evolve into the real application. This is especially the case when using a RAD development environment like Visual C++.

Setting Expectations for Prototyping

Good communication is key when prototyping. The customer might want to work with the prototype on their own. It's important that they understand that the prototype is not a real program. To them, when they see the forms on the screen and the colorful buttons, it seems like a real program. The customer needs to know that the prototyping process is simply an aid in defining the requirements of the project, in the same way that a flowchart would be used. This is an important point. If the customer views the prototype as a real piece of software, they may end up pushing the development team into rushing the prototype into a production piece of software. Customers become impatient during software development. Remember that unless the customer has some history of software development, to them, the process of building a program is a complete mystery. As far as they're concerned, if you have a form that shows up with some data, it's a working program. They may not fully appreciate the next two months that you need to spend putting code behind all of those buttons and grids. In the end, keeping the expectations of the customer realistic during the prototyping process requires good communication.

CHAPTER 10

Database Design

Introduction

A large percentage of software development in the real world is geared toward developing database applications. When building a database application, you should put as much care into designing the database as you would in designing the software itself. When designing your tables, records, and queries, you are still working with objects, and the way these objects are designed will have as great an impact on your application as any class or control would.

Great care needs to be used when building the database to ensure that it has a solid structure and good relationships between the tables. Designing a database in this manner will involve the process of *normalization*, which will help keep the data organized in an efficient manner. It will also involve the construction of indexes and queries, which will aid the user when sorting and retrieving data or working with subsets of the data. Once the database design is completed, you can start thinking about the software, which is using Visual C++ to build the front end. The front end will be the dialog boxes and code that will provide the user with a means to manipulate the database.

Many database programs use Microsoft Access to store the data. Also, since it is a relational database system, we can learn a lot about the general principles of good database design by examining Access files. For this reason, we will focus on using this type of database. In this chapter we'll focus on what elements a Microsoft Access database will have, and we'll investigate some good design principles that should be followed when structuring the data. This is by no means a complete examination of Microsoft Access; we will be focusing on the elements that will be used in Visual C++ coding. As such, we will not cover Access forms, reports, and modules. At the end of the chapter, we will see how to create a database from scratch. Since this can't be done with Visual C++, we will examine the Visual Data Manager, a utility that comes with Visual Basic.

Overview of Database Design

A database is simply a file or files used to store data. In Microsoft Access, a database is just a single file with an *.mdb* extension. Inside that file you'll find all the objects needed to store and manipulate information. This will include tables, queries, forms, and reports. If the user has

Microsoft Access or a runtime version of Access installed, the database can include everything the user needs, including forms and the code behind them.

At this point you might be asking yourself, if an Access database has everything in it, why do I need to use a programming tool like Visual C++? The answer to this question depends on the situation, and as a developer, you'll have to use your judgment in deciding which tool to use. Typically, Visual C++ is good to use if you want to have a self-contained application, where the user is not required to have any preexisting tools, as in Access. In this case, as far as the user is concerned, the Access database is just a file that comes with your app. The speed advantages provided by a Visual C++ program is also a consideration. You may also want to take advantage of the strongly object-oriented nature of C++. In the end, the choice may simply come down to your preference. Many programmers would rather write C++ apps than use Access or Visual Basic. No matter what language you choose to develop in, the first step is to determine what data needs to be stored and how to organize it.

Determining the End User's Needs

The first step in designing a database is to meet with the customer and discuss what their needs are. Some items to keep in mind during the initial planning stage are as follows:

- What specific data elements need to be stored? This will include items such as name, address, or monthly salary.
- What possible ranges will the data elements take? As you should do in declaring variables in code, when designing the database you'll need to make sure that it can hold the largest-possible (and still valid) value the user might enter. You'll also need to keep efficiency in mind; variables with larger ranges take more storage space.
- What will be used to uniquely identify the data?
- How can the data be organized, so as to break it down into different tables?
- How will the different categories of data interact? In other words, how do the individual tables relate to one another?
- In what ways will the user want to sort the data?
- What types of queries will the user want to "ask" the database?

- Does the user have MS Access or some other database on his or her system?
- Will the user need to transfer data between different storage formats (i.e., between different types of databases)?
- Will the application be a local app or client/server?

The design of the database needs to be taken just as seriously as any step in the software development cycle. Also, you should have the design of the database completed before you move on to building the application in Visual C++. This will help ensure that the software development cycle moves as smoothly as possible. If there are problems in the database, redesigning the data means redesigning your software as well, which can turn into a real headache.

Organizing the Data

Once you've determined what data needs to be stored, the next step is to organize that data into distinct but related categories that can be turned into tables (see below). The user might already have some idea of how they want this done, but chances are you will have to make sure that the data is arranged in such a way to maintain efficiency and develop good relationships between each category. Consider a database for a local high school that will track students, the classes offered, and what classes each student is taking. Let's say the school administrator wanted to track the following information:

- Social Security number
- Name, address, home phone, and parents' work phone for each student
- The grade level, date of enrollment, and expected date of graduation for each student
- A list of classes offered by the school, with class name and scheduled time
- The classes each student is taking

Looking at this data, we can divide it into three distinct categories:

- *Students* This table will maintain the list of students and store the Social Security number, name, address, phone number, grade level, date of enrollment, and expected date of graduation for each student.

Chapter 10: Database Design

- *Classes*   This table will maintain the list of classes offered by the school.
- *Schedules*   This table will track which classes each student is enrolled in.

When we actually build the database, each of these categories would become a table in the database. The tables will be related through indexing.

The Elements of a Database

As mentioned earlier, an Access database file can contain just about everything the user needs to store, view, and manipulate data. If you open an MDB file with Access, you'll find that it contains the following elements:

- *Tables*   This is where the data is actually stored. A table is a collection of information relating to a specific category. Tables are arranged in a row column format, with each row representing a *record*, and each column representing a *field*. A record is a single entity of related data. For example, in a list of students, a particular student record will contain all of the information for one particular student. Each piece of information is a field, such as Name, Address, or Phone Number. Typically, a table will be indexed, which will allow the database to uniquely identify each record and sort the data.
- *Queries*   A query is basically a question you can ask about a database. For example, you might ask "How many students are in the sophomore class?" Queries usually return a subset of the data in a table, or they can combine the data from several different tables. Queries can be built in Microsoft Access or in code using a special language called structured query language (SQL). We'll be discussing SQL in the next chapter.
- *Forms*   Access allows you to build forms to provide a user interface as part of the database. A form is like a dialog box in C++. Since we'll be building the user interface with Visual C++, we will ignore forms in Access.
- *Reports*   Access reports provide a format to view and print data. You can create or call up reports in a Visual C++ program, so we won't be talking about Access reports.

- *Macros* A macro is a single command that allows you to perform several tasks in Access at once.

- *Modules* An Access module is a code module where you can add subroutines and functions. This is similar to a code module in Visual Basic.

Let's start by looking at tables.

Organizing Data into Tables

An Access database is a single disk file, and the database file contains data stored in one or more tables. Each table represents a collection of related data, such as an employee list, a list of office locations, or a list of job positions. Data in tables is organized in a row-and-column format, much like an Excel spreadsheet. Each row in the table is a called a *record*. A record is a collection of data that belongs to a single object in the table. Each column in the table represents a *field*, which is an individual piece of data, such as somebody's phone number. A record could represent an employee, a customer order, an item in inventory, or any other object. The individual characteristics of the object are the fields.

Let's consider a simple example. A table that tracked product inventory for an office supply store might contain the following fields:

- Product ID
- Product Name
- Description
- Quantity

The table will then contain one column for each of these fields. The products that the user enters into the database will be the rows or records in the table, and each record will have a value specified for each of these fields. When data has been entered in the table, it might look something like this:

Product ID	Product Name	Description	Quantity
1001	Computer disks	3.5" floppy diskettes, IBM formatted	2000
1002	Pencils	No. 2 pencils	300
1003	College-ruled notebook	100-page college-ruled notebook	50
1004	Office desk	ABC company office desk	5

Chapter 10: Database Design

The row identified by ProductID 1002 represents an individual record in this table, while each column, for example, Product Name, is a field in the table.

In summary, there are two things to remember about tables:

- Each row or record is an individual object stored in the table, such as an employee.
- Each column or field represents one aspect of a record, such as name or phone number.

Data Types in an Access Database

If you are familiar with Visual Basic, you will immediately recognize the data types used in Access. Each field in a table will have a data type, just like a variable in Visual Basic. This means that you will think about the same kinds of issues that you would when choosing the data types for Visual Basic variables or the variables in your C++ programs. That means giving a field a meaningful name and weighing efficiency issues. Following are some good ideas to keep in mind:

- *Use good judgment when selecting a field size.* There are two considerations here, and you've faced this before when choosing data types for variables in your C++ programs. First, you want to make sure that you allocate enough space for the range of values the data might take. For example, when storing the population of a city, an integer will not be large enough, so a long integer would be a better choice. Another consideration, however, is that you don't want to waste disk space when you can avoid it. When saving test scores with a range of 0 to 100, it is more efficient to store this as type byte rather than using an integer, which takes 2 bytes of storage. Of course, on today's computers where hard disk space is cheap, this isn't as much of a concern as it was in the past.
- *For numbers that don't require calculations, use text fields.* Examples of when this a good idea include Social Security numbers, part serial numbers, and phone numbers.
- *Think about sort order.* If this is a field that will be used in an index, think about how a particular data type will sort. For example, a string will sort differently than a number will.
- *Give meaningful, descriptive names to each field.* An Access field name can be up to 64 characters in length. You should give field

names a reasonably sized but descriptive name. We don't use Hungarian notation when naming fields; just give a straightforward name that you would use in everyday language. Don't forget the user will see the field names when working with the database. This means you should avoid using cryptic field names.

There are 10 types of fields that you can use in Access:

- *Text* Use for strings, or numbers that won't be used in calculations. A text field can be up to 255 characters in size. The default size is 50 characters.
- *Memo* A memo field is used to hold large chunks of text data, when you think the field will require more than 255 characters. A memo field can hold up to 64,000 characters.
- *Number* Number fields hold numeric data. The field size for a number field corresponds to the Visual Basic data types. In other words, you can have an integer, long integer, byte, single, or double. These correspond to the C++ types `short`, `int`, `char`, `float`, and `double`, respectively.
- *Date/Time* A date/time field can store dates in the range of January 1, 100 to December 31, 9999.
- *Currency* This field is the same as the Visual Basic currency type. Stores numeric data with 4 decimal places.
- *AutoNumber* An autonumber field is used by Access to automatically provide a number to identify each record. Each time you add a record to the database, Access increments the value it will place in the autonumber field.
- *Yes/No* This field corresponds to the VB Boolean data type. Yes/no fields display in Access with a checkbox, with checked meaning yes and unchecked meaning no.
- *OLE Object* An OLE object field is a large binary field that can store data such as pictures or sound files.
- *HyperLink* This type of field can store a Web link.
- *Lookup Wizard* This lets you create a field that can be used to select a value from a list of choices in another table. For example, you could have a table that stored the state abbreviations for the 50 U.S. states. In another table, say, a list of customers, when entering the address of each customer, the State field could be a lookup field that retrieves the values from the U.S. States table.

Chapter 10: Database Design

Field Properties

Each field in the table will have the following properties:

- Name
- Type
- Size
- Ordinal position
- Validation text
- Validation rule
- Default value

We discussed the name, type, and size properties of a field earlier. Let's explore some of the other attributes that a field can have, focusing on items that will concern you when building a front end with Visual C++.

Ordinal Position

The Ordinal Position property will determine where a field will appear when you load the table in a data grid. This is done in a left-to-right order. While you can arrange the order of fields in your grid during design or runtime, things will be easier if you think about the order in which you want the data to appear on screen when you are designing the table.

Validation Rule

The Validation Rule property determines what type of data will be accepted in the database. For example, if we had a field to track the hourly wage of an employee, we could define a validation rule that made sure that the pay rate was at least the minimum wage. We could use the following validation rule:

```
>= 5.25
```

This would ensure that the wage had to be at least $5.25 per hour. When tracking a text field, we can provide a list of valid choices. For example, if we were maintaining a list of college students, we could use the following validation rule for the Class field:

```
IN(FR,SO,JR,SR)
```

This way, the user will only be able to enter one of the choices from this list. You can also use the `Like` keyword to test for similar text strings or to validate date ranges.

Validation Text

If the Validation Rule property is violated, we can specify a message to display to the user by setting the Validation Text property. If the user did not enter one of the class abbreviations that we specified in our list, we could display the error message:

```
Class Must Be One of FR,SO,JR, or SR.
```

Allow Zero Length

If you want to allow the user to enter a null value for a field, select the Allow Zero Length checkbox.

Indexes

A table will have one or more indexes. The primary key is used to determine the default sorting order of the table and to uniquely identify each record. Indexes can also be used for speedier access to a record. This is just like using a Rolodex to store your phone numbers or, you guessed it, looking up a subject in the index of a book. By categorizing and ordering the names in your phone number list, they can be located much more quickly and easily. An index in the table works much the same way.

Each index is made up of one or more fields in a table. For example, if we had a list of students, we could use the Social Security number of each student as the primary key. This is because each student has a unique Social Security number. Indexes can also consist of more than one field and can be used to relate two different tables, to achieve a different sorting order, or to speed searching on frequently used fields. Keep in

Chapter 10: Database Design

mind that a large number of indexes can add a lot of overhead to a database, so they should be used judiciously.

The Primary Key

Each table must have a way to uniquely identify the data it contains. This is done by specifying a primary key. Just like any other index, a primary key can be made up of just a single field, or it can contain multiple fields. Use a single field if a table contains one field that can uniquely identify each record.

Sometimes more than one field will be required to uniquely identify a record. Earlier we considered a class schedule at a local high school. A table that tracked the classes each student was taking might contain the following fields:

- Social Security Number
- Class ID
- Class Name
- Homework Grade
- Test Grade

Obviously, the Social Security Number field cannot be used because a student will likely enroll for more than one class. Class ID can't be used because several students will sign up for the same class, say, history. In this case, to uniquely identify a record, we need to consider two fields, Social Security Number + Class ID. This will ensure that every record in the table is unique, that each student only signs up for a class once, and that every student can sign up for multiple classes.

In summary, each record in the table will have its own unique value of the primary key. If possible, use a single field to define the primary key. If a record can't be uniquely identified with a single field, however, multiple-field primary keys can be used.

Foreign Keys and Relating Tables

If a field is used as the primary key of one table and it is included as a field in a second table, that field is known *in the second table* as a *foreign key*. The power of a database is the ability to relate the data in one or more tables, and it is the foreign key that helps us do this. For example, consider a Vendors table, along with the related table of products that the vendors supply. Let's say the Vendors table had the following fields:

Vendors

Vendor ID

Name

Address

Phone Number

Contact Person

Terms

Now let's consider the Products table. The Products table has its own primary key, *productID*, but is related to the Vendors table by the VendorID field. VendorID is the primary key of the Vendors table, so it is a foreign key in the Products table. The Products table might look like the following:

Products

ProductID

Description

VendorID

Quantity

Storage Location

In summary, foreign keys are used to define relationships between common fields of data in two or more different tables.

One-to-Many Relationships

The type of arrangement we described above is known as a *one-to-many relationship*. One record in the Vendors table, which can be thought of as

Chapter 10: Database Design

the master table, relates to multiple records in the Products table, which can be thought of as a lookup table.

Queries

As mentioned, a query is a question that the user can ask about the data. A query can be used to sort the data in a particular way or to retrieve a subset of the data. Queries are where the power of a relational database really becomes apparent. The most common query is called a *select query*. A select query can be used to retrieve a subset of the data in a table and to join data from multiple tables together. Some example queries are as follows: How many customers are from California? How many cars in the inventory are blue? Who are the students in the junior class?

Queries can be built in Access with the Query Wizard, manually, or through code. We will be concerned with building queries in Visual Basic code. This is done by using a special language called *structured query language*, or SQL. In the next chapter, we'll see how to use SQL in a Visual C++ program.

Views

When you are working inside Access, there are different ways to look at the structure of the database, or different views. This includes Design View, where you can build the structure of a table or query. Datasheet View displays the data in a table or query in a spreadsheet, or row-column, format.

Stored Procedures

Stored procedures provide a means to perform various functions on a database. Basically, it is an SQL query that is stored as a part of the database rather than including it in code. A stored procedure fits in with the idea of object-oriented design and encapsulation, by hiding what's going on in the database from the rest of the our application. This provides a data layer that is separate from the C++ code. This means that we can change the implementation of the data processing without having to change the C++ code. This fits in nicely with the idea of object-oriented design—remember that we want to relate between objects only though an interface while not worrying about how the object is actually implemented. The specifics of stored procedures will depend on the DBMS (database management system) that you are using.

Normalization

In the previous section we saw how to organize data into tables and how the tables are related through indexing. This type of arrangement is what makes relational databases so powerful, and understanding how to organize your data in this manner is central to maintaining the integrity of your database. Splitting your data into different tables is known as *normalization*.

The central goal in normalization is to avoid placing data in a table that should be placed in a table of its own, or that should be calculated at runtime or when generating reports. For example, in a database that tracked customer orders, it would not be advisable to place the products ordered by the customer in the same table that maintains the list of customers. Every time a customer placed a new order, the customer's phone number and address would be added again for each product, making the database bloated and inefficient. It would make more sense to place this data in its own table, say, OrderDetails, and relate the two tables through indexing.

There are three types of normalization used by most programmers. We'll explore each of these by considering the following simple example. Let's say that we need to design a database to track the club membership of the students at a local high school. We might track the following information:

- Student ID number
- Last name
- First name
- Phone number
- The clubs each student belongs to
- Membership dues, monthly and annual

Chapter 10: Database Design

First Normal Form

The most fundamental type of normalization is known as *first normal form*. The central idea behind first normal form is making the fields in a table *atomic*. Generally, for a field to be atomic, it must meet two conditions. First, it cannot store a listing of values in a single column or field. Second, the table must not have repeating fields of data, such as Order1, Order2, and Order3.

In our example, let's say we started our design by building a students table that looked like this:

StudentID	Last Name	First Name	Phone	Clubs	Monthly Dues	Dues/YR
0001	Jones	Sandra	555-5555	Chess, Drama, Debate	$25	$300
0002	Smith	Frank	555-9010	Tennis, Chess	$15	$180
0003	Garcia	Stephanie	555-7363	Tennis, Ski Club	$10	$120
0004	Newman	Chris	555-4990	Debate	$5	$60

The data in the Clubs field violates first normal form, because we have a list of values for almost every student. This is not desirable because it places limits to what we can do with the data. For example, we might want to view students who belong only to the chess club, and to do so would require parsing the Clubs field for each student.

We could organize the data by placing, say, three club fields in the table:

StudentID	Last Name	First Name	Phone	Club1	Club2	Club3	Monthly Dues	Annual Dues
0001	Jones	Sandra	555-5555	Chess	Drama	Debate	$25	$300
0002	Smith	Frank	555-9010	Tennis	Chess		$15	$180
0003	Garcia	Stephanie	555-7363	Tennis	Ski Club		$10	$120
0004	Newman	Chris	555-4990	Debate			$5	$60

However, as you can see, this arrangement could cause lots of problems. Many students might belong in more than three clubs, and this database can't handle that situation without the programmer going in and adding a new field. Also notice that many students don't belong to the maximum number of clubs, so the database is wasting a great deal of space. This really wouldn't help our searching criteria either; we would have to check all three club fields to extract the members of the chess club. By using only one club field with a single value for each record, we can place the database in first normal form:

Student ID	Last Name	First Name	Phone	Club	Monthly Dues	Annual Dues
0001	Jones	Sandra	555-5555	Chess	$10	$120
0001	Jones	Sandra	555-5555	Drama	$10	$120
0001	Jones	Sandra	555-5555	Debate	$5	$60
0002	Smith	Frank	555-9010	Tennis	$5	$60
0002	Smith	Frank	555-9010	Chess	$10	$120
0003	Garcia	Stephanie	555-7363	Tennis	$5	$60
0003	Garcia	Stephanie	555-7363	Ski Club	$5	$60
0004	Newman	Chris	555-4990	Debate	$5	$60

In summary then, for a database to be in first normal form, it must meet these conditions:

- All fields must be atomic.
- Fields should not store a list of values.
- Columns should not be repeated in a table.

Second Normal Form

While we have improved the situation, this table design is far from optimal. You might notice that we are wasting a lot of space with repeated data. The Last Name, First Name, and Phone Number fields are entered for every record, which is not necessary or efficient. It would make more sense to split the database into two tables, one that contained student information and another that contained the clubs each student belonged to. The two tables could then be related by the StudentID field.

This brings us to the concept of *second normal form*. In second normal form, all nonprimary key fields in each table are directly dependent on the primary key. Data that is not directly dependent on the primary key should be moved to a separate table.

Chapter 10: Database Design

In our example, the most sensible arrangement would be to first create a Students table that tracked StudentID, last and first names, and phone number. The table would look like this:

StudentID	Last Name	First Name	Phone
0001	Jones	Sandra	555-5555
0002	Smith	Frank	555-9010
0003	Garcia	Stephanie	555-7363
0004	Newman	Chris	555-4990

The primary key in this table is StudentID. Each field that we have put in the table, Last Name, First Name, and Phone Number, is completely dependent on the primary key—which specifies who the student is. Another way to look at this is that for each student ID there is one and only one last name, first name, and phone number.

The Clubs table will contain all the clubs each student belongs to. To relate the two tables, we'll use the primary key from the Students table, StudentID, which will be the foreign key for the Clubs table. The primary key for this table would be the StudentID + Club fields. The Clubs table would look like this:

StudentID	Club	Monthly Dues	Annual Dues
0001	Chess	$10	$120
0001	Debate	$10	$120
0001	Drama	$5	$60
0002	Chess	$5	$60
0002	Tennis	$10	$120
0003	Ski Club	$5	$60
0003	Tennis	$5	$60
0004	Debate	$5	$60

The database is now in second normal form. To summarize, for a database to be in second normal form, each table should only contain data that is directly related to the primary key. Fields that are only indirectly related should be placed in a separate table.

Third Normal Form

You'll notice that the Clubs table contains the monthly and annual dues required for each club. Storing the data in this manner is a waste of space because we can derive the annual dues from the monthly dues with a simple calculation. Also, whenever the monthly dues change, we would have to go into the Annual Dues field and update the value in the table.

This brings us to the concept of *third normal form*. In third normal form, all nonkey fields must be independent of one another. This means that a field that contains data derived or calculated from other nonkey fields in the table is kept out of the table. Instead, the calculation is done at runtime. The calculated data can be displayed on forms or reports as necessary, without wasting space in the table and having to go in and write to the database every time the calculation changes.

It makes more sense to calculate the Annual Dues at runtime or when displaying a report. The Annual Dues field should be removed from the Clubs table, so the Clubs table would then look like this:

StudentID	Club	Monthly Dues
0001	Chess	$10
0001	Debate	$10
0001	Drama	$5
0002	Chess	$5
0002	Tennis	$10
0003	Ski Club	$5
0003	Tennis	$5
0004	Debate	$5

Third normal form is the easiest type of normalization to implement. Just remember one simple fact: If a field is derived from data in another field, leave it out of the database. Calculate the value at runtime for display on a form or generate the value in a report.

Here is a summary of normalization:

- *First normal form*   Never allow a single field to contain a listing of values, and never create repeating fields.

- *Second normal form*   Every nonkey field depends on the primary key, and the database is in first normal form.

Chapter 10: Database Design

- *Third normal form*   Each nonkey field in the table is independent of the other nonkey fields. Never create a field whose value can be calculated from the values stored in the other fields. A table should be in second normal form before it can be in third normal form.

There are higher levels of normalization; however, third normal form is adequate for most database designs.

Denormalizing a Database

While you should use the first three forms of normalization when designing most databases, there are occasions when normalization is not the best design approach. Let's return to our example of the Students and Clubs tables. To locate the clubs for a particular student, we have to look up the student record and then retrieve the clubs for that student from the Clubs table. If our data set is particularly large, this may end up being a slow process. On an inadequate computer system the delay of such a search operation may outweigh the benefits achieved by normalization. In this case, it might be easier to simply use first normal form, where all the records are centrally located in one table.

Another situation where normalization may not be the best approach involves the use of calculated fields. There could be a situation where you will need to design a report that can't be built in such a way as to perform the calculations you need when the report is generated. In this case, it would be easier to store the calculations in a table and simply have the report read those values. There also could be a situation in which the calculations slow down the report so much that it's more user-friendly to place the calculations in the database. Once this is done, the report will load much faster.

As a final example, consider the requirement of first normal form that we avoid repeating fields. If the number of repeating fields is always constant and is small, it may make more sense to keep the repeating fields in the table rather than splitting them off to another table or creating multiple records. For example, if we tracked multiple phone numbers for a client, it makes more sense to have three phone number fields, Phone1, Phone2, and Phone3 or Home_Phone, Work_Phone, and Mobile, rather than splitting the phone numbers off in a separate table. In any case, the decision to denormalize a database should not be taken lightly. If you decide to denormalize a database, keep the following in mind:

- You should have a strongly compelling reason for doing so. Generally normalization will increase the efficiency of a database.
- The reason for denormalizing should be carefully documented. This will prevent a new programmer from coming along and normalizing the database, which will probably be his or her first impulse.

Using the Visual Data Manager

Visual C++ does not allow you to create Access databases. This leaves the developer with two choices, either use Microsoft Access or use the Visual Data Manager that comes with Visual Basic as an add-in (see Figure 10-1). Since many developers will work with both Visual Basic and Visual C++, we will examine the Visual Data Manager here.

The advantage of using the Visual Data Manager is that you don't need to have MS Access installed in order to create an Access database. The first step is to create the database file, which is done by executing the following steps:

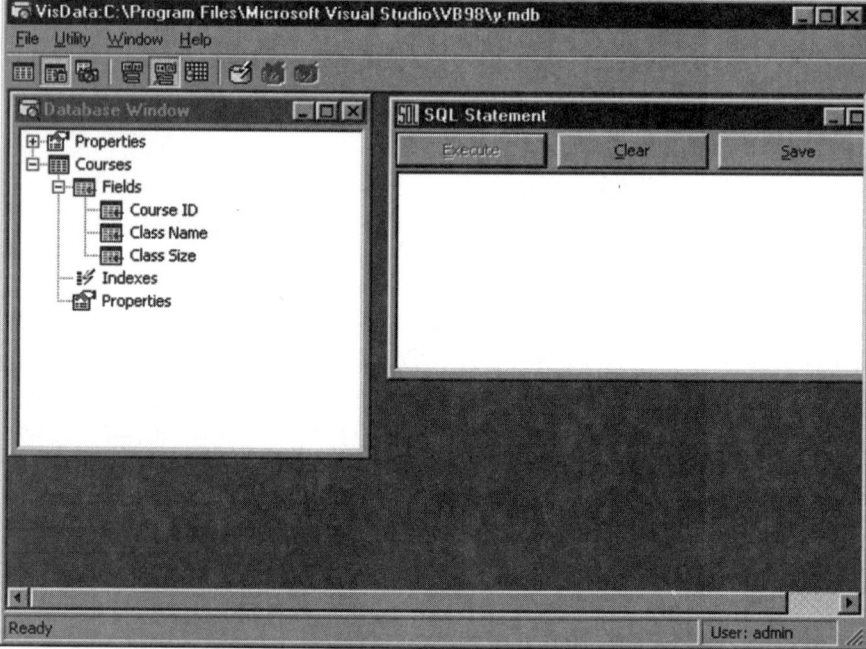

Figure 10-1
The Visual Data Manager.

Chapter 10: Database Design

- Select *New* from the *File* pull-down menu.
- Specify the type of database you want to create. We will select *Microsoft Access Version 7.0 MDB*.
- Type in the name you want to give the file, and click the *OK* button.

When the database is created, you'll see the database window open on the screen, with one object, labeled *Properties*. You can click open the *Properties* icon to view and edit certain properties of the database.

Adding a Table

To add a new table to the database:

1. Select the *Properties* icon in the database window.
2. Right-click and select *New Table*.

The New Table window will then appear on your screen (see Figure 10-2).

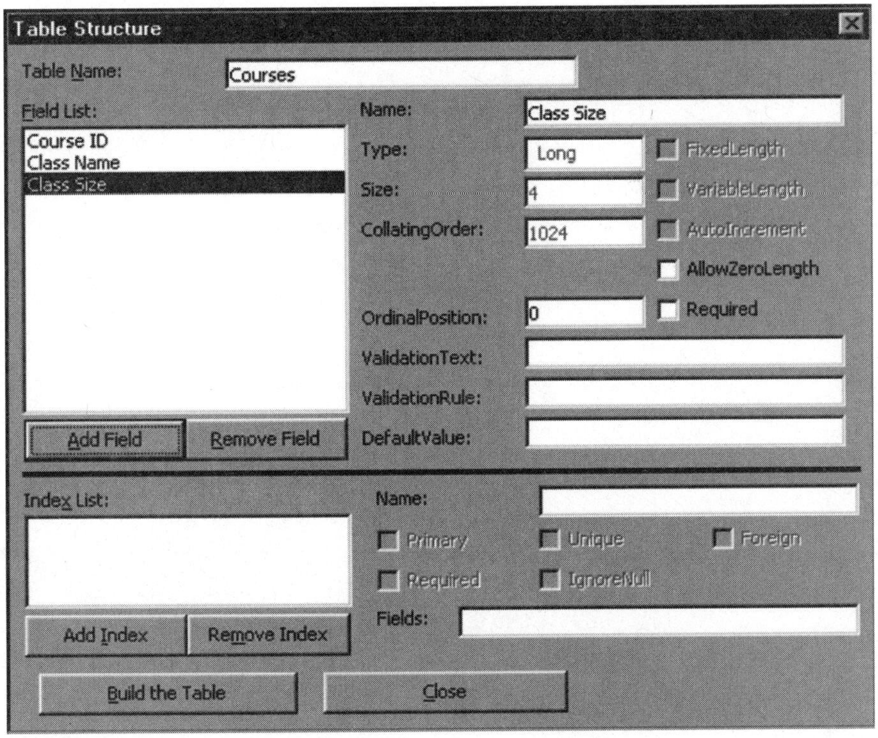

Figure 10-2
Creating a table.

Figure 10-3
The Add Field dialog.

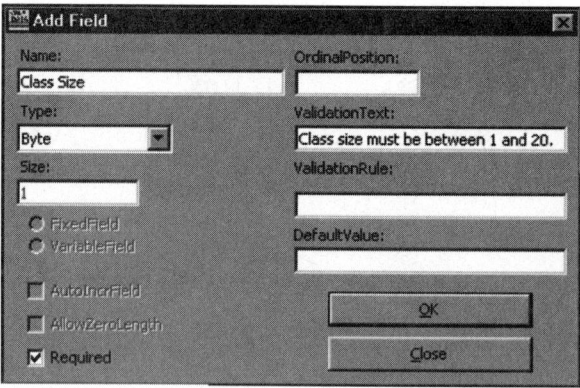

Adding Fields to the Table

Now we can add fields to the table. To add a field, follow these steps:

1. Click the *Add Field* button. A new dialog will open (see Figure 10-3).
2. Specify the field name, up to 64 characters in length.
3. Specify the data type for the field. This will be one of the Access data types that we discussed earlier.
4. Specify field size, if appropriate.
5. If you will allow zero-length or null data for this field, click the *Allow Zero Length* box.
6. If this field will be required, click the *Required* box.
7. Specify the ordinal position, if desired. If you don't, Access will assign ordinal position based on the order in which the fields are added to the database.
8. Specify the validation rule and validation text for this field.
9. Enter a default value.
10. Click the *OK* button.

Once the fields have been added to the table, you can define one or more indexes for the table. This is done by clicking the *Add Index* button. The Add Index To dialog box will open, as shown in Figure 10-4. You can specify if the index is a primary index, if the index will require unique values, or if it will allow null values. Select the fields you want to include in the index from the Available Fields list. You must also specify a name for the index.

Chapter 10: Database Design

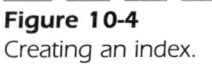
Figure 10-4
Creating an index.

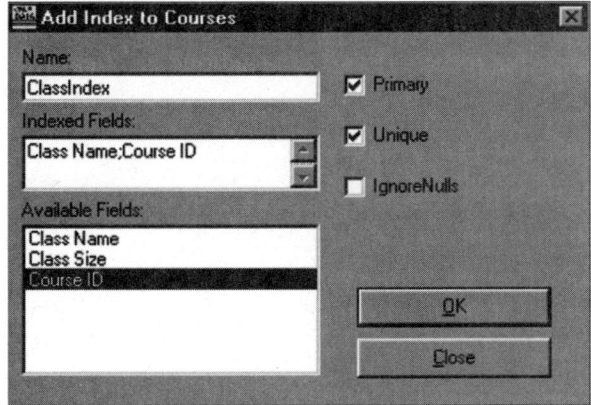

Repeat each of these steps as necessary to create your tables and fields. The Visual Data Manager also provides facilities for building and saving SQL statements and viewing/editing the data in your tables. We will be doing these tasks with C++.

CHAPTER 11

Data Access

Introduction

Almost any type of program you develop with C++ will need to access stored data. This is true for the entire range of applications, from a business database front end to a scientific or graphics program. While the applications you create with the MFC App Wizard will come with some file-saving capabilities built in, this is not adequate for many applications. Specifically our concern here will be with applications that use some form of structured data access. These include flat files and databases.

In the first part of this chapter, we will tackle the use of flat files. A *flat file* is a regular text or binary file that is not a part of a relational database. We will review the older methods of file access used in the C language such as `fprintf` and file pointers. Next, we will consider the `fstream` class, which makes the handling of files in C++ very simple.

In the second part of this chapter, we will take a look at using Visual C++ to manage relational databases. In this section we will consider the database technologies that can be used such as OLE DB and ADO. We will also consider the use of SQL and the issues that may come up when working in an environment with multiple users.

Flat Files

Visual C++ allows the programmer to work with flat files, which, as mentioned, are simply nondatabase files. A flat file is "flat" because it has no relationships within the file or with other files in the way that a relational database like Microsoft Access does. A flat file can be just about anything, from a simple text file to an image. In this chapter, we will focus mainly on using C++ to work with files that have some type of structure, which might include numerical data and text. There are two ways that you can work with these types of files in C++:

- By using the older C functions such as `fscanf` and `fprintf`.
- By using the `fstream` class.

We will briefly consider the use of the old C file routines and then take a look at the `fstream` class, which is the preferred method.

Chapter 11: Data Access

Basic File I/O Using C

Reading from and writing to files in the C language can be done with a file pointer. A *file pointer* is a pointer variable of type FILE that you can use to open, read from, and write to files. The basic file I/O routines can be used in a Visual C++ program by including the header file *<stdio.h>* in your program. You can declare a file pointer just like any other variable, as shown here:

```
FILE *fp; //fp is a file pointer
```

To open a file, we use the fopen function. The syntax of the fopen function is as follows:

```
FILE *fopen(const char *filename, const char *mode);
```

This function returns a pointer of type FILE. You can use the mode parameter to specify the type of access that will be allowed for the file; for example, you can open it for reading or writing. The mode is passed as a character string, which must be one of the following:

Mode	Definition
"r"	Open a text file for reading.
"w"	Create a text file for writing.
"a"	Append to a text file.
"rb"	Open a binary file for reading.
"wb"	Create a binary file for writing.
"ab"	Append to a binary file.
"r+"	Open a text file for read-and-write access.
"w+"	Create a text file for read-and-write access.
"a+"	Open a text file for read or append.
"rb+"	Open a binary file for read or append.
"wb+"	Create a binary file for read-and-write access.
"ab+"	Open a binary file for read access and append.

To create a new file named *mydata.dat*, we could use the following code:

```
FILE *fp;

fp = fopen("mydata.dat", "w");
```

The `fopen` function can be used to ensure that the file opened successfully. If a file cannot be opened, `fopen` will return a NULL pointer. We can test this condition in an `if` statement:

```
FILE *fp;

fp = fopen("mydata.dat", "w");

if(fp == NULL)
{
    messagebox("ERROR: CANNOT OPEN FILE", "ERROR", MB_OK);
    return;
}
```

This example attempts to open the file, and then tests to see if `fopen` was successful. If not, an error message is displayed to the user and we exit the function. When including path information, we need to use two backslashes when calling `fopen`, as we illustrate here:

```
FILE *fp;

fp = fopen("C:\\DataDir\\mydata.dat", "w");
```

This is because C/C++ uses the backslash character to indicate a command sequence or special characters, such as the end line character, which is represented by \n. The double backslash tells the compiler that this is a directory path. We can use string variables to pass the file information:

```
CString filename, mode;
FILE *fp;

filename = "C:\\DataDir\\mydata.dat";
mode = "r";

fp = fopen(filename,mode);
```

Once we have the file open, we can read from or write to the file, depending on which mode we used. We are primarily concerned with

Chapter 11: Data Access

structured or formatted files, and the easiest way to work with such a file is to use the `fprintf` function. The syntax of `fprintf` is as follows:

```
int fprintf(FILE *fp, const char *format,...);
```

The format string includes both text you want to write to the file as well as a list of format specifiers that you want C++ to apply to the data contained in any variables that you will write to the file. For example, if we want to add the following string to a file:

```
Hello it is November 2 The Temperature is 34
```

we could use the following code:

```
CString Month;
FILE *MyFilePointer;
short day, temp;

Month = "November";
day = 2;
temp = 34;

MyFilePointer = fopen("C:\\MyDir\\Temps.txt", "w");

if(MyFilePointer != NULL)
    fprintf(MyFilePointer, "Hello it is %s %d The Temperature is %d",
Month, day, temp);
```

From this example you can see that we pass the format string with any text we want to write to the file and insert format specifiers where we want each variable to print. After we terminate the format string with a double quote and comma, we include a comma-delimited list of variables in the proper order.

The following list includes the valid format specifiers that can be used with `fprintf`:

Code	Definition
%c	Single character or variable of type `char`
%d	Signed decimal integer
%i	Signed decimal integer
%e	Floating point, scientific notation, lowercase e
%E	Floating point, scientific notation, uppercase E
%f	Decimal floating point

Code	Definition
%g	Uses the shorter of %e or %f
%G	Uses the shorter of %E or %f
%o	Unsigned octal
%s	Character string
%u	Unsigned integer
%x	Unsigned hex
%X	Unsigned hex, uppercase
%p	Pointer
%n	Pointer to an integer, with number of characters written so far
%%	Prints a % character

We close a file using the `fclose` function, which takes a file pointer as its single argument:

```
fclose(fp);
```

In the following program, we will create a file and use the `fprintf` function to write a series of student names and test scores. The data is stored in a structure with the following definition:

```
struct Student
{
    CString Name;
    int score;
};
```

The scores are stored in an array of these structures:

```
bconst int MAX= 5;
Student TheClass[MAX];
```

Here we open the file and write the array elements to it using a `for` loop:

```
FileName = "C:\\TestScores.Dat";
    //open the file
    fp = fopen(FileName, "w");

    //make sure it's not null
```

Chapter 11: Data Access

```
        if( fp != NULL)
        {
            //if not null, write the data
            for(int i=0; i < MAX; i++)
            {
                fprintf(fp,"Student : %s %c",
TheClass[i].Name,newline);
                fprintf(fp, "Score : %d %c",
TheClass[i].score,newline);
                fprintf(fp, " %c", newline);
            }//next i
            //close the file

            fclose(fp);

}//end if fp != NULL
```

To read from a file, we can use the `fscanf` function. The syntax is as follows:

```
int fscanf(FILE *fp, const char *format,...);
```

If you understand `fprintf`, you will have no problem working with `fscanf`. It works in pretty much the same way, except that we are reading from a file. The function returns the number of arguments that were assigned values from the file. If the return value is `EOF`, this means that the end of the file was reached and the operation could not be completed. The format specifiers are the same as `printf`, except you can use `%[]` to scan for a set of characters. The format specifiers are matched left to right with the arguments you pass. The `fscanf` function will skip over white-space characters.

The arguments you pass to `fscanf` must be addresses. Therefore, you can either pass a pointer or use the address of operator `&`. For example, we can read in two integers with the following:

```
int total, *ave;
fscanf(fp,"%d%d", &total, ave);
```

If we are reading from a comma-delimited file, we must read in the commas as well. We can use the character combination `%*` to tell `fscanf` to skip over a character. For example, to read the following from a file:

```
820, 17
```

we can use the following:

```
int total, average;

fscanf(fp, "%d%*c%d", &total, &average);
```

With `fprintf` and `fscanf`, we have the tools we need for file I/O. However, C++ provides a class known as `fstream`, which we can use for very easy file access. We consider `fstream` in the next section.

Using `fstream` for File I/O

C++ provides an easier and more flexible means that can be used to read and write to files. This is done with the `fstream` class, which works in much the same way as `iostream` (`iostream` can be used for output to the screen in a console application). The `fstream` class works by using overloaded operators to write to and read from files. To use the `fstream` class, include *fstream.h* in any project files that use it:

```
#include <fstream.h>
```

Opening a File with `fstream`

When using `fstream`, a file is opened by a call to the `open` function. This function has the following syntax:

```
void fstream::open(const char *filename, openmode mode);
```

where `mode` is one of the following:

```
ios::app        //appends output to the end of a file
ios::ate        //causes a seek to the end of file when opened
ios::binary     //opens a binary file for I/O operations
ios::in         //opens a text file for input or reading
ios::out        //opens a text file for output or writing
ios::trunc      //destroys the contents of a file and sets it to zero
                length
```

These values can be combined together with a logical OR operation. In the following example, we open a file for reading named *namelist.txt*:

```
CString myfile;
fstream fp;

myfile = "C:\\namelist.txt";

fp.open(myfile, ios::in);
```

In the next example, we open the same text file so we can write to the file:

Chapter 11: Data Access

```
CString myfile;
fstream fp;

myfile = "C:\\namelist.txt";

fp.open(myfile, ios::out);
```

To read or write to a binary file named *myimage.dat*, we can open the file in binary mode:

```
CString myfile;
fstream fp;

myfile = "C:\\myimage.dat";

fp.open(myfile, ios::binary);
```

We can test the `fstream` object to see if the file was opened successfully by using the `good` member function. This function returns an `int` and has the following syntax:

```
int good();
```

We can use the result in an `if` statement. For example, we can display a message to the user and exit the current function if the file could not be opened:

```
if(!myfile.good())
{
   MessageBox(NULL, "Can't Open.", "Open File", MB_OK);
   return(false);
}
```

Alternatively, we could only work with the file if it opened correctly:

```
if(myfile.good())
{
   //code to process the file here
   ...
   return(true);
}
```

Closing a File with `fstream`

To close a file with an `fstream` object, simply use the `close()` member function. This function takes no parameters. The following example illustrates how to use the `close()` function:

Part 2: Designing Visual C++ Software

```
#include <fstream.h>
...
fstream FilePointer;

FilePointer.open("C:\\Nums\\Data.TXT", ios::out);

//code to write file
...

//close the file
FilePointer.close();
```

Reading from `fstream`

To read data from a file with an `fstream` object, we use the overloaded `>>` operator. For example, we can read three integers from a file with the following code:

```
int *x, *y, *z;

fstream myfile;

myfile.open("C:\\mydat.txt", ios::in);

if(!myfile.good())
{
   MessageBox(NULL, "Can't Open.", "Open File", MB_OK);
   return(false);
}

myfile > *x;
myfile > *y;
myfile > *z;
```

In the next example, suppose we had the following data file:

```
11      2       29
4       6       90
88      31      7721
1       0       0
765     22      100
```

We can read the file into an array by using the `>>` operator:

```
#include <fstream.h>
...
CString filename;
fstream myfile;
short mydata[5][3];

filename = "C:\\DataDir\\Numbers.dat";
```

Chapter 11: Data Access

```
myfile.open(filename, ios::in);

if(!myfile.good())
{
   MessageBox(NULL, "Can't Open.", "Open File", MB_OK);
   return(false);
for(int i = 0; i < 5; i++)
   for(int j = 0; j < 3; j++)
      myfile > mydata[I][j];
```

Writing a File with `fstream`

To write data to a file with an `fstream` object, simply use the overloaded `<<` operator. You can specify the number of spaces for each item written to the file by using the `setw` operator. For example, suppose that we wanted to write the contents of an array to a file, including the number of rows and columns in the array. We can use the following code:

```
#include <fstream.h>
#define MAX 100
...

bool SaveFile(CString FileName, int myarray[][MAX], int rows, int cols)
{

   int k,l;
   fstream myfile;
   char newline = '\n';
myfile.open(FileName, ios::out);

if(!myfile.good())
{
    messagebox(NULL,"Cannot Open File", "SaveFile", MB_OK);
    return(false);
}

//write number of the rows and columns
myfile << rows; //write rows
myfile << setw(12) << cols; // add some space before next variable, write cols
myfile << newline; //add a new line before writing array data

//write the array
for(k=0; k < rows; k++)
{
   for(l=0; l < cols; l++)
   {
      myfile << setw(12) << myarray[k][l];
   }
   //move to a new line
   myfile << newline;
}
```

```
//close the file, return success
myfile.close();

return(true);

}//end function save file
```

When writing floating-point variables or values of type `double`, we can use the `setprecision` member to specify the number of decimal places to write in the file. This can be used in combination with the `setw` operator:

```
fstream myfile;
double max, min;

...

myfile << setprecision(14) << max;
myfile << setprecision(14) << setw(30) << min;
```

To work with scientific notation, set the `scientific` flag. Flags can be set with the `setiosflags` member function.

Working with Text Strings

We can also use the `fstream` class to work with text strings. In this example, we write name and Social Security numbers for an array of employees:

```
#include <fstream.h>
#define MAX 100

struct Person
{
   char first[10];
   char last[20];
   char SSN[11];
}
...

fstream myfile;
Person employees[MAX];
char newline = '\n';

//code to load employees data
...

myfile.open("C:\\textdata.txt", ios::out);
//write the data
for(int i =0; i < 10; i++)
{
```

Chapter 11: Data Access

```
        myfile << employees[i].first << newline;
        myfile << employees[i].last << newline;
        myfile << employees[i].SSN << newline;
        myfile << newline;
}

myfile.close();
```

This example produces a text file like the following:

John
Jones
999-99-9999

Fred
Smith
999-99-9999

Mary
Jones
999-99-9999

Susie
Smith
999-99-9999

John
Garcia
999-99-9999

Joe
Martinez
999-99-9999

Nancy
Barnes
999-99-9999

We will explore reading strings from a text file in the next example.

Example: Programming with Flat Files

In this example we will illustrate how to use classes in combination with data read from a file using `fstream`. Our example will be a simple bank simulator. The program will run through the day at the bank, with customers coming in to make deposits and withdrawals. The program was created with the MFC App Wizard and is a dialog-based application.

The bank customers will be represented by a `customer` class. There will be an array of these class objects, with each array element representing one customer. The class definition is rather simple and is shown here:

```
//File Customers.h
//Description : Defines customer class

#define ASIZE 5
#define MAXSIZE 100
#define DEPOSIT -1
#define WITHDRAWAL 0

class customer
{

public:

    float balance;
    CString name;
    CString account_number;
    bool inbank;
    int transactiontype;    //DEPOSIT or WITHDRAWAL
    float tamount;    //amount of current transaction
    customer() { balance=0; inbank=false;}
    customer() {}

    bool withdrawl();
    void deposit();
    void arrive();
    void leave();
    void reset_amount(); //initializes transaction amount to zero

};//end class customer

bool customer::withdrawl()
{

    float result=0;

    result = this->balance - this->tamount;

    if(result < 0)
        return(false);
    else
    {
        this->balance = result;
        return(true);
    }

}//end withdrawl

void customer::deposit()
{

    this->balance += this->tamount;
```

Chapter 11: Data Access

```
        return;
}
void customer::arrive()
{
        this->inbank = true;

        return;

}
void customer::leave()
{
        this->inbank = false;

        return;

}

void customer::reset_amount()
{
        this->tamount = 0;
}

customer mylist[MAXSIZE];
```

Each `customer` object has member variables to track the customer name, balance, and account number. You will also notice a member variable named `inbank` of type `bool`. This true/false variable will be set to true if the customer is in the bank and to false otherwise. There are also member functions to handle a deposit or withdrawal, as well as functions that can be used to add or remove customers from the bank when they arrive or leave. An array of these objects named `mylist` is declared at the bottom.

The data for the customer list is stored in a text file. The file has a structure similar to the following, where we show just a few customers:

70
John Smith
10201
550.55

Jane Dolanski
00000
21900

Bob Jones
00001
14550

The first element in the file is the number of customers that are actually stored in the file. Following this number you will see the actual customer list. The customer's name is listed, followed by his or her bank account number and the balance in the account. The first step we need to take when running this program is to load the data from the file into our `mylist` array. This is done with the regular C++ function `ReadCustomers`, which we have included in the dialog box source code file:

```
void ReadCustomers(CString FileName, int *numcustomers)
{
    CString temp;
    fstream bankfile;
    char buffer[30];
    float *amount;

    bankfile.open(FileName, ios::in);

    if(!bankfile.good())
    {
        MessageBox(NULL,"ERROR OPENING FILE", "ERROR", MB_OK);
        return;
    }

    //read the number of bank accounts
    bankfile > *numcustomers;

    //read in the data
    for(int i=0; i<*numcustomers; i++)
    {
    //read in the first name
    bankfile.getline(buffer,100);
    mylist[i].name = buffer;

    //read in the last name
    bankfile.getline(buffer,100);
    mylist[i].name = mylist[i].name + " " + buffer;

    //read the account number
    bankfile.getline(buffer,6);
    mylist[i].account_number = buffer;

    //read in the balance
    bankfile > *amount;
    mylist[i].balance = *amount;

    //skip blank line
    bankfile.getline(buffer,2);

    }//end for loop

    //close the file

    bankfile.close();
```

Chapter 11: Data Access

```
    return;
}
```

The first item of business in this function is to declare the local variables we will need and open the file:

```
fstream bankfile;
char buffer[30];
float *amount;

bankfile.open(FileName, ios::in);

if(!bankfile.good())
{
    MessageBox(NULL,"ERROR OPENING FILE", "ERROR", MB_OK);
    return;
}
```

We will need an `fstream` object to work with the file, so we declared the `bankfile` variable. We will also use two temporary variables to read from the file, which we have named `buffer` and `amount`. The `buffer` array will be used to read in text strings, while the float pointer `amount` will be used to read in each balance. We open the file with the file name passed to the function in the `CString` variable `FileName`, and we specify that we are reading from the file by passing `ios::in` for the file mode.

Once the file is opened successfully, we read in the number of customers stored in the file. This is placed in the `numcustomers` pointer, which will be used later to set the maximum number of iterations on the `for` loop used to read the data:

```
//read the number of bank accounts
bankfile > *numcustomers;
```

Next, we use the `for` loop to read in the data from the file. Pay special attention to the next couple of lines, which are used to read in the name of the customer:

```
//read in the first name
bankfile.getline(buffer,100);
mylist[i].name = buffer;

//read in the last name
bankfile.getline(buffer,100);
mylist[i].name = mylist[i].name + " " + buffer;
```

To read a text string from a file, we use the `getline` function. The syntax of `getline` is as follows:

```
istream &getline(char *buf, streamsize num);
```

This is a member function of the `fstream` class. We use the `buffer` variable, which is an array of `char`s, to read in the string. The `getline` function reads to the next white space character, which in this case will be the blank space in between the first and last name. When we read in the last name, we concatenate it to the first name that we read in earlier. Notice that the `name` member variable of the customer class is of type `CString`, so we can use the overloaded + operator to concatenate the strings. If a white space character is not encountered, the `getline` function will read until num-1 characters have been read.

We can also call `getline` with the following syntax:

```
istream &getline(char *buf, streamsize num, char delim);
```

where `delim` is the character you want to use to stop the reading process. In this case, `getline` will read until either `delim` is encountered or num-1 characters are read in. To read in an entire line of text, you could set `delim` to be the end-of-line character.

Remember that `getline` reads num-1 characters. Since our account number has five characters, to read in the account number, we need to set num = 6:

```
//read the account number
bankfile.getline(buffer,6);
mylist[i].account_number = buffer;
```

Since the `account_number` member variable is an array of type `CString`, we can use the overloaded operator = in place of the `strcpy` function to copy the contents of `buffer` into the `account_number` member variable.

Next, we read in the account balance and then skip the blank line that separates each customer:

```
//read in the balance
bankfile > *amount;
mylist[i].balance = *amount;

//skip blank line
bankfile.getline(buffer,2);
```

Remember that `getline` reads in num-1 characters. Since a blank line contains one character, the newline character, we pass 2 to `getline`. The function ends by closing the file, which is done by calling the `fstream` function `close()`:

Chapter 11: Data Access

```
//close the file
bankfile.close();
```

Once we have the data read from the file, we can run the simulation. The program consists of a single dialog box, with a button labeled *Run Simulation* (see Figure 11-1). The user can start the simulation by clicking here.

The code for this simple simulation is in the `OnButtonClick` event function for this button:

```
void CBankDlg::OnRun()
{
        //Function : OnRun
        //Runs the bank simulator

        //variables to track
        //simulated time
        short hours, mins;

        CString filename;
        //char anum[ASIZE];
        CString anum;
        int maxsize=0;
        int myrandomvar=0;

        filename = "customers.txt";
        //read the customer list
        ReadCustomers(filename,&maxsize);

        srand(100);
```

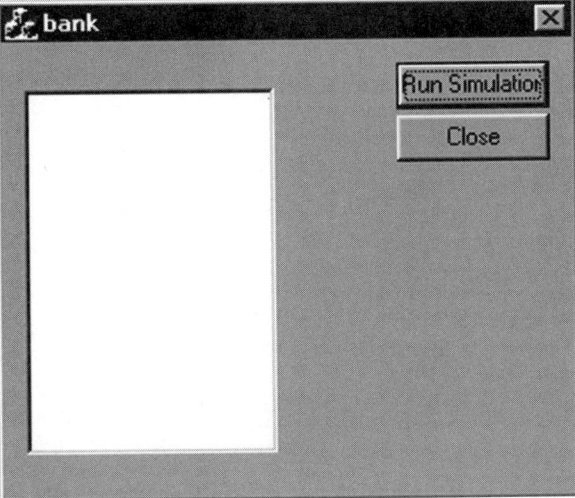

Figure 11-1
The Bank simulator.

```cpp
        //initialize bank time to 9AM
        hours = 9;
        mins = 0;

//run the simulation until 3 PM
    while(hours < 15)
    {

        //see if we should add a customer to the
        //line
    myrandomvar = rand(); //get a random number

        //adjust it
        myrandomvar = myrandomvar/1000;

        //if in defined range, customer enters
        //bank
        if(myrandomvar < MAXSIZE)
        {
            if(mylist[myrandomvar].inbank == false)
                {
                    mylist[myrandomvar].arrive();
                    if(myrandomvar < 4)
mylist[myrandomvar].transactiontype = DEPOSIT;
                    else

mylist[myrandomvar].transactiontype = WITHDRAWAL;
                    mylist[myrandomvar].tamount = (float)-
                    (myrandomvar*10);

m_acctlist.AddString(mylist[myrandomvar].account_number);

            }//end if mylist inbank = false

        }//end if random var in range

        //process first customer in line

        if(m_acctlist.GetCount() > 0)
        {
            m_acctlist.GetText(0,anum);

        //find customer in class array
        for(int l=0; l <maxsize; l++)
            {
            if(anum == mylist[l].account_number)
                {
                if(mylist[l].transactiontype == DEPOSIT)
                    mylist[l].deposit();
                else
                    mylist[l].withdrawl();
                break;
                }
            }//next l

    //remove customer from line
      m_acctlist.DeleteString(0);
      mylist[l].leave();
      mylist[l].reset_amount();
```

Chapter 11: Data Access

```
            }//end if get count > 0

            //increment minutes by ten

            mins += 10;

            //if we have gone 60 mins,
            //move to next hour
            if(mins > 59)
            {
                hours++; //hours = hours + 1
                mins = 0;
            }//end if mins > 59

        }//end while loop

        //report simulation completed
        MessageBox("FINISHED SIMULATION", "RUN", MB_OK);

        //save customer list
        WriteCustomers(maxsize);

}
```

Our main concern here is reading from and writing to text files, so we will briefly examine the code here. The first thing to notice is that we use a random-number generator to randomly select an element from the `mylist` customer array. First, we initialize or seed the random-number generator by calling the `srand()` function:

```
srand(100);
```

This function accepts an integer argument and can be used to initialize the random-number generator. Each time through the loop, we use the `rand()` function to generate a random number. Next, we adjust the value by dividing by 1000. This is because the numbers that are generated will have a large range, and we want a reasonable probability that the number generated will be within the range of our array:

```
myrandomvar = rand(); //get a random number

//adjust it
myrandomvar = myrandomvar/1000;
```

Next, we test to see if the random number falls within the valid range. If so, we use it to select an element from the `mylist` customer array. If that customer is not currently in the bank, we can have the customer enter by calling the `arrive` member function. We can test to see if the customer is in the bank by examining the `inbank` member variable, which is of type `bool`. If the random value generated was less than a certain value, we will allow a deposit. Next, we set the transaction amount based on the random number, and then add the customer's account number to a list box, which is used to maintain a list of customers waiting to see the teller. The list box is represented by the `m_acctlist` member variable, which is of type `CListBox`.

```
//if in defined range, customer enters
//bank
if(myrandomvar < MAXSIZE)
{

    if(mylist[myrandomvar].inbank == false)
    {
       mylist[myrandomvar].arrive();
       if(myrandomvar < 4)
         mylist[myrandomvar].transactiontype = DEPOSIT;
       else
         mylist[myrandomvar].transactiontype = WITHDRAWAL;
       mylist[myrandomvar].tamount = (float)(myrandomvar*10);

m_acctlist.AddString(mylist[myrandomvar].account_number);

}//end if mylist inbank = false
```

Our next task is to process the first customer in line. First, we test to see if any customers are waiting. This means that we need to find out how many customers are in the list box. We can use the `GetCount` member function of the list box control to find out this information. If there are customers in the list, we use the `GetText` function to retrieve the account number stored in the list box. `GetText` takes two parameters: the index of the item we want to retrieve from the list and a text string where we want that data stored. We place the account number in a string variable named anum. Next, we locate that customer in the `mylist` array and perform the appropriate transaction, using the member variables and functions. When done with that customer, we use the `DeleteString` list box function to remove the account number from the list box. `DeleteString` takes a single argument, the index of the item that you want removed from the list box. Since we are removing the first customer in line, we pass 0, because the index used in a list box is 0 based.

```
if(m_acctlist.GetCount() > 0)
   {

         m_acctlist.GetText(0,anum);

      //find customer in class array
      for(int l=0; l <maxsize; l++)
         {
            if(anum == mylist[l].account_number)
```

Chapter 11: Data Access

```
            {
            if(mylist[l].transactiontype == DEPOSIT)
                mylist[l].deposit();
            else
                mylist[l].withdrawal();
            break;
            }
        }//next l

    //remove customer from line
      m_acctlist.DeleteString(0);
      mylist[l].leave();
      mylist[l].reset_amount();

    }//end if get count > 0
```

We finish the while loop by incrementing our time variables. After the simulation is finished, we call the WriteCustomers function to write the contents of the array to a disk file. The code for WriteCustomers is listed here:

```
void WriteCustomers(int numcustomers)
{

    fstream bankfile;
    CString FileName;
    char newline = '\n';

    FileName = "OutFile.txt";
    bankfile.open(FileName, ios::out);

    if(!bankfile.good())
    {
        MessageBox(NULL,"Cannot Open File","WriteCustomers", MB_OK);
        return;
    }

    //save number of customers to file
    bankfile << numcustomers << newline;

    for(int i=0; i < numcustomers; i++)
    {
      bankfile << mylist[i].name << newline;
      bankfile << mylist[i].account_number << newline;
      bankfile << mylist[i].balance << newline;
      bankfile << newline;
    }

    //close the file
    bankfile.close();
    return;
}//end write customers
```

First, we save the number of customers to the file by writing the numcustomers variable. Next, we use a for loop to write the contents of the array to the file. Writing to text files with `fstream` is simple, you just use the overloaded << operator. Finally, we close the file by using the `fstream` `close()` function.

Working with Databases

Visual C++ version 6.0 is a big improvement over its predecessors when it comes to building database applications. This improvement has largely been achieved by the introduction of the ADO (ActiveX Data Objects) and OLE DB technologies, which provide an increased ease of use and power for the developer when creating database apps. OLE DB forms the base of this new technology. It is OLE DB that actually provides the interface or communication with the database through COM. ADO provides a wrapper for OLE DB, so you use ADO to access the underlying functions that OLE DB provides. You will see this when you use an ADO data control to connect to a database. While you can work directly with OLE DB, ADO makes it much easier to develop database applications.

When it comes to OLE DB technology, there are different categories that you need to be aware of. Two that are important are as follows:

- *Data Consumer*   A data consumer is a program or user that uses the information contained in the database.
- *Data Provider*   This is you, the developer. A data provider is a developer who creates an OLE DB provider by using the OLE DB software development kit (SDK).

When you create database apps, you will be working with OLE DB through using ADO controls and ADO objects. Included with these new technologies are the same types of data-bound controls found in Visual Basic. This means that it is easy to create database programs in Visual C++. Unfortunately, Visual C++ is still not as thorough and flexible with databases as Visual Basic. If you are strictly doing database programming, Visual Basic might be a better choice. However, the improvements that have been made make Visual C++ a more attractive choice than it has been in the past. If you have the Enterprise edition of Visual C++, you will be able to use the ADO Data-Bound Dialog Wizard to quickly create data-bound dialog boxes. In this chapter we will be investigating the techniques that can be used to manually create database applications.

When creating a database application in Visual C++, there is more than one route you can follow. One is to create a dialog-based application and insert the appropriate controls needed for database access. The second method is to have the App Wizard create an SDI or MDI database application for you. You can also create a database project. We will examine some simple dialog-based applications using the ADO data control. This will give us a good feel for database programming in general.

With the introduction of ADO and OLE DB, older data access technologies like DAO and ODBC have become less important. However, they are still in use, so we will take a brief look at these older types of data access as well.

A Brief Note on Database Options and File Support

If you create a database application with the MFC App Wizard, you will be presented with a few choices. The choice you make will depend on the level of database support you want, how detailed your design is at the time you're creating the new application, and how flexible you want to be in the future. The options you need to be aware of are as follows:

- *Header Files Only* If you choose this option, Visual C++ will create an application and include the header files required for database programming. You will be required to create your own database classes with the Class Wizard and write any code to interact with the database.

- *Database View without File Support* If you select this option, you can create an application that is limited to the specific data source that you use to build the application. The user will not be able to use your application to open and work with other files.

- *Database View with File Support* Selecting this option will create an application that will give users the most freedom. They will be able to work with the data source you specify when you create the application, and in addition they will be able to open and use external files. What they can do with those files will depend on how you design the program. Visual C++ will provide the basic support, but it will be up to you to design the user interface.

These options are only available if you create an SDI or MDI application. If you create a dialog-based application, the App Wizard will not ask you about database support. When you create a dialog-based application, you can use ActiveX controls to provide database support and design forms in much the same way that you would in Visual Basic. This is the method I prefer when creating database applications with Visual C++.

Programming with the ADO Data Control

Let's start our examination of database programming by taking a look at the ADO data control. This is an ActiveX control that you can add to your projects by using the Components and Controls Gallery. This is done by following the same steps for adding an ActiveX control that we explained in Chapter 9. When you add the control to your project, Visual C++ will create the appropriate classes for use in your code, and then you can use the Class Wizard to create a member variable for the control.

The ADO data control is used to establish and manage a connection to a database. The control will be found in the Registered ActiveX Controls folder, labeled *Microsoft ADO Data Control, version 6.0 (OLE DB)*, as shown in Figure 11-2. To actually provide the user interface to the data, you will need to add the appropriate bound controls. These include the following:

- *Microsoft Data Combo Control, version 6.0 (OLE DB)*   This control is a combo box or drop-down list that can be used to display data stored in a table. It can be used as a lookup list, which may grab data from another table and bind the selected value to a field in the original table. For example, if a user is ordering a product, the order form, which is bound to the Orders table, can use a Data Combo control to look up product ID numbers.

- *Microsoft Data Grid Control, version 6.0 (OLE DB)*   This control can be used to display the data in a table in grid format.

- *Microsoft Data List Control, version 6.0 (OLE DB)*   This is a list box, which can be bound to a field in a database.

When you insert each control, Visual C++ will create the appropriate classes that you will need to use the control. For example, we can add a Data List control (see Figure 11-3). Visual C++ will display the source code or implementation file and the header file that will be used to represent the control. You can figure out how to use the control by examining the methods and properties (member functions and variables) of the class used. Once these files are created, the control is available in the

Chapter 11: Data Access

Figure 11-2
Adding the OLE DB control.

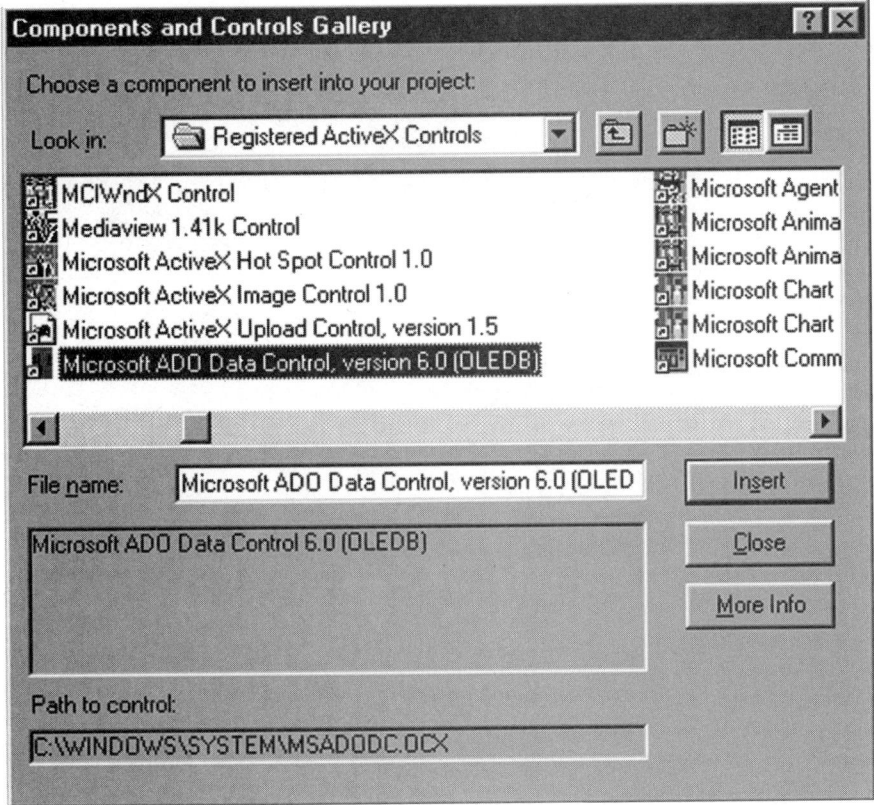

toolbox and can be added to your dialog boxes, as we have done with an ADO data control in Figure 11-4. With these controls, we have just about everything we need to build fully functional database front ends. Let's take a look at the ADO data control first.

The first step is to add the ADO data control (ADO DC) to a dialog box. We have created a new dialog-based project with the MFC App Wizard named *Biblio*. We will use the project to create a simple database interface using a Microsoft-created Access database, *Biblio.mdb*. This database contains a listing of authors, books, and publishing companies. Let's start out by displaying the authors in a Data Grid control.

Let's take a look at the properties of the ADO data control. You can view the properties of the ADO DC by right-clicking on the control and selecting Properties. Some of these are as follows:

- *ID* This is the control ID that will be used to identify the control. This ID will be used in the Class Wizard when you create a member

Figure 11-3
Confirming classes for the Data List control.

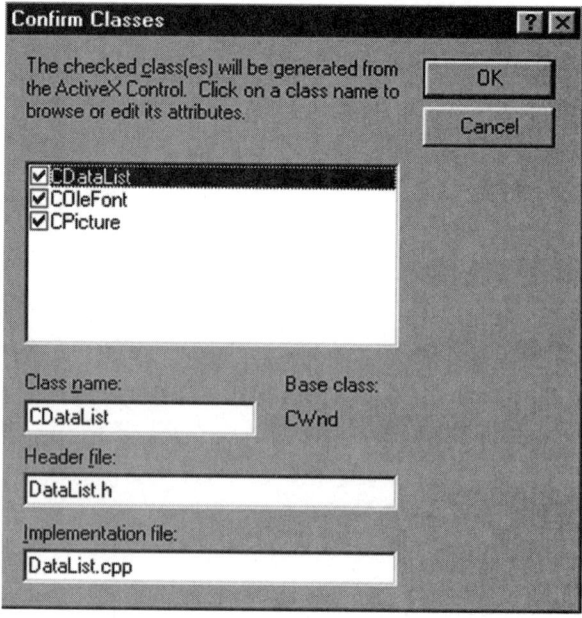

variable to represent the control in code. Give the ID property a meaningful name so that you know it represents an ADO DC and which database or table it is connected to. For example, for the ADO DC that we will use to connect to the *Bibio.mdb* file, we set the ID property to *IDC_ADODCBIBLIO*.

Figure 11-4
Adding the ADO DC to a dialog box.

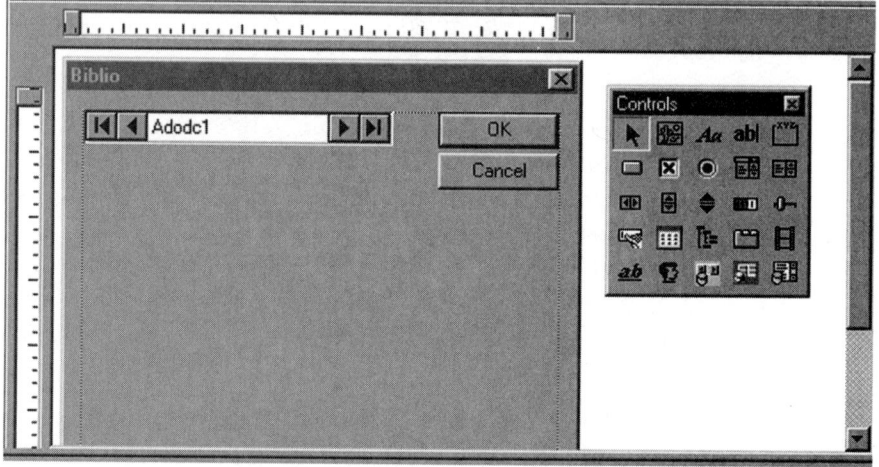

Chapter 11: Data Access

- *Caption* The Caption property is displayed to the user. Generally, you may want to set the Caption to a text string representing which table the ADO DC is connected to.

There are several tabs on the Properties dialog for the ADO DC. One important tab is the Control tab, which is used to specify the database connection used for the control (see Figure 11-5). There are three choices:

- Use Data Link File
- Use ODBC Data Source Name
- Use Connection String

For this example, select *Use Connection String*. When selecting this option, you need to click the *Build* button to create the connection string. This will open the Data Link Properties dialog box (see Figure 11-6). When building an Access front end, the easiest thing to do is use the Microsoft Jet Engine. You can do this by selecting Microsoft Jet 4.0 OLE DB Provider.

To select the database used, click on the *Connection* tab (see Figure 11-7). You can type in the name and path of the database or click the ellipsis button (...) to locate the database on your system. Select the *Biblio.mdb* file. If there is a user name and password required to log in to the database, you can enter that information here. Click the *Test Connection* button in the lower right corner to make sure that everything is in proper working order.

On the Advanced tab, you can specify certain behaviors for the database, such as setting the permissions or connection time out for the database. When done with the Data Link Properties dialog, select the *OK* button to save your settings. The next tab of interest on the ADO DC

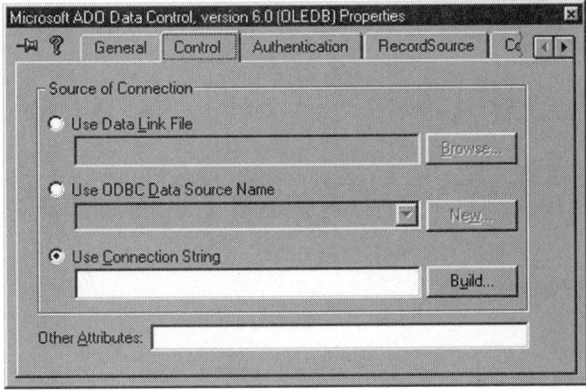

Figure 11-5
The ADO Data Control Properties dialog.

properties dialog is the Authentication tab. Again, here you can provide user name and password information if required.

The RecordSource tab is used to either select the table where you want to get your data or stored procedure, or to use an SQL statement. SQL statements can be entered in the Command Text (SQL) input box. Use the Command Type drop-down list to select the appropriate type of record source. In our case, we select *adCmdTable*, since we will simply open a table in the database. You will then see the Table or Stored Procedure Name drop-down list become enabled. Click this list open to select the appropriate table. We will select *Authors*.

Other tabs on the ADO DC properties dialog include Color, Font, and All. You can use these tabs to set display properties of the control, such as the font. The All tab can be used to view all of the properties of the control, in a similar way that the properties of a control are displayed in Visual Basic.

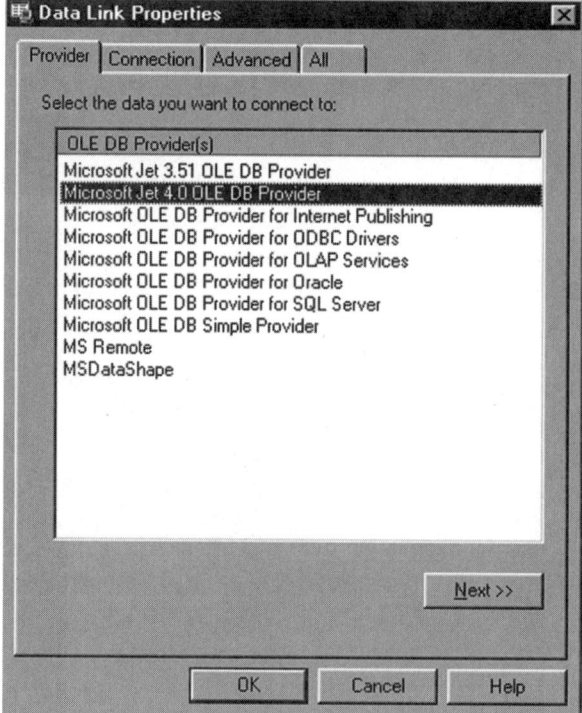

Figure 11-6
Setting the ADO connection.

Chapter 11: Data Access

Figure 11-7
Selecting the database.

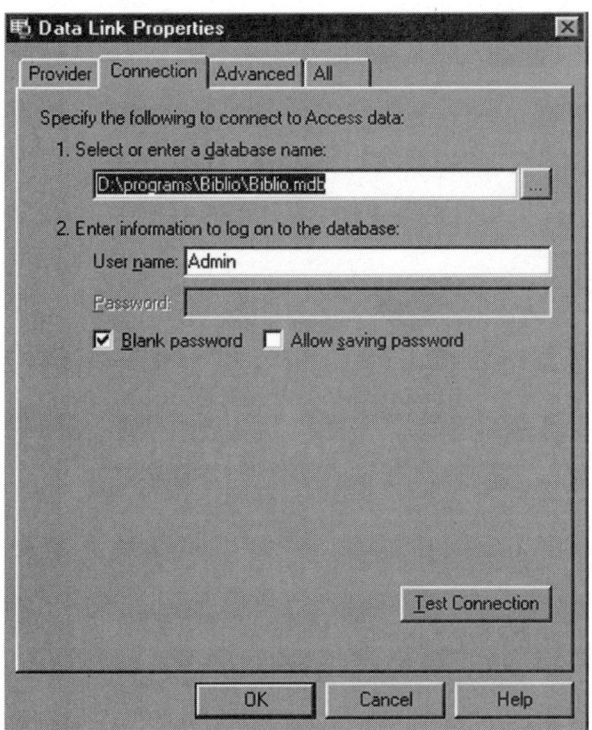

Connecting Data Bound Controls

The ADO DC provides us with a means to connect to the database. Now we need to display that data to the user. This is done with the data-bound controls provided by Microsoft. For example, we can add a grid to the dialog box in our Biblio project and connect it to the ADO DC that we created earlier. This will provide us with a ready-made means to display data to the user.

First, we add a Data Grid control to the surface of the dialog box (see Figure 11-8). To display data in a data-bound control, we need to set the Data Source property of the control. You can find the Data Source property on the All tab. We can display the Authors table that is connected to our ADO DC control by setting the Data Source property of the Data Grid to the ID of the ADO DC, which is IDC_ADODCBIBLIO. This will give us a functional program with access to the data, as shown in Figure 11-9.

Figure 11-8
Adding a data grid.

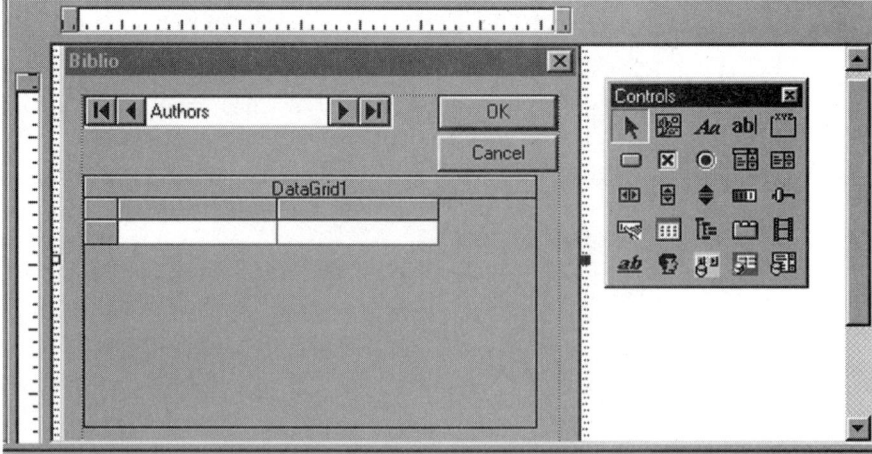

Figure 11-9
The Biblio program.

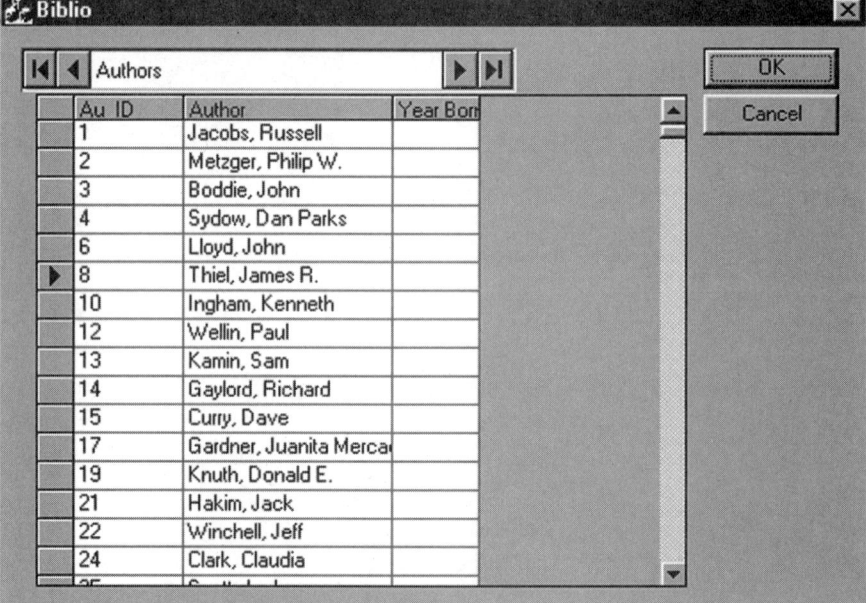

Programming the ADO Data Control in Code

While the simple application we just created displays the data from the Authors table, it doesn't do much in the way of functionality. To really

Chapter 11: Data Access

create a database application, we need to work with the controls in code. This will allow us to add new records, delete records, search, and more.

To illustrate how to work with the data control in code, we begin a new project named *Biblio2*. This project is also a dialog-based application; however, we are displaying the data with edit boxes, instead of by using a grid (see Figure 11-10). This method will display the records one at a time. Also notice that we have included a set of buttons on the bottom of the screen, which will allow the user to perform specific tasks such as adding a new record. If we wish to write code to perform these types of tasks, we will need to be familiar with the member functions of the ADO data control. We will also need a member variable to represent the control in code, so we create one of type CAdodc named m_Biblio2.

When you are programming a database, the key object you are working with is called the *recordset*. A recordset is exactly what the name says: it is a set of records. This can be a single table from the database, or it can be a subset of records created with an SQL statement. The recordset is an object that belongs to each ADO data control in your project, and you will access the recordset through the ADO data control. When you add the ADO data control to a Visual C++ project, it creates header files and source code files to represent the control. One of the files it creates is *recordset.h*. By examining the C_Recordset class, we can see the types of operations that can be performed on a recordset object:

```
// C_Recordset wrapper class

class C_Recordset : public COleDispatchDriver
{
public:
    C_Recordset() {}                    // Calls COleDispatchDriver
```

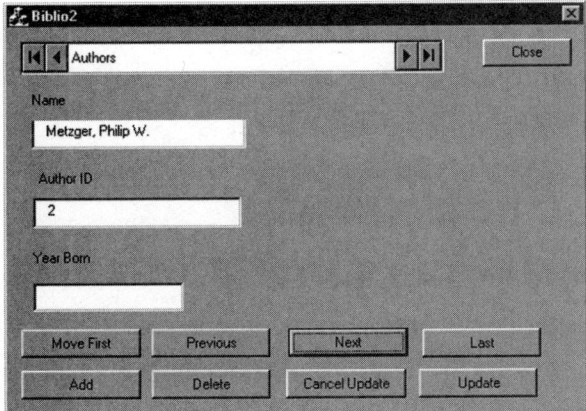

Figure 11-10
Displaying data one record at a time.

```
    default constructor
        C_Recordset(LPDISPATCH pDispatch) :
COleDispatchDriver(pDispatch) {}
        C_Recordset(const C_Recordset& dispatchSrc) :
COleDispatchDriver(dispatchSrc) {}

// Attributes
public:

// Operations
public:
        CProperties GetProperties();
        long GetAbsolutePosition();
        void SetAbsolutePosition(long nNewValue);
        void SetRefActiveConnection(LPDISPATCH newValue);
        void SetActiveConnection(const VARIANT& newValue);
        VARIANT GetActiveConnection();
        BOOL GetBof();
        VARIANT GetBookmark();
        void SetBookmark(const VARIANT& newValue);
        long GetCacheSize();
        void SetCacheSize(long nNewValue);
        long GetCursorType();
        void SetCursorType(long nNewValue);
        BOOL GetEof();
        CFields GetFields();
        long GetLockType();
        void SetLockType(long nNewValue);
        long GetMaxRecords();
        void SetMaxRecords(long nNewValue);
        long GetRecordCount();
        void SetRefSource(LPDISPATCH newValue);
        void SetSource(LPCTSTR lpszNewValue);
        VARIANT GetSource();
        void AddNew(const VARIANT& FieldList, const VARIANT& Values);
        void CancelUpdate();
        void Close();
        void Delete(long AffectRecords);
        VARIANT GetRows(long Rows, const VARIANT& Start, const VARIANT& Fields);
        void Move(long NumRecords, const VARIANT& Start);
        void MoveNext();
        void MovePrevious();
        void MoveFirst();
        void MoveLast();
        void Open(const VARIANT& Source, const VARIANT& ActiveConnection, long CursorType, long LockType, long Options);
        void Requery(long Options);
        void Update(const VARIANT& Fields, const VARIANT& Values);
        long GetAbsolutePage();
        void SetAbsolutePage(long nNewValue);
        long GetEditMode();
        VARIANT GetFilter();
        void SetFilter(const VARIANT& newValue);
        long GetPageCount();
        long GetPageSize();
        void SetPageSize(long nNewValue);
        CString GetSort();
        void SetSort(LPCTSTR lpszNewValue);
```

Chapter 11: Data Access

```
        long GetStatus();
        long GetState();
        void UpdateBatch(long AffectRecords);
        void CancelBatch(long AffectRecords);
        long GetCursorLocation();
        void SetCursorLocation(long nNewValue);
        C_Recordset NextRecordset(VARIANT* RecordsAffected);
        BOOL Supports(long CursorOptions);
        long GetMarshalOptions();
        void SetMarshalOptions(long nNewValue);
        void Find(LPCTSTR Criteria, long SkipRecords, long
SearchDirection, const VARIANT& Start);
        void Cancel();
        LPUNKNOWN GetDataSource();
        void SetRefDataSource(LPUNKNOWN newValue);
        void Save(LPCTSTR FileName, long PersistFormat);
        LPDISPATCH GetActiveCommand();
        void SetStayInSync(BOOL bNewValue);
        BOOL GetStayInSync();
        CString GetString(long StringFormat, long NumRows, LPCTSTR
ColumnDelimeter, LPCTSTR RowDelimeter, LPCTSTR NullExpr);
        CString GetDataMember();
        void SetDataMember(LPCTSTR lpszNewValue);
        long CompareBookmarks(const VARIANT& Bookmark1, const VARIANT&
Bookmark2);
        C_Recordset Clone(long LockType);
        void Resync(long AffectRecords, long ResyncValues);
};
```

For example, you will notice member functions that can be used to navigate the recordset:

```
void MoveNext();
void MovePrevious();
void MoveFirst();
void MoveLast();
```

To access the recordset through the ADO data control, you use the `GetRecordset()` ADO Data Control member function. This function has a return type of `C_Recordset`:

```
C_Recordset GetRecordset();
```

You will find this member function in the header file that Visual C++ created to represent the ADO data control, named *adodc.h*.

Recall that we created a member control variable to represent the ADO data control on our form named *m_Biblio2*. To move to the next record in the table, we call the `GetRecordset()` member function, which in turn can be used to access the member functions of the `C_Recordset` class. This means we can call the `MoveNext()` member function like this:

```
m_Biblio2.GetRecordset().MoveNext();
```

We can access the other member functions in a similar manner. We have given the buttons on the Biblio2 dialog box the following object IDs:

- `IDC_First`
- `IDC_Previous`
- `IDC_Next`
- `IDC_Last`
- `IDC_ADD`
- `IDC_Delete`
- `IDC_CancelUpdate`
- `IDC_Update`

For each button, we use the Class Wizard to create a member function to respond to a user click event (see Figure 11-11).

Once we have done this, we can add the appropriate code to the `On` member function for each button, using the `GetRecordset()` ADO data control member function in combination with the appropriate recordset method. One nice feature found in Visual C++ 6.0 not found in the ear-

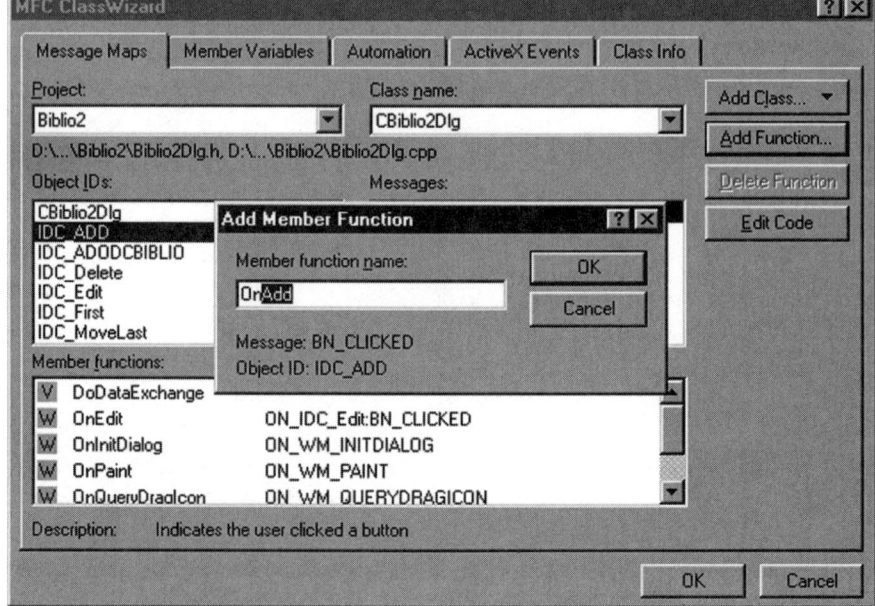

Figure 11-11
Adding a function to respond to a button click.

Chapter 11: Data Access

lier versions is that when we use the dot syntax when typing our code, the member functions for that object will be displayed in a drop-down list (see Figure 11-12), so we won't have to spend effort trying to remember what they are. Visual C++ will also display the function header for you when you type the opening parentheses for each function.

The code for each button is as follows:

```
void CBiblio2Dlg::OnAdd()
{
    // Add a new record
    m_Biblio2.GetRecordset().AddNew();
}

void CBiblio2Dlg::OnDelete()
{
    // Prompt for delete
    int result=0;

    result = MessageBox("Delete This Record?","DELETE",
MB_YESNOCANCEL);

    if(result == IDYES)
```

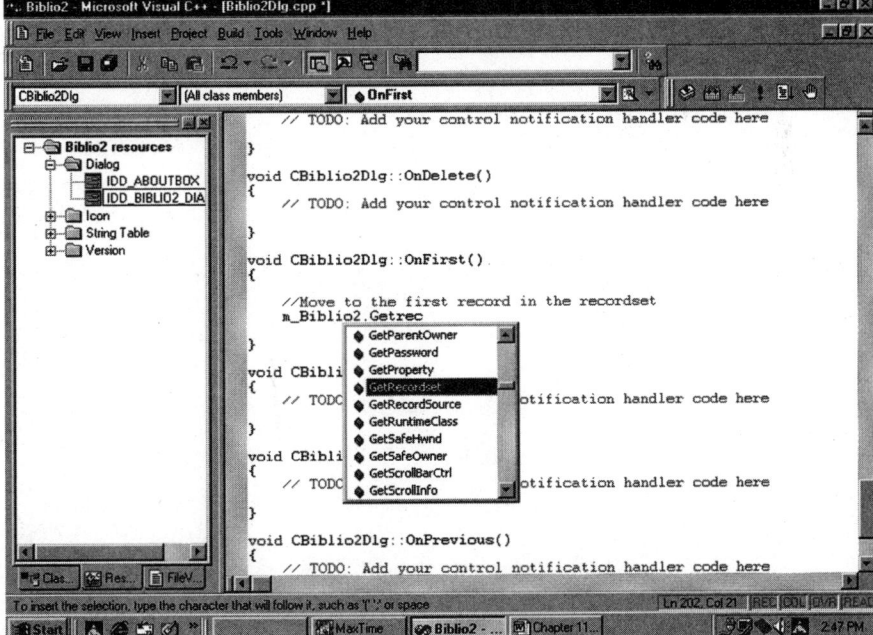

Figure 11-12
Accessing methods of the ADO data control.

```cpp
                m_Biblio2.GetRecordset().Delete;
}

void CBiblio2Dlg::OnFirst()
{
        //Move to the first record in the recordset
        m_Biblio2.GetRecordset().MoveFirst();
}

void CBiblio2Dlg::OnMoveLast()
{
        // Move to the last record
        m_Biblio2.GetRecordset().MoveLast();

        //test EOF condition, move to last
        //record if necessary
        if(m_Biblio2.GetRecordset().GetEof())
              m_Biblio2.GetRecordset().MoveLast();
}

void CBiblio2Dlg::OnNext()
{
        //Move to the next record
        m_Biblio2.GetRecordset().MoveNext();
}

void CBiblio2Dlg::OnPrevious()
{
        // Move to the previous record
        //Check for BOF condition, if true
        //move to first record

        m_Biblio2.GetRecordset().MovePrevious();

        if(m_Biblio2.GetRecordset().GetBof())
              m_Biblio2.GetRecordset().MoveFirst();
}
void CBiblio2Dlg::OnUpdate()
{
        // Save the record. Prompt the user first.
        int result=0;

         result = MessageBox("Save Record?","UPDATE", MB_YESNOCANCEL);

         if(result == IDYES)

                m_Biblio2.GetRecordset().Update();

}

void CBiblio2Dlg::OnCancelUpdate()
{
```

Chapter 11: Data Access

```
//Abort Update
m_Biblio2.GetRecordset().CancelUpdate();
}
```

Important ADO Data Control Events

If you want to build robust and professional database applications, you will have to familiarize yourself with the member functions of the ADO data control. This is because you will need to have your code respond to certain events, such as when the user moves off a record. For example, you might want to prompt the user before saving any changes. If you are familiar with the member functions of the ADO data control, you will know when and where to implement these types of actions. The functions we are interested in are the events of the control, which we find by examining the messages for the ADO data control in the Class Wizard. Note that you can see a short description of what each message means at the bottom of the Class Wizard when you select it in the Messages list.

To respond to the appropriate events, you will need to add a member function for each one using the Class Wizard. This is done by following the usual steps. For example, one important event is when the user reaches the end of the recordset. We can configure the behavior of the ADO data control by adding code to the `EndOfRecordset` member function. To do this, you would use the following steps:

1. Open the Class Wizard.
2. Select the object ID for the ADO data control you wish to program.
3. Choose *EndOfRecordset* from the Messages list.
4. Click the *Add Function* button.

The Class Wizard will then create a member function to respond to this event. Following is a list of events that are useful when building database applications with an ADO data control:

- `WillMove` This event fires just before the recordset moves to the next row.
- `MoveComplete` The `MoveComplete` event fires when the new row becomes the current row.

- `WillChangeField` The `WillChangeField` event will fire when the contents of a field are about to be changed. You can use this function for data validation and abort the change if necessary.
- `FieldChangeComplete` This event fires after a change to a field has been completed.
- `WillChangeRecord` This event fires just before a record change. You can use this event to prompt users to make sure they want to save the changes. The `adReason` parameter will tell you why the record is being changed.
- `Error` The `Error` event fires when a data access error occurs but no code is executing. In other words, the error was generated by the use of the data control. You can write code inside the `Error` member function to respond to the error.
- `EndOfRecordset` As stated earlier, this event fires when the `recordset` pointer reaches the end of the recordset, which can be the beginning of the file (*BOF*) or the end of the file (*EOF*). You can write code to respond to this condition, such as moving to the first record.

By examining the function headers for some of these functions, you can see how they might be used. For example, look at the function header for `MoveComplete`:

```
void CBiblio2Dlg::OnMoveComplete(long adReason, LPDISPATCH pError,
long FAR* adStatus, LPDISPATCH pRecordset);
```

The first parameter, `adReason`, can be tested to see why the recordset is being moved to a new row. This parameter is one that is used in many of the functions, it can take on one of the following enumerated values: `adRsnAddNew`, `adRsnDelete`, `adRsnUpdate`, `adRsnUndoUpdate`, `adRsnUndoAddNew`, `adRsnUndoDelete`, or `adRsnFirstChange`. The `pError` parameter can also be examined for error conditions. The `adStatus` parameter can be examined to see if the status is OK or if an error has occurred. When reading `adStatus`, it will have one of the following enumerated values: `adStatusOK`, `adStatusErrorsOccurred`, or `adStatusCantDeny`. If status is `adStatusCantDeny`, this means that you cannot cancel the operation. If status is not set to this value, you can cancel the operation by setting `adStatus` to the enumerated value `adStatusCancel`. For example, in the `WillChangeRecord` event, you could prompt users and make sure they want to save the changes. If they select no, you can cancel the changes by setting the `adStatus` parameter:

Chapter 11: Data Access

```
void CBiblio2Dlg::OnWillChangeRecord(long adReason, long cRecords,
long FAR* adStatus, LPDISPATCH pRecordset)
{
int result = 0;

result = MessageBox("Save Changes?","UPDATE", MB_YESNO);

if(result == IDNO)
  *adStatus = (long)adStatusCancel;

}
```

Notice that we have used a cast, because the enumerated types are defined as hex. These constants are defined in the header file *ADOINT.h*. For example, we have the EventStatusEnum typedef:

```
enum EventStatusEnum
    {       adStatusOK          = 0x1,
        adStatusErrorsOccurred  = 0x2,
        adStatusCantDeny        = 0x3,
        adStatusCancel = 0x4,
        adStatusUnwantedEvent   = 0x5
}   EventStatusEnum;
```

In the event of an error condition, you can take the appropriate action to respond. To see how this might be done, consider the EndOfRecordset function:

```
void CBiblio2Dlg::OnEndOfRecordset(BOOL FAR* fMoreData,
long FAR* dStatus, LPDISPATCH pRecordset)
{

    //Check the status
    if(*adStatus == (long)adStatusOK)
        m_Biblio2.GetRecordset().MoveFirst();
    else if(*adStatus == (long)adStatusErrorsOccurred)
        //code to handle error
    else
        //code here for other status conditions
}
```

In this example, we check the status to make sure everything is fine. This will be the case if the adStatus parameter is set to the predefined constant adStatusOK. If it is, we move the pointer to the first record. We use the else-if clause to check for errors and can include code here to respond to the error condition.

From these examples, you can see how you can add code to your database projects to make them more robust and reliable. This will reduce the risk of errors and data corruption. While Visual C++ makes it easy to create database apps by just adding a few controls, keep in mind that it is the code you put behind it that will make your application professional.

Creating a Database Project

Another way to work with a database in Visual C++ is to select *Database Project* in the New Project dialog (see Figure 11-13). A database project will allow you to work with and edit data contained in the database from within the Visual C++ IDE. When you create this type of project, Visual C++ will prompt you for a data source (see Figure 11-14).

You have two choices, *File Data Source*, which is a file that refers to an ODBC driver installed on your machine, and *Machine Data Source*, which is a data source specific to your machine. In this example, we select MS Access Database from the Machine Data Source list. This causes Visual C++ to prompt us for the database file (see Figure 11-15). You can specify that the database be opened Read Only or for Exclusive access, if desired.

Figure 11-13
Starting a database project.

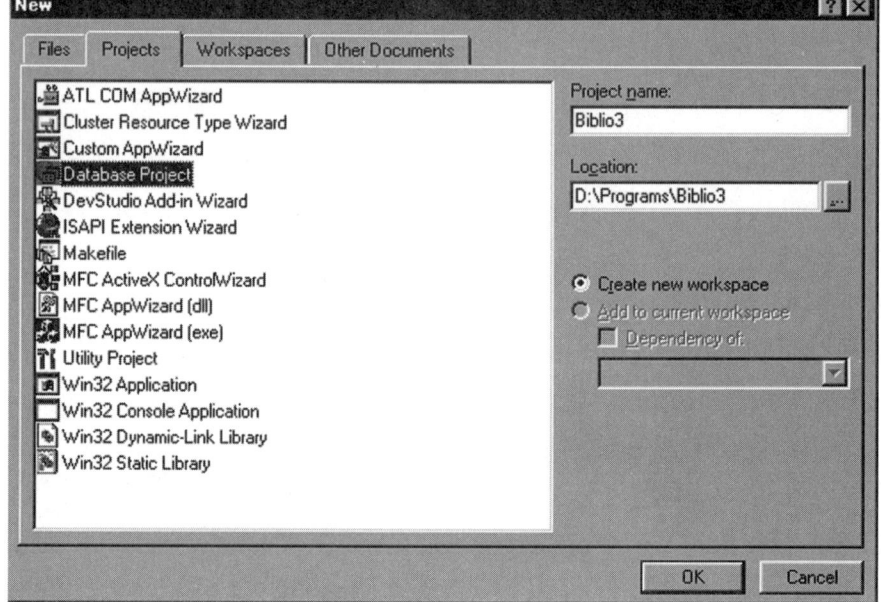

Chapter 11: Data Access

Figure 11-14
Selecting the data source.

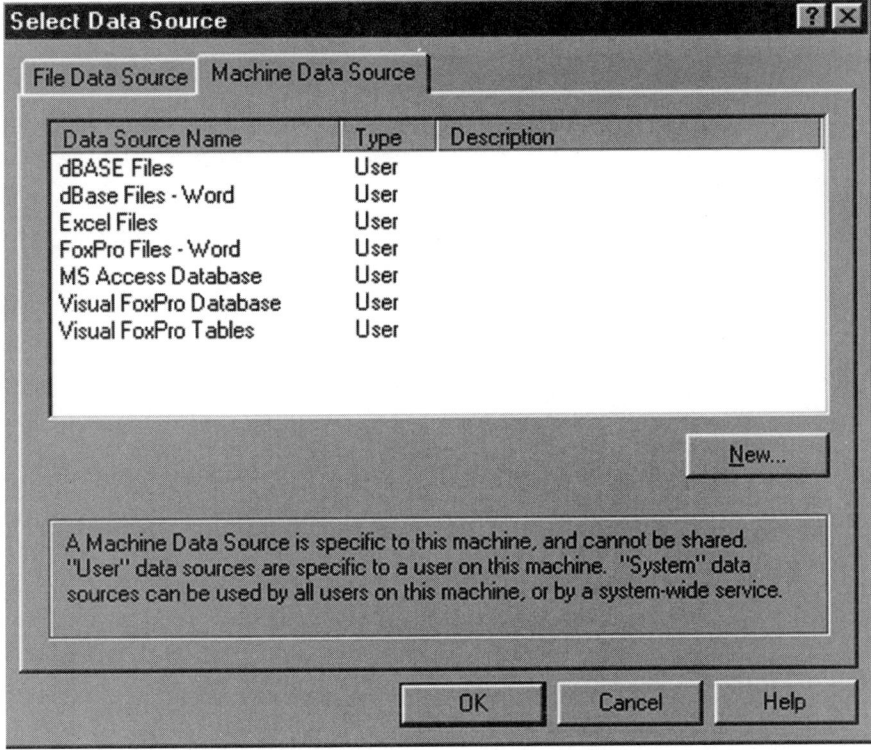

Figure 11-15
Selecting an Access database.

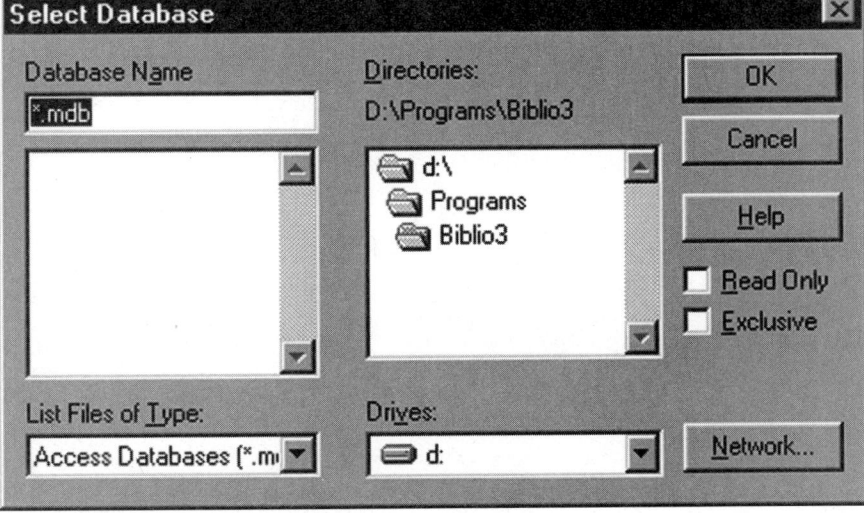

Visual C++ then provides two views, File View and Data View. In Data View, you can view the tables and fields contained in the database. You can open tables and view the data, and run queries against the database (see Figure 11-16).

Programming a Database with DAO

In the previous example, we didn't use regular edit boxes to build our user interface. Instead, we cheated a little bit by using Microsoft Forms TextBox controls. If you also have Visual Basic or Microsoft Access installed on your system, you will probably be able to use text box controls to automatically bind to a database. To add a text box to your project, open the Components and Controls Gallery and click on the Registered ActiveX Controls folder. Then look for the Microsoft Forms 2.0 controls. Here you will find the Microsoft Forms 2.0 TextBox control, which is just the good old Visual Basic TextBox, built ready-made for use with an ADO data control. You can bind the text box to a data control by setting its Data Source property on the All tab of the properties dialog for the control. To select which field you want the text box to display, set the

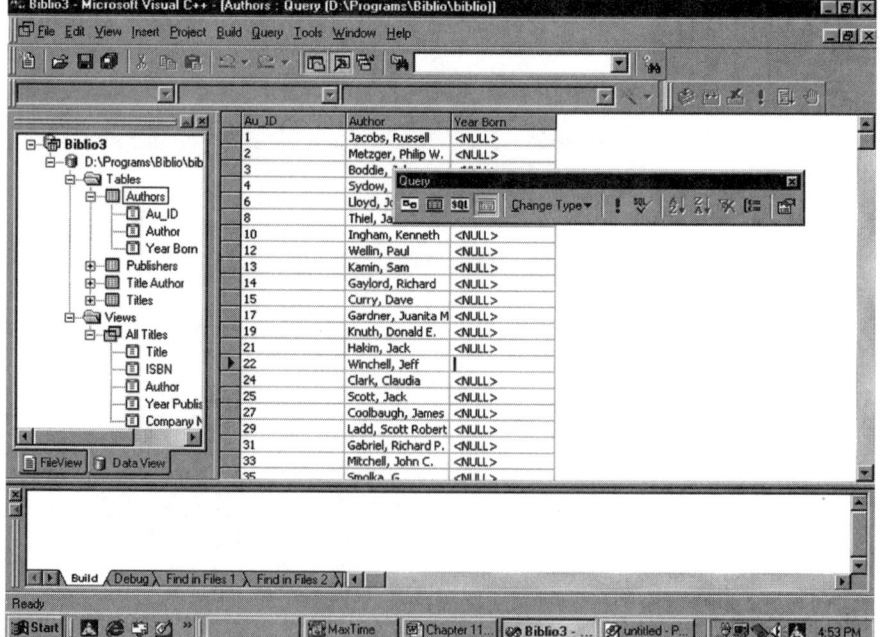

Figure 11-16
Running queries.

Chapter 11: Data Access

Data Field property. Be sure to connect your ADO data control to a database first.

Once this is done and you bind a text box to your database, when you click on the Data Field property, a drop-down list will open allowing you to select a field from the database. If you don't have the Microsoft Forms controls available, you can use the Rich TextBox Control, version 6.0. This ActiveX control can be used to bind to and display the data. Note that this is a different control than the Rich Edit control found by default in your toolbox. See your Microsoft documentation for the details on which controls can be used for data binding and how they work with the different technologies—ADO, RDO, and DAO.

In this section we will see another way to create a database application by using the MFC App Wizard to create a database SDI app. This is the old-fashioned way of creating database apps in Visual C++; in this application, we will build a DAO application. Again, we will work with the Biblio database, but this time we will use the Publishers table. This application is called the Publishers project. This project was created with the Database View without File Support selected on Step 2 of the wizard. Here you will be asked to select your data source, and if you choose OLE DB, the process will be the same as it was when connecting the ADO data control. In this example, however, we select DAO. You can select the type of support from the Database Options dialog box (see Figure 11-17).

If you select DAO, you can choose your database file by clicking on the button with the ellipsis, as shown in the figure. You will also be asked to select the Recordset Type. There are three options with DAO:

- *Snapshot* This is a read-only copy of the data. Can be of a single table or from a query.

Figure 11-17
Selecting a DAO data source.

- *Dynaset* The default option, this is read-write. Can be built from a single table or from a query. A Dynaset uses the Find methods for searching.
- *Table* Select this option to open a single table only. A table uses the Seek method of searching with DAO.

On the last step of the wizard, if you click on the `CPublishersView` class, you will see that it is based on the `CDAORecordView` class, which will provide the database functionality for the application.

When the wizard creates our application, it does not completely build the user interface for us. If we want to display the data in the underlying database, we need to add the controls to do so. This is done on the database form that the wizard added to the project. In this case, the project is named Publishers and the form is named IDD_PUBLISHERS_FORM. This is just a blank surface—a dialog box with no controls (with the exception of a label the App Wizard has placed there, telling us to add controls to the form). Our task is to add the controls necessary to view the data, just like we did when creating a dialog-based app with the ADO data control.

We are using this application to view the Publishers table in the Biblio database. This table has several fields, but we will concern ourselves with the following:

- PubID
- Name
- Company
- Address
- City
- State
- Zip

To build the form, we add a static text label for each field, along with an accompanying edit box that will display the data and allow the user to perform edits. With the controls added, the form looks like the one shown in Figure 11-18.

The first thing we need to do is provide a meaningful ID for each edit box. The ID of the edit box should correspond to the name of the field in the underlying database it will be bound to. For example, for the City field, we add an edit box and set its ID property to IDC_CITY. Once this is done for each edit box, we need to bind the edit boxes to the database.

Chapter 11: Data Access

This is done by opening the Class Wizard and selecting the *Member Variables* tab.

Now we will create a member variable for each edit box. This time, when you bring up the Add Member Variable dialog, you will see a drop-down list for the Member Variable Name. When you click it open, you will see that the Class Wizard has already loaded some pointer variables to the fields in the underlying database (see Figure 11-19).

All we need to do is make the appropriate selection for each edit box. The category for each member variable we are creating should be Value. When you select the appropriate member variable name from the list, the Class Wizard will automatically set the correct variable type for you. After we added all of the member variables for the Publishers form, the Class Wizard looks like that shown in Figure 11-20.

If you open the source code for the view for the project, which in this case is *PublishersView.cpp*, you can see how Visual C++ binds the controls. This is done in the `DoDataExchange` member function of the `CPublishersView` class. Visual C++ will create this code for you; you don't have to do any more work to bind the controls. The code looks something like this:

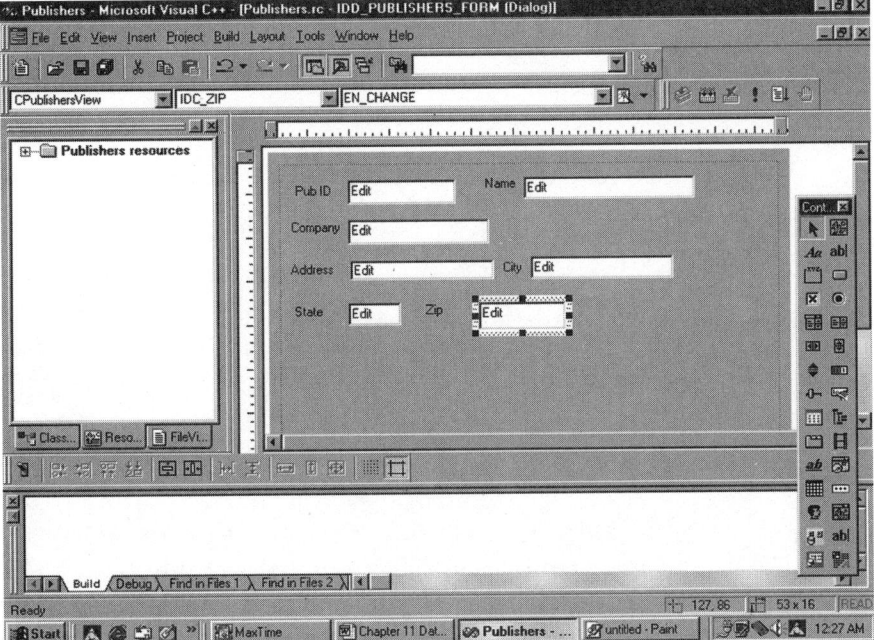

Figure 11-18
Setting up the Publishers dialog.

Figure 11-19
Mapping member variables to database fields.

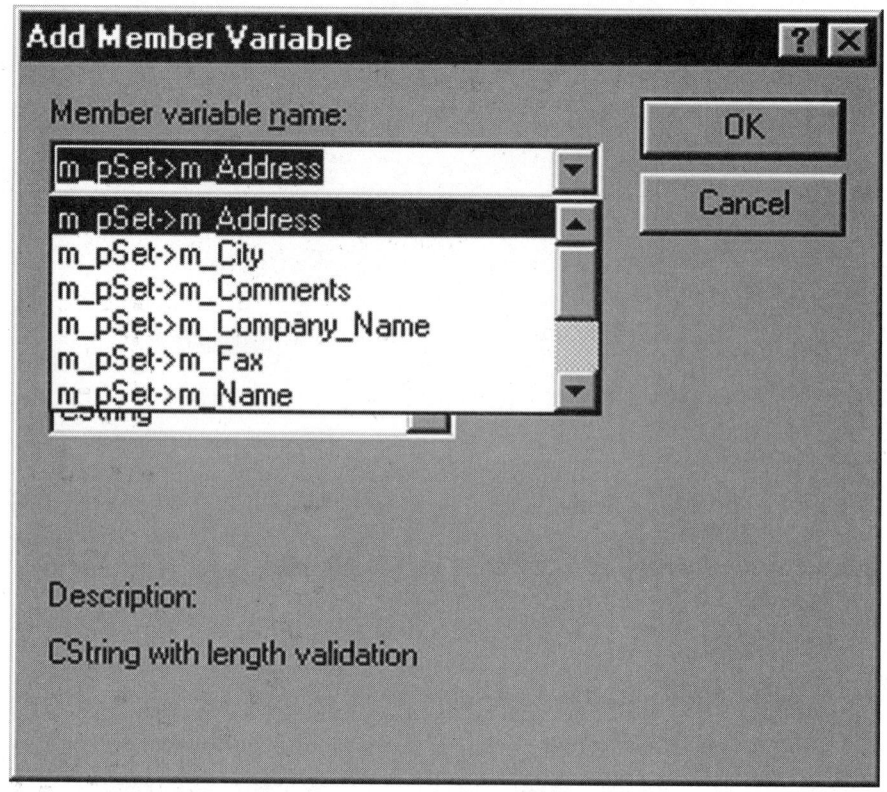

```
void CPublishersView::DoDataExchange(CDataExchange* pDX)
{
    CDaoRecordView::DoDataExchange(pDX);
    //{{AFX_DATA_MAP(CPublishersView)
    DDX_FieldText(pDX, IDC_ADDRESS, m_pSet->m_Address, m_pSet);
    DDX_FieldText(pDX, IDC_CITY, m_pSet->m_City, m_pSet);
    DDX_FieldText(pDX, IDC_COMPANY, m_pSet->m_Company_Name, m_pSet);
    DDX_FieldText(pDX, IDC_Name, m_pSet->m_Name, m_pSet);
    DDX_FieldText(pDX, IDC_PubID, m_pSet->m_PubID, m_pSet);
    DDX_FieldText(pDX, IDC_STATE, m_pSet->m_State, m_pSet);
    DDX_FieldText(pDX, IDC_ZIP, m_pSet->m_Zip, m_pSet);
    //}}AFX_DATA_MAP
}
```

Here you see how the DDX_FieldText function uses the ID we assigned to each edit box to connect it or bind it to the member variables we just created. The member variables are pointers to the fields in the underlying database.

Chapter 11: Data Access

Figure 11-20
Member variables mapped to fields in the database.

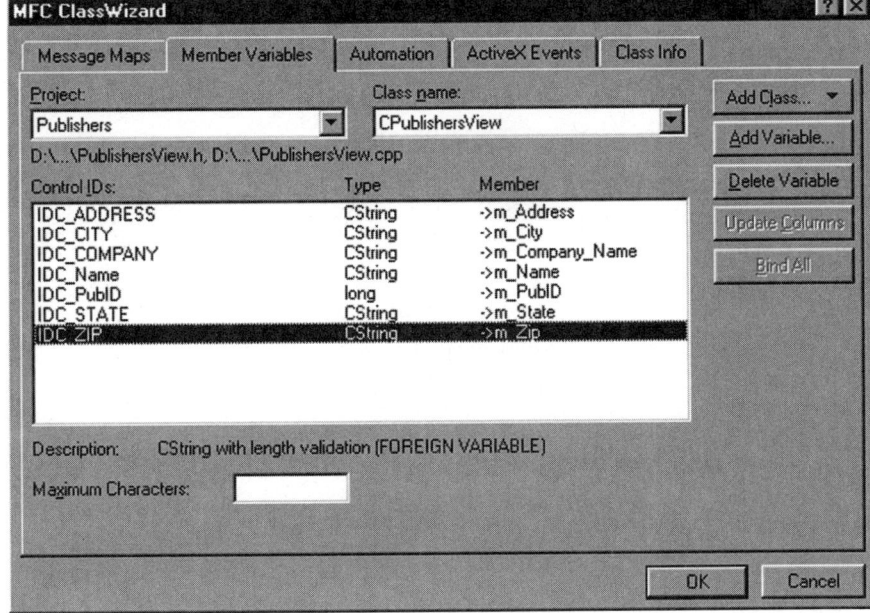

That's all there is to creating a DAO application and binding the controls. The application is shown in Figure 11-21. Creating an ODBC application is done in much the same way, except an ODBC application is based on the `CDatabase` class.

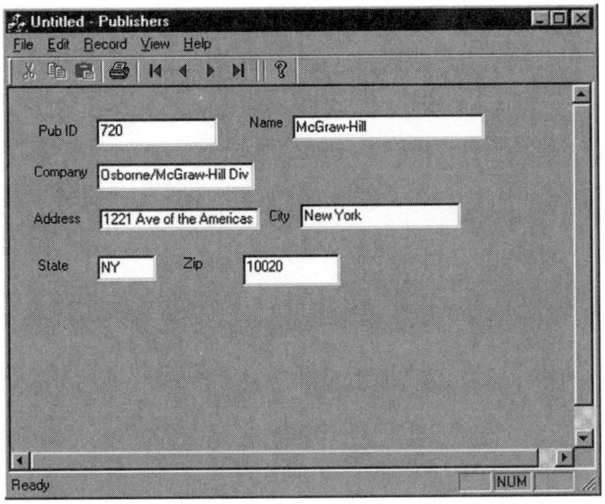

Figure 11-21
Running the Publishers program.

What Type of Data Access Should You Use—ADO, DAO, or ODBC?

The question now arises as to which type of data access you should use when creating a database application with Visual C++. This will depend on several factors, mainly what type of database is being used and what kind of environment the application will be running in. ADO is the most modern technology, and as such, it offers more to the developer in the way of methods, objects, and features. While there may be some reduced performance with ADO, in today's world of cheap computing power, the benefits gained will generally outweigh the cost in speed. If you are working with a database that is on a server that has no OLE support, you will need to use ODBC. Keep in mind that using ADO also provides access to the Jet engine, which can help automate many tasks. Generally, if you can use ADO, you should; it is the new technology and has the most-advanced features.

Structured Query Language (SQL)

A query can be used to retrieve a subset of the information stored in a database. Users can retrieve the data in a different sort order, retrieve only a subset of the fields in a table, or retrieve a set of records that only meet a specified criteria. Data from different tables can even be combined and displayed to the user. It is the query that helps bring out the power of storing information in a database.

One way to work with queries is to use a special language known as *structured query language*, or SQL. SQL is an especially powerful tool to use when writing database apps. It allows you to build the queries at runtime in response to user requests. This is called *dynamic SQL*. We can also create and use queries that are part of the database itself, or *embedded queries*. You can set the data source of an ADO data control to a query instead of a table, or you can open a `CRecordset` object in code using an SQL statement.

We will investigate both types of queries in this section. First, we'll learn about SQL and see what the rules are for building SQL statements. Next, we'll take a brief look at embedded SQL.

Building `Select` Queries

There are several types of queries that you can use when working with Access databases. The most common type of query is known as a `Select` query. A `Select` query allows us to specify which rows and columns to return from a table or tables, and in what order to sort the records. We can also construct queries to update records, add new records to the database, or delete a set of records. For many of our examples, we'll consider a phone number database that stores names, addresses, and phone numbers of clients in a table called Contacts.

We can start by imagining a simple query that only specifies which fields to return from the table. This is the minimal `Select` statement that can be used. At this point, we won't be worried about filtering the records returned. This type of query will have two elements, a `Select` clause and a `From` clause. The `Select` clause specifies which fields to return from the table, while the `From` clause specifies the name of the table where the data can be found. An SQL statement of this type has the form:

```
SELECT Field FROM Table
```

We can build a query like this to retrieve the names in our contact database:

```
Select Name From Contacts
```

When specifying more than one field in a query, place commas between each field name. The syntax of the SQL statement then becomes:

```
SELECT Field1, [Field2],...[FieldN] FROM Table
```

For example, to return names and phone numbers from the Contacts table of the phone database, we would write a query like this one:

```
Select Name, Phone from Contacts
```

To return every field in a table, you use an asterisk in place of the field list. To return all fields from the Contacts table, we write:

```
Select * from Contacts
```

If there are one or more blank spaces in the name of a field, enclose it in square brackets. Suppose that the Contacts table has a field named Zip Code. We can retrieve this field in a query with the following statement:

```
Select Name, Phone, [Zip Code] from Contacts
```

We can also specify the table name for each field, though this is optional. You will do this when building queries from multiple tables. The table name for each field is specified using the dot syntax *tablename.fieldname*. For example, we could rewrite the above query like this:

```
Select Contacts.Name, Contacts.Phone, Contacts.[Zip Code] from Contacts
```

Again, you won't do this unless you are building a query that retrieves fields from more than one table. To specify a query that returns every field from the table, we again use an asterisk:

```
Select Contacts.*
```

Aliasing

You can rename or *alias* field names that are returned by a query. This is done with the As keyword. For example, consider the *Biblio.mdb* database. The Publishers table has a Name field and a Company Name field. Suppose that we want to display the Name field as Division. We could write the query like this:

```
Select Name As Division, [Company Name] from Publishers
```

Aliasing is helpful when you are building a query with fields from multiple tables. Different tables may have fields with the same name. By using an alias, you can provide meaningful and unique names for each field.

Restricting the Records Returned with a Where Clause

Usually, when building a query, you will only want to return a subset of the records that are in the table. This will be based on the values con-

Chapter 11: Data Access

tained in certain fields. For example, in a table of students, you may only want to look at the students who are in the junior class. With this type of query, the records returned will be chosen based on a criteria that you supply with a Where clause. The form of the SQL statement then becomes:

```
SELECT Field1, [Field2],_,[FieldN] FROM Table WHERE Expression
```

The expression used in a Where clause will be a conditional expression similar to that used in an if statement. Like an if statement, the Where clause will use comparison operators as a filter. These are greater than (>), less than (<), equal to (=), greater than or equal (>=), less than or equal (<=). We can also use an inequality operator (<>) or not equal (!=). The expression will compare a field to some value we are using as a filter. Comparison values must follow these rules, based on the data type:

- Strings must be delimited by single quote marks.
- Dates must be delimited by the # character.
- Numeric values are not delimited.

The field name supplied does not need to be returned with the query. We consider each type of data with the following examples.

SQL Example: Searching Text or String Fields, Data Fields, and Numeric Data

Returning to the previous example, say we only wanted to return records from the Contacts table only if the client was living in California. We could use this SQL statement:

```
Select * from Contacts where State = 'CA'
```

Note the single quotation marks used to delimit the comparison value, which is a string.

SQL Example: Fields that Contain Date/Time Data

Dates in an SQL statement are delimited with the # character. Consider an Orders table for a small business. This table has a field named Date, which records the date the order was placed. If we only want to return orders placed since March 1, 1998, we can use the following query:

```
Select * from Orders where Date > #3/1/98#
```

Recall that the * character specifies that this query will return every field in the table.

SQL Example: Numeric Fields

As another example, let's return to a table that maintains a list of students. This table has string fields for last name and first name, and a numerical field that holds the students' GPAs. For our query, say we only wanted to return students with GPAs greater than 3.5. This can be done with this SQL statement:

```
Select Last, First from Students where GPA > 3.5
```

Remember, numerical values do not need to be delimited by quotes.

Using the Like Operator

Partial string searches can be done using the Like operator. You can use the Like operator in SQL statements to compare text strings with wildcards or a character list. To return all students whose last name starts with *J*, we can write:

```
Select * from Students where Last_Name Like 'J%'
```

The wildcard character % tells the query engine to return any string that begins with *J*. Single-digit wildcards can be built with the underscore character. For example:

```
Select Name From Contacts Where State Like 'C_'
```

will return contacts from any state beginning with the letter *C*.

You can also use Like to compare text fields to a list of characters. A character list is delimited in brackets. For example, suppose we wanted to return all records from the Contacts table where the name of the person was Tim or Tom. The SQL statement would look like this:

Chapter 11: Data Access

```
Select * from Contacts where Name Like 'T[io]m'
```

Like can also be used to leave out records that have characters found in a character list. This is done by including the ! character at the beginning of your list. The following statement returns all names that start with S, but only those that do not have a or u as the second letter:

```
Select * from Contacts where Name Like 'S[!au]*'
```

So names like Susan or Sam would not be returned by the query.

Returning Records that Fall Only within a Certain Range

When working with numerical values or dates, you can define an inclusive range of values by using the BETWEEN operator. This is used in conjunction with the AND keyword. To return the records for all Cub Scouts between the ages 7 and 10, we write:

```
Select Name, Age from Scouts where Age Between 7 And 10
```

where Scouts is the name of the table and Name, Age are fields within the Scouts table. The BETWEEN operator also works with date fields:

```
Select * from Orders where Date Between #1/1/98# And #12/31/98#
```

This query would return all orders placed in the year 1998.

Using the IN Operator

You can use the IN operator in your SQL statement to select among a group of values. This is basically a shorthand for using the OR operator several times. The list of choices is placed in between parentheses. As an example, let's write an SQL statement that selects contacts from California *or* Texas. Using the IN operator, it would look like the following:

```
Select Name, Phone from Contacts Where State IN ('CA','TX')
```

You can include as many values in the IN clause as test cases. This saves a lot of typing and makes your SQL statements easier to read if there are several OR choices.

Sorting the Records Returned by a Query

You can add an ORDER BY clause to an SQL query to tell the query engine how to sort the records. This can be based on whatever field you choose and is not necessarily determined by indexing. You do this by specifying which field or fields to sort on.

Returning to the previous example of a Scouts table, suppose we want to sort the scouts by age. We can do this by rewriting the query as follows:

```
Select Name, Age from Scouts where Age Between 7 And 10 ORDER BY Age
```

If we wanted to sort by name, the query would read as:

```
Select Name, Age from Scouts where Age Between 7 and 10 ORDER BY Name
```

ORDER BY sorts records in ascending order by default. To sort the same query in reverse order, you can add the DESC keyword:

```
Select Name, Age from Scouts where Age Between 7 And 10 ORDER BY Name DESC
```

Note that the field that you sort on with the ORDER BY clause does not need to be returned with the query. For example, we can still sort the scouts by age, but only return their names and phone numbers:

```
Select Name, [Phone Number] From Scouts ORDER BY Age
```

Building More-Complicated Queries with Logical Operators

We can extend the Where clause by using the AND and OR keywords to combine one or more expressions. Suppose we want to return records

Chapter 11: Data Access

from the Contacts table if the person lived in California and that person was entered in the database after November 1, 1998. The following statement would return the desired records:

```
Select Name, Phone from Contacts where State = 'CA' AND Date > #11/1/98#
```

If we want to return phone numbers for contacts in California and Texas, we can use the OR keyword:

```
Select Name, Phone from Contacts where State = 'CA' OR State = 'TX'
```

We can also use the NOT operator to keep certain records out of a query. To retrieve all clients except those from Texas, we could write:

```
Select Name, Phone from Contacts Where NOT State = 'TX'
```

We can build up increasingly complicated queries by combining the logical operators. This is done in the same way that we would when constructing an `if` statement.

Grouping Records

Often it will be necessary to group records together. This can be done by using a Group By clause. This type of clause is used with an aggregate function. *Aggregate functions* are functions that can be applied to a data set to perform some operation, such as counting the number of records. For example, if we wanted to count the number of students who had a GPA greater than 3.0, we could use the Count function:

```
Select Count(*) As "Honor Roll Students" From Students Where GPA > 3.0
```

We have used the As keyword to give a name to the field that will contain the result of the Count function. Other aggregate functions include SUM, AVG, MIN, and MAX. The GROUP BY clause can be used with an aggregate function to group the records together. For example, we can group the students together by class (freshman, sophomore, junior, senior) and use the Count function to count the number of students in each class:

```
Select Name, Count(*) As "Number of Students" From Students GROUP BY Class
```

Editing, Adding, and Deleting Records

SQL can be used to update, add, or delete groups of records in a single statement. To update a group of records, we use an UPDATE statement. The syntax is as follows:

```
UPDATE Table SET Field = Value [Where Condition]
```

A typical UPDATE statement might look like the following:

```
UPDATE Contacts SET State = 'AZ' WHERE ContactID > 188
```

We use the UPDATE keyword to tell the query engine that we will be updating the records. Next, we specify the table that we want to update. The SET clause specifies which field or fields to change, and the WHERE clause is used to define a criteria to select which records to update. In this example, we have specified that all contacts whose ID is greater than a certain value have the value in the State field set to Arizona. We can also update to a single record. For example, consider an inventory table named Products. We can change the price for a single item in the inventory with this statement:

```
UPDATE Products SET Price = 6.5 WHERE ProductID = 'A300L29'
```

To add records to a table with an SQL statement, you can use the INSERT keyword. You can specify the values that each field will take by using the VALUES keyword. The syntax is as follows:

```
INSERT INTO Table (Field List) VALUE (Value List)
```

For example, to add a record to the Contacts table, we can use this statement:

```
INSERT INTO Contacts (ContactID, LastName, FirstName) VALUES
(200,'Jones','Tim')
```

Deleting a record or group of records is done with a DELETE statement. A DELETE statement uses this syntax:

```
DELETE FROM Table WHERE Expression
```

To delete all contacts whose state of residence is California, we can use this statement:

```
DELETE FROM Contacts WHERE State = 'CA'
```

Each of these statements can be built up with more complexity in the same way that a `Select` statement is by following the same rules.

Joining Data from Different Tables

Up to this point, we've been building simple queries that retrieve a subset of data from one table. However, the ability to relate data in two tables is at the core of database design, and the design of queries would not be complete without being able to join the data from tables together. This is done with a `JOIN` statement. There are two types of joins. To distinguish between the joins, we consider an example. Consider a database with a Customers table and an Orders table. The Orders table has the orders each customer has placed. However, not every customer has placed an order (some may have requested a catalog but not yet ordered).

- *Inner Join* When an inner join is created, only records that have a match in both tables are included in the result of the query. If we build an inner join on our example database, the only records that will be included are those that match for both tables, which means that only the customers who have placed an order are listed.

- *Outer Join* With an outer join, all records from a master table are included in the result, while only the matching records from a lookup table are included. In this case, all customer records are listed, regardless of whether or not they placed an order. The fields from the Orders table will simply be blank for those customers.

To perform an inner join, you use a `Select` statement and specify the criteria you want to use to join the tables in the `Where` clause. As an example of an inner join, consider the *Biblio.mdb* database. The Titles table and the Publishers table can be linked on the pub_id field. An inner join would look like this:

```
Select Titles.*, Publishers.pub_id, Publishers.Name From Titles, Publishers Where Titles.pub_id = Publishers.pub_id
```

Notice that we used the familiar dot syntax to specify which table we are talking about. Using the asterisk tells the query engine to retrieve all fields.

When building an outer join, you can use a left join or a right join. This tells the query engine which table is the "master" table and which table is the "lookup" table. An outer join uses an ON clause instead of a Where clause. For example, let's build a query with the Titles table as the "master." This means that the query will return every Title record, regardless of whether or not there is a match in the Publishers table. The query will look like this:

```
Select Titles.*, Publishers.* From Titles Left Join Publishers On
Titles.pub_id = Publishers.pub_id
```

A right join works the same way, except the other table is considered the "master."

Multiuser Considerations

When developing multiuser applications, we need to concern ourselves with the problem of several users trying to access the same data at once. This is known as a *concurrency problem*. Concurrency problems are managed by using record locking. This prevents users from accessing a record for a certain period during which it is locked. While the record is locked, the user who locked the record can save their data. There are several types of locking that can be used in database programming. Most of the time you will choose between pessimistic and optimistic locking.

Pessimistic Locking

The first type of locking strategy is known as *pessimistic locking*. This can be done by setting the LockType property of an ADO data control to adLockPessimistic. This locks the record immediately after a call to the Edit method has been issued. The record remains locked, and it is therefore inaccessible to other users until the record is saved with an Update method.

Optimistic Locking

Another type of locking strategy we are concerned with is known as *optimistic locking*. This type will lock the record for a shorter time period.

Chapter 11: Data Access

With optimistic locking, the record is only locked when a call to the Update method is issued. This type of locking may be less secure, since other users can make changes to the record while the first user is editing it. You can use optimistic locking by setting the `LockType` property to `adLockOptimistic`.

Read-Only

The default lock type is `adLockReadOnly`. This makes the recordset read-only. This is useful in situations where data changes aren't necessary. For example, you can use read-only locking when generating a report.

Batch Optimisitc

Batch optimistic locking is similar to optimistic locking. However, in this case, it requires the use of an UpdateBatch rather than the Update method. To use batch optimistic locking, set the `LockType` property to `adLockBatchOptimistic`.

Database Transactions

Database transactions enable the developer to make several changes with a single command. Transactions can be used to group together a set of program statements, which can then be canceled or "rolled back" if the transaction fails. This can help make your code more robust.

To use database transactions, there are three commands that can be used: `BeginTrans`, `CommitTrans`, and `RollbackTrans`. `BeginTrans` starts the transaction. `CommitTrans` is used in an attempt to commit the transaction, while `RollbackTrans` can be used to cancel it. Transaction methods are members of a connection object. A transaction should be used when a large number of commands or a large amount of data will be used. If the network goes down or the user's application crashes, the transactions are rolled back and data loss is avoided.

CHAPTER 12

Putting It All Together

Introduction

In the last chapter we focused primarily on using the ADO data control to develop a database application. Most database applications will be more substantial than that, however. This usually means that you will have to do some processing of the data in code and probably filter the data with SQL statements. In this chapter we will explore how to program with data in code and how to open recordsets with SQL statements. The examples in this chapter will be DAO examples.

Programming with a Recordset

In this section we will write a program that will loop through a recordset and read the data. The program, shown in Figure 12-1, opens the Authors table in the *Biblio.mdb* database. The project is called TAuthors and the dialog box is called TAuthorsDlg. When the user clicks on the *Load Data* button, the program opens the Authors table and loads the data into the grid. This program operates without a data control. This is

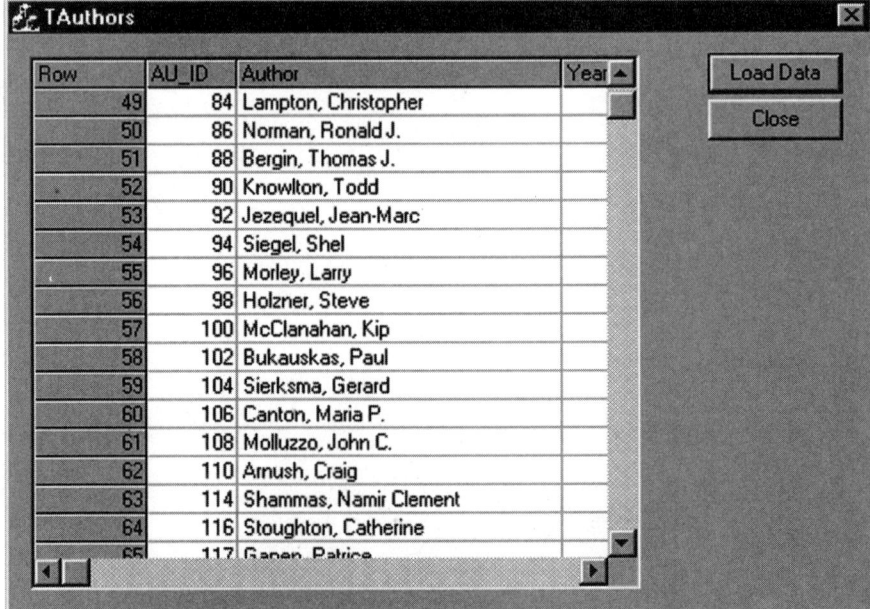

Figure 12-1
The Authors table.

Chapter 12: Putting It All Together

done by creating a `CDaoRecordSet` object. The `CDaoRecordSet` class allows you to create, open, and work with recordsets, which are sets of data from a table or tables. They can be a single table, a subset of the data created with an SQL statement, or a set of tables linked together with a `JOIN` statement.

The easiest way to program with a recordset in code is to create your own `RecordSet` class with the Class Wizard and use the `CDaoRecordSet` class as the base class. This way the Class Wizard will automatically set up important objects for you, such as the default database for the recordset and member variables that are mapped into the fields in the table you are using. To start the process, open the Class Wizard and select the *Add Class* button in the upper right corner. When you are prompted to create a *New* class or one From a Type Library, select *New*. This will open the New Class dialog box, shown in Figure 12-2.

Since we are creating the class to work with the Authors table, we call this class `CAuthors`. When you type in the class name, you will notice that Visual C++ inserts the name of the source code file that will implement the class for you. If you begin your class name with a *C*, the wizard will name the source and header files after your class name but leave the leading *C* off. In this case it will create *Authors.h* and *Authors.cpp* files. If you don't like the names it has selected, click the *Change* button and type in a new name.

The next step is to select the base class for our new class. This is done by clicking open the drop-down list, where you will see the Microsoft

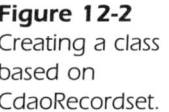

Figure 12-2
Creating a class based on CdaoRecordset.

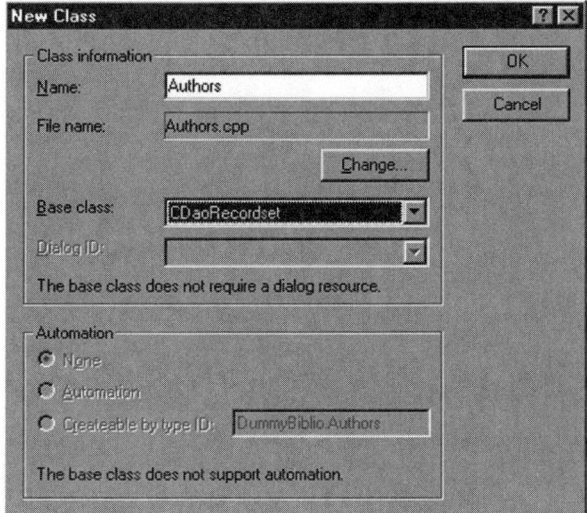

classes listed. Since we are going to be using DAO and working with a recordset, select *CDaoRecordSet* as the base class. When you make this selection, the other options on the dialog will be grayed out since this class does not require a dialog resource or support automation. Click *OK* to create the class.

When you click the *OK* button, the Class Wizard will prompt you for a data source (see Figure 12-3). Since we are working with DAO, the DAO radio button is selected. You can click the ellipsis button to select the database file, which in this case is *Biblio.mdb*. For recordset type, select *Dynaset*. When you click on the *OK* button, the wizard will ask you which table(s) to select. In this example, we are only working with one table, so select *Authors* and click *OK*.

This will create the class. If you look at your project in File View, you will see the *Authors.cpp* and *Authors.h* files have been added to your project. Next, we need to add the appropriate header file, which is *afxdao.h*. This header file is where the base class, CDaoRecordset, is contained. Otherwise you will get an error when you try to compile the project. Add the header file with an #include statement at the beginning of the *Authors.h* file. The code should look like this:

```
// Authors.h : header file
//
#include <afxdao.h>
/////////////////////////////////////////////////////////////////////
////////
// Authors DAO recordset

class Authors : public CDaoRecordset
{
public:
    Authors(CDaoDatabase* pDatabase = NULL);
    DECLARE_DYNAMIC(Authors)
```

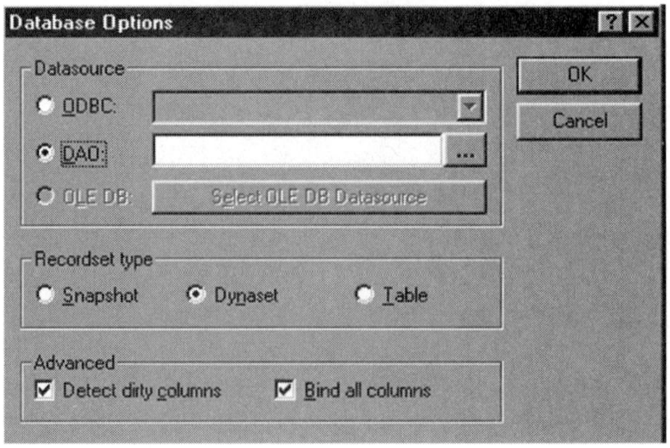

Figure 12-3
Selecting the DAO data source.

Chapter 12: Putting It All Together

```
// Field/Param Data
    //{{AFX_FIELD(Authors, CDaoRecordset)
    long m_Au_ID;
    CString m_Author;
    short m_Year_Born;
    //}}AFX_FIELD
```

With the *afxdao.h* file included, the compiler will know what `CDaoRecordset` means. Now look below to the `//Field` section. The thing to notice here is that the Class Wizard has created member variables in our derived class that correspond to the fields in the Authors table. By using the Class Wizard we have saved ourselves a lot of work, letting it define and map all the variables rather than having to create our own class and do the work from scratch. All that remains now is to create a variable of type `CAuthors` and program it.

To view the data, we have added an MSFlexGrid 6.0 control to our project with the Controls and Components Gallery. Visual C++ created header and implementation files to represent the control in *msflexgrid.h* and *msflexgrid.cpp*. We will write code to open the database and load the data from the Authors table into this grid.

The dialog box used in this project has two command buttons:

- IDLOAD
- IDCLOSE

The Close command button is simple; we will unload the dialog when the user clicks on it. One easy way to do this is to use the OnCancel method of the `CDialog` class. The code for the Close button looks like this:

```
void CTAuthorsDlg::OnClose()
{
    //close the dialog box
    CDialog::OnCancel();
}
```

The Load Data button will call another function, called `LoadData`, where we will place the code to read the data and load the grid. We will make this function a part of the class used to represent the dialog box in our project. We simply add the function header to the `Public` section of the TAuthorsDlg class:

```
// CTAuthorsDlg dialog

class CTAuthorsDlg : public CDialog
{
```

```
// Construction
public:
    CTAuthorsDlg(CWnd* pParent = NULL);   // standard constructor
    void LoadData();
```

We call the function when the user clicks on the *Load Data* button:

```
void CTAuthorsDlg::OnLoad()
{
    this->LoadData();
}
```

Notice that we have used the `this` pointer to emphasize that we are calling a member function of the class. While this isn't strictly necessary, it makes our code more readable. The code to implement the `LoadData` function is added to the *TAuthorsDlg.cpp* file:

```
void CTAuthorsDlg::LoadData()
{
    //recordset variable

    CAuthors authors;

    long nNumRows=0; //variable to track # rows in dataset

    //counter to move
    //through grid
    long nRowCounter=0;

    //constants to define
    //column indexes for grid
    const int ColIndex = 0;    //column 0 is row #
    const int ColID = 1;       //column 1 is Author ID
    const int ColName = 2;     //column 2 is Author Name
    const int ColYR = 3;       //column 3 is Year Born

    //temp string to copy
    //data from database
    char temp[50];

    //set the number of rows and
    //columns in the grid
    m_AuthorGrid.SetCols(4);

    //load column headers

    m_AuthorGrid.SetRow(0);
    m_AuthorGrid.SetCol(ColIndex);
    m_AuthorGrid.SetText("Row");
    m_AuthorGrid.SetCol(ColID);
    m_AuthorGrid.SetText("AU_ID");
    m_AuthorGrid.SetCol(ColName);
    m_AuthorGrid.SetText("Author");
```

Chapter 12: Putting It All Together

```
        m_AuthorGrid.SetCol(ColYR);
        m_AuthorGrid.SetText("Year Born");
        authors.Open(AFX_DAO_USE_DEFAULT_TYPE);

        //move pointer to last record
        //to get total record count
        //add one row for titles
        authors.MoveLast();
        nNumRows = authors.GetRecordCount() + 1;

        //set row number in grid
        m_AuthorGrid.SetRows(nNumRows);

        //move back to first record to
        //traverse list
        authors.MoveFirst();

    while(authors.IsEOF() == false)
    {
        //advance the row counter to the next row
        nRowCounter++;
        m_AuthorGrid.SetRow(nRowCounter);
        m_AuthorGrid.SetCol(ColIndex);

        //load the row index
        _ltoa(nRowCounter,temp,10);
        m_AuthorGrid.SetText(temp);

        //load the author ID
        m_AuthorGrid.SetCol(ColID);
        _ltoa(authors.m_Au_ID,temp,10);
        m_AuthorGrid.SetText(temp);

        //load the author name
        m_AuthorGrid.SetCol(ColName);
        m_AuthorGrid.SetText(authors.m_Author);

        //load year born
        m_AuthorGrid.SetCol(ColYR);
        _itoa(authors.m_Year_Born,temp,10);
        m_AuthorGrid.SetText(temp);

        //move to the next record
        authors.MoveNext();
    }//end while loop
        //close the recordset
        authors.Close();

}
```

We won't be worrying too much about the code that operates on the MSFlexGrid control, which we have represented by the m_AuthorGrid member variable. Instead, we will be focusing on the recordset object. For this code to work, we need to add #include statements to the beginning of the *TAuthorsDlg.cpp* file for the MSFlexGrid control and the `CAuthors` class that we created with the wizard. The `#include` statements should look like this:

```
// TAuthorsDlg.cpp : implementation file
//

#include "stdafx.h"

#include "msflexgrid.h"
#include "Authors.h"
#include "TAuthors.h"
#include "TAuthorsDlg.h"
```

Now let's focus on the problem at hand: using a recordset. The first step is to declare an object variable of the class that we created earlier with the Class Wizard. This is done at the beginning of the `LoadData` function:

```
CAuthors authors;
```

To work with the data, we have to open the database first. With a `CDaoRecordset` variable, this is done in one step, we don't have to worry about a database variable, workspaces, or anything like that. We can open it with one simple call to the Open method:

```
authors.Open(AFX_DAO_USE_DEFAULT_TYPE);
```

We have passed the constant `AFX_DAO_USE_DEFAULT_TYPE` to tell the compiler to open the recordset using the settings we selected when creating the class. If we take a look at the `CAuthors` class, we will see how the file is opened. The `CAuthors` constructor sets the recordset type to `Dynaset` and initializes the member variables:

```
CAuthors::CAuthors(CDaoDatabase* pdb)
    : CDaoRecordset(pdb)
{
    //{{AFX_FIELD_INIT(CAuthors)
    m_Au_ID = 0;
    m_Author = _T("");
    m_Year_Born = 0;
    m_nFields = 3;
    //}}AFX_FIELD_INIT
    m_nDefaultType = dbOpenDynaset;
}
```

The constructor was created by the Class Wizard for us, we didn't have to write any of this code on our own. The default database name is returned by the `GetDefaultDBName` function. Again, the wizard created

Chapter 12: Putting It All Together

this for us, but I'm showing it here so you can understand how this works:

```
CString CAuthors::GetDefaultDBName()
{
    return _T("D:\\programs\\Biblio\\Biblio.mdb");
}
```

When we open the recordset in the `LoadData` function and tell it to use the defaults, it knows from the constructor and `GetDefaultDBName` function what to do. Once the recordset is open, we need to obtain the number of rows in the table so that we can adjust our flex grid to the proper size. To do this, we must move the recordset pointer to the last record. This is because a recordset only keeps a count of the number of records that have been accessed. By moving to the last record, we can access all of the records in the table and set the number of rows in the grid. We add one to this value, since the grid will have a header:

```
authors.MoveLast();
nNumRows = authors.GetRecordCount() + 1;

//set row number in grid
m_AuthorGrid.SetRows(nNumRows);
```

Next, we move back to the first row in the table, by calling the MoveFirst() method. Then we use a `while` loop to move through the records. The `while` loop will test for `end of file` and will terminate when this condition is reached:

```
authors.MoveFirst();

while(authors.IsEOF() == false)
```

The code inside the `while` loop is pretty simple. We set the text displayed in the grid with a string variable. For each field in the Authors table, we read the data and convert it to a string if necessary, by storing it in temp. To access each field in the table, we use the member variables of the `CAuthor` class. For example, here we copy the data from the Year Born field into the temp variable and then add it to the grid:

```
//load year born
m_AuthorGrid.SetCol(ColYR);
_itoa(authors.m_Year_Born,temp,10);
m_AuthorGrid.SetText(temp);
```

The `_itoa` function converts an integer into a character array. At the bottom of the `while` loop, we take the all-important step of moving to the next record, so that we can load all of the data into the grid and eventually terminate the `while` loop by hitting *end-of-file*:

```
//move to the next record
authors.MoveNext();
```

When the `while` loop terminates, we are done reading the data and can close the recordset:

```
authors.Close();
```

That's all there is to it. Now we have the data loaded in our C++ program, and we can manipulate it and then write it back out to the database later. This type of programming allows us to make our code more modular and take advantage of the speed offered by C++. In other words, we can build applications that separate the database from the rest of the program. You can design one tier of your application to read the data from the database into a class, work with the data using the class, and then write it out to the database when done.

Opening a Recordset with SQL

Now suppose that we wanted to open only a subset of the data. As we discussed in the last chapter, this can be done with an SQL statement. SQL statements can be built up to almost arbitrary complexity. Our task here, however, is simply to illustrate the process that can be used to create an SQL statement in code and open the recordset.

Suppose that we wanted to open the recordset and only read the first 100 authors. The authors are keyed on the AU_ID field, which is of type `long`. We will also suppose that we want to return all fields from the table. To do so, you will recall from the last chapter that we use an asterisk (*) to tell the SQL engine that we want all fields returned. We can create and store the SQL statement in a string variable. For example:

```
CString strSQL;

strSQL = "Select * from Authors where AU_ID < 101";
```

All we need to do is pass our string to the Open method of the `CAuthors` recordset object. We can use the `strSQL` statement to create

Chapter 12: Putting It All Together

any type of valid SQL statement, as we discussed in the last chapter. To open a recordset with the `strSQL` string, we use the following:

```
CString strSQL;
strSQL = "Select * from Authors where AU_ID < 101";
authors.Open(AFX_DAO_USE_DEFAULT_TYPE,strSQL);
```

By opening the recordset this way, we can restrict the records returned in any way deemed necessary.

PART 3

Implementation

CHAPTER 13

The Microsoft Foundation Class Library

Introduction

Almost every 32-bit Windows application created with Visual C++ is built by using the Microsoft Foundation Class Library (MFC). While we could create a Windows project without using MFC, it would be a tremendous amount of work. The advantage of using MFC is that you can build your applications based on the classes that Microsoft has already created. This saves time and effort, while at the same time allowing you to take advantage of the power of Windows and the efficiency that MFC provides. We have already worked with MFC, when using the App Wizard to create new projects or when using the Class Wizard to create derived classes. In this chapter we will provide a brief overview of MFC so you can have an idea of the larger picture within which applications created with the App Wizard fit.

Overview of MFC

MFC works by taking advantage of the object-oriented nature of C++. This means that simple base classes can be created, and then more complicated or specialized classes can be derived from them. You can also derive your own classes, using an MFC class to base it on. This allows you to take advantage of the power that is already there in the Windows operating system, and it saves you a lot of trouble in doing everyday kinds of tasks such as using menus or performing file handling. There is no sense in reinventing the wheel; a programmer may as well take advantage of what Microsoft has to offer.

One advantage of MFC over other libraries is that it has a small overhead. This provides the developer with the advantages of object-oriented programming and the ability to use inheritance while achieving the same tight and fast code that you would get from a C Windows application. MFC also provides support for dialog boxes, message boxes, menus, and other user interface elements. You saw how much work this saves when we created an SDI application. The menus are already there for us to manipulate, and many menu items are already fully functional. MFC also provides good exception handling, making your applications less likely to crash (although I am sure they still will much of the time).

Much of the basis of MFC can be found in the CObject class. This class can be found in the *afx.h* file, which ships with Visual C++. You can

Chapter 13: The Microsoft Foundation Class Library

find this and other MFC header files in the *MFC/Include* directory in the folder in which Visual C++ was installed. Many important classes are derived from the `CObject` class. One such class is the `CGdiObject` class, which forms a basis for drawing objects such as `CPen` or `CFont`. `CGdiObject` is found in the *afxwin.h* file.

The `CObject` class also forms the basis for many other important classes, including the `CException` class, which is used for important classes to handle many types of exceptions such as `CFileException` and `CMemoryException`, which can be found in *afx.h*. Other important classes include the `CMenu` class, `CDatabase` class, and `CWnd` class. The `CWnd` class, which is found in *afxwin.h*, forms the basis for the Windows and dialog boxes used in your applications. This includes the `CFrameWnd` class, which is used as a base class for MDI child windows, and `CDialog`, which is used to create dialog-based applications.

By examining the overall structure of the relationships between the classes, you can get a good idea of how the MFC classes work and interrelate. Here is an abbreviated listing of classes derived from the `CObject` class:

```
CGdiObject
     CPen
     CBrush
     CFont
     CBitmap
     CPalette
     CRgn

CException
     CMemoryException
     CFileException
     CArchiveException
     CDaoException
     CNotSupportedException
     CUserException
     COleException
     COleDispatchException
     CDBException
     CResourceException

CDC
     CClientDC
     CWindowDC
     CPaintDC
     CMetaFileDC

CFile
     CStdioFile
     CMemFile
     COleStreamFile
     CSocketFile
```

```
CMenu
CArray
CByteArray
CWordArray
CDWordArray
CPtrArray
CObArray
CStringArray
CUIntArray
CList
CPtrList
CObList
CStringList
CMap
CMapWordToPtr
CMapPtrToWord
CMapPtrToPtr
CMapWordToOb
CMapStringToPtr
CMapStringToOb
CMapStringToString
CDatabase
CRecordSet
CLongBinary

CDocument
    COleDocument
        COleLinkingDoc
            COleServeroc
                CRichEditDoc
CDocItem
    COleClientItem
        CRichEditCntrItem
    COleServerItem

CWnd

    CFrameWnd
    CControlBar
    CSplitterWnd
    CPropertySheet
    CDialog
    CView
        CCtrlView
            CEditView
            CListView
            CRichEditView
            CTreeView

CButton
CBitmapButton
CComboBox

CEdit

CListBox
    CheckListBox
    CDragListBox
```

```
CListCtrl
COleCtrl
CProgresCtrl
CRichEditCtrl
CScrollBar
CSliderCtrl
CSpinButtonCtrl
CStatic
CStatusBarCtrl
CTabCtrl
CToolbarCtrl
CToolTipCtrl
CTreeCtrl
```

This is not a complete list, but it should give you an idea of how the objects in Windows are derived from the base class `CObject`. This allows each item to take advantage of the functionality provided by the `CObject` class and add to it. The classes derived from these classes do the same, expanding the power of MFC even further.

Window Classes

One important class that is derived from `CObject` is the `CWnd` class. This class forms the basis of most of the user interface in Windows. If you take a look at the classes derived from `CWnd`, you will notice that this list includes many controls and other types of windows you use in your programs. It is helpful in your programming to think of a control, such as an edit box, as a kind of window. This way you can keep the fact that you can use the base window functions in mind when programming with these objects. This is why we use the `SetWindowText` function to set the text displayed in an edit box.

One of the more important classes derived from `CWnd` is the `CDialog` class. This class is important because dialog boxes are used frequently in Windows programs; it is impossible to think of a Windows program without at least one dialog box. The class hierarchy looks like this:

```
CDialog
    CCommonDialog
        CColorDialog
        CFileDialog
        CFindReplaceDialog
        CFontDialog
        COleDialog
            COleInsertDialog
            COleChangeIconDialog
```

```
                    COlePasteSpecialDialog
                    COleConvertDialog
                    COleBusyDialog
                    COleLinksDialog
                    COleChangeSourceDialog
                    COlePageSetupDialog
                    CPrintDialog
            COlePropertyPage
            CpropertyPage
```

Here we see that many common dialogs, such as a color, font, or file, are derived from the `CDialog` class. When you create a dialog box in your projects, or you create a dialog-based project with the MFC App Wizard, your dialog will be based on the `CDialog` class. This gives your dialogs a great deal of built-in functionality, such as the ability to show itself modally.

The Application Class

Windows applications are built around an application class. The `CWinApp` class forms the basis of MFC applications. For example, when we created the `TAuthors` program in the last chapter, the MFC App Wizard created a `TAuthorsApp` that is based on the `CWinApp` class:

```
/CTAuthorsApp:
// See TAuthors.cpp for the implementation of this class
//

class CTAuthorsApp : public CWinApp
{
public:
    CTAuthorsApp();

// Overrides
    // ClassWizard generated virtual function overrides
    //{{AFX_VIRTUAL(CTAuthorsApp)
    public:
    virtual BOOL InitInstance();
    //}}AFX_VIRTUAL

// Implementation

    //{{AFX_MSG(CTAuthorsApp)
        // NOTE - the ClassWizard will add and remove member
functions here.
        // DO NOT EDIT what you see in these blocks of generated
code !
    //}}AFX_MSG
    DECLARE_MESSAGE_MAP()
};
```

Chapter 13: The Microsoft Foundation Class Library

```
///////////////////////////////////////////////////////////////
///////
//{{AFX_INSERT_LOCATION}}
// Microsoft Visual C++ will insert additional declarations
immediately before the previous line.

#endif //
!defined(AFX_TAUTHORS_H__86C8E0A0_62C4_11D3_856B_90CE7CF9DE51__
INCLUDED_)
```

This class forms the basis of our application. You will notice that there is a section for overrides. When doing object-oriented programming, you will find yourself overriding the members of base classes often; this is one way that you can extend and redefine an object. The `InitInstance` member function can be overridden to provide customized initialization for your applications.

Using MFC Wizards

In the previous chapters we have already been using the MFC App Wizard to generate our applications. This is the simplest way to create Windows applications. The wizard does all the dirty work for you; it creates the application class and includes all of the appropriate header files. In summary, the MFC App Wizard can be used to create:

- Single-document, or SDI, applications, with or without database support
- Multiple-document, or MDI, applications, with or without database support
- Dialog-based applications, which can be extended with the use of ActiveX controls

The MFC App Wizard can also be used to specify the level of OLE support you want your application to have. MFC can also be used for project types other than the standard Windows or database programs we have looked at so far. In the next chapter, we will see how to use MFC wizards to create:

- Dynamic-link libraries, or DLL files
- ActiveX controls

By using the MFC wizards, you can save yourself a lot of time and effort when creating Windows applications.

CHAPTER 14

Advanced Topics—Multithreading, DLLs, ActiveX Controls, and Web Programming

Introduction

Visual C++ is a powerful programming tool, and that power goes beyond simple database programming and object-oriented design with classes. Much of the power that comes from Visual C++ is the ability it gives the developer to create programs that take advantage of Windows features like OLE and multithreading. Visual C++ also allows the creation of ActiveX controls, allowing the developer to create tools and objects that can be readily used in other programs and even other development languages. In this chapter we will investigate the use of Visual C++ to create these types of projects. The main topics that we will discuss include:

- Using multithreading
- Using OLE; creating containers and servers
- Creating a dynamic-link library (DLL)
- Creating an ActiveX control using MFC and ATL
- Programming for the Web

Throughout the chapter, we will use the App Wizards that come with Visual C++.

Threads, Processes, and Asynchronous Program Flow

Microsoft Windows is a multitasking environment. This means that the user can have several applications open at once, even several different instances of the same application. The user can switch between applications with the click of the mouse, use one app while another is busy printing or processing data, and share data among different applications. This is part of the power of Windows; it gives the user maximum flexibility and the ability to work with several programs. One important aspect of the Windows operating system that we will explore in this section is *multithreading*. Before we do anything else, let's try to understand what a process and a thread are in the Windows environment.

Processes and Threads

A *process* consists of a single executing application and all of the resources that have been allocated for it by Windows. In the imaginary scenario we painted above, each of the applications that the user has open on his or her desktop is a separate process. For example, if you have Microsoft Word, Paint, and an Internet provider application open on your computer, each one of these applications is a process. An executable program that you create and compile with Visual C++, when executing, is also a process. Each process runs inside its own virtual computer, where the application thinks that it has the entire computer to itself. The application, or process, will have its own memory or address space that is separate from every other process in Windows.

A *thread*, meanwhile, is a single path of execution in the computer. A thread belongs to a process. Each process has at least one thread, and in the 32-bit Windows operating system, a process can actually have multiple threads. All of these threads can be running at the same time, and this is the basis of multithreading. So, to summarize, an application running in Windows is a process, and each process has one or more threads. A thread belongs to one and only one process.

Advantages of Multithreading Applications

Each thread will get a *time slice* of the microprocessor, which is an allotted time for the thread to execute. Inside Windows, threads are prioritized by the operating system. When a thread's time slice is up, Windows will choose the thread with the highest priority and give it the processor. To determine thread priority, Windows considers the thread's internal priority as well as whether or not the thread is waiting for something, such as a background print job. You can see from this model that threads will not only be competing with the "outside" for processor time, they also compete with other threads from the same application, if that application is multithreaded.

There are a variety of circumstances when multithreading can be useful to an application. The first factor to consider is the possibility of running the application on a machine with two or more processors. If this is what you will be doing, your application is a good candidate for multithreading. In this kind of scenario, Windows will be able to allocate one thread to each processor, which can drastically improve the performance of the application. In the ideal case, the number of threads used should be matched to the number of microprocessors on the machine. If you are running an application on a machine with a single processor, multithreading is probably not a good idea. In fact, it might actually hurt the performance of the application. This is because

Windows will have to take time to swap threads in and out with the same microprocessor, wasting time that would be better spent computing with a single thread.

The next question to ask when considering multithreading is what type of work the application will be doing. A type of application that might be suitable for multithreading is one in which there are several tasks that need to be completed but that can run concurrently. This is especially true if the application you are developing does a great deal of number crunching. Say that you were running calculations on an extremely large chunk of data that could be stored in an array. Also suppose that the calculations on each element are independent of the calculations done on the other elements. We could speed things along by splitting the data into two chunks, and then using a separate thread to process each chunk on a machine with two processors. This will run much faster than if we had just processed the whole data set on a single processor.

Another area where number crunching might benefit from multithreading is when you have a series of operations that operate in assembly-line fashion. Let's suppose that we have operations A, B, and C. Each operation is processed in sequence, so A acts on a piece of data, which is then fed to B, and when B finishes, the data is passed onto C. As operations B and C begin to crunch the numbers, operation A has fetched more data to operate on, which it again feeds to B. The process will continue until A runs out of data. Now imagine that this application happens to be running on a machine with three processors. You can also see that the application will benefit from multithreading if you assign a thread to each process, A, B, and C. The operating system will try to assign each thread to its own processor, which means that each of these operations will be running simultaneously, resulting in an application that is much faster.

The final situation that we will consider where multithreading can be useful is when you are performing some background task, such as printing or disk I/O. This results in the "hurry up and wait" situation that users love. When an application is on a machine with multiple processors, however, we can take advantage of multithreading to build faster and more user-friendly applications. The "background" task, such as disk I/O, can be sent off in its own thread and can run independently on the other processor while the "main" thread can operate on the other processor. This way the user does not suffer from having the resources of the computer diverted. To get the speed boost from this type of operation, keep in mind that you should be on a machine with more than one processor; otherwise, performance may actually get worse.

Apartment Model Multithreading

One type of multithreading you will see used with ATL COM controls is *apartment model threading*. In this type of multithreading, the objects in each thread run in a space known as an *apartment*. Each apartment is completely isolated from all others. The isolation includes global data; each thread will get its own copy. While this increases the safety of operation, it means that you cannot use global data to communicate between threads. Apartment model multithreading can be set with the ATL COM Object Wizard.

Multithreading in C++

Visual C++ comes with the ability to use MFC to create multithreaded applications. A thread in an MFC application is represented by the `CWinThread` class, which is inherited from `CCmdTarget`. There are two types of threads that you will be concerned with when creating a multithreaded MFC application: user interface and worker threads.

A *user-interface thread* can be used to process some user action while other threads are executing in the background. For example, this type of thread might be useful in the scenario described above where you are using a thread to perform some disk I/O or to spin off a print job. You can use a user-interface thread to get some user input or respond to user actions while this is going on. You can create your own multithreaded classes by using the Class Wizard. The class may represent some object or document in your application, and it will be based on the `CWinThread` class.

Programming with OLE

Object Linking and Embedding, or OLE, is a technology that can be used to share information between applications. This might mean sharing documents, images, or the services provided by an application. For example, you can embed an Excel chart in a word-processing document, or you can use OLE to program Microsoft Word behind the scenes, using the Word object library.

The MFC App Wizard makes it easy to add OLE to your applications. There are two ways you can do this. The simplest way is to create a container, which means that your application will be able to contain and use objects from other applications, which function as servers. The second method is to create a server application. Unfortunately, there isn't space in the chapter to explore the creation of a server, but we will create a container application with the MFC App Wizard so that you can get an idea of how the process works.

Creating a Container

In this section we will create a container application called SDIContainer. This project will be an SDI-type application created with the MFC App Wizard. You tell the wizard whether or not you want your application to have OLE capabilities on Step 3 (see Figure 14-1). In this step, the wizard will ask you what type of compound document support your application will support. To have it act as a container, click the *Container* radio button. You can include active document support by selecting the *Active Document Container* checkbox.

The wizard will create the usual source code and header files for the SDI app that we are familiar with from previous chapters. One of those files is named *SDIContainerDoc.cpp*. This file contains a message map that enables the application to be an OLE container. The code is displayed here:

```
//////////////////////////////////////////////////////////////////////
////////
// CSDIContainerDoc

IMPLEMENT_DYNCREATE(CSDIContainerDoc, CRichEditDoc)

BEGIN_MESSAGE_MAP(CSDIContainerDoc, CRichEditDoc)
    //{{AFX_MSG_MAP(CSDIContainerDoc)
        // NOTE - the ClassWizard will add and remove mapping macros here.
        // DO NOT EDIT what you see in these blocks of generated code!
    //}}AFX_MSG_MAP
    // Enable default OLE container implementation
    ON_UPDATE_COMMAND_UI(ID_OLE_EDIT_LINKS,
CRichEditDoc::OnUpdateEditLinksMenu)
```

Chapter 14: Advanced Topics

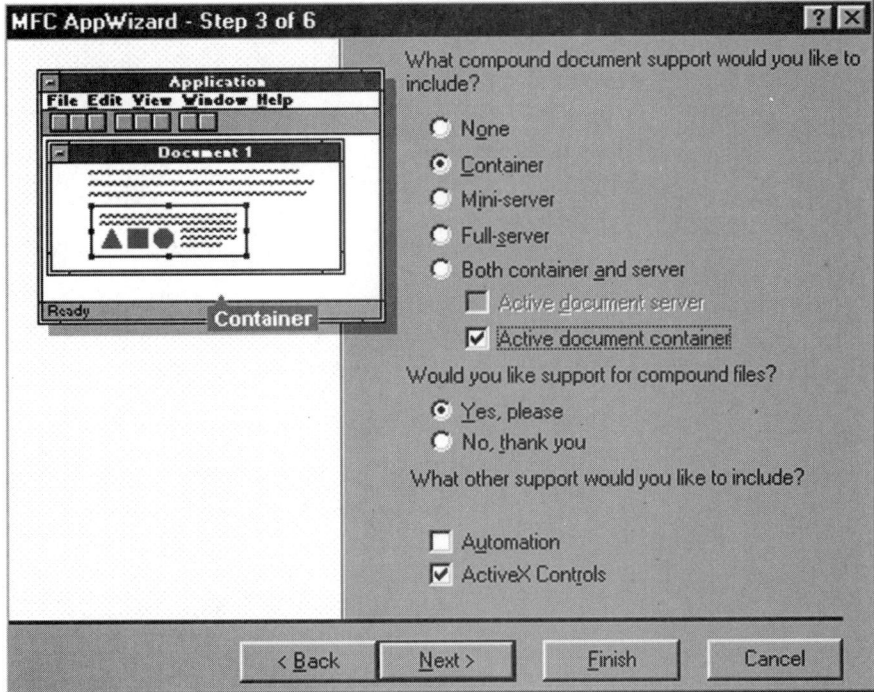

Figure 14-1
Creating an Active document container.

```
     ON_COMMAND(ID_OLE_EDIT_LINKS, CRichEditDoc::OnEditLinks)
     ON_UPDATE_COMMAND_UI_RANGE(ID_OLE_VERB_FIRST, ID_OLE_VERB_LAST,
CRichEditDoc::OnUpdateObjectVerbMenu)
END_MESSAGE_MAP()

/////////////////////////////////////////////////////////////////////
///////
// CSDIContainerDoc construction/destruction

CSDIContainerDoc::CSDIContainerDoc()
{

     // Use OLE compound files
     EnableCompoundFile();

     // TODO: add one-time construction code here

}

CSDIContainerDoc::~7ECSDIContainerDoc()
{
}

BOOL CSDIContainerDoc::OnNewDocument()
{
     if (!CRichEditDoc::OnNewDocument())
        return FALSE;
```

```
        // TODO: add reinitialization code here
        // (SDI documents will reuse this document)

        return TRUE;
}

CRichEditCntrItem*
CSDIContainerDoc::CreateClientItem(REOBJECT* preo) const
{
        // cast away constness of this
        return new CSDIContainerCntrItem(preo, (CSDIContainerDoc*) this);
}

/////////////////////////////////////////////////////////////////////
///////
// CSDIContainerDoc serialization

void CSDIContainerDoc::Serialize(CArchive& ar)
{
        if (ar.IsStoring())
        {
                // TODO: add storing code here
        }
        else
        {
                // TODO: add loading code here
        }

        // Calling the base class CRichEditDoc enables serialization
        // of the container document's COleClientItem objects.
        // TODO: set CRichEditDoc::m_bRTF = FALSE if you are serializing
as text
        CRichEditDoc::Serialize(ar);
}

/////////////////////////////////////////////////////////////////////
///////
// CSDIContainerDoc diagnostics

#ifdef _DEBUG
void CSDIContainerDoc::AssertValid() const
{
        CRichEditDoc::AssertValid();
}

void CSDIContainerDoc::Dump(CDumpContext& dc) const
{
        CRichEditDoc::Dump(dc);
}
#endif //_DEBUG

/////////////////////////////////////////////////////////////////////
///////
// CSDIContainerDoc commands
```

There isn't anything we need to do to the code for our application to work as a container. When we compile the project and run it, if we click

Chapter 14: Advanced Topics

Figure 14-2
Inserting an object.

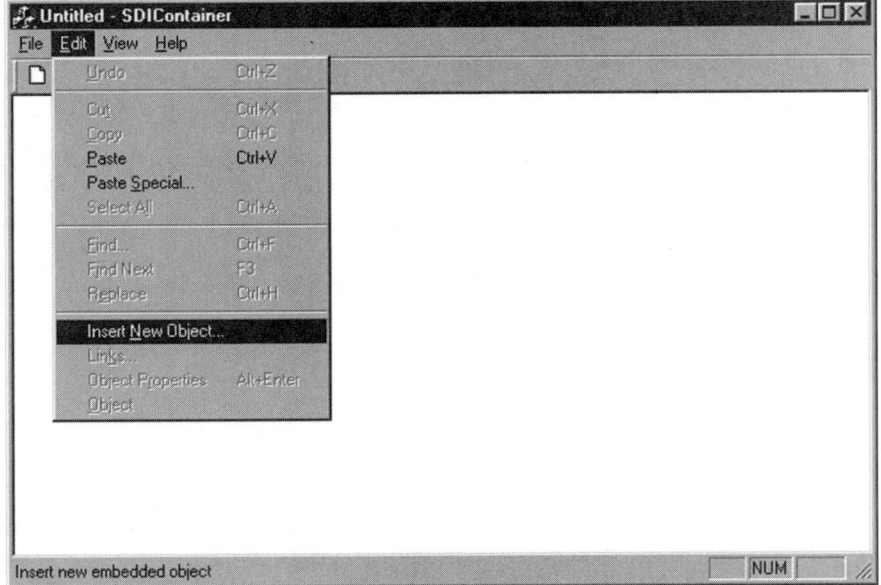

on the *Edit* pull-down menu, we see a new menu item, Insert New Object (see Figure 14-2).

You may be familiar with this menu item; you have probably seen it in some Windows applications that you have used. If we click on it, this will bring up the Insert Object dialog (see Figure 14-3).

Figure 14-3
The Insert Object dialog.

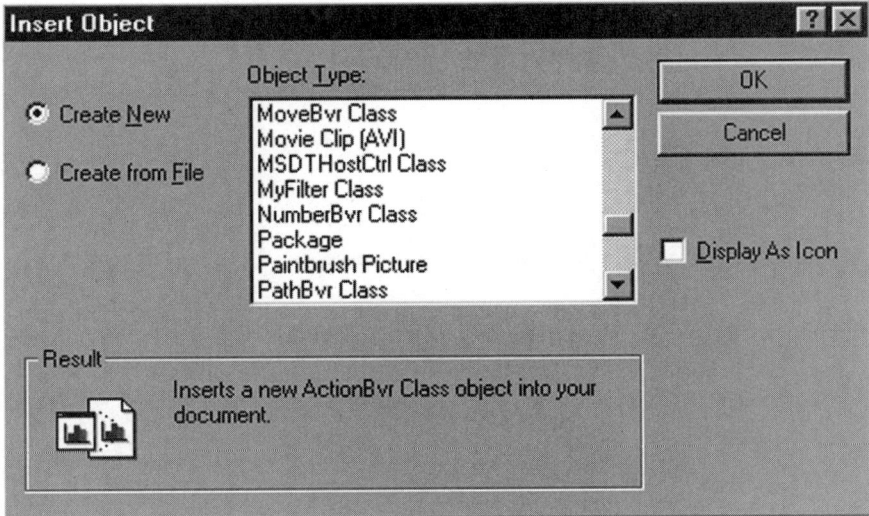

Part 3: Implementation

This will display a list of OLE servers on your system. These servers are applications that can provide objects you can embed in the document or that you can link with to work with them from within your app. You can either create a new object or create from a file.

For our example, select a new Paintbrush picture. What you will find is that when you click the *OK* button, the SDI app created with the MFC App Wizard suddenly takes on the menus and toolbars of the Paintbrush application. You can work with Paintbrush right inside the SDI app to create the object. The object is inserted as a rectangular area in the upper left corner of the document. When you click on this area, the interface of Paintbrush appears, allowing you to work with and modify the object (see Figure 14-4).

Keep in mind that every feature you add to your applications will have to be paid for somewhere, usually in terms of larger file size. However, adding OLE container support to your applications is very easy. If your application works with documents, this will provide a nice user-friendly feature by allowing the user to work with objects from other applications. In today's Windows environment, the user will probably expect some form of container support anyway.

Figure 14-4
Running Paint inside our project.

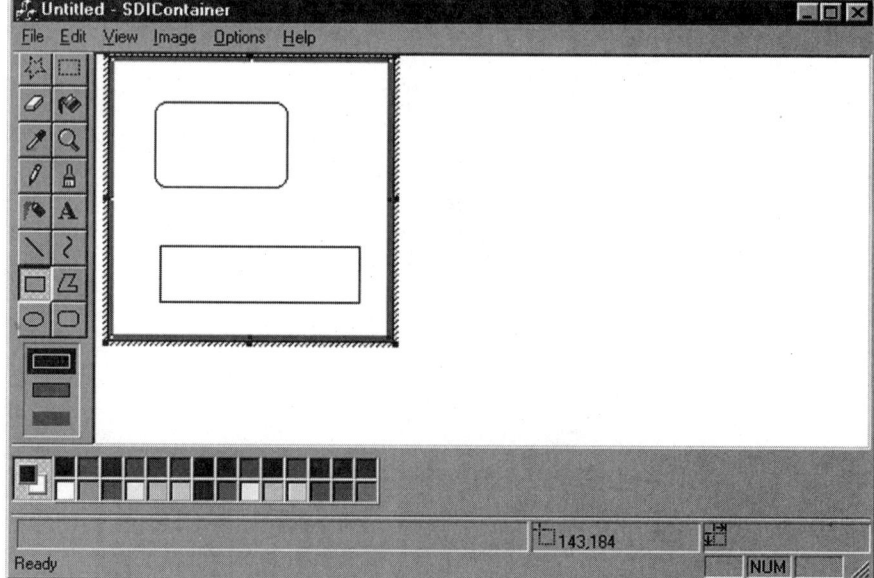

Creating a Dynamic-Link Library

One of the ways that Windows facilitates flexibility and code reuse is through *dynamic-link libraries*, or DLLs, which have a *.dll* extension. If you look in your *Windows/System* directory, you will see that your computer has many DLLs already installed. A DLL is basically a library of functions that is linked together with another application at runtime. This is done instead of linking together the object code when you link and compile the executable, in which case you would be using a *static* library.

With a dynamic-link library, when an application makes a function call to a function in the DLL, the library is loaded into memory. A DLL can be shared among many different applications, promoting code reuse and saving on resources. A single copy of the DLL is loaded into memory and shared among any applications that need to use it. This saves on resources, since only one copy of the library is taking up memory. If the library had been statically linked, each application that uses it would have the library as part of its executable, making each program larger and therefore consuming more resources.

Creating a DLL with Visual C++ is fairly straightforward. The first choice you will have to make is whether to make it an MFC DLL or just a plain Win32 DLL. Let's explore both types, taking a look at the Win32 DLL first.

Creating a Win32 DLL

A plain Win32 DLL is a dynamic-link library that does not use MFC. There are many times that you will not need to use MFC—say, to create your own library of math functions. In this section we will see how to create a Win32 DLL, what elements it needs to have, how to export functions, and how to compile and use it.

You can create a Win32 DLL by selecting *Win32 Dynamic-Link Library* from the New Projects dialog (see Figure 14-5).

This will open a wizard that will allow you to choose whether to create an empty DLL project (in which case you will need to create the appropriate files yourself), a simple DLL project, or a DLL that exports some symbols (see Figure 14-6). We will select the last option, a DLL that exports some symbols. Our project is called Win32Stats2.

There are two elements that a DLL must have. Every DLL must have a `DLLMain` function, and it must export one or more functions, classes, or

Figure 14-5
Creating a dynamic-link library.

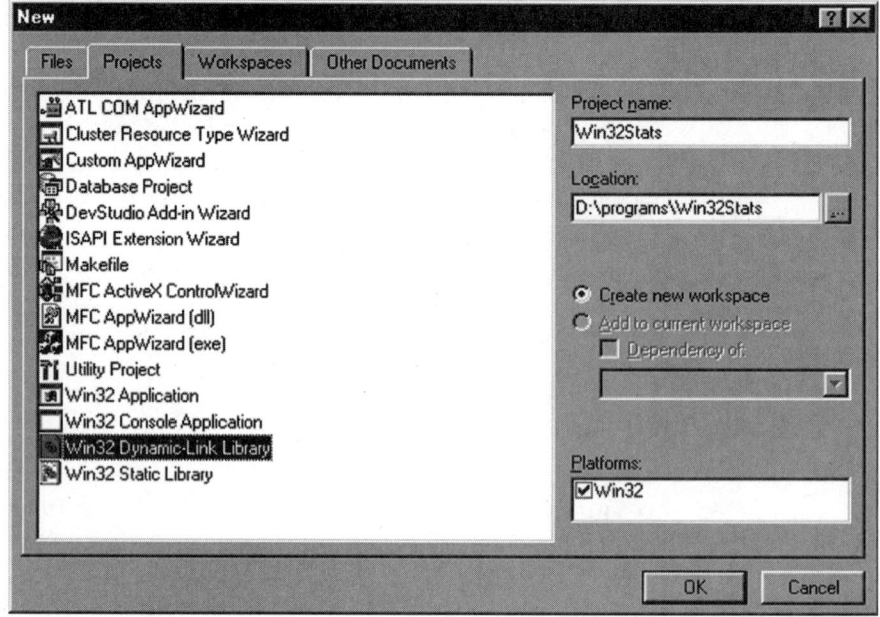

variables. The DLL main function is called whenever a process or thread calls the DLL or detaches from the DLL. When we created the Win32Stats32 DLL, Visual C++ created the `DLLMain` function for us. The code looks like this:

```
BOOL APIENTRY DllMain( HANDLE hModule,
                      DWORD ul_reason_for_call,
                      LPVOID lpReserved
                     )
{
    switch (ul_reason_for_call)
    {
        case DLL_PROCESS_ATTACH:
        case DLL_THREAD_ATTACH:
        case DLL_THREAD_DETACH:
        case DLL_PROCESS_DETACH:
            break;
    }
    return TRUE;
}
```

For most applications, you won't have to worry about the `DLLMain` function and can just use the code that the wizard created. However, if your DLL needs to take some special action based on why it was called, you can use this function. As you can see from this example, the `ul_Reason` parameter can be used to see why the DLL was called.

Chapter 14: Advanced Topics

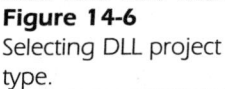

Figure 14-6
Selecting DLL project type.

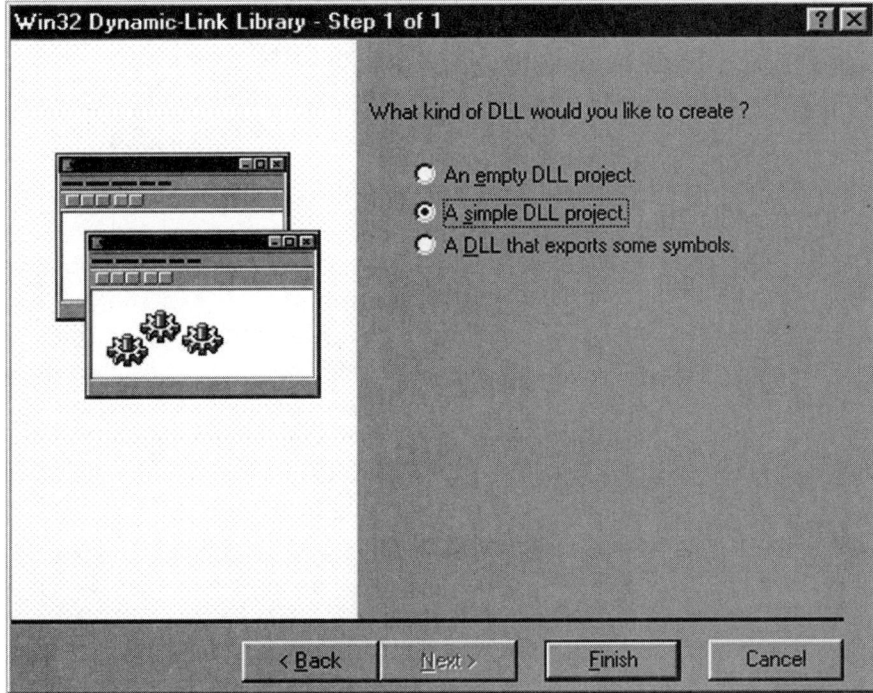

Visual C++ has already added a `switch` statement to the `DLLMain` function that we can use to add code to handle each case. For example, if we need to add some initialization code when a process calls the DLL, we can add it to the case `DLL_PROCESS_ATTACH` block.

Earlier we stated that a DLL must export something; otherwise, it can't be of much use. Usually, a DLL is used to export one or more functions, which can then be called by other applications. When we created the Win32Stats2 DLL, Visual C++ created a class named `CWin32Stats2` and it also added one function we can examine to see how to export. The code for that function is listed here:

```
// This is an example of an exported function.
WIN32STATS2_API int fnWin32Stats2(void)
{
    return 42;
}
```

The key is the `WIN32STATS2_API` specifier that we see before the usual function header. This is a macro that tells the compiler to export the function. The definition of the macro can be found in a header file that Visual C++ added to the project for us when we created it. This is in the *Win32Stats2.h* file. When we open that file, we see the following preprocessor definition:

```
#ifdef WIN32STATS2_EXPORTS
#define WIN32STATS2_API __declspec(dllexport)
#else
#define WIN32STATS2_API __declspec(dllimport)
#endif
```

The key is the `dllexport` keyword. This keyword is used to tell the compiler to export the function. When the project was created, Visual C++ created the macro `WIN32STATS2_API`, which can be used in place of the `dllexport` keyword. To export a function, we simply include the macro before the usual function header. The function will then be available as part of the library when we compile it to a DLL file.

For our example, we will create a small statistics library. The library will perform the following functions:

- Average
- Variance
- Standard deviation
- Mean absolute deviation

We can write functions to perform each of these tasks, and then export them so that our statistics library can be used by other applications. We can either include them in the class that was created or export them in the same manner as the sample function. We will choose the latter.

We begin by defining function headers for each task. Each function will operate on a one-dimensional array of type `double`. Each function will accept two parameters: the array and a `short` representing the number of elements in the array. The function headers are as follows:

```
WIN32STATS2_API double Average(double *in_data, short NumItems);
WIN32STATS2_API double Variance(double *in_data, short NumItems);
WIN32STATS2_API double StdDeviation(double *in_data, short NumItems);
WIN32STATS2_API double MeanAbsDev(double *in_data, short NumItems);
```

Notice that we have preceded each function declaration with the `WIN32STATS2_API` macro, which tells the compiler that each function will be exported. The function declarations are included in the *Win32Stats2.h file*.

The function bodies for each task will be placed in the source code file, *Win32Stats2.cpp*. Again, remember that we need to precede each function header by the macro used to define the `dllexport` specifier. The code for the functions is as follows:

Chapter 14: Advanced Topics

```c
WIN32STATS2_API double Average(double *in_data, short NumItems)
{
    //Function : Average
    //Description : Returns the average of the elements
    //contained in the in_data array.

    double ave=0; //return value for function
    double sum=0; //holds sum of array elements
    short j; //loop counter
    for(j=0; j < NumItems; j++)
        sum += in_data[j];

    ave = sum/(double)NumItems;

    return(ave);

}

WIN32STATS2_API double Variance(double *in_data, short NumItems)
{

    //Function : Variance
    //Description : Returns the variance for
    //array in_data

    short j; //loop counter
    double sumx=0, sumsquared=0;
    double variance=0;

    for(j=0; j < NumItems; j++)
    {
        sumx += in_data[j];
        sumsquared += pow(in_data[j],2); //sum squares of elements
    }//next j

  variance = (sumsquared -
(pow(sumx,2)/(double)NumItems))/((double)NumItems -1.0);

  return(variance);

}//end function variance

WIN32STATS2_API double StdDeviation(double *in_data, short NumItems)
{
    //Function : StdDeviation
     //Returns standard deviation for elements
     //in in_data array.

    double variance=0;
    double std_deviation=0;

    //find the variance
    variance = Variance(in_data,NumItems);

    //return standard deviation
    std_deviation = sqrt(variance);

    return(std_deviation);

}//end function standard deviation
```

```
WIN32STATS2_API double MeanAbsDev(double *in_data, short NumItems)
{
    //Function : MeanAbsDev
    //Finds the mean absolute deviation

    double sumdeviation=0;
    double deviation=0; //deviation for each array element
    double ave=0; //average for the array
    double mad=0; //return value
    short j; //loop counter

    //find the average
    ave = Average(in_data,NumItems);
    //find individual deviations
    for(j = 0; j < NumItems; j++)
    {
        deviation = (double)abs(in_data[j] - ave);
        sumdeviation += deviation;
    }//next j

    mad = sumdeviation/NumItems;

    return(mad);

}//end function mean absolute deviation
```

Notice that we use the `pow` and `sqrt` functions. These functions are in the *math.h* file, so we add the following #include statement to our *Win32Stats2.cpp* file:

```
#include <math.h>
```

The `abs` function, which returns the absolute value of an expression, is found in the *stdlib.h* file.

Compiling a DLL

Now that we have added the functions we will export, we are ready to compile the library. This is done in the usual manner; you can click the *Execute* icon on the Visual C++ toolbar or select *Build Win32Stats2.DLL* or *Execute* from the Build pull-down menu. When you do this, if your project compiles successfully, Visual C++ will create a DLL file. Be sure to note where the DLL file is placed. If you are creating a debug version of your project, the DLL file will be located in the */Debug* directory of your project. If you selected Execute, you will be prompted to select an executable file to run the DLL. Before we get to that point, we need to see how to use a DLL in another Visual C++ application.

Chapter 14: Advanced Topics

Importing from a DLL

Once you have your DLL written and successfully compiled, you will need to build an application to test it. This will probably include another Visual C++ application, but you may also write DLLs for use with other languages, such as Visual Basic. If you are writing a generic DLL, you may want to test the DLL in multiple-language platforms before releasing it, to ensure that your variable passing works correctly no matter which tool is used with your DLL. Here we will focus on using a DLL in another Visual C++ program.

Actually, using a DLL in another Visual C++ program is quite simple. As usual, you will need to include function headers, just like you would for any function you use in a C++ program. In this case, however, we use a special keyword, extern, which tells the compiler that we are getting the function from the outside. This keyword is placed immediately preceding the function declaration, in a similar manner to the macro we used to represent __declspec(dllexport) when creating the DLL. In fact, we will just copy and paste the function declarations from the *Win32Stats2.h* file into the new project. We created a Win32 console application to test the DLL, but you could use any type of Windows app. Here we placed the function declarations just before the main function of our console program, including the extern keyword:

```
extern double Average(double *in_data, short NumItems);
extern double Variance(double *in_data, short NumItems);
extern double StdDeviation(double *in_data, short NumItems);
extern double MeanAbsDev(double *in_data, short NumItems);
```

Now we can write code to use the functions. Since this is a test program, we will just load a dummy array with some data and call each function. Next, we will print the results to the screen. This code is included in the main function of our console app:

```
int main(int argc, char* argv[])
{
    double mydata[MAX];
    double myave=0;
    double myvariance=0, mystddev=0, meandev=0;
    //load some numbers
    for(int i=0; i < MAX; i++)
        mydata[i] = (double)i;

    //find the average, variance,
    //standard deviation and mean absolute
```

```
//deviation
myave = Average(&mydata[0],MAX);
myvariance = Variance(&mydata[0], MAX);
mystddev = StdDeviation(&mydata[0],MAX);
meandev = MeanAbsDev(&mydata[0], MAX);

//report the answers
cout << "\nAverage : " << myave;
cout << "\nVariance : " << myvariance;
cout << "\nStandard Deviation : " << mystddev;
cout << "\nMean Absolute Deviation : " << meandev;

return 0;
}
```

Everything is pretty straightforward. Once you have the function declarations in your project, you can write code to call the functions as if they were a part of your project. As an aside, note how we pass the array to each function. We declared the array as a pointer of type `double` in each function declaration. This means that the function is expecting an address, which points to a type `double`. We can pass an array to a function like this by passing the address of the first element of the array. We did this when we called the `Average` function:

```
myave = Average(&mydata[0],MAX);
```

When the function `Average` executes, the address of the first element of the array will be passed to it. It can then use that address to locate the rest of the array.

At this point, we have almost done everything we need to for our DLL to work properly. There are only a few more things we need to do. First we need to open the Project Settings dialog for the application that will use the DLL. We need to tell the linker where it can find the library. This is done by clicking on the *Link* tab and providing a path to the LIB file that is associated with the DLL. When you compile the DLL, the compiler creates the LIB file for you. It will have the same name as the DLL project, so in this case the file is named *Win32Stats2.lib*. The LIB file name must be entered in the Object/Library Modules input box of the Link tab, as shown in Figure 14-7.

You will need to include the full path. In this case, since we compiled a debug version of the DLL, the LIB file is located in the Debug folder, which we have indicated. If Visual C++ has included other LIB or OBJ files in this input box, just place the cursor at the end and type in the needed information. No commas or other characters are needed to delimit the various libraries; just use a space. Once you have typed in the correct path and file name, click the *OK* button.

Chapter 14: Advanced Topics

Figure 14-7
DLL Project Settings.

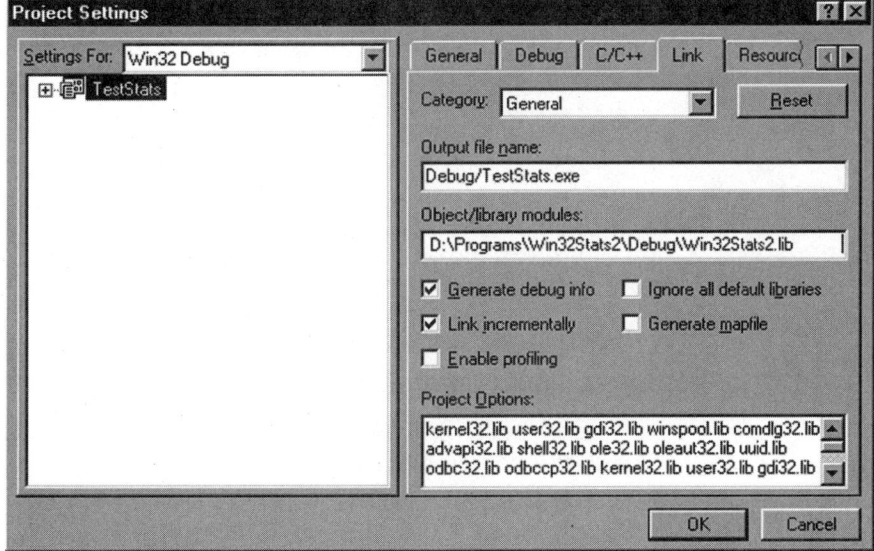

Next, we need to place the DLL somewhere our test program can find it. Most DLLs are placed in the *Windows/System* directory. For testing, you can simply copy the DLL file and place it in the *Debug* directory of your test program. That is all there is to it. We are ready to compile our test program and run the code that calls the DLL. In summary, here are the steps required to use a DLL in a Visual C++ program:

1. Include the function declarations for each DLL function you will call. Precede each function declaration with the `extern` keyword.
2. Write the code to call the functions as needed. There is nothing special that needs to be done here.
3. Open the dialog under *Project | Settings* and click on the *Link* tab. Enter the path and file name of the LIB file for the DLL in the Object/Library Modules input box.
4. Place the DLL in a location where your program can find it. A good place is in the *Debug* directory where the executable will be placed.

Once you have compiled a test executable, you can also run it from the DLL project. When you click the *Execute* icon in your DLL project, a dialog box will open named Executable for Debug Session (see Figure 14-8). Click on the small arrow on the right side of the Executable File Name input box, and locate the executable file you will use. This way, you can test and debug your DLL with the DLL project open. I usually set the output file name for the DLL project to the directory I am using for my

Figure 14-8
Selecting the Executable file for testing.

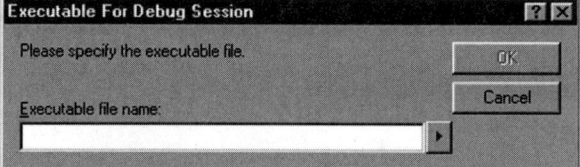

test application, so that I can recompile the DLL as necessary without having to copy the DLL to that location.

MFC App Wizard DLLs

If you will be using MFC in your DLL, you can use the MFC App Wizard to create the DLL instead. To create a DLL using the MFC App Wizard:

1. Open the dialog under *New | Projects*.
2. Select *MFC App Wizard(dll)*.
3. Type in a project name and click *OK*.

The next step is to specify how you want to link with MFC, as shown in Figure 14-9. The choices are as follows:

- Regular DLL with MFC statically linked
- Regular DLL using shared MFC DLL
- MFC extension DLL (using shared MFC DLL)

The choice you will make basically comes down to two things. First, if you are going to actually extend the MFC Library, then you will want to create an MFC extension DLL. If you will not be extending the MFC Library but only using it, create a regular DLL. If you are creating a regular DLL, use shared MFC DLL if you want to minimize your file size. You can use static linking to increase your performance a bit; however, this will greatly increase the size of your file, since the MFC Library will have to be linked to your DLL at compile time. You will also be able to use automation and Windows Sockets in your DLL if desired. When you click the *Finish* button, the App Wizard will generate the files for your project. You can then go about writing the functions that you will export in the same way that we did in the previous example.

One important difference you will notice when you create a DLL this way is the presence of a DEF file in the project. This is just a text file that is used to tell Visual C++ which files we will export. In a DLL that

Chapter 14: Advanced Topics

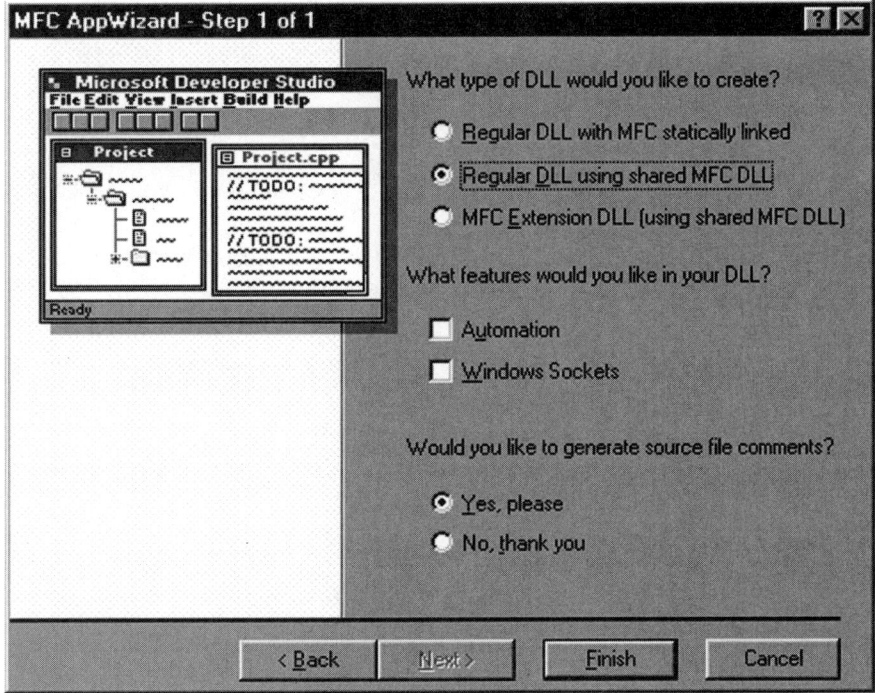

Figure 14-9
Creating a DLL with the MFC App Wizard.

uses a DEF file, you don't need to use the __declspec(dllexport) macro with your function declarations. Instead, you just write your functions like you would in any regular C++ program. You use the DEF file to specify which functions will be exported. For example, if we created a DLL called MFCDLL for our stats library using the MFC App Wizard, we would tell the compiler to export the functions we wrote in the DEF file, like this:

```
; MFCDLL.def : Declares the module parameters for the DLL.


LIBRARY "MFCDLL"
DESCRIPTION 'MFCDLL Windows Dynamic Link Library'

EXPORTS
    ; Explicit exports can go here
    Average
    Variance
    StdDeviation
```

Initially, the EXPORTS section will be blank. After the line with a semicolon (which represents a comment), you simply place the function name of each function that you want to export. When you compile the DLL, Visual C++ will then automatically export each function. The function declarations themselves look pretty normal:

```
double __stdcall Average(double *in_data, short NumItems);
double __stdcall Variance(double *in_data, short NumItems);
double __stdcall StdDeviation(double *in_data, short NumItems);
```

as do the function bodies. (Note, however, that we are using the `stdcall` calling convention here, so that we can use the functions with Visual Basic; see your Visual C++ documentation for a discussion on calling conventions.) For example, here is how the `Average` function looks in a DLL with a DEF file:

```
double __stdcall Average(double *in_data, short NumItems)
{
    //Function : Average
    //Description : Returns the average of the elements
    //contained in the in_data array.

    double ave=0; //return value for function
    double sum=0; //holds sum of array elements
    short j; //loop counter

    for(j=0; j < NumItems; j++)
        sum += in_data[j];

    ave = sum/(double)NumItems;

    return(ave);

}
```

The `WIN32STATS2_API` macro that we created in the previous example is not required here, since the DEF file tells the compiler to export the function.

You can also use a DEF file when you create a non-MFC Win32 DLL. To do so, after you create your project, add a regular text file to the project. Then save it with a *.def* file extension. Next, you need to add three lines, in all caps:

- LIBRARY
- DESCRIPTION
- EXPORTS

After the `LIBRARY` keyword, include the name of the compiled DLL file without the file extension in double quotes. Next to `DESCRIPTION`, include a description of the library in single quotes. Following the

EXPORTS keyword, you can add the names of the functions that you want to export.

For another example, consider a DLL named *MyFile.DLL* that exports the following functions:

```
void SaveFile(CString FileName);
bool OpenFile(CString FileName);
void PrintFile();
```

The DEF file would look like this:

```
LIBRARY "MYFILE"
DESCRIPTION `MyFile Windows Dynamic Link Library'

EXPORTS
   SaveFile
   OpenFile
   PrintFile
```

To include any comments, use a semicolon.

ActiveX Controls

Perhaps no other feature of Windows programming illustrates the concepts of code reuse and object orientation better than an ActiveX control. The ActiveX control provides the developer with a simple means for creating a sophisticated user interface with little or no programming required. The control literally is an object that can be inserted into just about any type of Windows program and can be used across development platforms. You can create an ActiveX control in Visual C++ and then use it in Visual Basic, Microsoft Access, or Delphi. Since the control is compiled to an OCX file, the developer who uses the control in his or her projects really sees the control as a black box; the code that makes it work is completely hidden. The only way to access the control is through the interface of methods, properties, and events. If the control is updated, code written to work with the old version of the control will still work; the new version of the control is simply dropped into a project, and the developer can then take advantage of the new features without abandoning the old interface. ActiveX controls are truly an object-oriented method of software development.

The controls that are available have a wide range of complexity and functionality. Simple controls let you add extended versions of the standard controls, such as labels, command buttons, and text boxes. More-sophisticated controls, such as word-processor controls, communications controls, or advanced graphing tools, let a developer quickly add complex behavior to a project with a minimal amount of programming. This saves a great deal of time; having to build such complex behavior from scratch would take hundreds of programming hours or more.

Recent versions of Visual C++, including version 6.0, provide the developer with two ways to create ActiveX controls. The first method is to use the MFC ActiveX Control Wizard. You can also create a control using the Active Template Library, or ATL. After going over the basic concepts used in ActiveX control design, we will create a simple ActiveX control using the two methods.

Control Basics

You begin the process of creating an ActiveX control in the same way that you begin every other task in Visual C++, by starting a new project. There are two options available when creating an ActiveX control:

- ATL COM App Wizard
- MFC ActiveX Control Wizard

The first step in creating your control is to decide which method of control creation is the best to use for the control. The MFC ActiveX Control Wizard is easier to use because it provides a ready-to-use control skeleton. If you are new to Visual C++, this is probably a point to consider; you will be able to develop controls in less time using MFC.

An experienced Visual C++ user may be more inclined to use ATL. An ATL control will have less premade code created by Visual C++, so in a sense it is more your creation than an MFC control would be. You will have more direct influence over every aspect of the control with ATL.

In addition, an ATL control will in general be smaller than one created with MFC. A client application may also require the presence of MFC libraries in order to use the control, adding some overhead. If the size of the file and using the MFC Library would create problems, then ATL may be a more attractive choice. However, if you are looking for a faster way to create a control and like the ease of use that the MFC wizards provide, an MFC-based control is an attractive choice.

Before we illustrate how to create a control with an example, let's take a look at an overview of the process, as well as at some basic characteristics that ActiveX controls have.

Chapter 14: Advanced Topics

Overview of Creating an ActiveX Control

If you are creating an ActiveX control with MFC, you will generally use the following steps:

- Start a new project by launching the MFC ActiveX Control Wizard.
- Specify how many controls will be in your project. You can create a project with multiple controls if desired, but each control will still be a separate entity.
- Specify if you want the control to require a runtime license.
- Choose a base class, if desired, for your control. By including a base class, you can take advantage of the functionality already available in MFC classes like `CEditBox`, `CListBox`, and so on.
- Define any custom methods and events that your control will support.
- Add custom properties to the control.
- Edit the About dialog box and property page for the control.
- Compile the control to an OCX file and test it. You can test it with the ActiveX Control Test Container found on the Tools menu.
- Modify any resources if necessary, such as the bitmap used to represent the control in a developer's toolbox.

The Control Class

MFC ActiveX controls are based on the `COleControl` class. This class will be given a name based on what you called the project. The class will include the properties, methods, and events that you define for the control. For example, here we see the class header for an ActiveX control named `xcontrol`. The control has one custom method, `mymethod`, one custom property, `myproperty`, and one custom event, `myevent`:

```
// CXcontrolCtrl : See XcontrolCtl.cpp for implementation.

class CXcontrolCtrl : public COleControl
{
    DECLARE_DYNCREATE(CXcontrolCtrl)
    // Constructor
public:
    CXcontrolCtrl();

    // Overrides
        // ClassWizard generated virtual function overrides
        //{{AFX_VIRTUAL(CXcontrolCtrl)
```

```cpp
        public:
            virtual void OnDraw(CDC* pdc, const CRect& rcBounds,
const CRect& rcInvalid);
            virtual BOOL PreCreateWindow(CREATESTRUCT& cs);
            virtual void DoPropExchange(CPropExchange* pPX);
            virtual void OnResetState();
            //}}AFX_VIRTUAL

    // Implementation
    protected:
        CXcontrolCtrl();

        DECLARE_OLECREATE_EX(CXcontrolCtrl)     // Class factory and guid
        DECLARE_OLETYPELIB(CXcontrolCtrl)       // GetTypeInfo
        DECLARE_PROPPAGEIDS(CXcontrolCtrl)      // Property page IDs
        DECLARE_OLECTLTYPE(CXcontrolCtrl)       // Type name and misc
status

        // Subclassed control support
        BOOL IsSubclassedControl();
        LRESULT OnOcmCommand(WPARAM wParam, LPARAM lParam);

    // Message maps
        //{{AFX_MSG(CXcontrolCtrl)
            // NOTE - ClassWizard will add and remove member functions
here.
            //     DO NOT EDIT what you see in these blocks of generated
code !
        //}}AFX_MSG
        DECLARE_MESSAGE_MAP()

    // Dispatch maps
        //{{AFX_DISPATCH(CXcontrolCtrl)
        float m_myProperty;
        afx_msg void OnMyPropertyChanged();
        afx_msg BOOL MyMethod(short Test);
        //}}AFX_DISPATCH
        DECLARE_DISPATCH_MAP()

        afx_msg void AboutBox();

    // Event maps
        //{{AFX_EVENT(CXcontrolCtrl)
        void FireMyEvent(short EventParam)
            {FireEvent(eventidMyEvent,EVENT_PARAM(VTS_I2), EventParam);}
        //}}AFX_EVENT
        DECLARE_EVENT_MAP()

    // Dispatch and event IDs
    public:
        enum {
        //{{AFX_DISP_ID(CXcontrolCtrl)
        dispidMyProperty = 1L,
        dispidMyMethod = 2L,
        eventidMyEvent = 1L,
        //}}AFX_DISP_ID
        };
};
```

Chapter 14: Advanced Topics

```
//{{AFX_INSERT_LOCATION}}
// Microsoft Visual C++ will insert additional declarations immedi-
ately before the previous line.

#endif //
!defined(AFX_XCONTROLCTL_H__0E043B6E_66D2_11D3_856B_A5AF83992E53__
INCLUDED)
```

The class created to represent your control has two interesting sections:

- `Dispatch maps`, used for custom properties and methods
- `Event maps`, used for custom events

Unless you are an experienced developer, don't edit the code here directly. Use the Class Wizard to manipulate the class. If you look at the `Dispatch maps` section, you will see the representation of the custom property, `myproperty`, by a member variable named `m_myProperty`. You will also notice a function header definition for the custom method we created, named `MyMethod`. We defined the method to accept one parameter of type `short`, named `Test`. The custom event we created is defined by the `FireEvent` defined in the `Event maps` section. We will see how to add custom properties, methods, and events to a control later in this chapter.

Subclassing a Control

We mentioned above that you can base the control on an existing MFC class. This can be helpful when creating simple controls; you can take advantage of the functionality already present in the parent class and use the appearance of that class to determine how your control will appear. When you create your control with the MFC Wizard, you will be asked which class you want to base your control class on.

Custom Methods, Properties, and Events

Before we continue, let's get a good handle on what methods, properties, and events are. In our discussion on object-oriented programming in Chapter 6, we used an example of a car to explain what these concepts mean. Let's quickly review them here.

A *property* is some characteristic an object can have. For example, a car has several properties such as weight, color, make, and model. When you create an ActiveX control, it will also have properties associated with it. For example, it may have height and width properties that the developer can modify to resize the control. Another useful property might be the background color of the control. You can add properties to your control by right-clicking in the Class View window. A property will be represented by a member variable of the control class. You can create properties that are based on standard properties like BackColor, Caption, or Enabled, or you can create your own properties from scratch.

A *method* is something that we can do to the object or an action we can make the object take. Think back to the car example. Filling the car with gas can be represented by a method. Or perhaps pressing the accelerator is another method. In code, a method is represented by a function, and it can accept parameters. You can add methods based on the methods of the base class, such as DoClick, or you can create your own methods from scratch.

An *event* is something that can happen to an object. In our car example, one event that we imagined was an accident. With a control, an event is something initiated by a user, such as a mouse click, or something initiated by the operating system. You can define custom events for your control and determine what parameters are passed to the event, but the developer who uses your control in a project of his or her own will write the code to respond to the event.

Ambient, Stock, and Extender Properties

Ambient properties are those that can be used to obtain information about the environment of the ActiveX control. In other words, ambient properties provide information about the form or container control where your control has been sited by the developer. Examples of ambient properties include BackColor, ForeColor, or Font. An ambient property is accessed by a call to the COleControl::GetAmbientProperty function. This function accepts three parameters. The syntax is as follows:

```
COleControl::GetAmbientProperty (DISPID dispatchID, VARTYPE tag, void* retvalue);
```

Some of the useful ambient properties are as follows:

- *BackColor*—The background color of the form or container control where your control has been sited

Chapter 14: Advanced Topics

- *AmbientDisplayName*—The name the user has assigned to your control
- *UserMode*—A Boolean property that tells you whether the control is in the design environment or user mode (i.e., a running program).

In the following code example, we determine which mode the control is currently in, design more or user mode:

```
bool bMode; //user mode is false at design time

GetAmbientProperty(DISP_ID_AMBIENT_USERMODE,VT_BOOL,&bMode);

if(bMode == true)
  //code for runtime here
else
  //code for design mode here
```

We can obtain the display name of the control by calling the `AmbientDisplayName` function, which returns the display name as type `CString`:

```
CString MyControlName;
MyControlName = AmbientDisplayName();
```

The ambient properties are obtained from the `COleControl` class member functions. See your online documentation for more information.

Another useful type of property is a stock property. A *stock property* is a basic property such as BackColor, Caption, or Font that many controls have. Stock properties are automatically supported by the parent class, if you used one to create your control. You can create a stock property for your control by clicking open the *External Name* drop-down list when you create the property and selecting one of the properties from the list. Then select *Stock* for the implementation.

Finally, there are extender properties. An *extender property* is one that is provided by the container where the developer has placed your control. These properties have been "extended" to your control, hence the name. These are built-in controls that every control has, and they depend on where the user puts your control on a dialog box, for example. The extender properties include:

- Index
- Left
- Top
- TabIndex

Each of these properties is determined by the container that hosts the control. There are also built-in extender events, such as `GotFocus` and `LostFocus`. As the developer of the control, you generally won't be concerned about the extender properties; they are there for the benefit of the developer who is using your control.

Drawing a Control

If you are not using a base class for your control (such as `CListBox`, for example), you will have to draw your control. This is done by adding code to the `OnDraw` member function that is part of the class created to represent your control. This function will be added to the control by the MFC ActiveX Control Wizard. For example, when we created the `xcontrol` object, a generic draw function was added to the class:

```
// CXcontrolCtrl::OnDraw - Drawing function

void CXcontrolCtrl::OnDraw(
            CDC* pdc, const CRect& rcBounds, const
CRect& rcInvalid)
{
    DoSuperclassPaint(pdc, rcBounds);
}
```

If you need to customize the appearance of your control, you can add the code here and use the regular drawing methods of Visual C++.

Example: A Simple MFC ActiveX Control

We will now look at how to create a simple ActiveX control using the MFC ActiveX Control Wizard. We will create a control that displays the current date and time within a rectangular border. Start by opening the *New Projects* dialog, and select *MFC ActiveX Control Wizard*. We will call the project DateTime.

The first step of the MFC ActiveX Control Wizard is shown in Figure 14-10. Here we are asked how many controls we want to include in the project, whether or not we want to include a runtime license, and whether or not we want comments and help files included with the project. We will just accept the default settings.

Chapter 14: Advanced Topics

Figure 14-10
The MFC ActiveX Control Wizard.

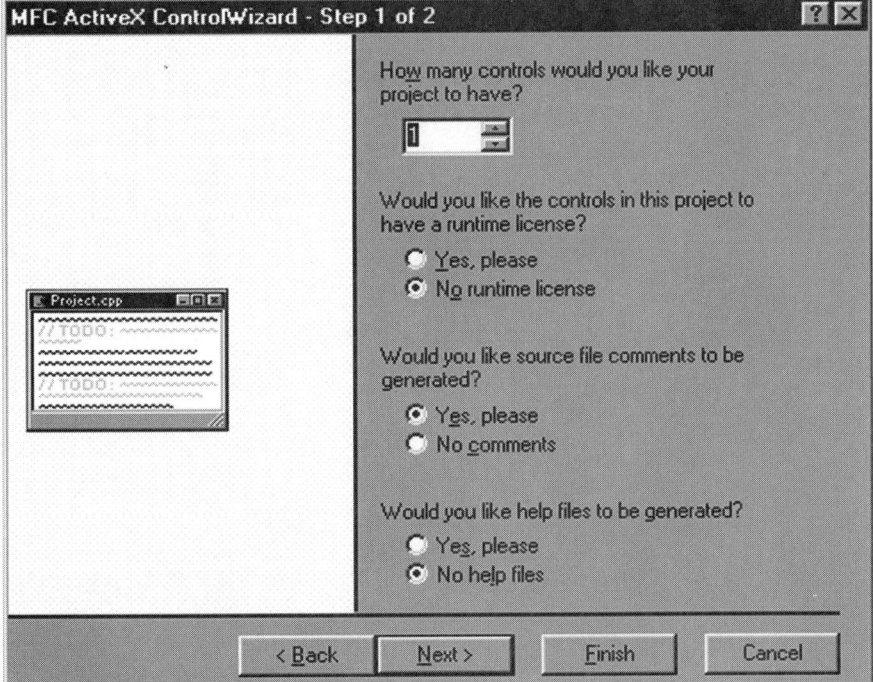

In Step 2 of the wizard, shown in Figure 14-11, we can specify some features that we want the control to have and choose a base class to use for the control. Our control will not subclass any other controls, so we accept the default value of NONE. If you wanted to base your control on one of the basic controls such as a list box, you would click open the subclass list and choose LISTBOX. Other choices include BUTTON and EDITBOX. If desired, we can change the names given to the files and class used to represent the control and modify the Advanced settings. We won't use any advanced settings, so we click the Finish button. The wizard will then create the necessary classes for use in the project. The class created by the wizard to represent the DateTime control is called `CDateTimeCtrl`.

Maintaining the Control's Appearance

If you subclass one of the basic controls, such as a button, this will determine the appearance of your control. If you start from scratch, how-

Figure 14-11
Step 2 of the ActiveX Control Wizard.

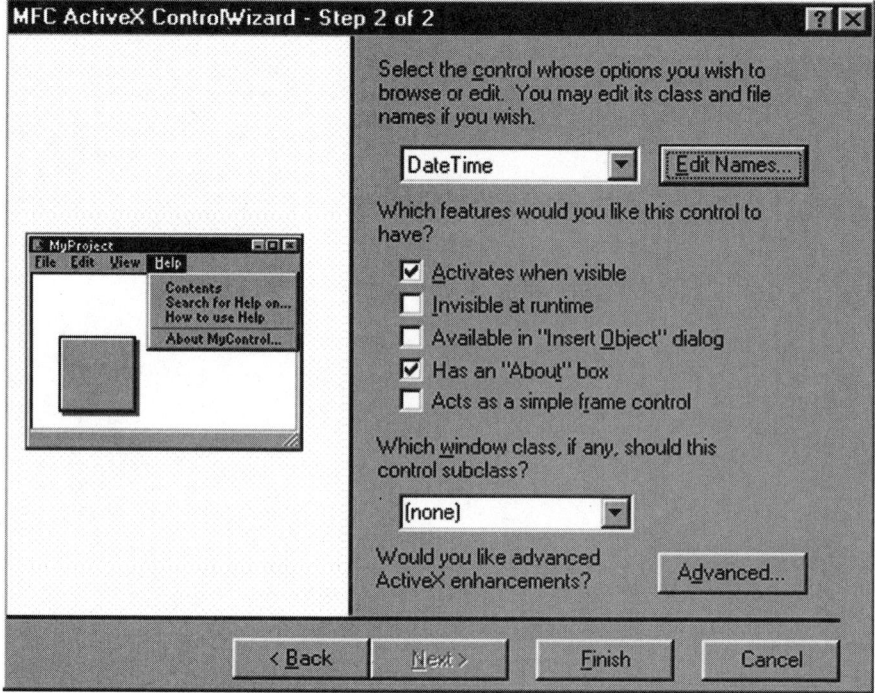

ever, you will need to maintain the appearance of your control with the `OnDraw` member function. When the wizard creates your control, the `OnDraw` function looks like this:

```
// CDateTimeCtrl::OnDraw - Drawing function

void CDateTimeCtrl::OnDraw(CDC* pdc, const CRect& rcBounds, const
CRect& rcInvalid)
{
// TODO: Replace the following code with your own drawing //code.
    pdc->FillRect(rcBounds,
CBrush::FromHandle((HBRUSH)GetStockObject(WHITE_BRUS H)));
    pdc->Ellipse(rcBounds);
}
```

As it stands now, the control will appear as a white rectangle with an ellipse in the center. We will need to modify this function to draw it the way we want. For this example, we will have the control paint a light-gray background and display the caption of the control.

Chapter 14: Advanced Topics

Adding Properties to the Control

You can add properties, methods, and events to your control by using the Class Wizard. Click *Class Wizard* from the View menu, and select the *Automation* tab (see Figure 14-12). This is where you can add the methods and properties for your control. A list displaying the external names for each member is shown on the left side. The external name is the name that developers who use your control will see in the toolbox for properties and when programming your control if they want to invoke a method.

For our example, we will add a property that we will use to display a text string in the center of the control. First, click the *Add Property* button on the Automation tab of the Class Wizard. This opens the Add Property dialog box, shown in Figure 14-13. To add a new property, use the following steps:

1. Specify the external name for the property. This is the name that the developer who uses your control will see in the toolbox, or when referencing the property in code.

Figure 14-12
The Automation tab of the Class Wizard.

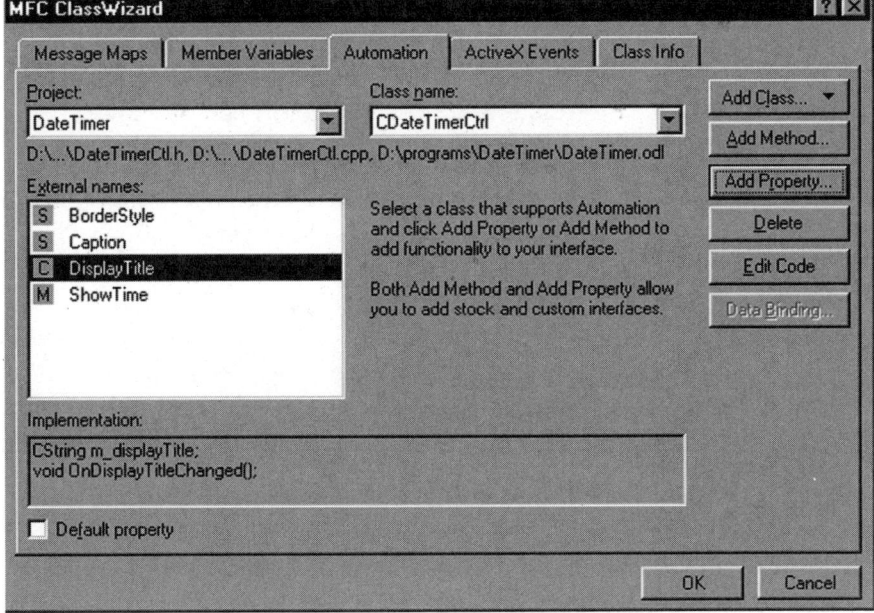

Figure 14-13
The Add Property dialog.

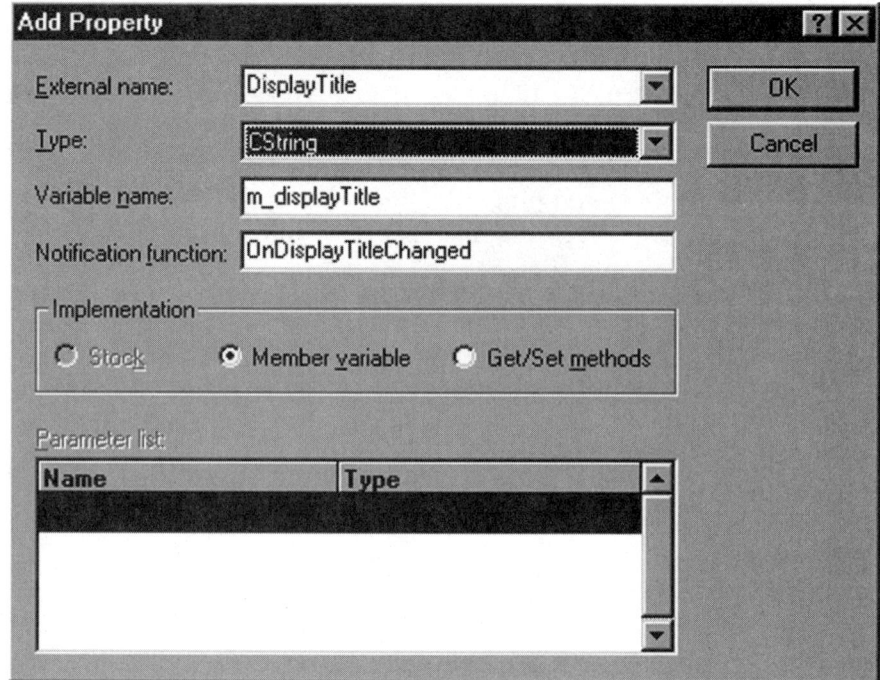

2. Specify the data type for the property by clicking the *Type* drop-down list. The DisplayTitle property will be a text string, so we select type `CString`. This will be the data type of the member variable used to hold the property's value.

3. Edit the member variable name given for the property if desired.

4. In the Implementation frame, select the type of implementation as *Member Variable* or *Get/Set Methods*. If you select *Get/Set Methods*, the property will be maintained by two functions, a `Get` function, which can be used to retrieve the value of the property, and a `Set` function, which can be used to set the property's value. If you want to create a read-only property, you can use Get/Set implementation and leave off the `Set` function. For our example, we will implement the property as a member variable.

5. Click *OK* to add the property.

Earlier I mentioned that a control can use a set of stock properties, which are properties given to the control from the `COleControl` class. Stock properties are familiar standard properties that many controls have such as BackColor, Caption, or Enabled. We will add a BorderStyle

Chapter 14: Advanced Topics

property to our control that will allow the developer to set the border style to NONE or FIXED SINGLE. To add the BorderStyle stock property, use the following steps:

1. Open the Add Property dialog.
2. Click open the *External Name* drop-down list. This will reveal a list of stock properties that are available.
3. Select *BorderStyle*.
4. The Type, Get Function, and Set Function input boxes will be grayed out, while the Implementation box will be set to Stock Property. Select *OK*.

The BorderStyle property will be handled automatically by Visual C++ once the control is compiled.

Adding Custom Methods

Custom and stock methods can also be added to your control from the Automation tab of the Class Wizard. We will add a custom method to the DateTimer control that will display the current system time to the user in a message box. To add a custom method:

1. Click the *Add Method* button on the Automation tab of the Class Wizard. This will open the Add Method dialog box, shown in Figure 14-14.
2. In the External Name input box, type in the name you will use for the method. For our example, we type "ShowTime."
3. If desired, specify an internal name by which the method will be known to the code that is part of your control. Generally, it makes sense to have the same internal and external name for the method, which is the default behavior.
4. Click open the *Return Type* drop-down list, and select a return type for the method. A method is nothing more than a function, so it must have a return type. For this example, select *void*.
5. At the bottom of the screen you will see the Parameter list. It is here where you can specify the name and data type of each parameter that will be passed to the function that represents this method. You must enter the parameters now. If you try to do it later, it will cause problems. To add a parameter, click on the *Name*

Figure 14-14
The Add Method dialog.

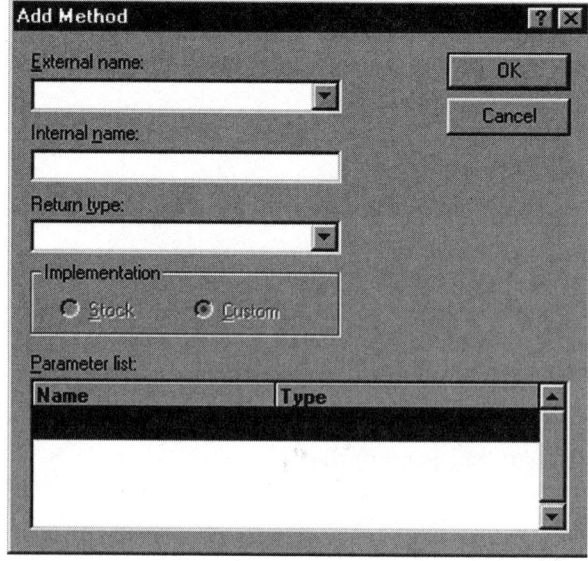

column and type the name of the parameter. We will specify one parameter, named IsLocal. Next, click on the *Type* column. A drop-down list will open allowing you to select a data type for the variable. Select *BOOL* for this example.

6. Click *OK* to create the method.

The way the method will work is users can either display the local time or the Greenwich mean time. If they want to display the local date and time, they can pass TRUE to the method. To make the method work, we need to add some code to it. To do this, select the method name from the External Names list on the Automation tab of the Class Wizard and click the *Edit Code* button. This will bring up the function body that will implement the method. Our task here is pretty simple. We need to do the following:

- Retrieve the system time.
- If the IsLocal variable is set to TRUE, convert that time into the local time; otherwise, display the Greenwich mean time.
- Show the time string in a message box.

We can accomplish these tasks by using the time functions found in the *time.h* header file. First, we need to add this header file to the *DateTimerCtl.cpp* source code file. Next, we add the following code to the ShowTime member function:

Chapter 14: Advanced Topics

```
void CDateTimerCtrl::ShowTime(BOOL IsLocal)
{
    // TODO: Add your dispatch handler code here
    time_t timer;
    struct tm *mytime;
    CString strDateTime;

    time(&timer); //retrieve the system time

    //convert to local time
    //if IsLocal is true,
    //otherwise display greenwich mean time
    if(IsLocal)
        mytime = localtime(&timer);
    else
        mytime = gmtime(&timer);
    //convert the time to a string
    strDateTime = asctime(mytime);

    //show it to the user
    MessageBox(strDateTime,m_displayTitle,MB_OK);

}
```

The code is pretty straightforward. To add more methods to your control, follow the same procedure. You can add stock method as well.

Adding Events

Events are also added to a control with the Class Wizard. Open the Class Wizard and click on the *ActiveX Events* tab (see Figure 14-15).

To add an event, use the following steps:

1. Click the *Add Event* button. The Add Event dialog box will open (see Figure 14-16).
2. Either enter the name of your custom event in the External Name input box, or click open the drop-down list and choose a stock event. We will add a `Click` event for the control, which is a stock event.
3. If necessary, fill in the parameter list for the event handler.
4. Click *OK* to add the event.

The code in an event handler is the responsibility of the developer who uses your control. You provide event handlers to allow them to respond to events as they deem necessary. For example, our `Click` event could be used by the developer to invoke the ShowTime method of the control, so that the user can view the date and time by clicking the control.

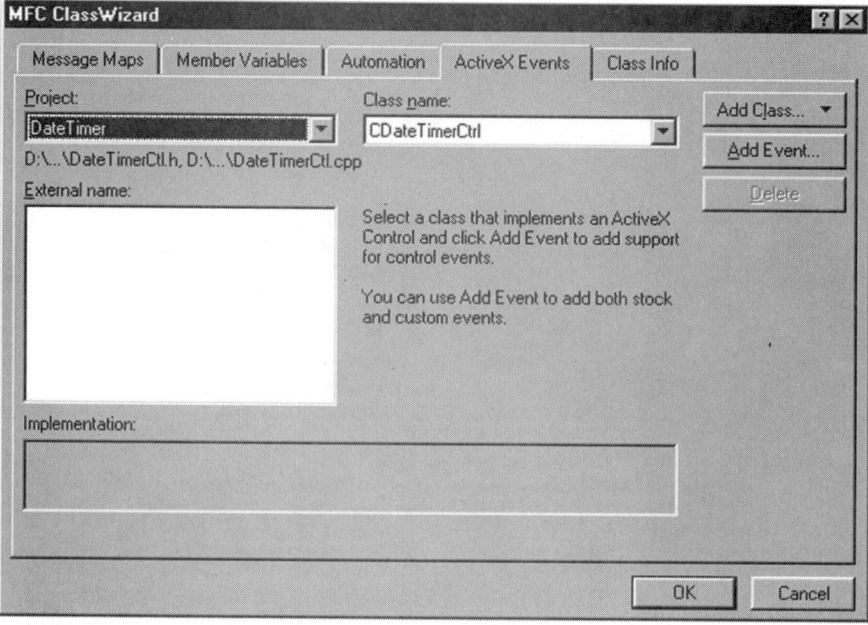

Figure 14-15
The Events tab of the Class Wizard.

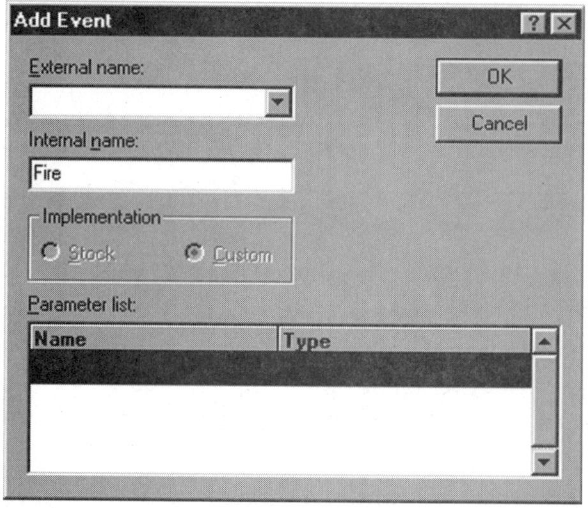

Figure 14-16
The Add Event dialog.

Fixing the `OnDraw` Member Function

Now that we have added the properties, methods, and events for this control, we need to customize the `OnDraw` function. We will have the function display the text string that stores the DisplayTitle property. First, we need to initialize the DisplayTitle property so that it has a

Chapter 14: Advanced Topics

default value when the developer adds the control to a form or dialog box for the first time. We can do this in the constructor for the `CDateTimerCtl` class. We will simply set the DisplayTitle property to "Date Timer." This is done by setting the member variable used to represent the property:

```
// CDateTimerCtrl::CDateTimerCtrl - Constructor
CDateTimerCtrl::CDateTimerCtrl()
{
    InitializeIIDs(&IID_DDateTimer, &IID_DDateTimerEvents);

    // Initialize the display title
    m_displayTitle = "Date Timer";
}
```

Now we turn our attention to the `OnDraw` function. Here we use drawing methods of Visual C++ to paint a light-gray rectangle and display the text stored in `m_displayTitle` on the control surface. We won't go into the graphics methods, but the code looks like this:

```
// CDateTimerCtrl::OnDraw - Drawing function

void CDateTimerCtrl::OnDraw(
            CDC* pdc, const CRect& rcBounds, const CRect& rcInvalid)
{
    // Draw gray background and print string
    //"Date Timer" in center

    CRect rect;
    TEXTMETRIC tMetric;
    CString ControlLabel=m_displayTitle;
    CBrush hitbrush;
    CBrush* pOldBrush;

    hitbrush.FromHandle((HBRUSH)GetStockObject(LTGRAY_BRUSH));

    pdc->SetBkMode(TRANSPARENT);
    pOldBrush = pdc->SelectObject(&hitbrush);
    GetClientRect(rect);

    pdc->Rectangle(rect);
    pdc->GetTextMetrics(&tMetric);
    pdc->SetTextAlign(TA_CENTER | TA_TOP);
    pdc->ExtTextOut((rect.left + rect.right)/2,(rect.top + rect.bottom - tMetric.tmHeight)/2, ETO_CLIPPED, rect,
ControlLabel, ControlLabel.GetLength()-1, NULL);
    pdc->SelectObject(pOldBrush);

}
```

The control will display whatever text is stored in the `m_displayTitle` member variable. The contents of the variable are ini-

Part 3: Implementation

tialized to "Date Timer" and can be modified if the developer chooses to change the DisplayTitle property.

Modifying the About Box and Property Page

When you create an ActiveX control with the MFC ActiveX Control Wizard, it adds two useful dialog boxes to the project: an About box and a property page. These two dialogs can be found in the usual place, the Dialogs folder from the Resource View window. The About box can be used to display information about the control, such as version number or company name. The dialog can be modified using the usual methods.

The property page is also a normal dialog; however, we will need to bind the properties of the control to it. This is done by creating an OLE connection between the controls we place on the property page and the property we wish to set. We will add two controls, an edit box to hold the DisplayTitle property and a combo box for the BorderStyle property (see Figure 14-17).

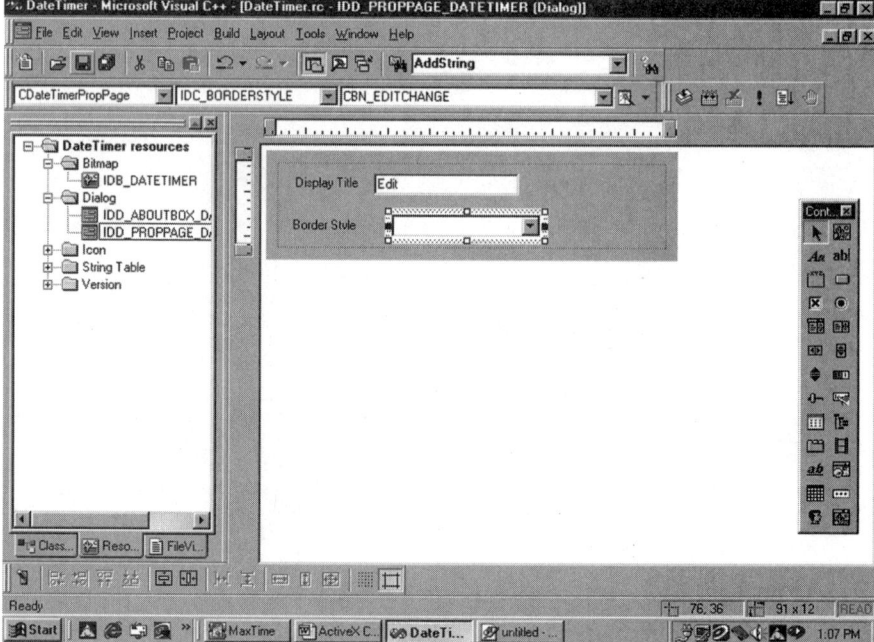

Figure 14-17
Property page.

Chapter 14: Advanced Topics

To bind each control to a property, use the following steps:

1. Open the Class Wizard and select the *Member Variables* tab.
2. Select a control to bind from the Control IDs list. The Add Member Variable dialog box will open, as shown in Figure 14-18.
3. To bind a custom property, type in the name of the member variable used to represent the property in the Member Variable name input box. For example, to bind the DisplayTitle property, we enter "m_displayTitle" here. This was the member variable name chosen earlier when the property was created.
4. Leave the Category and Variable Type boxes alone; accept the default settings.
5. In the Optional Property input box, type in the external name for the property. For this property, we type "DisplayTitle." If you are setting up a stock property, such as the BorderStyle property, click open the drop-down list and choose the stock property name.
6. Click the *OK* button.

To bind a stock property, we follow the same steps but click open the Optional Property list and choose the appropriate stock property. We bind the combo box to the BorderStyle property in this manner. We also need to set the combo box so that it contains the available border styles in the drop-down list. Finally, we need to set up the property exchange function and make the properties persistent. This is done in the

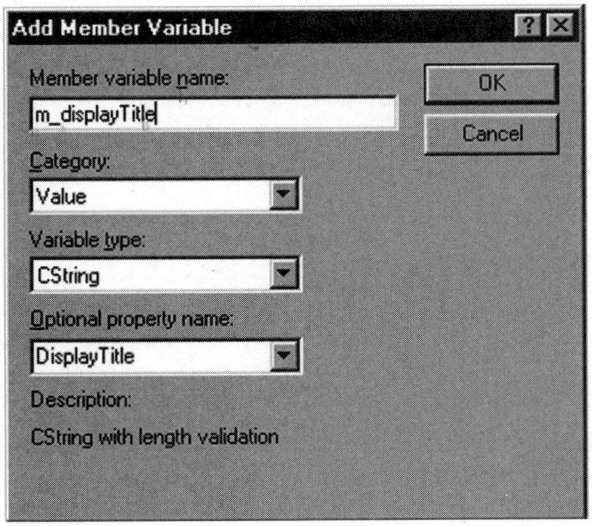

Figure 14-18
Adding a member variable to represent a property.

DoPropExchange member function. To make the DisplayTitle property persistent, we modify the code to look like this:

```
void CDateTimerCtrl::DoPropExchange(CPropExchange* pPX)
{
    ExchangeVersion(pPX, MAKELONG(_wVerMinor, _wVerMajor));
    COleControl::DoPropExchange(pPX);

    //Call PX_ functions to make custom
    //properties persistent
    PX_String(pPX,"DisplayTitle",m_displayTitle);

}
```

When the user modifies the properties of the control, the `OnDraw` function will be invoked automatically. As a result, we do not need to explicitly redraw the display title whenever it is changed.

Modifying the Toolbox Icon

Every control in the toolbox is represented by a small bitmap. Your control is assigned a default bitmap that will be used in the toolbox. The bitmap is just a gray square with "OCX" displayed in the middle. You will probably want to give your control a customized look; this is done by opening the Bitmap folder and selecting the IDB_DATETIMER bitmap from the Resources View. When you open this bitmap, a set of drawing tools will appear on the right side of the screen. You can use these drawing tools to customize the bitmap's appearance. You won't want to resize the bitmap, since it has been sized to fit inside the icon of the toolbox. However, you probably want to replace the "OCX" characters with either a custom drawing or text string.

Compiling the Control

An ActiveX control must be compiled just like any other Visual C++ project. ActiveX controls are compiled into OCX files. The control must also be registered; this is done by the compiler for you. To compile your control select *Build ProjectName.ocx* from the Build pull-down menu, where *ProjectName* is the name you assigned to the control with the MFC ActiveX Control Wizard. If the control compiles successfully, the compiler

Chapter 14: Advanced Topics

will register it for you. You can then test the control with the ActiveX Control Test Container, in another Visual C++ project, or in a Visual Basic project. The control should also be tested for Internet use in a Web page.

Using the ActiveX Control Test Container

The ActiveX Control Test Container is available from the Tools menu (see Figure 14-19). The first step is to insert your control. This is done by clicking on the *New Control* button on the toolbar. The Insert Control dialog will open, where you can select the control you want from the list of registered controls.

The control will then be inserted into the view area of the Test Container. You can then manipulate the control by setting properties, invoking methods, and raising events. An icon for each task is available on the toolbar of the Test Container. You can invoke methods and try different parameter values, and set different values for the properties to make sure the behavior is as you expect and to make sure your property

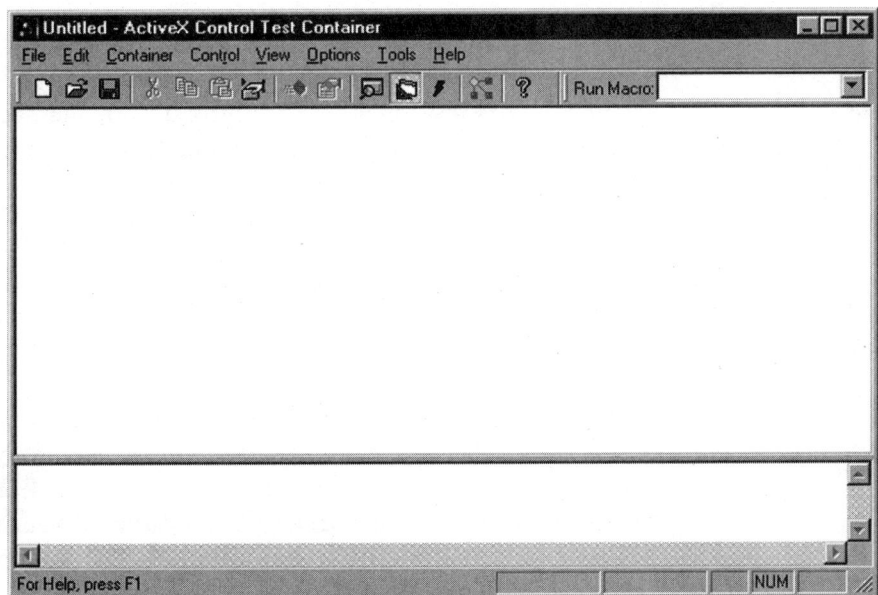

Figure 14-19
The ActiveX Control Test Container.

page is correctly bound. You can save the session by clicking on *Save Session* from the File pull-down menu.

Testing the Control in a VB App

When we compiled the control, Visual C++ automatically registered the control on our machine. We can now test the control in another language or development system to see how it behaves. For our test, we will choose Visual Basic. First, we start Visual Basic and start a new standard EXE project. If we open the Components dialog, we will see the DateTimer control listed. We can then proceed to add the control to the project. The control is then available from the Visual Basic toolbox, where we can select it to add to a form. We can set properties of the control, such as the border style.

The methods of the control can be invoked in code. Here we invoke the ShowTime method in the `Click` event of a command button we have placed on the form:

```
Private Sub cdmShow_Click()

  DateTimer1.ShowTime (True)
End Sub
```

We can also use the VB environment to test the property page and make sure the control works as expected as properties are set, and methods and events are invoked. In Figure 14-20, you see a Visual Basic program that invokes the ShowTime method.

Creating an ActiveX Control with ATL

The second method that can be used to create an ActiveX control in Visual C++ is by using the Active Template Library (ATL). To do this, start a new project and select *ATL COM App Wizard* from the New Projects dialog. We won't go into the details of creating a control, but we will outline the general steps. The ATL COM App Wizard, shown in Figure 14-21, allows you to select which type of server you want to create.

Chapter 14: Advanced Topics

Figure 14-20
Testing the control.

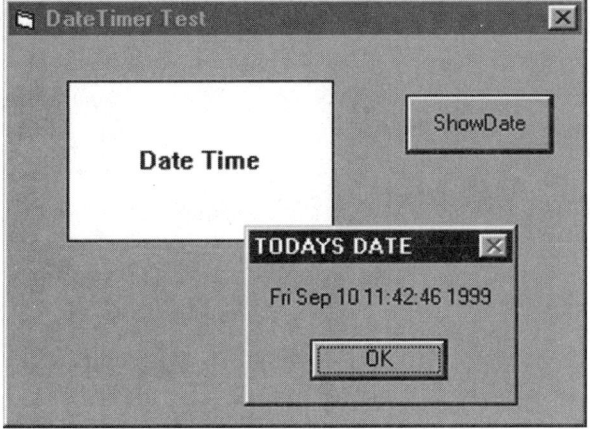

To create a control, select *DLL*. This will create a basic framework that can be used to create the control. The next step is to add a control to the project. This is done by clicking on the *Insert* pull-down menu, and selecting *New ATL Object*. The ATL Object Wizard will open (see Figure 14-22). Click on the *Controls* category and select *Full Control*. Then click the *Next* button.

Figure 14-21
The ATL COM App Wizard.

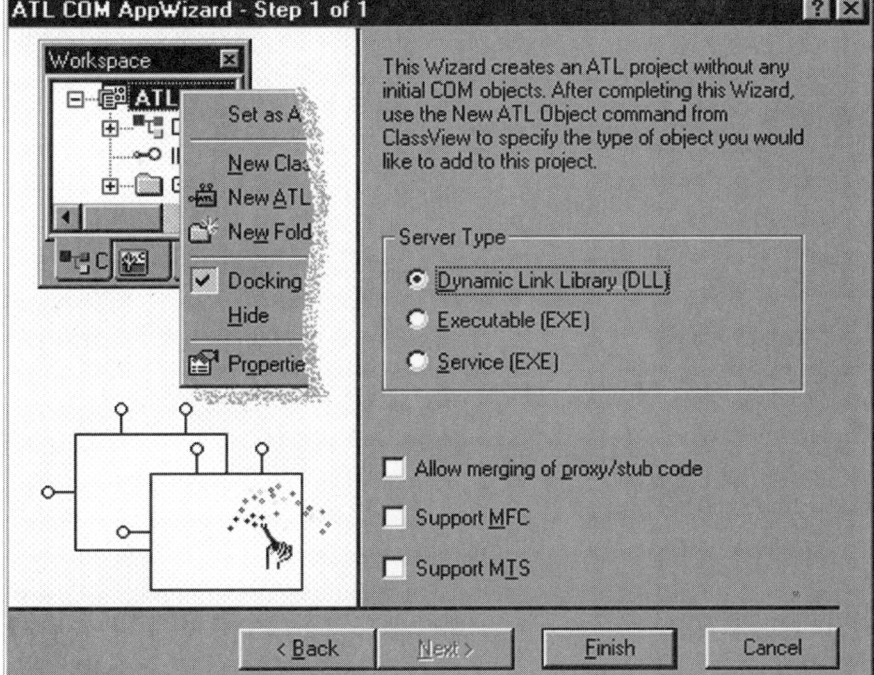

Figure 14-22
The ATL Object Wizard.

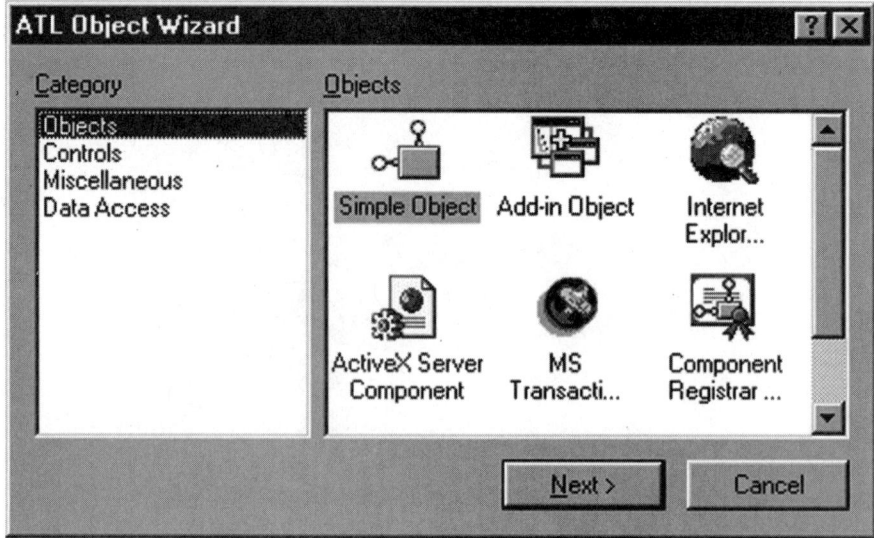

The next step is to enter the properties and attributes for the control. First, we need to enter the short name that will identify the control. We will choose *DateTimer2*. The file names and COM information are entered automatically. On the Attributes tab, you can specify the threading model, interface, and aggregation. You can select stock properties by clicking on the *Stock Properties* tab (see Figure 14-23). We add the stock properties BackColor, BorderStyle, and Font.

On the Miscellaneous tab, you can base the control on other controls such as a ListBox or ScrollBar. If you want to create a control based on these items, select the item you want from the drop-down list. You can also specify whether you want the control to be invisible at runtime or act like a button or label. When finished with your settings, click the *OK* button.

Adding a Property to an ATL Control

To add a property to the control, right-click on the control short name in the Class View window and select *Add Property*. The Add Property to Interface dialog box will open (see Figure 14-24). Properties in ATL controls are implemented with Get/Put functions, like they are in Visual

Chapter 14: Advanced Topics

Figure 14-23
Selecting stock properties.

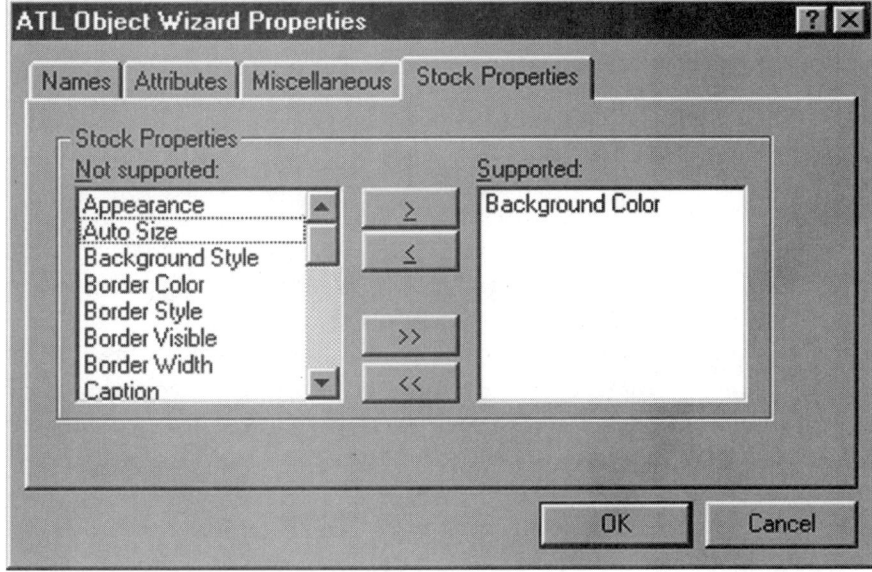

Figure 14-24
Adding a property.

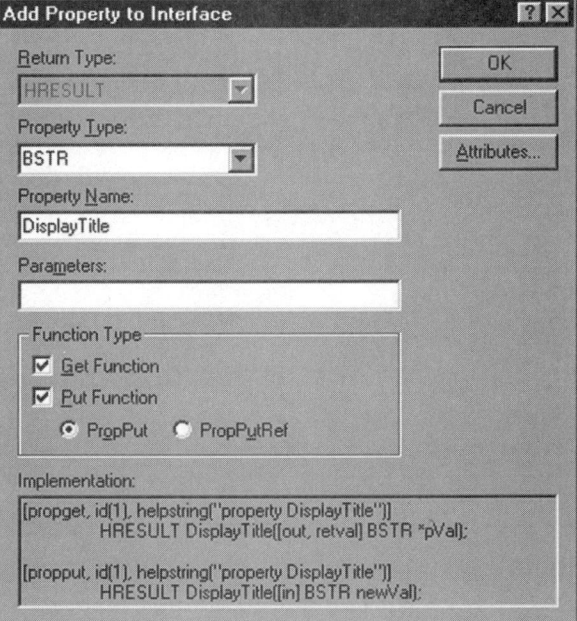

Basic. If you click the *Attributes* button, you can set several attributes of the property, such as bindable or hidden.

Adding a Method to an ATL Control

To add a method, right-click on the control short name in the Class View window and select *Add Method*. The Add Method to Interface dialog box will open, as shown in Figure 14-25.

You can set the parameters passed to the function in the Parameters input box and set attributes by clicking on the *Attributes* button. You can then find the method in the Class View window and double-click to edit the source code. The ShowTime function looks like this:

```
STDMETHODIMP CDateTimer2::ShowTime(bool IsLocal)
{
    AFX_MANAGE_STATE(AfxGetStaticModuleState())

    // TODO: Add your implementation code here

    return S_OK;
}
```

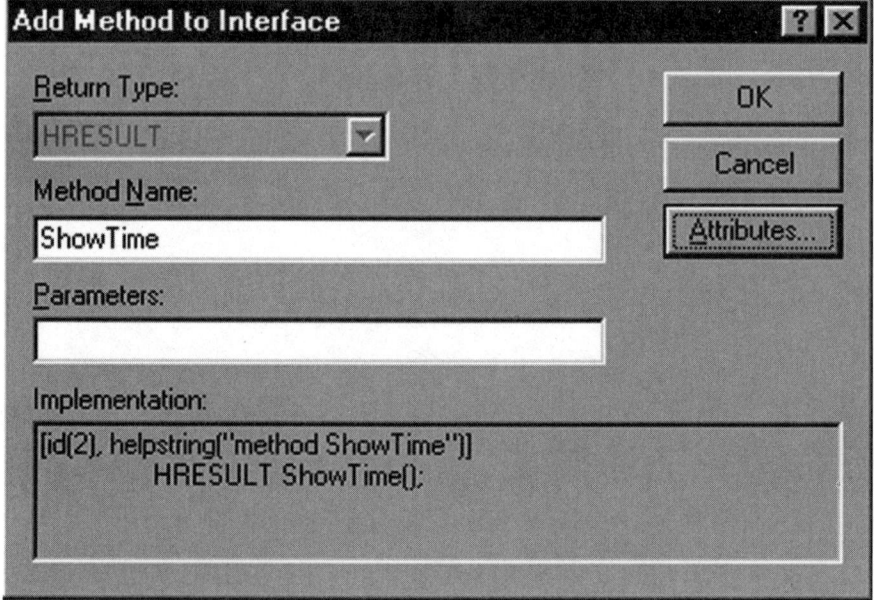

Figure 14-25
Adding a method.

Chapter 14: Advanced Topics

After the TODO comment, we can add the code to implement the method. We will add the same code that we used to create the first DateTimer control. Again, we manage the control's appearance with the `OnDraw` member function.

Internet Programming

The Internet continues to grow in popularity, and tools you create with Visual C++ such as ActiveX controls will have a large role to play in Internet software. Some of the important technologies include:

- ActiveX documents
- URLs and monikers
- Internet information servers
- DHTML (Dynamic HTML)
- JavaScript
- ActiveX controls on Web pages

Unfortunately there isn't space to deal with these complex issues here. For a good overview of Internet programming, see *Visual C++ 6 from the Ground Up* by John Paul Mueller (Osborne/McGraw-Hill, 1998).

CHAPTER 15

Debugging

Introduction

When a new software project is completed, even the most carefully written program will contain errors that keep it from running properly. These errors are known as *bugs*, and the process of locating and correcting these errors is known as *debugging*. Debugging even a moderately sized software project can be quite time-consuming. In the past, a programmer would have to compile a program and run it several times, perhaps printing out error messages along the way in an attempt to locate the bug. Modern software tools like Visual C++, however, come complete with an extensive set of built-in debugging tools that make the debugging process easier. Not only that, they allow the developer to debug right from the IDE, allowing you to step through code and examine variables in real time.

When thinking about bugs, we must also consider errors that will crop up during runtime as a result of the actions of the user or system configuration that cannot be prevented by debugging. For example, a user might attempt to open a file on a floppy drive when no disk is present in the drive. These types of errors are called *runtime errors*. The C++ language provides a means to deal with this type of error, and we will learn how to trap and rectify them in code.

In general, there are three types of errors encountered in software development:

- *Syntax errors* A syntax error is an invalid statement in your program that won't compile. Often, a syntax error is nothing more than a typing mistake. For example, you might have misspelled a keyword or used the incorrect capitalization. Or perhaps you left a closing brace of an `if` statement block. In any case, the compiler will find and alert you of syntax errors and provide suggestions you can use to correct them.

- *Runtime errors* A runtime error occurs after a program has successfully compiled and is up and running. At this point, the program has all the correct syntax and logic, but some action is taken, perhaps by the user, that might cause the software to crash. The user may try to open a nonexistent file, for example. This type of error is dealt with by including error trapping in your code. We will investigate how to do this later in the chapter.

- *Logic errors* A logic error is an error in the way your program is designed. In other words, it does not do exactly what you think it

Chapter 15: Debugging

should be doing. All but the simplest of programs will have logic errors.

Tracking down bugs is a difficult and time-consuming process. In a complicated project, you may spend as much time debugging as you do in the actual creation of the software. Fortunately, Visual C++ provides the developer with an effective integrated debugger.

When debugging, fixing logic errors will be the primary focus. In this chapter, we will explore the process used when debugging a C++ project, which will usually involve one or more of the following:

- Setting breakpoints
- Using watches to track the value of a variable as the program runs
- Stepping through code
- Tracking down and killing bugs
- Using error trapping to handle runtime errors

In Visual C++, you can find the debugging tools from the Build pull-down menu. The Debug toolbar (see Figure 15-1) can also be used to access debugging tools.

Setting Breakpoints and Starting the Debug Process

When you run your program using the debugger, you have the ability to step through code one line at a time. This provides you with the ability to watch the logic of the program flow and to examine the contents of variables as the program executes. Generally, a program will only have bugs limited to certain areas of the program. This means that you prob-

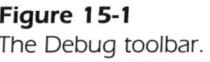
Figure 15-1
The Debug toolbar.

ably won't want to single-step through each line of code right from the beginning.

To get around this situation, Visual C++ allows you to set a *breakpoint* in your code. A breakpoint is a specified line of code that tells Visual C++ to pause execution. When Visual C++ reaches a breakpoint line, execution is paused and the line of code containing the breakpoint is displayed. Note that execution is paused before the breakpoint line is executed. You can then use debugging tools to single-step through code and examine the contents of variables and registers. Visual C++ allows you to set a breakpoint anywhere in code, except on a comment line. A line with a breakpoint is indicated by a red circle to the left of that line in the code window (see Figure 15-2). You can set breakpoints before executing a program with the debugger, or while you are single-stepping through code with the debugger.

To set a breakpoint, use these steps:

1. Place the cursor on the line of code where you want execution to pause.
2. Right-click the mouse.
3. Select *Insert/Remove Breakpoint* from the pop-up menu.

To remove a breakpoint, use the same steps, but select *Remove Breakpoint* or *Disable Breakpoint*.

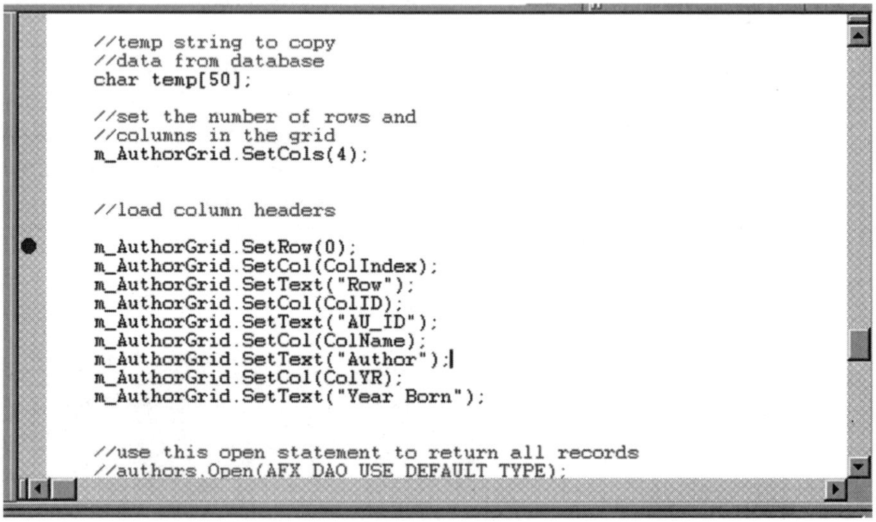

Figure 15-2
A breakpoint.

```
//temp string to copy
//data from database
char temp[50];

//set the number of rows and
//columns in the grid
m_AuthorGrid.SetCols(4);

//load column headers

m_AuthorGrid.SetRow(0);
m_AuthorGrid.SetCol(ColIndex);
m_AuthorGrid.SetText("Row");
m_AuthorGrid.SetCol(ColID);
m_AuthorGrid.SetText("AU_ID");
m_AuthorGrid.SetCol(ColName);
m_AuthorGrid.SetText("Author");
m_AuthorGrid.SetCol(ColYR);
m_AuthorGrid.SetText("Year Born");

//use this open statement to return all records
//authors.Open(AFX_DAO_USE_DEFAULT_TYPE);
```

Chapter 15: Debugging

Generally, you should set your breakpoints a few lines of code ahead of where you think a problem is located. For example, if you have a `while` loop that executes indefinitely, set the breakpoint a few lines before the `while` statement.

Stepping through Code

Visual C++ provides you with several methods you can use to single-step through the code in your project. Single-stepping through code will allow you to see the flow of execution of the program. This will aid you in determining which code the program will run through and where it will pause, so you can examine the contents of variables or see where a crash occurs. The debugger lets you control the flow of your program with the following methods, each of which can be selected from the Debug toolbar, from the Debug pull-down menu in Visual C++, or by using the indicated key combination:

- Step Into (press F11)
- Step Over (press F10)
- Step Out (Shift + F11)
- Run to Cursor (Ctrl + F10)
- Stop Debugging (Shift + F5)
- Restart (Ctrl + Shift + F5)

The first two methods, Step Into and Step Over, can be used to launch a program, although this is not advisable unless you are specifically debugging initialization code. Note that at any time you can resume normal execution by pressing the F5 key. If there are other breakpoints in the current function, this will take you to the next breakpoint.

Let's examine each of these stepping methods in more detail.

Step Into

During break mode, which is entered when Visual C++ encounters a breakpoint, using Step Into allows you to execute the code one line at a time. If Step Into encounters a function call, it will enter that function and continue to execute code one line at a time. Keep in mind that your programs, when using MFC, will make many function calls to the underlying code. This means that using this method may take you into MFC code, which you probably do not want to do unless you are an advanced user who has modified some MFC code. If this happens, use Step Out or Step Over to avoid entering the function calls.

Step Over

Using Step Over will also execute the code one line at a time. However, when a function call is encountered, Step Over treats the function call as a single line of code and does not enter the function. The function executes in its entirety in a single step, and the debugger continues to execute code one line at a time in the current function.

Step Out

Step Out lets you execute the current function. If you select this option, the remaining lines in the current function will be executed at once and the debugger will pause on the line of code following the line where this function was called. For example, suppose you had the following lines of code:

```
X = 32;
Average(&Avg);
Y = X + Avg;
```

Now suppose the debugger was executing code one line at a time in the `Average` function, perhaps inside a `for` loop:

```
for(int j=0; j < MAX; j++)
{
    sum += data[j]; //breakpoint is right here
    //more code
   ...
}
```

Now suppose you are paused on the line where the breakpoint is indicated, inside the `Average` function. If you select *Step Out* by pressing SHIFT + F11, the debugger will execute the remainder of the `Average` function and return control to the code that called it. Execution will pause on the next line, which in this case is Y = X + Avg;

Chapter 15: Debugging

Run to Cursor

If you are stepping through code and you want to skip over a number of statements and select another line of code on which to pause execution, you can use Run to Cursor. To use this option, place the cursor on the line of code (in the current function) where you want execution to pause. Then choose *Run to Cursor* by pressing CTRL + F10.

Using Watch Expressions and Examining the Contents of Variables and Memory

One of the most powerful methods that can be used is the ability to view and track the contents of variables, registers, and memory while debugging. This is done primarily through the use of *watch expressions*. You can also examine the contents of variables in the current function by viewing the Variables window (see Figure 15-3).

In this window, the variables and their contents that are currently in use are displayed. You can click open the *Context* drop-down list to select

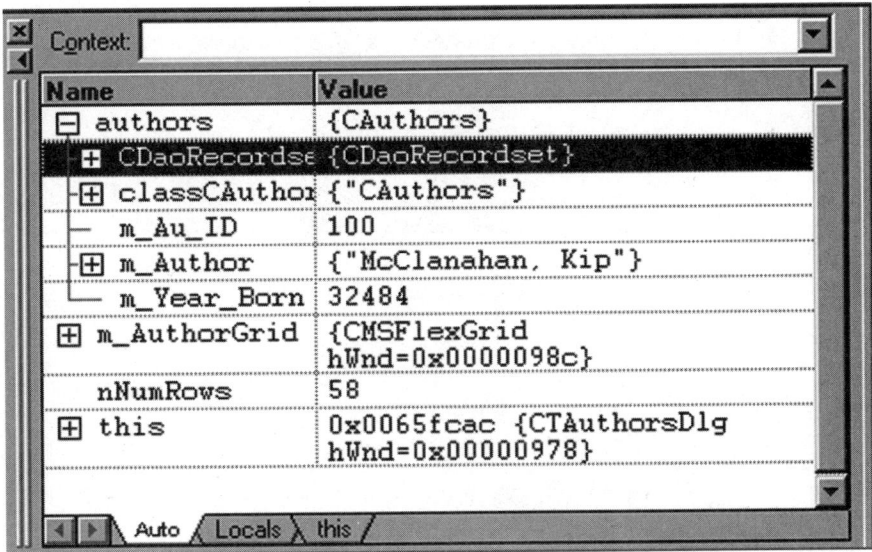

Figure 15-3
Viewing Variables.

a desired function. By clicking on the *Locals* tab, at the bottom of the window you can view the contents of local variables in the current function. The contents of this pointer can also be examined. This window is usually found in the lower left corner of the IDE during debugging. Also note that you can examine the contents of a variable by placing and holding the mouse pointer over the variable name in the source code while you are debugging. This information will be displayed as a ToolTip.

To display the contents of a pointer (and not its memory address), click and highlight the variable name, including the indirection operator (*). Then hold your mouse pointer over it. The value pointed to by the pointer will then be displayed.

Each of the options listed below can be opened from the Debug toolbar or by clicking open the *View* pull-down menu.

Adding a Watch

A watch expression can be used to display the value of a variable or expression while you are running the debugger. You can create a watch expression by using the QuickWatch window (see Figure 15-4).

Type in the expression you want to monitor, and click the *Add Watch* button. The watches you have created will be displayed in the Watch window, usually found in the lower right corner of the IDE (see Figure

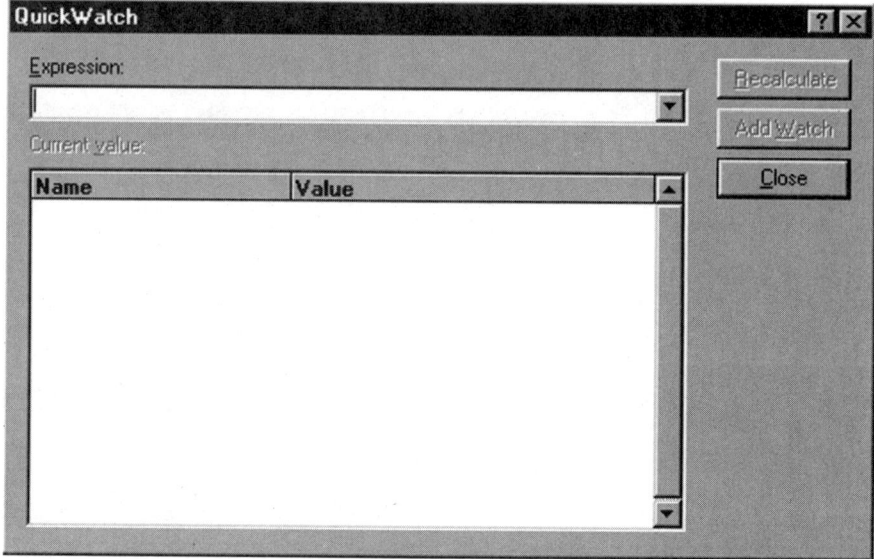

Figure 15-4
The QuickWatch dialog.

Chapter 15: Debugging

Figure 15-5
Watches.

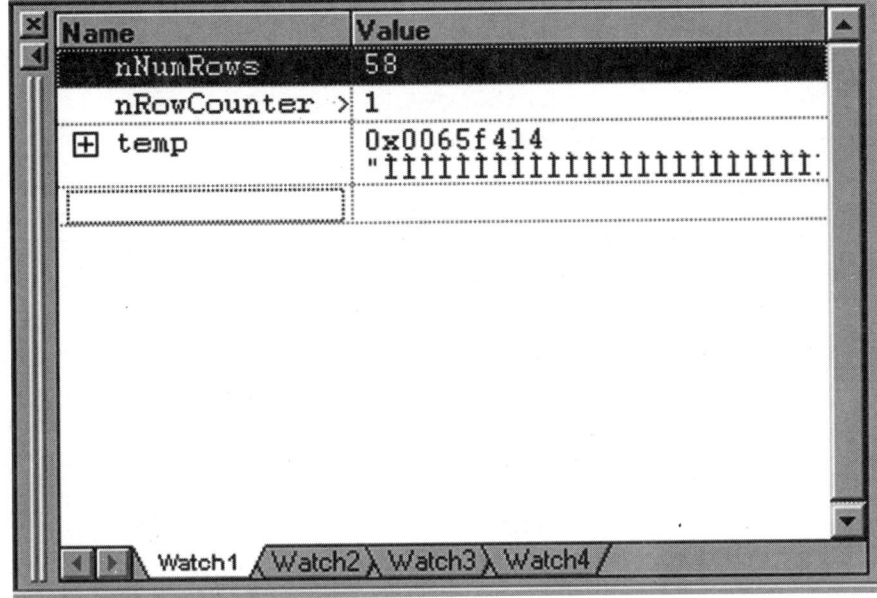

15-5). You can also use the QuickWatch window to modify the contents of a variable. You might want to do this to see how the performance of the program is affected by certain values, for example.

Registers

While debugging, you can view the contents of various registers in the CPU by clicking the *Registers* icon on the Debug toolbar. This will open the Registers window, as shown in Figure 15-6. This window displays each register along with its contents in hexadecimal form. The contents

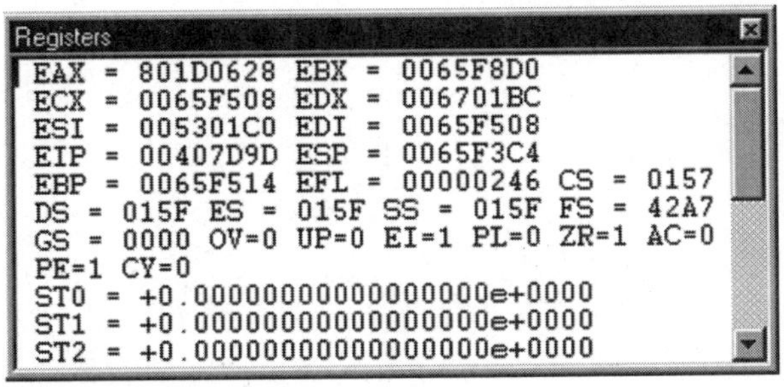

Figure 15-6
Registers.

of the floating-point stack are also displayed, as ST0, ST1, and so on. You can right-click to view/close the floating-point stack.

Memory

The contents of memory can be examined by clicking on the *Memory* icon of the Debug toolbar. This will open the Memory window, shown in Figure 15-7.

This window displays each memory location and the contents, which can be displayed in either byte, short hex, or long hex format. Position the mouse pointer over the window and right-click to make your selection. The window will show you the memory contents starting at an address that you type in the Address input box at the top of the window. The window will open with the address 0x00000000 displayed. The contents of memory locations in your program's address space can be viewed by using the scroll bar on the right side of the window.

The Call Stack

The call stack, which can be viewed during break mode by selecting the *Call Stack* icon on the Debug toolbar, is shown in Figure 15-8. This win-

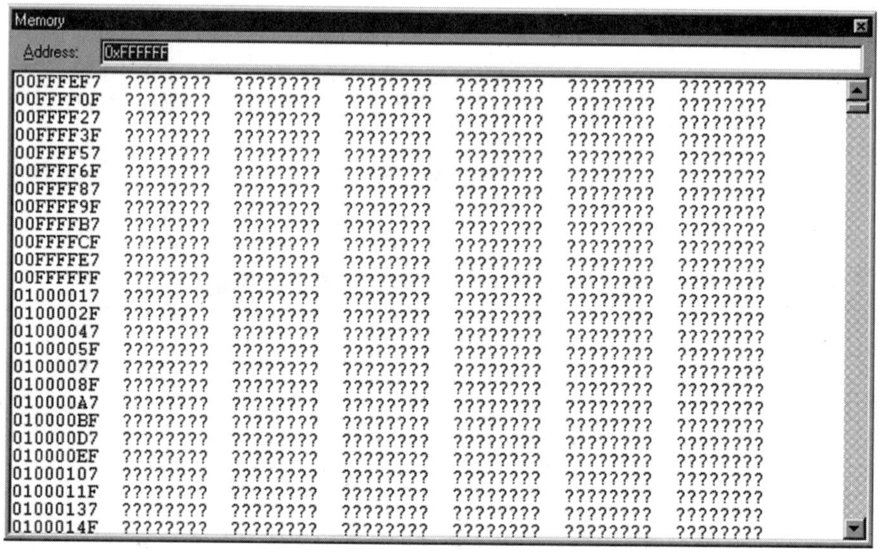

Figure 15-7
Viewing Memory.

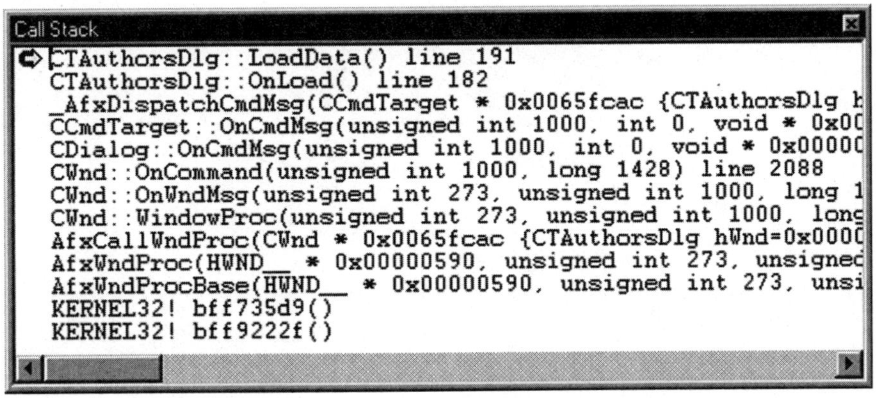

Chapter 15: Debugging

Figure 15-8
The call stack.

```
Call Stack
⇨ CTAuthorsDlg::LoadData() line 191
  CTAuthorsDlg::OnLoad() line 182
  _AfxDispatchCmdMsg(CCmdTarget * 0x0065fcac {CTAuthorsDlg
  CCmdTarget::OnCmdMsg(unsigned int 1000, int 0, void * 0x0
  CDialog::OnCmdMsg(unsigned int 1000, int 0, void * 0x0000
  CWnd::OnCommand(unsigned int 1000, long 1428) line 2088
  CWnd::OnWndMsg(unsigned int 273, unsigned int 1000, long
  CWnd::WindowProc(unsigned int 273, unsigned int 1000, lon
  AfxCallWndProc(CWnd * 0x0065fcac {CTAuthorsDlg hWnd=0x000
  AfxWndProc(HWND__ * 0x00000590, unsigned int 273, unsigne
  AfxWndProcBase(HWND__ * 0x00000590, unsigned int 273, uns
  KERNEL32! bff735d9()
  KERNEL32! bff9222f()
```

dow will show you all of the functions that are currently loaded into memory. This will include a list of parameters, with the function that is currently executing listed at the top of the window. You can move to a given function and display the source code, variable, and watch windows for that function by double-clicking on its name in the Call Stack window. A green arrow on the left side of the function names will indicate which function is being displayed, while a yellow arrow and breakpoint symbol indicates where execution is currently paused.

Disassembly

This option is for advanced users. You can select it by clicking on the Disassembly icon of the Debug toolbar, or by pressing the ALT + F8 key combination. This will display the code in your program in assembly language (see Figure 15-9).

Line numbers are displayed on the left side of the screen. You will see each line of source code in your files, along with comments, followed by the corresponding assembly language commands. For example, you can see the following code, which is a set of constant declarations, and how this translates into assembly language statements:

```
//constants to define
201:         //column indexes for grid
202:         const int ColIndex = 0;    //column 0 is row #
00407C30     mov          dword ptr [ebp-0C0h],0
203:         const int ColID = 1;       //column 1 is Author ID
00407C3A     mov          dword ptr [ebp-0C4h],1
204:         const int ColName = 2;     //column 2 is Author Name
00407C44     mov          dword ptr [ebp-0C8h],2
```

Figure 15-9
Disassembly.

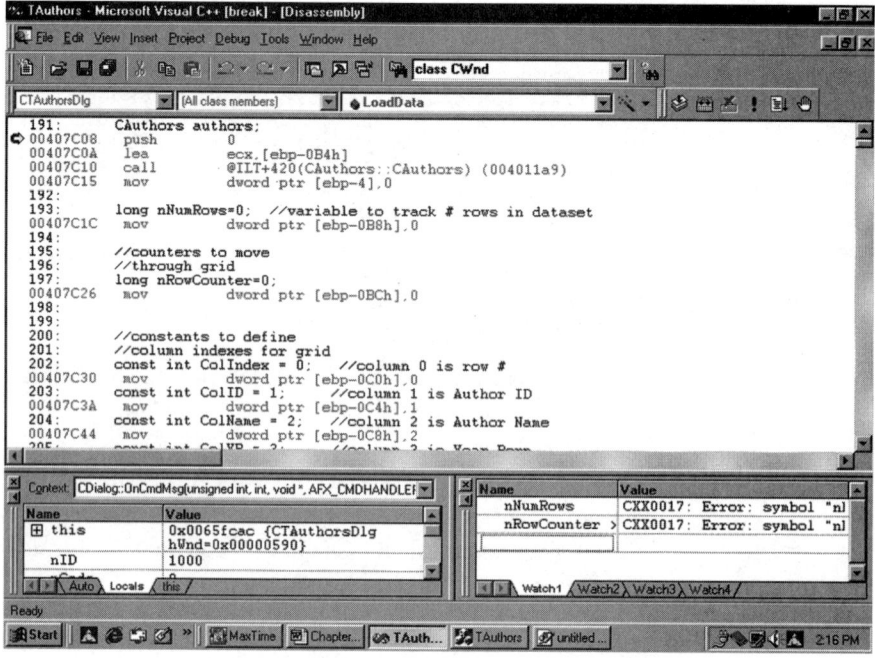

```
205:         const int ColYR = 3;     //column 3 is Year Born
00407C4E     mov          dword ptr [ebp-0CCh],3
```

The meaning and methods of assembly language programming are beyond the scope of this book. However, if you understand assembly language, you can use this debugging tool to aid in the process of getting your code to run correctly.

Error Trapping and Handling Exceptions

In the previous sections we went over the tools that you can use to track down logic errors and strange behavior in your programs. The second important area we need to consider is that of runtime errors. As stated in the introduction, a runtime error is one that occurs after a program is up and running successfully. There is nothing wrong with the program itself, but it may encounter a situation that will cause an error to occur during the normal course of operation. For example, the user may

Chapter 15: Debugging

request that a file be opened on the floppy drive, but no disk is present in the drive. This can cause problems, or at the very least result in unfriendly code, if your program does not handle this situation properly. The idea is that you write code that allows the user to correct the situation by inserting a floppy disk, and then the operation is tried again. If a situation arises where the program cannot recover, you can also have friendly code report the problem to the user in clear language and allow the program to exit gracefully, rather than just letting it crash.

The try Block

Statements that are bound to throw exceptions can be included in a try block. A try block is initiated by including the try keyword, with the possibly offending code enclosed in braces. The syntax is as follows:

```
try
{
     //code here which is risky
     ...
}
```

When code may cause an exception, we say that it will "throw" an exception. When code can throw an exception, there must be a way to deal with it, and this is done with the catch keyword. A catch statement is placed immediately after the try block. The general syntax of a complete try-catch block looks like this:

```
try
{
   //code here which is risky
   ...
}
catch (type1 arg)
{
   //catch block to respond to exception
   ...
}
...
catch (typeN arg)
{
  //catch block for type N
}
```

The code that you are worried about is included in the try block. If an error occurs, it is handled by the appropriate catch block. Program control is transferred from the `try` block to the `catch` block, and execution is resumed from that point. You can have multiple `catch` blocks with one `try` block, as we have indicated. When an exception occurs, the `arg` parameter receives a value representing the exception. The `catch` block that is used is selected based on the type of argument that the exception generates. The argument that is thrown to the `catch` block is generated in code with a `throw` statement. The `throw` statement is included in the `try` block where you expect an error can occur. For example, you can throw an error number, say, error 55, by using the following `throw` statement:

```
throw 55;
```

You can catch the error by including the appropriate `catch` statement, which in this case will accept an integer:

```
catch(short num)
{
   _itoa(num, temp, 10);
   strcat(strError, temp);
   MessageBox(strError, "FILE", MB_OK);
}
```

For a more concrete example, suppose we have a function that opens a file on the floppy disk. The function header looks like this:

```
short OpenDiskFile(CString FileName);
```

This function returns a `short` that represents an error code. It returns 0 if the function returned successfully. We can use a `try-catch` block to handle an error condition:

```
try
{
   short returnvalue=0;

   returnvalue = OpenDiskFile(strFileName);
   if(returnvalue != 0)
      throw returnvalue;
}
catch(short errornum)
{
   char temp[10];

   _itoa(errornum, temp, 10);

   MessageBox("ERROR OPENING FILE", temp, MB_OK);

}
```

Chapter 15: Debugging

This code block will display a message box with the appropriate error number to the user if an error occurs. If the `OpenDiskFile` function returns 0, indicating success, the `catch` block is skipped over. Keep in mind that the `catch` block is not a function call, even though it appears to be one since it takes a parameter. This is simply a block of code, just like an `if` statement or `while` loop. Control is only directed to the `catch` block if an error is thrown.

In summary, there are many conditions that will cause runtime errors, including dividing by zero, attempting to open a nonexistent file, assigning an out-of-range value to a variable, or exceeding the bounds of an array, just to name a few. The fact is, no matter how carefully you design your software, it's just impossible to account for every situation the program will encounter while being operated by end users. In Visual C++, you can insulate your code against these problems by including `try-catch` blocks. This approach allows you to guard against risky code, to identify and report errors, and to take corrective action if necessary. You should include error-handling code in each function where risky behavior is possible. Otherwise, your program may be unstable and subject to repeated crashes.

You should include exception handling in your code by following these rules:

- Enclose risky code blocks inside a `try` block.
- Provide a `catch` block to respond to errors appropriately.
- Display clear error messages to the user with a message box.
- Include an error number or code with your message. This way the errors can be easily tracked by tech support.
- Recover from the error gracefully if possible.

By including error handling in your programs, you can ensure that they will behave in a professional and user-friendly manner.

PART 4

Testing and Distribution of Visual C++ Software

CHAPTER 16

Testing Applications

Part 4: Testing and Distribution of Visual C++ Software

Introduction

There comes a time in the life of a software project when the coding is completed and we are sure that the code corresponds well to the specified design requirements. It is at this point that formal testing can begin. Testing, just like any other aspect of RAD, is a phase that requires careful planning. In the real world, I've seen too many programmers get seduced by the illusion that a RAD environment is capable of producing: If an application looks good, it must be working correctly. Testing the project seems like an afterthought. With this assumption in mind, the product gets shipped out the door before it's really ready to go. Just like any other aspect of the RAD design process, it's important to avoid falling victim to this kind of behavior. You do so by maintaining a rigorous testing protocol.

Before beginning a testing program, you should ask yourself what the goal of testing is. Most developers would probably agree that the goal of testing is to show that the software is free of defects. However, writers such as Roger Pressman have suggested that successful testing involves the uncovering of errors in the software. Pressman states:

Testing cannot show the absence of defects; it can only show software defects are present.

With this in mind, we can approach the subject of testing software in a more realistic manner. Bugs and errors are inevitable in the design of software that's of any substantial complexity. If a testing process is uncovering those errors, this isn't necessarily an indication of bad software design; it just means that the testing process is an effective one. Testing can be broken down into two distinct areas:

- *Internal operations testing*   This entails testing the internal operations of the various components to ensure that they perform according to specifications. This is known as *white box testing*.

- *Higher-level or interface testing*   Here we test to ensure that the software behaves as expected. Does it accept data input correctly and produce the correct output? This is known as *black box testing*.

Testing a Visual C++ project will involve both types of testing. Your project will use many built-in Windows components, as well as several ActiveX controls. We aren't worried about the internal functioning of these objects; we want to make sure that they have been integrated correctly so the program produces the expected output. This means we will do a lot of black box testing. However, a Visual C++ project is made up of many individual windows, dialogs, resources, old-style functions, and classes. You will write the code that makes these units function. In this case, you will do white box testing to make sure that the internal operations of each component work as specified in the design requirements. The functioning of each of these elements will then be tested in the larger context of the entire project, meaning that we will do more black box testing.

In any programming language, testing should proceed through the following phases:

- Testing for proof of concept
- Unit testing
- Batch testing
- Integration testing
- System testing
- Beta testing
- Regression testing

As testing proceeds, it tends to move in an inside-out fashion. We start our testing process at the lowest levels, the level of the code inside each function and subroutine. Testing then moves to the level of the file or class, to see if all modules are integrated correctly. Only then do we test the system as a whole, under different configurations of hardware and software. Once the testing process by the developer is complete, we expand the testing to include the end user. The testing process must be repeated as code is maintained and modified. In this chapter, we will explore each testing phase.

The Importance of Documenting the Testing Process

The testing process should be formalized. This means developing a standard series of testing phases and documenting each step. Documentation should include a list of what tests were done, what data was used, the expected results, and the actual results. Standardizing the testing process will make it easier to implement it in the future and will save time. By maintaining good documentation, we can ensure that we will be able to go back and repeat the *exact* same tests if necessary.

Testing for Proof of Concept

Above all, a software product must be tested to ensure that it meets any architectural and design specifications. This is known as testing for *proof of concept*. In other words, does the software do what it's supposed to do? Testing for proof of concept will involve examining the following areas:

- Does the software accept the data the customer expects it to?
- Does the software produce the proper output and reports?
- Are the correct algorithms and data formats used? Sometimes developers don't understand exactly what the customer wants, so it's important to make sure that the problem solved is on target. As a simple example, a customer might expect data to be output in square meters while the program uses square feet.
- Is the user interface what the customer expects? Does each dialog box display the data fields expected?

Testing for proof of concept is not something that begins when the program is finished. Rather, it will go on throughout the entire development life cycle. When we are sure the program does what the design requirements specify, we are ready to begin the testing of each component.

Unit Testing

The start of any effective testing program begins with *unit testing*. This is a testing process that focuses on testing individual units of code. In the past, this would probably involve testing a suite of subroutines or functions. In an object-oriented language like Visual C++, this type of testing is facilitated by the way that the language is structured. Consider the fact that a Visual C++ project can include one or more of the following elements:

- Classes
- Conventional functions
- Dialogs
- ActiveX controls or DLLs
- Objects such as user documents

This means that we can approach unit testing by testing the behavior of each class, function, or object on an individual basis. This enables a robust testing process, because we can ensure that each item is in good working order before testing the project as a whole. As mentioned, when we are testing the individual units of the program, we are engaging in white box testing. Testing can proceed in an orderly fashion, ensuring that dialogs or functions work as expected one by one. When it comes time to test the entire project, the testing process is reduced to making sure that each element interacts with the others correctly.

The object-oriented nature of Windows programming also aids in speeding the unit testing process. If a dialog box has several controls on it, such as a calendar, an ADO data control, some edit boxes, and some command buttons, we don't have to worry about whether or not these objects work; that was already done by the manufacturer. Since we know that these "black box" elements already function properly, our focus shifts to worrying about whether they are configured and integrated correctly. This means we can add a great deal of functionality to our programs without adding an additional cost to the testing process.

Integration Testing

After we test each individual unit or component in the project, we need to see how these units work together. This brings us to the concept of *integration testing*. In integration testing, the focus starts to shift from the individual units to the software architecture as a whole. Integration testing is a form of black box testing. Each unit in the project has already been tested to ensure that the internal "parts" are working. Now we are testing to see how each unit interfaces with the other units with which it must interact.

Black box techniques are used that focus on the required output. For example, suppose we know from unit testing that a dialog box gets the user input correctly, and a function in another file crunches numbers and produces the right output. In the integration phase, we will see what happens when the dialog box passes the data to the function, and then the function returns the output for display to the user. Many errors are uncovered during this phase of testing, because such data interchanges were not planned correctly.

System Testing

After the integration process is complete, the next stage involves *system testing*. System testing involves testing at a higher level, which may involve more than the components of the software. This means testing with different hardware configurations, operating systems, and databases is necessary. System testing will involve one or more of the following:

- Testing the software on single-user machines.
- Testing the software on a network, as well as on various network configurations.
- Trying different memory and hard disk configurations.
- If the software uses multithreading, testing on single- as well as multiple-processor machines to ensure that performance is not compromised.
- Testing on different processors, such as Pentium, Pentium II, or AMD chips.
- Testing with different operating systems. For example, the code may perform differently under Windows 95/98 than it will under Windows NT 4.0.
- If this is an Internet application, testing with different browsers.

Some aspects of system testing may be beyond the reach of small companies. In that case, the system and beta testing phases can overlap. For example, if your company does not have a network, arrangements can be made with a customer to test the product under these conditions.

Beta Testing

Once the software team has pushed a product through its own round of testing, it's time for real-world customers to have a chance at it. Given the opportunity to use the product under real-world conditions, customers will inevitably uncover several faults in the software. This process is known as *beta testing*. During beta testing, a "prerelease" version of the software is provided to a subset of customers. The understanding is that they will use the product and attempt to discover remaining bugs or errors. This puts the product through the paces of day-to-day use, giving the developer an opportunity to correct many problems before the product actually hits the market. This is an important phase of the testing process. No matter how careful the software team is during testing, a developer simply can't anticipate every action the end user will take or what kind of data might be encountered. The only way to push the software to the limit is to have real users get a chance to break the product.

The size of the beta testing pool will vary widely depending on what kind of market you are developing for. If you're designing customized software as a consultant, beta testing will only involve one customer. In this case, beta testing follows naturally as the feedback between the client and developer continues through the testing process.

In a vertical or widespread software market, where the number of customers can range from a few hundred to millions, beta testing can be done by selecting a subset of clients that represent a cross section of users. A free version of the software can be provided in exchange for the knowledge gained by the customer using the software under real-world conditions. As updates or new versions of the software are released, beta testers can provide feedback on user interface changes or performance.

An effective beta testing program should involve the following:

- *Choose a representative subset of customers.* They should reflect a cross section of your market, including both large and small clients and different levels of usage. If possible, the beta testers should be spread out among rural and urban clients, as well as government and commercial users. The goal is to maximize the variety of conditions under which the software will be used.

- *Customers should receive the complete product, including documentation such as users manuals.* Don't forget that the users manual and online help system are part of the beta testing process as well. If users find the help confusing or don't like the manual, this is the time to find out.

- *A reasonable time period for evaluation should be given.* This will depend on many factors such as market size or pressure to get the product out. However, don't rush the beta process; it's better to take your time and release a software product that works well, rather than simply getting to market as quickly as possible.

- *Beta testers should maintain a "bug" or error log, where they make a detailed entry every time they run into a problem.* The information recorded should include a detailed description of the error. What data was being entered or what user action was taking place when the error occurred? Did the program crash? If the program reported an error message, what was the error number and description?

- *Beta testers should report their overall impressions of the product.* Did they like the user interface? Was it difficult to use? Did they approve of the manual?

Many companies cringe at the thought of giving away their software. If we imagine a vertical software product where we expect to sell a few hundred copies per year, we might be taken aback by the lost revenue. However, the payback from letting 15 or 20 real customers test the software over a reasonable amount of time will be enormous. They will unearth many bugs and discover problems the developer never thought of. Feedback on the user interface and overall flow of the software will be invaluable. By cleaning up the product after the beta process is complete, we've ensured that the software is as ready for market as it can be. Happy beta testers will push the product to their friends in the industry, and in exchange for the free software, positive customer comments can be used in marketing materials.

Many smaller companies try to avoid beta testing. They figure they can "wing it," fixing problems as they go along and simply shipping out a "patch" to the client. However, failure to use an effective beta testing program will result in higher costs later on. This means more technical support calls, more time spent fixing bugs *after* the product has been released, and more customer complaints. If you're continually shipping patches to your customers, after a while they'll start to question your abilities and judgment. The time and resources that will have to be directed toward continually fixing under-tested software will mean fewer resources are available to develop new products. For these reasons, a highly structured and carefully planned beta testing program is recommended.

Beta testing will likely involve many successive iterations as the software gets closer and closer to an acceptable level of performance. When the beta testers can no longer find errors, the software is ready to be released.

Regression Testing

During the life cycle of a software product, it will undergo many modifications as customers demand new features or the software team dreams up new innovations. Another factor that needs to be considered is that despite our best testing efforts, users will continue to discover new bugs during the course of product use. As a result, continued coding and testing will be required.

Whenever such modifications are made to a software product, previous testing procedures must be repeated. This process is known as *regression testing*. The purpose of regression testing is to ensure that any code maintenance or modification has not introduced new errors into previously functioning software. To engage in regression testing, you must maintain a detailed record of testing procedures. By documenting the testing procedures used, you can repeat the same tests to make sure that the software still behaves as expected. Regression testing is also important when using an incremental software development model. It can be applied at each increment or release of the software. This way, old tests are repeated to maintain the integrity of the software as new features are added. At each stage or increment, the battery of tests used will have to be expanded. Since most software products follow the incremental model, they will need to use regression testing.

CHAPTER 17

Distribution of Software

Once the application has been developed, debugged, and thoroughly tested, it's time to distribute it to the end user. There are many ways this can be done, including via disk media, over the Internet, or on a network. In this chapter we will explore the issues involved in deploying an application, such as the choice of media and method of distribution. We'll also explore the use of InstallShield for Microsoft Visual C++ 6, a third-party package that comes with Visual C++. It can be used to create professional installation programs for your applications. Finally, we'll discuss issues involved in providing patches or updates to existing users.

Identifying the Target Audience

Being aware of the needs of the target audience is an important factor when distributing an application. One concern is the level of technology available to the user. For example, a few years ago it would be an important question to ask if the average user would have access to a CD-ROM drive, or if distribution on 3.5-inch disk would be necessary. Today, that focus is more likely to shift to issues involving the Internet. There are several issues to keep in mind:

- What is the level of technological sophistication of the end user?
- What level of hardware technology will the average user have? For example, will they have CD-ROM drives?
- Does the average end user frequently browse the Internet?
- If so, is Internet distribution feasible?
- Will the program be used on a network?

Answering questions like these will help you develop an effective deployment strategy. For example, what if most users browse the Internet, but they tend to have 33-Kbps modems? If your program is large and would take a long time to download, Internet deployment may not be the ideal method to use.

Creating a Setup Program for the Application

The development of the setup program is the final stage of rapid application development. Just like every other phase, it needs to be taken seriously. The ease with which setup wizards can be used to build a setup program can give the developer a smug feeling, leading to the temptation to simply speed through the steps of the wizard without adequate testing and planning.

Once the setup program is complete, it is important to test it in a wide variety of scenarios that might be encountered by users. A system should be used that does not have Visual C++ or a previous version of your program installed. This is necessary because Windows programs have a large number of dependencies in the form of DLLs, OCXs, and other files. By testing the installation on a clean system, you can make sure that you've included every DLL, OCX, or database file that your program requires for operation. If a computer that has not been exposed to Visual C++ (and other Visual Studio tools, such as Visual Basic that may also use the same ActiveX controls) or your application is not available, you may consider renting one to test the setup program. In any case, careful planning and documentation must be done to develop a listing of dependencies for your program.

One way to determine a control's dependencies is by reading a *dependency file*. A dependency file is a text file that is set up like an INI file. For example, an OCX control may have a dependency file that provides information about DLLs the OCX requires, CAB file information, and the CAB file URL. Incomplete, missing, or incorrect dependency files can lead to errors in the DLL, OCX, or other files that are loaded by a setup wizard for your project. Therefore, it's always a good idea to sit down and work out the dependencies before running the setup wizard. Most ActiveX controls will have some documentation to help you do this.

Another important point to keep in mind is the licensing requirements for any ActiveX controls used. Make sure that you have the right to distribute the control before including it in your setup program.

Don't forget that the setup program will give customers the first impression that they have of your program. First impressions often leave the deepest impact, so it's important to make sure your setup program is professional and runs smoothly.

Determining the Dependencies

Before you begin the process of creating the setup program, take some time to determine which dependencies your application has. As mentioned earlier, this means dynamic-link libraries (DLLs), ActiveX controls (OCXs), database or other files (MDB, TXT, etc.), as well as any other files specific to your application. Each ActiveX control in your project may itself have dependencies—DLL files that it must use to function. Check the documentation of any third-party ActiveX controls for a list of any dependencies they may have, or examine the dependency file (.dep) for each control. If you attempt to distribute your application without all of the supporting files it depends on, it will not function on the destination computer.

One way you can determine the DLL files that your application uses is to view the Import table for your project. The Import table can be viewed by using the Windows QuickView utility. This will list each DLL and the functions within each DLL that your application uses. See your Windows documentation for information on using QuickView.

Compiling the Final Version of Your App

After you have completed all of your testing, be sure to compile a release version of your application. Do this before you run InstallShield. Open the *Project Settings* dialog in Visual C++, and select *Win32 Release* to specify the settings for the release version of your application. Then recompile your project.

Getting Started with InstallShield

Visual C++ comes with InstallShield for Microsoft Visual C++ 6, a version of the InstallShield product made by InstallShield Software Corporation for use with applications created with Visual C++. You can launch InstallShield by clicking on the InstallShield for Microsoft Visual C++ 6 icon on the toolbar. This will bring up the InstallShield program, shown in Figure 17-1.

The easiest way to get started is to launch the Project Wizard, by double-clicking on its icon found in the main window of InstallShield. This will bring up the Welcome screen, which you can use to fill out some basic information about your project (see Figure 17-2). The information you will be required to enter in the Welcome screen includes:

- Name of your application.
- Company name.

Chapter 17: Distribution of Software

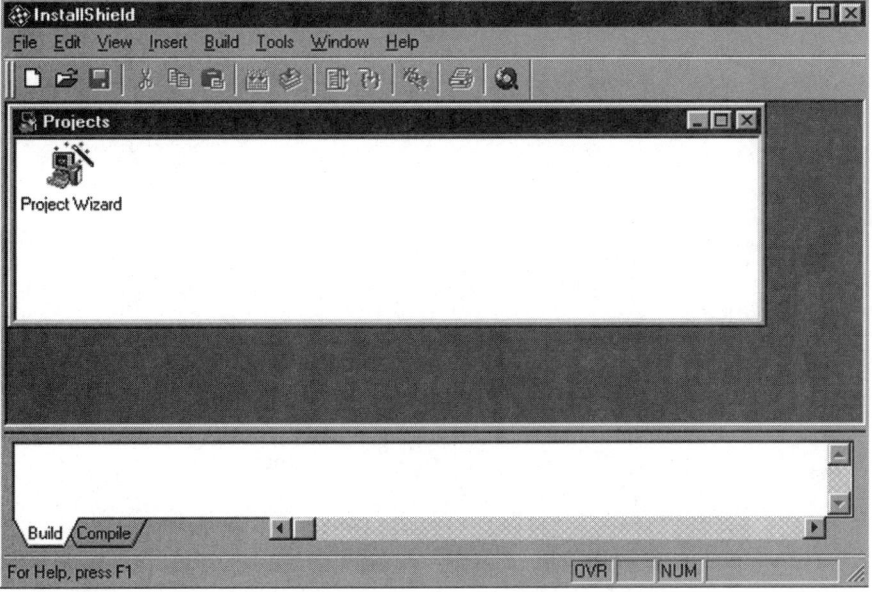

Figure 17-1
InstallShield.

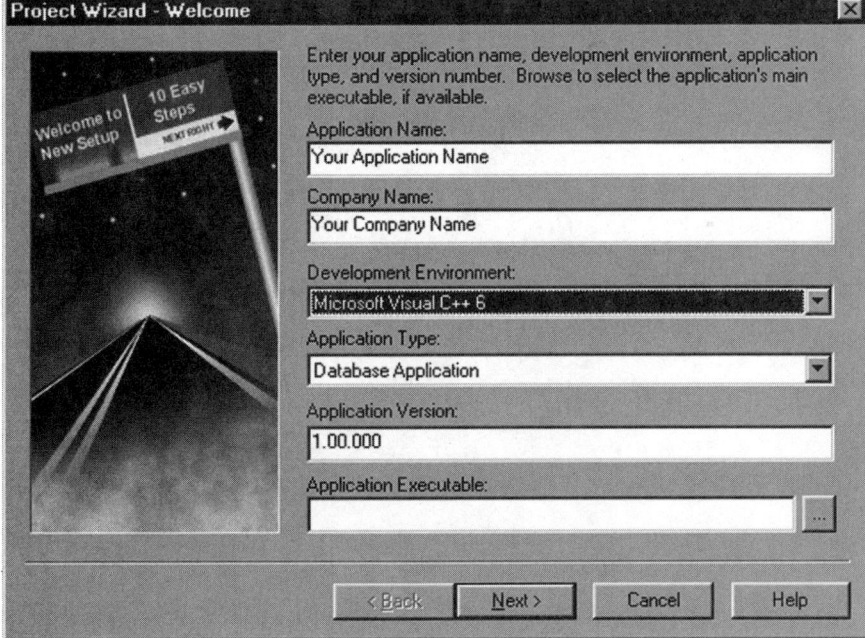

Figure 17-2
The InstallShield Project Wizard.

Part 4: Testing and Distribution of Visual C++ Software

- Development environment; this defaults to Visual C++.
- Application type; choose from the drop-down list.
- Application version.
- Application executable; click the ellipsis button to locate your executable file.

Choose Dialogs

The next screen is the Choose Dialogs screen, shown in Figure 17-3. You use this screen to specify which dialogs will be included in the installation program. This will include dialogs like the following:

- Software License Agreement
- Readme Information
- Setup Type (i.e., typical, custom, etc.)

Select one or more of these dialogs depending on how you want your installation program to operate. You can click the *Preview* button to see how the dialog box will look.

Figure 17-3
Selecting the InstallShield dialogs to include in your install program.

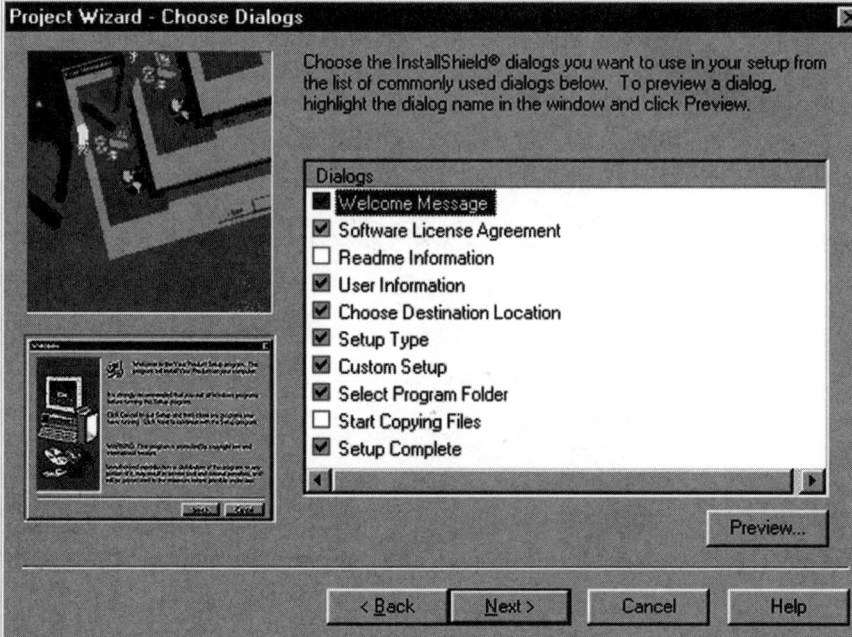

Chapter 17: Distribution of Software

Choose Target Platforms

The next screen, shown in Figure 17-4, is the Choose Target Platforms screen. This screen allows you to specify which target platforms your application will be installed on, such as Windows 95. If you want your application to be available for all of the target platforms listed, accept the default setting. You can deselect a target platform if desired. For example, if you will only be installing on Windows 95 machines, you can deselect the Windows NT 3.51 and Windows NT 4.0 options. This will reduce the size of your installation program.

Languages

The next screen is the Specify Languages screen. The free edition of InstallShield that comes with Visual C++ only supports English, so that is our only choice available here.

Figure 17-4
Choosing target platforms.

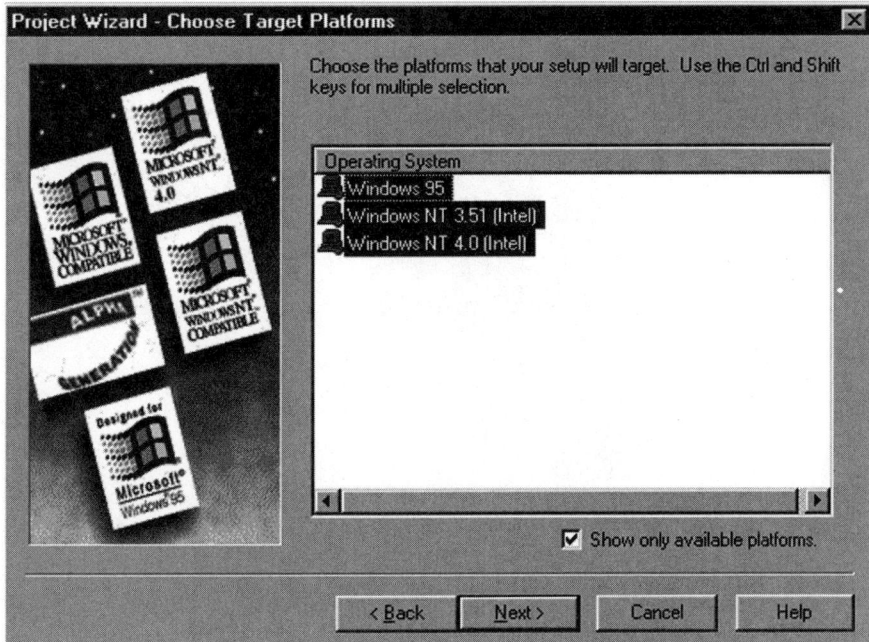

Specify Setup Types

In Figure 17-5, you will see the Specify Setup Types screen. This allows you to select one or more setup type options for your installation program. You are probably familiar with the setup types from installing programs on your own system, such as Compact, Typical, and Custom. Other options that you may want to give your users include Administrator and Network.

Specify Components

The next screen is Specify Components, shown in Figure 17-6. This is where you specify the different components that you will install along with your application. In other words, components are used to define different setup types, such as compact or typical. This includes your program files, any example files, help files, and shared DLLs.

You can also add your own component categories if desired. In our example, we will be shipping a database file, so we have added a database file component to the list. The actual files for each component are

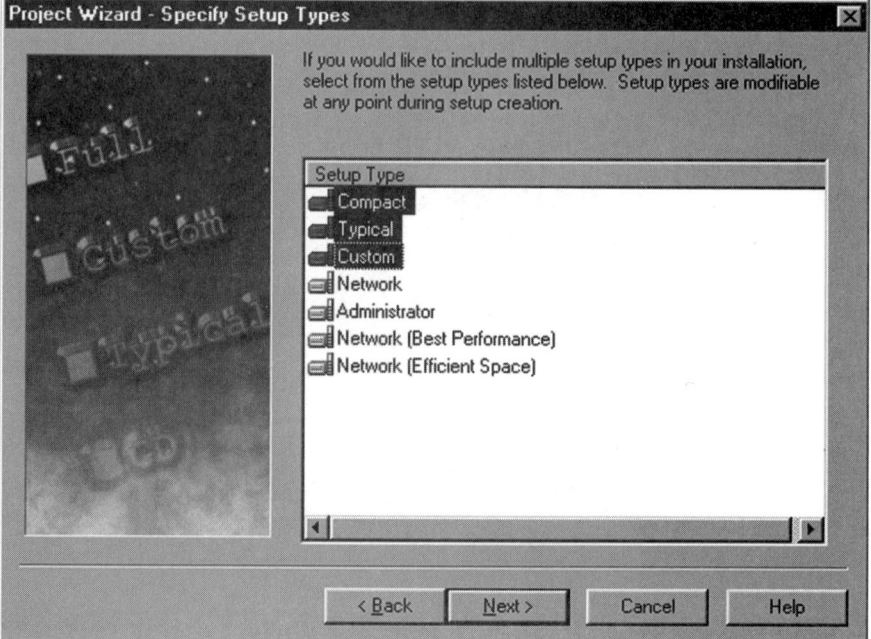

Figure 17-5
Selecting setup types.

Chapter 17: Distribution of Software

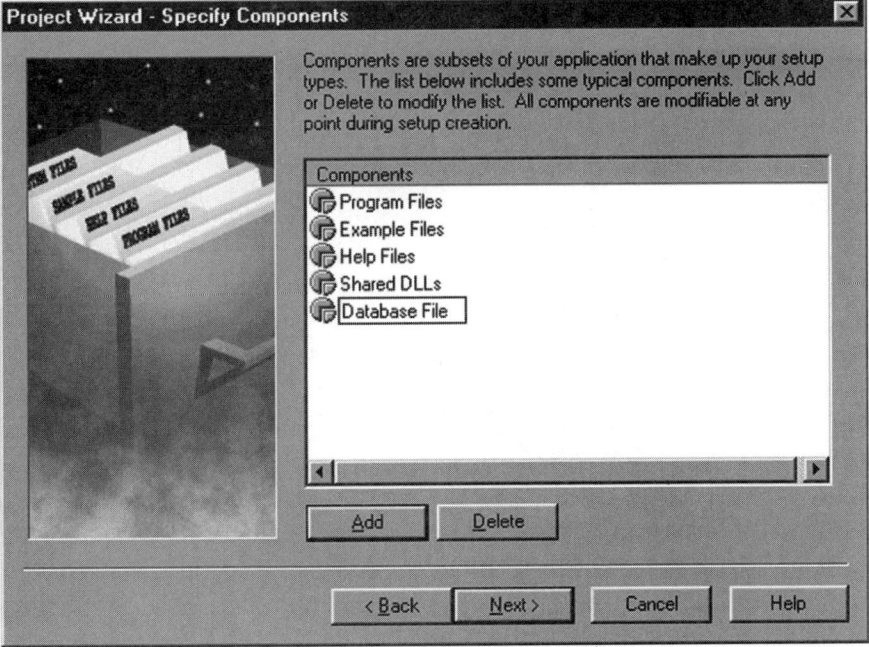

Figure 17-6
Choosing components for your application.

filled in later. The components listed here are just categories of files that users will be able to select or deselect for custom installation. For example, they may want to save disk space and not install your help files.

Specify File Groups

The next screen is the Specify File Groups screen. File groups are logical groups of files that are included with your application, such as dynamic-link libraries or help files. When you click *Next*, you will be brought to the summary screen, shown in Figure 17-7. Click *Finish* so that InstallShield can create the installation program. InstallShield will then open the source code used to create it so that you can view and modify it if necessary.

Specifying the Components

Unfortunately, we aren't done yet with the installation program. We need to specify the components that will be used in the installation pro-

Figure 17-7
Project Wizard summary.

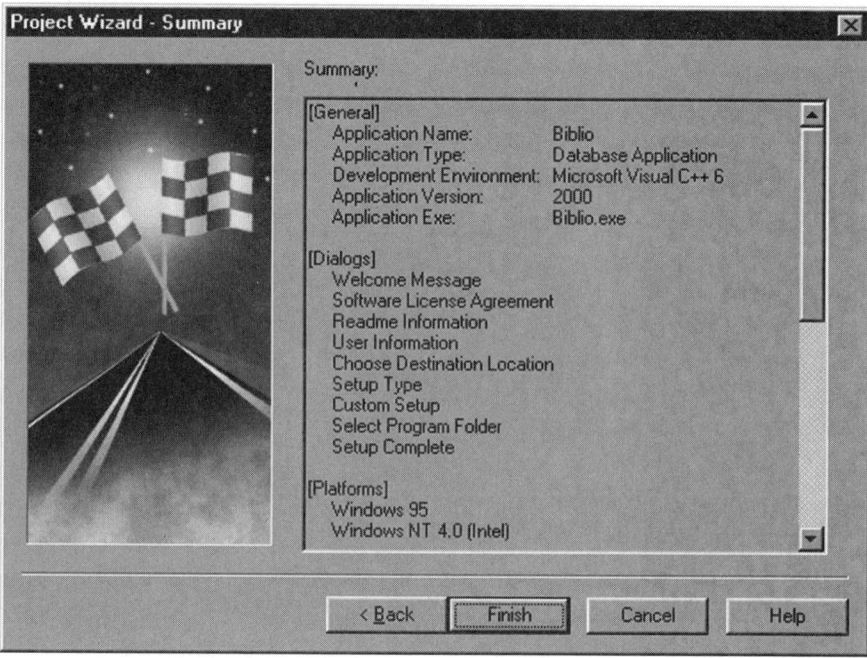

gram and build the distribution media. You will recall that the components are categories displayed for the user, such as program files, help files, or shared DLLs, that can be selected or deselected for installation usually based on some setup type, such as typical, compact, or custom. You need to configure the components before you build the distribution media. When you select the *Components* tab in InstallShield, the Components window will be displayed on the right side of the screen (see Figure 17-8).

You can select a component and view or set the values for that component. In the figure, we have selected the Program Files component by clicking on its folder in the left window pane. This brings up its Components window on the right, where you see properties such as Overwrite and Required Components. If you double-click on one of the properties—for example, the Description property—a Properties dialog will open, describing what to do with each property. Some of the important properties are as follows:

- *Destination* This is the destination directory where the files for this component will be installed. For example, shared DLLs will probably be installed in the user's system directory, while your program files will be installed in the target directory.

Chapter 17: Distribution of Software

Figure 17-8
Components.

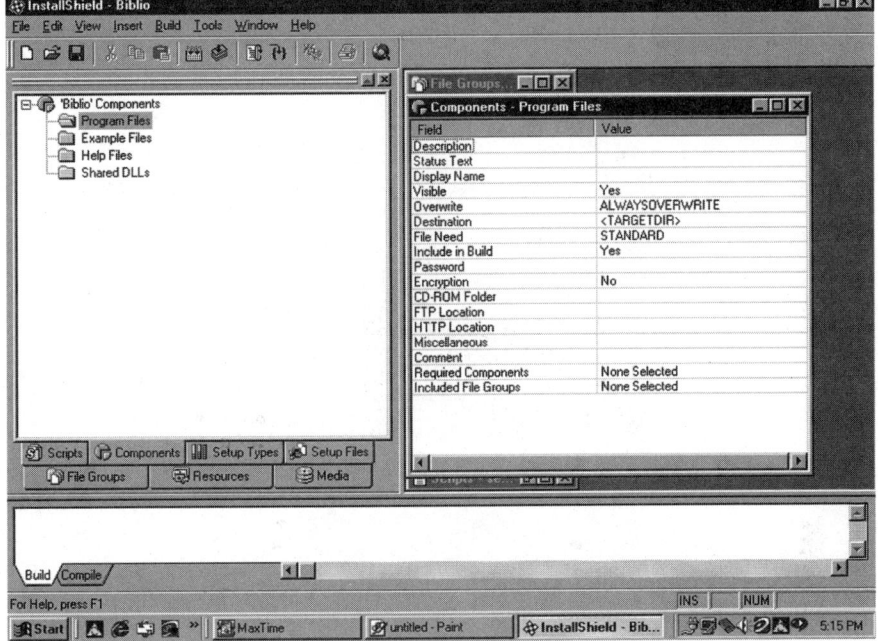

- *Required Components* Use this screen to specify dependencies between components. For example, if the user selects the Program Files component, the user will need to install the Shared DLLs component as well.

- *Status Text* This is a text string that users will see when that component is being installed on their machines.

- *Installation* This is an important setting; it is used to specify the behavior of your installation program when it attempts to install a file that is already on the user's machine, such as an ActiveX control. There are several options. For example, you can select NEWER VERSION/NEWER DATE to tell InstallShield to overwrite the old file if the file in your installation is a newer version.

- *Included File Groups* Use this property to assign the File Groups you created to the appropriate component. For example, if you have a help file and a DLL associated with your help system, you can assign these files to the Help Files component. While they belong to the same component, the help file may belong to the Help Files group, while the DLL belongs to the Shared DLLs group.

File Groups

If you look at the left window pane in InstallShield, you will see a tab at the bottom labeled File Groups. Click on this tab to specify which files will actually be installed with your application. Select a file group, such as Help Files, and click it open. Next, select the *Links* entry. This will bring up a dialog box that you can use to select the files that will be assigned to this group. It is here where you specify the EXE, DLL, OCX, HLP, MDB, and other files that will be shipped with your application.

To summarize, each file you want to distribute is selected in File Groups and assigned to one of the groups you created with the wizard. The file groups merely define the different types of files you will include with the installation program. Then each file group is associated with a component. A component can include one or more types of files. For example, a database component may include an MDB file and a set of DLL files that are necessary to open and use it. All of these files go with the database component, but the DLL files belong to the Shared DLLs file group, while the MDB file belongs to, say, the Example Files file group.

SetupTypes

In Figure 17-9, we are using InstallShield to edit the setup types for the application. You can select a setup type, say, Compact, and then specify which components will be associated with that setup type. In the example shown in the figure, we have selected Program Files, along with Shared DLLs, for the compact-type installation. This means that if the user selects this type of setup, the example files and help files will not be installed.

Selecting the Media and Building the Install Program

Once everything is configured correctly, the last step is to select the media type for distribution and build the installation disk. This can be done by launching the Media Build Wizard, shown in Figure 17-10. The first step is to type the name for your distribution media and click *Next*. We will select the default, which is 650 MB CD-ROM, shown in the Existing Media list.

Chapter 17: Distribution of Software

Figure 17-9
Setting properties for setup types.

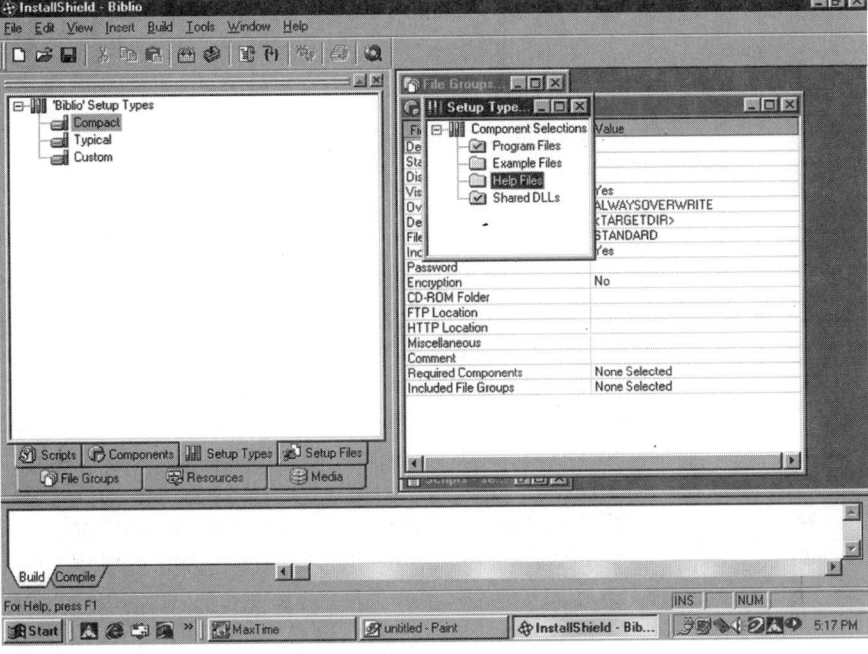

Figure 17-10
Choosing a media name.

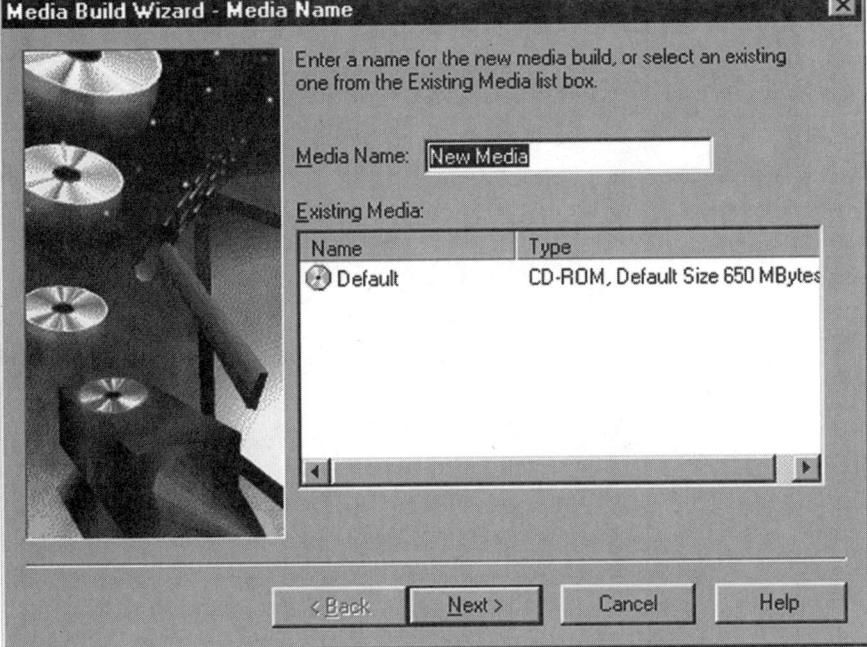

The next screen is the Disk Type screen, shown in Figure 17-11. Find the type of media you will use to distribute your software in the list and select it. Then click *Next*.

The next screen is the Build Type screen, shown in Figure 17-12. There are two options, Full Build and Quick Build. The Quick Build option is provided so that you can test the installation. This will let you see how the installation will work. To create a real installation, you need to select *Full Build*. This will create a set of CAB files and build the real install program.

The next screen is the Tag File screen. This screen will prompt you for information about the application and your company, which we already entered when we first launched InstallShield. The information that you entered there will be listed here, and you can edit it if necessary. This information will be placed in a tag file, which has a *.tag* file extension. The tag file will be placed on your installation disk.

Next, we encounter the Platforms dialog again, where you can choose the operating system platforms that you want the install program to support. Click *Next*, and you will see the Summary dialog, shown in Figure 17-13. If you click *Finish*, InstallShield will open the Building Media dialog and begin to compress and build the files for your installation disk.

Figure 17-11
Selecting the distribution disk type.

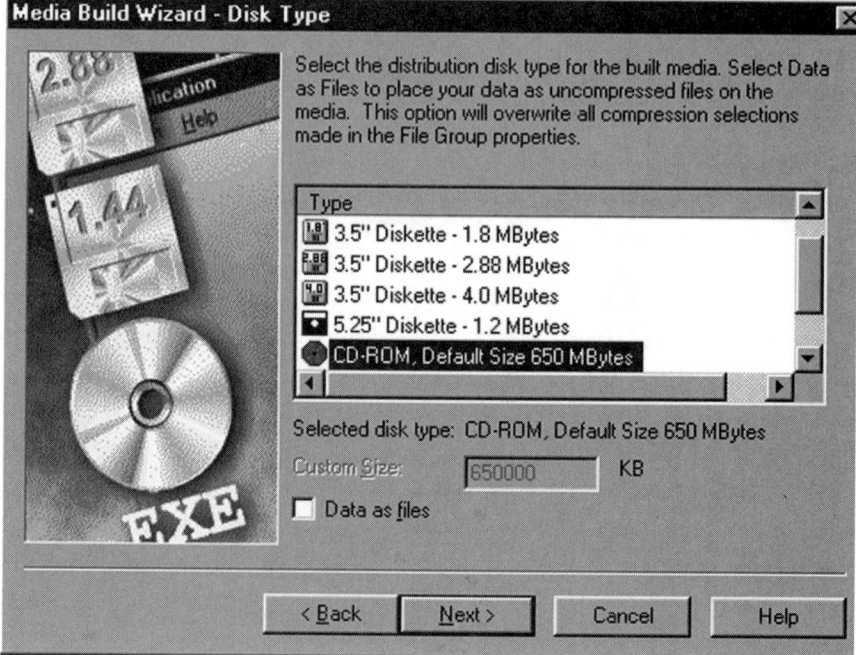

Chapter 17: Distribution of Software

Figure 17-12
Choosing the build type.

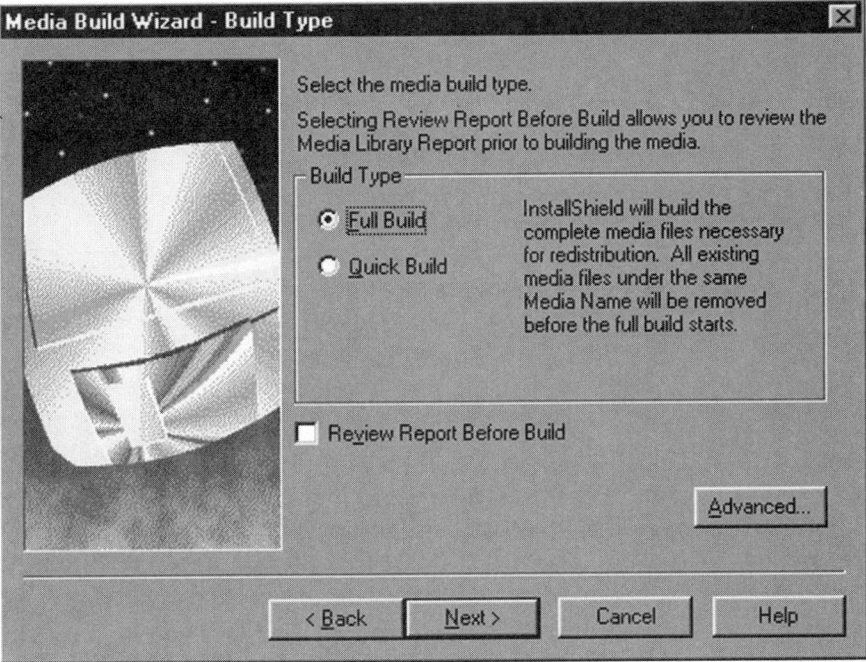

Figure 17-13
The Media Build Wizard summary screen.

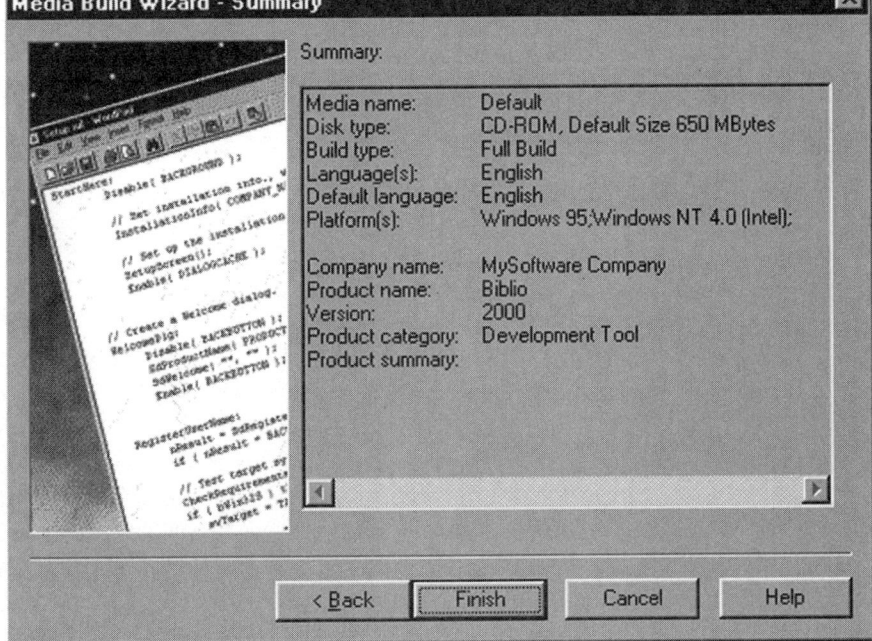

Once this process is complete, you are ready to begin copying CD-ROMS and distributing your software.

Other Third-Party Utilities

InstallShield for Microsoft Visual C++ 6 is an excellent choice for creating a setup program for your applications. However, many developers continue to find that other third-party setup tools are useful for their needs. Many third-party tools provide professional setup programs for your application and include many options, such as adding password protection, setting up screen customization such as different colors and fonts, creating a single executable file to use for installation, displaying licensing agreements, and adding typical, custom, and minimum setup options. If you work with multiple programming languages, you may find that owning a third-party setup tool is useful. Some of the most popular setup programs include Setup 98 from Sax Software, PC-Install from 20/20 Software, and Setup Factory from Indigo Rose Design Corporation.

Distribution of the Software— Selecting Media

In today's world, there are several methods that can be used to distribute a software product. The days of the 5¼-inch diskette are gone. In their place, today's software engineer is faced with a wide variety of possible distribution methods. This includes 3.5-inch disk, CD-ROM, the Internet, and network distribution. Generally, today's software is too large and complicated to make 3.5-inch disks a reasonable choice for distribution. This leaves us with the other possibilities: CD-ROM, the Internet, and network distribution. The choice that you make for distribution will depend on the users of the product and may involve one or more of the options that we listed. Distribution methods should be as flexible as possible, so that the end user can select the option that is most convenient.

CD-ROM vs. Floppy Disk

The CD-ROM is currently the most popular means used to deploy an application. CD-ROMs are low cost, yet provide ample storage space for most projects. The availability of low-cost CD writing devices makes the option of distribution on CD-ROM available to software companies of all sizes, from a large corporation all the way down to a single consultant. In addition, a CD-ROM is easier to ship than a set of floppy disks. If you need to distribute a large number of CDs, low-cost duplication services are available.

Distribution on CD-ROM also makes life easier for the end user. Instead of having to sit there and pop disks in and out during installation, they can just pop in the CD-ROM and let it run. Even the smallest application in 32-bit Windows is likely to take at least 10 floppy disks to install, so it is evident that a CD-ROM provides a more convenient means of distribution.

Despite the advantages and popularity of CD-ROM deployment, you are likely to come across some users who do not have a CD-ROM drive on their computer. As a result, it is a good idea to have installation using 3.5-inch disks available for these users. This means you may have to create two media builds for your application.

Internet Distribution

Internet distribution is becoming an increasingly attractive option for many software companies, especially small ones. This can provide a cost-effective means of distribution. The user can be provided a password that allows the software to be downloaded from a secure Web site. Another option that can be used is to have a "demo" version of the software. This demo can be downloaded by users free of charge, and if they like it, they can call for a password or ID to activate the software.

Internet distribution can save time and money by avoiding shipping costs and time spent packaging and duplicating disks. This option also has appeal for the end user, since they can get the feel of instant gratification, rather than having to wait for the product to arrive by mail. However, this option still remains limited. If your program is even of moderate size, the long download time may be unattractive. Users may also demand a printed manual, and they might prefer to have something "solid" to represent their purchase, such as the CD-ROM. Some users may not even have access to the Internet, although this is becoming less of a factor.

Workstation Duplication and Distribution

If you are developing applications for internal use by a large organization, you will probably use some form of network-based deployment. Arrangements can be made with the network administrator to provide a folder where the deployment will be stored and accessed. You can then use InstallShield to create the setup program, selecting *Network* from the Specify Setup Types screen.

Patches and Updating Applications

Throughout the lifetime of an application, chances are it will be updated as bugs are corrected and new features are added. To handle these situations, you will need to create new setup packages. The nature of these packages will be determined on a case-by-case basis. Patches can be divided into two cases: fixing bugs and adding updated components. For example, if you are correcting a bug in the application, you might only need to ship a new executable file. Rather than mailing it to your customers on CD, it may be more attractive to provide the file for download off the Web.

If your application uses any third-party ActiveX controls, new versions of these controls will be released from time to time. If they provide extended functionality, you may be interested in including the new controls in your application. This will require shipping a new executable, the OCX file, and any new DLL dependencies for the ActiveX control. Another scenario when a patch will be used to update a component can include an update to a DLL file that your application uses directly.

Software products typically go through several iterations or versions. As each version is released, it will be provided to existing customers in the form of an update. An update will require a different setup package than a full version provided to a new customer. The update might include a subset of project files, including new ActiveX controls and other dependencies. Data files and initialization files associated with the application will probably be left out of an update setup package.

APPENDIX

REFERENCES

McMahon, David. *Rapid Application Development with Visual Basic 6*. New York: McGraw-Hill, 1999.

Mueller, John Paul. *Visual C++ 6 from the Ground Up*. Berkeley, Calif.: Osborne/McGraw-Hill, 1998.

Neibauer, Alan. *Access 97 for Busy People*. Berkeley, Calif.: Osborne/McGraw-Hill, 1997.

Pappas, Chris H. and William H. Murray. *Visual C++ 6: The Complete Reference*. Berkeley, Calif.: Osborne/McGraw-Hill, 1998.

Pressman, Roger S. *A Manager's Guide to Software Engineering*. New York: McGraw-Hill, 1993.

Schildt, Herbert. *C/C++ Programmer's Reference*. Berkeley, Calif.: Osborne/McGraw-Hill, 1997.

Sodhi, Jag and Prince Sodhi. *Software Reuse, Domain Analysis and Design Process*. New York: McGraw-Hill, 1999.

INDEX

#@ (charizing operator), 77
(concatenation operator), 77
? (ternary operator), 84

A

Abstraction, 126
Access specifiers, 135
Active Template Library (ATL),
    35, 394–399
  adding methods to, 398–399
  adding properties to, 396–398
ActiveX Control Test Container,
    26
ActiveX controls, 29, 206, 373–399
  About box, 390
  adding, 233–234
  adding custom methods to,
      385–387
  adding events to, 387–388
  adding properties to, 383–385
  ambient properties of, 378–379
  ATL controls, 394–399
  and COleControl class,
      375–377
  compiling, 392–393
  creating, 374–375, 394–396
  drawing, 380
  example of, 380–382
  extender properties of, 379
  maintaining appearance of,
      381–382

ActiveX controls (*Cont.*):
  and object-oriented programming, 377–378
  OnDraw function, customization of, 388–390
  programming with, 232–240
  property page of, 390–392
  stock properties of, 379
  subclassing, 377
  Test Container, 393–394
  testing, 394
  toolbox icon, modifying, 392
ActiveX Data Objects (ADO), 35,
    290 (*See also* ADO Data
    Control)
Addressof operator, 72–73
Admin utility (Visual Source
    Safe), 33–34
ADO (*see* ActiveX Data Objects)
ADO Data Control:
  code, control, 298–305
  connecting to databases with,
      297–298
  creation of project, 308–310
  member functions of, 305–308
  programming with, 292–297
Aggregate functions, 323
Aliasing, 318
Ambient properties, 378–379
Analysis, 43–48
  and estimating, 44
  requirements, 40
  and scheduling, 44–46

449

Analysis (*Cont.*):
  and staffing, 46–48
AND operator (C++), 68, 85–86
Anonymous structure types, 106
Apartment model multithreading, 355
Application development, layered, 55–58
Applications, distributed, 55
Architecture:
  client/server, 53–59
  modular, 55
  software, 55–58
  systems, 52–53
Arrays:
  in C++, 78–80
  initializing, 80
  multidimensional, 79
  passing, 97–100
Arrow operator, 108–109
Assembly language, viewing, 411–412
ATL (*see* Active Template Library)
ATL COM App Wizard, 17

B

Batch optimistic locking, 327
Beta testing, 424–426
Bitmap files, 20
Bitwise operators (C++), 68–70
Block structures, indenting, 188
Booch method (*see* Grady Booch object-oriented design method)
`bool` data type, 62
`bool` keyword, 36
Breakpoints, 403–405

"Brute force" software development, 12–13
Burnout, 48
Business Logic layer, 52, 57–58
Business services tier, 57

C

C language, 10
C++ class, 134–135
C++ header files, 20
C++ language, 10
C++ programming language, 60–119
  address of operator in, 73–74
  arrays in, 78–80, 97–100
  bitwise operators in, 68–70
  casting in, 66
  charizing operator in, 78
  comments in, 81–82
  concatenation operator in, 77
  control structures in, 82–90
  data types in, 60–62, 103–106
  declaring constants in, 65
  defining new type names in, 71–72
  dynamic memory allocation with, 102–103
  funtion overloading in, 101–102
  good programming practices with, 115–117
  `if` statements in, 82–84
  increment/decrement operators in, 66–68
  loops in, 86–89
  `for` loops in, 86–87
  modular programming with, 90–115
  multithreading in, 355

Index

C++ programming language, (*Cont.*):
 one's complement operation in, 70–71
 passing parameters in, 93–94
 pointers in, 72–74, 100–101, 108–109
 preprocessor directives in, 75–77
 programming pitfalls with, 118–119
 programming strings in, 80–81
 prototyping in, 94–96
 relational operators in, 85–86
 source files, 20
 `switch` statement in, 89–90
 ternary operator in, 84
 variables in, 63–64, 96–97
 `void` return type in, 91–93
Call stack, viewing, 410–411
Casting, 66
`CDialog` class i, 347–348
CD-ROM, 445
`CException` class i, 345
`char` data type, 61–62
Charizing operator (#@), 77
CHTML MFC class, 36
`class` keyword, 135
Class View (Workspace window), 30
Class Wizard, 31–32
Class(es), 125–126, 134–172
 adding member functions to, 138–139
 and constructor/destructor functions, 141–142
 creating, 134–136
 defining data/function members of, 136–137
 derived, 145–154

Class(es) (*Cont.*):
 and `friend` functions, 156–162
 inheritance-based, 144–145, 167–171
 and inline functions, 140–141
 instances of, 131
 and multiple inheritance, 167–171
 and overloaded operators, 163–165
 pointers with, 165–166
 and polymorphism, 154–156, 166
 public vs. private members of, 137–138
 variables, defining/using, 142–144
 and `virtual` functions, 166–167
ClassID, 129
Client/server model, 53–54, 126–127
Coad/Yourdon object-oriented design method, 130
`CObject` class i, 344–347
Code libraries, 129–130
Code reuse, 124, 129–130
Code reviews, 189–190
Coding standards (*see* Standards)
`COleControl` class, 375–377
COM (*see* Component object model)
Comments, 43, 115–116, 178–179
 in C++, 81–82
 in function headers, 185–186
 inline, 186–187
 for revision history, 187
 standards for, 184–187
Communication:
 among software team, 46

Communication (*Cont.*):
  and documentation, 41
  fostering, 47–48
  and prototyping, 242
Component object model (COM), 128–129
Components and Controls Gallery dialog box, 29
Concatenation operator (##), 77
Concurrency problem, 326
Constants, declaring (in C++), 65
Constructor functions, 141–142
Contain applications, 356–360
Context-sensitive help, 42
Control structures (C++), 82–90
  `do` loops, 88
  `if` statements, 82–84
  `for` loops, 86–88
  relational operators, 85–86
  `switch` statement, 89–90
  ternary operator, 84
  `while` loops, 88–89
Critical tasks, identification of, 45
Custom App Wizard, 17–18
Custom app wizards, 32
Customer demands, meeting, 46
Customize dialog box, 27–28
`CWinApp` class i, 348–349
`CWnd` class i, 347
Cyclic waterfall software development model, 12

D

DAO:
  programming databases with, 310–315
Data:
  displaying, 197, 199–201
  joining, 325–326
  organizing, 246–247
  tables, splitting into (*see* Normalization)
Data access (*see* Database(s); Flat files)
Data types, 249–250
Database layer, 50, 56
Database(s), 244–265
  adding records to, 324
  data types in, 249–252
  deleting records from, 324–325
  denormalization of, 261–262
  elements of, 247–248
  fields, adding, 264–265
  foreign keys with, 253–254
  grouping records of, 323
  indexes of, 252–253
  joining, 325–326
  multiuser considerations with, 326–327
  and needs of end user, 245–247
  normalization of, 256–261
  one-to-many relationships in, 254–255
  options with, 291–292
  organizing data in, 248–249
  primary key of, 253
  queries, 316–323
  queries in, 255
  recordsets, opening, 338–339
  recordsets, programming with, 330–338
  stored procedures for, 255–256
  tables, adding, 263–264
  transactions, database, 327
  updating records in, 324
  using DAO to program, 310–315
  views of, 255

Index

Database(s) (*Cont.*):
  Visual Data Manager with, 262–263
  working with, 290–291
  See also ADO Data Control
Date/time fields, queries with, 319–320
DCOM (Distributed COM), 129
Debug configuration, 21–22
Debugging, 402–415
  assembly language, viewing, 411–412
  call stack, viewing, 410–411
  definition of, 402
  and error types, 402–403
  memory, viewing contents of, 410
  registers, viewing contents of, 409–410
  with Run to Cursor, 407
  of runtime errors, 412–413
  setting breakpoints for, 403–405
  with Step Into, 405–406
  with Step Out, 406
  with Step Over, 406
  with `try` block, 413–415
  with watch expressions, 407–409
`decrement` operator (C++), 66–68
`#define` preprocessor statement, 75
Denormalization, 261–262
Dependencies, 431–432
Derived classes, 145–154
Destructor functions, 141–142
Dev Studio Addin Wizard, 18
Developer Studio, project vs. workspace in, 16
Dewire, D. Travis, 53

Diagrams, avoiding unnecessary, 48
Dialog boxes:
  adding menu items for, 231–232
  closing, 231
  creating, 218–231
Dialog-based interface programs, 194
Disassembly, 411–412
Distributed applications, 55
Distributed COM (DCOM), 129
Distribution, software, 430–446
  and dependencies, 431–432
  and InstallShield, 432–444
  media for, 444–446
  patches, 446
  release, recompiling for, 432
  and setup program, 430–431
  target audience, identification of, 430
  and third-party setup tools, 444
  updates, 446
DLL (*see* Dynamic link libraries)
`do` loops, 88
Documentation, 40–43
  in code, 43
  end user, 41–42
  as a living process, 43
  technical design, 43
  of testing, 421
Dot syntax, 105
`double` data type, 61
Dynamic link libraries (DLL), 361–373
  compiling, 366
  creating Win32, 361–366
  definition, 361
  importing from, 367–370
  MFC App Wizard, creating with, 370–373

Dynamic memory allocation (with C++), 102–103

E

Encapsulation, 127
End user(s):
  determining needs of, 245–247
  documentation for, 41–42
Environment, development, 48
Error Lookup, 26
#error preprocessor statement, 75
Errors:
  logic, 402–403
  runtime, 402, 412–413
  syntax, 402
  testing for, 117
Estimating, 44
Exclusive OR operator (C++), 69–70
Experience level (of staff), 47
explicit keyword, 37
Exposing (objects), 127
Extended Stored Proc Wizard, 18
Extended Stored Procedure Wizard, 37
Extender properties, 379

F

false keyword, 37
Fields, 248–251
  properties of, 251
  tables, adding to, 264–265
  types of, 250
File Groups (InstallShield), 437, 440
File types, 20
File View (Workspace window), 30
First normal form, 257–258
Flat files:
  basic I/O routines with, 269–274
  definition of, 268
  programming with, 279–290
  using fstream to work with, 274–290
float data type, 61
Floppy disk, 445
Font dialog box, creating, 217–218
for loops, 86–88, 116
Foreign keys, 253–254
Forms, 247
Free memory, 102
friend functions, 156–162
fstream class, 274–290
  closing files with, 275–276
  opening files with, 274–275
  programming with, 279–290
  reading file data with, 276–277
  text strings, working with, 278–279
  writing file data with, 277–278
Function headers, functions in, 185–186
Functions:
  aggregate, 323
  breaking down code into, 116–117
  constructor/destructor, 141–142
  declaring variables at beginning of, 117
  inline, 140–141
  passing structures to, 109–110
  pointer return type, using with, 119

Index

Functions (*Cont.*):
   `virtual`, 166–167

G

Get Latest Version (Visual Source Safe), 34–35
Global variables, avoiding, 115, 118
Grady Booch object-oriented design method, 130
Graphical user interface (*see* User interface)
Grid format, 199–201
Grouping records, 323

H

Header files, 75
Heap, 102
Help:
  context-sensitive, 42
  online, 42
HelpContextID property, 42
Hiding, information, 127
Higher-level testing, 420
HTML Page files, 20
Hungarian notation, 182–183

I

Icon files, 20
IDE (integrated development environment), 16
Identifiers, 63–64
`#if` preprocessor statement, 76
`if` statements, 82–84, 116, 177
`#include` preprocessor statement, 75

`increment` operator (C++), 66–68
Incremental software development model, 13, 14
Indenting, 116, 188
Indexes (of databases), 252–253
Indirection operator, 72
Individual records, displaying, 201–202
Info View (Workspace window), 31
Information hiding, 127
Inheritance, 123, 127–128, 144–145, 167–171, 180
In code documentation, 43
`In` operator, 321–322
Inline comments, 186–187
Inline functions, 140–141
Inline `if` statements, avoidance of, 177
Inner joins, 325
InstallShield, 432–444
  components, specifying, 436–439
  dialogs, choosing, 434
  file groups, specifying, 437, 440
  languages, specifying, 435
  Media Build Wizard, 440–444
  setup types, specifying, 436, 440
  target platforms, choosing, 435
Instances, 131
`int` data type, 60–61
`_int8` data type, 62
`_int16` data type, 62
`_int32` data type, 62
`_int64` data type, 62
Integrated development environment (IDE), 16
Integration testing, 423
Interface testing, 420

Internal operations testing, 420
Internet:
   programming for, 399
   software distribution via, 445–446
ISAPI Extension Wizard, 18

J

Jargon, avoiding, 48
Java, 8–9
Joins, 325–326

K

Keys:
   foreign, 253–254
   primary, 253
Keywords (in version 6), 36–37
Knowledge (of staff), 47

L

Language standards, 175–181
   comments, 178–179
   function prototypes, listing of parameters in, 177–178
   global variables, avoidance of, 180–181
   inline `if` statements, avoidance of, 177
   local variables, declaration of, 175–177
   with multiple inheritance, 180
   "negative logic," avoidance of, 177
   `switch` statements, 181
   `this` pointer, 179–180
LANs (*see* Local area networks)

Layered application development, 55–58
Layers, application, 52–53
Layout, screen, 197
`Like` operator, 320–321
Linear software development model, 11–12
Linker, 25–26
Local area networks (LANs), 53, 54
Local scope (of variables), 96
Local variables, declaration of, 175–177
Locking:
   batch optimistic, 327
   optimistic, 326–327
   pessimistic, 326
Logic errors, 402–403
`long` data type, 61
Loops:
   `for`, 86–88
   `do`, 88
   `while`, 88–89

M

Macros, 27, 248
`main` function, 90
Main window, 196, 198–199
`malloc` function, 119
Manuals, 41–42
MDI programs (*see* Multiple-document interface programs)
Media, software, 444–446
Media Build Wizard, 440–444
Meetings, 48
Member operator, 105
Members:
   class, adding to, 138–139
   private, 135–138

Index

Members (*Cont.*):
  protected, 136
  public, 136, 138
Memory:
  dynamic memory allocation, 102–103
  free, 102
  viewing contents of, 410
Menus:
  adding items to, 231–232
  coding items in, 213–217
  pull-down, 26–29, 196
Methods:
  ActiveX controls, adding to, 385–387
  ATL, adding to, 398–399
  MFC (*see* Microsoft Foundation Classes)
MFC ActiveX Control Wizard, 18
MFC App Wizard, 18–19, 203–209, 291, 356, 370–373
MFC Class Wizard, 209–213
MFC Tracer, 27
Microsoft Access, 9
Microsoft Foundation Classes (MFC), 17, 31, 344–349
  advantages of, 344
  application class in, 348–349
  `CObject` class, 344–347
  window classes in, 347–348
  wizards, MFC, 349
Microsoft Windows, 352
Min/max buttons, 197
Modular architecture, 55
Modular programming, 90–115
Modules, 248
MSDEV utility, 36
Mueller, John Paul, 399
Multidimensional arrays, 79
Multiple inheritance, 167–171, 180

Multiple-document interface (MDI) programs, 194
Multithreading, 352–355
  advantages of, 353–355
  apartment model, 355
  in C++, 355
Multitiered client/server architecture, 54
`mutable` keyword, 37

N

"Negative logic," avoidance of, 177
Networks, 53, 54
Normalization, database, 256–261
  and denormalization, 261–262
  first normal form, 257–258
  second normal form, 258–259
  third normal form, 260
NOT operator (C++), 86
Numeric fields, queries with, 320

O

Object Linking and Embedding (OLE), 355–360
  container application, creating, 356–360
  as technology, 355–356
Object Modeling Technique (Rumbaugh method), 130–131
Object-oriented programming, 122–131
  and ActiveX controls, 377–378
  classes in, 125–126
  and code libraries, 129–130
  and COM, 128–129

Object-oriented programming (*Cont.*):
  data/function members in, 136–137
  and inheritance, 123
  methodologies for, 130–131
  terminology of, 126–128
Objects, exposing, 127
OLE (*see* Object Linking and Embedding)
OLE/COM Object Viewer, 26–27
OLE-DB, 37
OnDraw function, 388–390
One's complement operation, 70–71
One-tiered model, 56
One-to-many relationships, 254–255
Online help, 42
operator keyword, 163
Optimistic locking, 326–327
Options dialog box, 28
Ordinal Position property, 251
OR operator (C++), 69
Outer joins, 325, 326
Overloading, 101–102, 128, 163–165

P

Parameters, passing, 93–94
Pass by reference, 93–94
Pass by value, 93, 117
Patches, 446
P-code, 26
Performance level (of staff), 47
Personality characteristics (of staff), 47
Pessimistic locking, 326

Pointers, 72–74, 165–166, 269
  to functions, 100–101
  passing arrays as, 99–100
  programming structures with, 108–109
Polymorphism, 128, 154–156, 166
#pragma preprocessor statement, 76–77
Preprocessor directives (preprocessor statements), 75–77
Pressman, Roger S., 44, 420
Primary keys, 253
Private members, 135–138
Processes, 352–353
Programming practices, good, 115–117
Project Settings dialog box, 21–25
  C/C++ tab of, 25
  Debug tab of, 23
  General tab of, 22
Projects, 16
  file types in, 20
  management of, 21
  scheduling, 44–46
  settings for, 21–25
  size of, 44
  structure of, 44
  types of, 17–20
Proof of concept, 422
Properties:
  ambient, 378–379
  ATL control, adding to, 396–398
  extender, 379
  stock, 379
Protected members, 136
Prototyping, 94–96, 240–242
  components of, 241–242
  reasons for, 241
  setting expectations for, 242

Index

Public members, 136, 138
Pull-down menus, 196

Q

Queries, 247, 255

R

Rapid Application Development (RAD), 4
  avoiding pitfalls of, 6–7
  cost vs. benefits of, 4–6
  tools for, 7–10
Readability, code, 187–189
Records:
  adding, 324
  deleting, 324–325
  displaying individual, 201–202
  grouping, 323
  updating, 324
Recordsets, 299
  opening, 338–339
  programming with, 330–338
Register Control, 27
Registers, viewing contents of, 409–410
Registry, COM and, 129
Regression testing, 426–427
Relational operators, 85–86
Release configuration, 21–22
Reliability, software reuse and, 124
Remote procedures call (RPC), 129
Reports, 247
Requirements analysis, 40
Resource View (Workspace window), 30–31
Reuse, software, 124, 129–130
Revision history, 187
Ritchie, Dennis, 10
Roles, establishing, 48
RPC (remote procedures call), 129
Rumbaugh method (Object Modeling Technique), 130–131
Run to Cursor, 407
Runtime errors, 402, 412–413

S

Scalability, 55
Scheduling, 44–46
SDI programs (*see* Single-document interface programs)
Second normal form, 258–259
`Select` queries, 317–318
Setup program, creation of, 430–431
Setup Types (InstallShield), 436, 440
`short` data type, 61
Single-document interface (SDI) programs, 194, 203–210
Size, project, 44
Software distribution (*see* Distribution, software)
Software life cycle models, 11–14
Software media, 444–446
Software reuse, 124, 129–130
Software team, communication among, 46
Source Browser, 26
Spiral software development model, 12
Splash screen, 195–196
Spy++, 27

SQL (*see* Structured Query Language)
Staffing considerations, 46–48
Standards, 174–191
  for code readability, 187–189
  coding, 7
  commenting, 184–187
  enforcement of, 189–191
  language, 175–181
  for naming, 182–183
`static` variables, 97
Status bars, 196, 199
Step Into, 405–406
Step Out, 406
Step Over, 406
Stock properties, 379
Stored procedures, 37, 255–256
`strcat` function, 80–81
Strings:
  programming with, 80–81
  working with, 278–279
Stroustrup, Bjarne, 10
Structs, 104, 134
Structure, project, 44
Structured Query Language (SQL), 316–323, 338–339
Subprojects, 21
Subroutines, 90
`switch` statements, 89–90, 181
Syntax errors, 402
System testing, 424
Systems architecture, 52–53

T

Tab key, 197
Tables, 197, 247–249
  adding, 263–264

Tables (*Cont.*):
  adding fields to, 264–265
  and foreign keys, 253–254
  joining data from different, 325–326
  primary key of, 253
Tag field, 104–105
Target audience, identification of, 430
Technical design documentation, 43
Ternary operator (?), 84
Test Container (ActiveX controls), 393–394
Testing, application, 420–427
  ActiveX controls, 394
  areas of, 420–421
  beta testing, 424–426
  documentation of, 421
  importance of, 420
  integration testing, 423
  for proof of concept, 422
  regression testing, 426–427
  system testing, 424
  unit testing, 422–423
Text files, 20
Third normal form, 260
Third-party setup tools, 444
`this` pointer, 165–166, 179–180
Threads, 353, 355 (*See also* Multithreading)
Three-tiered model, 56–58
Toolbars, 196, 198–199
Tools pull-down menu, 26–29
ToolTips, 196
Transactions, database, 327
`try` block, 413–415
Two-tiered model, 56
`typedef` keyword, 71–72
`typename` keyword, 37

Index

U

UI layer (*see* User interface layer)
`#undef` preprocessor statement, 77
Unified modeling language, 131
Unit testing, 422–423
Updates, 446
Use-case diagrams, 131
User interface, 194–242
   and ActiveX controls, 232–240
   and Class Wizard, 209–213
   data display, 199–201
   dialog boxes, creating, 218–232
   elements of good, 195–197
   Font dialog box, creating, 217–218
   individual records, display of, 201–202
   main window, 198–199
   menu items, adding, 231–232
   menu items, coding, 213–217
   prototyping, 240–242
   for single-document interface applications, 203–210
User interface tier, 52
User interface (UI) layer, 54, 57
User manuals, 41–42
User-interface threads, 355

V

Validation Rule property, 251–252
Validation Text property, 252
Variables:
   avoiding global, 115, 118
   declaring, 63–64, 117, 142–144
   initializing (in C++), 64
   left/right shifts of, 70–71
   lifetime of, 96–97
   local, 175–177
   naming, 115, 182–183
   pointers, declaring with, 72–74
   scope of, 96
Version control, 32–35
Views, 255
`virtual` functions, 166–167
Visual Basic, 7–8
Visual C++:
   advantages/disadvantages of, 9–10
   history of, 10
Visual Component Manager, 27
Visual Data Manager, 262–263
Visual Source Safe, 32–35
Visual Studios, 16
`void` return type, 91–93

W

Watch expressions, 407–409
Waterfall software development model, 11–12
`wchar_t` data type, 62
`Where` clause, 318–320, 322–323
`while` loops, 88–89, 116
White space, use of, 188–189
Wide area networks (WANs), 54
Win32 DLLs, 361–366
Workspace window, 30–31
Workspaces, 16
Workstations, software duplication on, 446
World Wide Web, programming for, 399

X

XOR operator (C++), 69–70

ABOUT THE AUTHOR

David McMahon is Microsoft Certified in Visual Basic and a software developer who writes hardware drivers for Windows NT and 95/98 with Visual C++.